Q. At what point during labor [illegible]
a woman become a יולדת?

יסוד הטהרה

Foundation of Purity

A Practical Comprehensive Guide to the Laws of Family Purity

First published 2007

Rabbi Chiya 9, P.O.B. 505
Bnei Brak 51104
Israel
Tel. 972-50-4101831

ISBN 978-1-58330-915-5

Design and typesetting:
MILLER PUBLISHING L.T.D & Miller Point Production
www.millerbooks.co.il

Distributed by:
FELDHEIM PUBLISHERS
P.O.B 43163 / Jerusalem, Israel

208 Airport Executive Park
Nanuet, NY 10954

www.feldheim.com

Printed in Israel

יסוד הטהרה

Foundation of Purity

A Practical Comprehensive Guide to the Laws of Family Purity

Based on the *shiurim*
of Rabbi Moshe Shaul Klein *shlita*
Dayan and *Moreh Tzedek* in the *Beis Hora'ah*
of *Maran HaGaon* Rav Shmuel HaLevi Wosner *shlita*

Compiled by Rabbi Hillel Wertheimer *shlita*

Published by
Machon Taharas Yisrael
The Institute for the Observance
of the Laws of Family Purity

Bnei Brak - 5767
ISRAEL

SHMUEL HALEVI WOSNER
RABBI OF
ZICHRON - MEIR, BNEI - BRAK

שמואל הלוי ואזנר
רב אב"ד ור"מ
זכרון־מאיר, בני־ברק

ב"ה, יום ב' פנחס תשנ"ה לפ"ק

מפי תלמידי המובהק הגאון ר' משה שאול קליין שליט"א שמעתי על ס' קיצור הלכות טהרה ויחוד שחיבר הה"ג ר' הלל ורטהיימר שליט"א לזכות את הרבים בכעשרה שיעורי הלכות טהרה שיסד ומלמד טהרת ישראל ע"פ פסקי דינים שלנו הרגילים בבית הוראה של זכרון מאיר. וכב' הג' רמ"ש קליין שליט"א עבר על הכל וניפה הכל להיות **סלת נקי' מוכן להוראת מעשה.**

והרני מברך את הה"ג ע"ז, וחפץ ה' בידו יצליח, כי הוא ת"ח יקר ראוי לתפארת ושבח.

ע"ז בעה"ח, מצפה לישועת ה'

שמואל הלוי ואזנר

הרב ש. י. נסים קרליץ
רמת אהרן
רח' ר' מאיר 6, בני-ברק

בס"ד, יום א' מנ"א תשנ"ה

הנני בדברי אלו להוקיר ולחזק פעולת
הרה"ג ר' הלל ורטהיימר לזכות את ישראל בלימוד
הלכות הנחוצות לכל בית ישראל הלכות טהרה
וגם חיבר ספר יסוד הטהרה קיצור הלכות
טהרה ויחוד, ספר שכשמו הוא ספר יסודי לדעת הלכות אלו
ויהי רצון שיזכה הרב המחבר שליט"א שאכן
רבים יתחזקו בלימוד ושינון הלכות אלו וזכות
הרבים יהי' תלוי בו.
נסים קרליץ

בס"ד, יום א' מנ"א תשנ"ה

הנני בדברי אלו להוקיר ולחזק פעולת הרה"ג ר' הלל ורטהיימר שליט"א לזכות את ישראל בלימוד הלכות הנחוצות לכל בית ישראל הלכות טהרה וגם חיבר ספר יסוד הטהרה קיצור הלכות טהרה ויחוד, **ספר שכשמו הוא ספר יסודי לדעת הלכות אלו.**

ויהי רצון שיזכה הרב המחבר שליט"א שאכן רבים יתחזקו בלימוד ושינון הלכות אלו וזכות הרבים יהי' תלוי בו.

נסים קרליץ

RABBI MOSHE SHOUL KLEIN
Dayan in Beth Din
of Hagaon Harav Wzner Shelita
And Rabbi of Or Hachayim are Bnei Brak

משה שאול קליין
מו"ץ בבד"ץ דמרן הגר"ש ואזנר שליט"א
ורב שכונת אור החיים בני ברק

בס"ד, כ"ו בתשרי תש"ס לפ"ק

בחורף תשנ"ה הגה ברוחו ידידי החשוב הרה"ג ר' הלל ורטהיימר שליט"א לעשות פעולות למען חיזוק הטהרה בבתי ישראל והקים למען מטרה נעלה זו את מכון "טהרת ישראל" וביקשני לנווט את פעולות המכון, וראיתי את גודל רצונו ללמד את בני ישראל דעת זה סדר טהרות וע"כ קיבלתי ע"ע את עול פעולות הגדולות של המכון.

לצורך זה נתאספו קבוצה גדולה ונכבדה של ת"ח מופלגים ומורי הוראה מובהקים בבית הרה"ג הלל ורטהיימר שליט"א, לשמוע שעורי הלכה והדרכה ודרכי הוראה, ע"פ מה שקבלתי ממו"ר מרן הגר"ש ואזנר שליט"א, כדי שידעו הדרך ילכו בה ואת המעשה אשר יעשון להורות לעם את דבר ד' זו הלכה. וב"ה כמה מהם נעשו לרבנים בקהילות ישראל בני תורה, ומורי צדק לרבים, ובעזרת ד' עוד היד נטויה.

ומאז ועד עתה זה כחמש שנים נאמרו עשרות רבות של שעורי הלכות טהרה ע"י האברכים מורי הוראות הנ"ל בכמה וכמה מקומות וישובים, הן בארץ ישראל המקומות הקרובים והרחוקים והן בארצות הגולה בכמה מקומות, וזכינו שעי"ז רבים נתחזקו מאד בשמירת הטהרה והקדושה.

והנה רבו השיעורים שנאמרו ע"י הרבנים הגאונים וע"י כב' הרה"ג הלל ורטהיימר שליט"א שנסע למקומות רחוקים ללמד דעת זה סדר טהרות לבני ישראל וכמו כן לימד הרבה, הלכות אלו ליחידים כמו חתנים וכדומה, וע"כ ראה הצורך הגדול שיהיה ספר פסקי הלכות בהלכות טהרה מסודד וערוך בשפה ברורה ובלשון צח ע"פ דרך ההוראה שקבלתי מאת מורי ורבי פוסק הדור ממעתיקי השמועה מרן הגאון רבי שמואל הלוי ואזנר שליט"א הגאב"ד ור"מ ז"מ ב"ב. וע"כ יגע טובא והשקיע כוחות עצומים זה כמה שנים להוציא לאור ספר הלכות טהרה וקרא שמו "יסוד הטהרה" שממנו ילמדו ברבים בכל שיעורי התורה דבר השוה לכל נפש.

והנה זה ברור שצריך יגיעה רבה להוציא ספר הלכה שיהיה מדוייק בתכלית הדיקדוק ומאחר שנקרא שמי עליו ע"כ יגעתי טובא לעבור עליו ולדקדק בלשון

כל סעיף וסעיף כדי שיהיו הדברים מסודרים ומחוורים כשמלה, ושיהיו מכוונים להלכה והיה לי לעזר ולסיוע ידידי הרב הגאון מו"ה משה טוביה דינקל שליט"א בעל מחבר ספר דבר חריף ועוד ספרים ורב שכונת בית ומנוחה בבית שמש אשר זה כמה שנים שבררנו יחדיו כמה וכמה סוגיות בהלכות טהרה, ובמסגרת לימודינו גם בירדנו הרבה פרטי ההלכה המופיעים בספר יסוד הטהרה ועברנו על הספר בעיון ככל האפשר עד מקום שידינו מגעת.

ותפילתנו שגורה בפינו שלא נכשל בדבר הלכה לעולם ושנזכה לכוין לאמיתה של תורה, (ובקשתנו לכל אחד ואחד שאם יראה איזה הערה בדבר הלכה שיכתוב למכון הנ"ל כי כבר אמר דוד המלך עליו השלום שגיאות מי יבין).

והנה איתא במסכת אבות פ"ה מי"ח כל המזכה את הרבים אין חטא בא על ידו, התנא הקדוש נתן לנו עצה נפלאה להנצל מן החטא. כי הרי שנינו באבות פ"ב מ"ד אל תאמין בעצמך עד יום מותך, וכבר אמרו חז"ל ברכות כ"ט. שיוחנן כ"ג שימש שמונים שנה בכהונה גדולה ולבסוף נעשה צדוקי, ואמרו חז"ל במסכת קידושין ל': יצרו של אדם מתגבר עליו בכל יום ויום ואלמלא הקב"ה עוזרו אין יכול לו, וא"כ מה יעשה אדם וינצל מן היצר האורב בכל פינה ופינה, וע"ז בא התנא הקדוש ללמדנו כל המזכה את הרבים אין חטא בא על ידו, הרי שזיכוי הרבים הוא עצה נפלאה ושמירה חזקה להנצל מן החטא.

וידוע שחז"ל גדלו ושבחו את מעלת רבי חייא בעבור שהקים עולה של תורה שלימד תורה ברבים וזכה שעל ידו לא נשתכחה תורה מישראל ולמדנו מזה שלהרבות תורה ודעת לבני ישראל גדול מכל, ועל כן גדולה מעלת המזכה את הרבים שאין חטא בא על ידו.

וע"כ כמה גדולים מעשי ידי ידידי הרה"ג הלל ורטהיימר שליט"א שמוציא לאור עולם ספר הלכה למען זיכוי הרבים ולמען הרבות הטהרה בישראל, ובודאי תהיה תועלת גדולה בספר הזה לכלל ישראל.

ויה"ר שנזכה בקרוב למה שכתוב "ומלאה הארץ דעה כמים לים מכסים" במהרה דידן, אמן.

הכותב וחותם למען חיזוק הטהרה בישראל
המצפה לחסדי ה'
[illegible] קליין

דברים שהוסיף מו"ר לקראת הוצאת ספר יסוד הטהרה באנגלית

משה שאול קליין

מו"ד בבד"ץ דמרן הגר"ש ואזנר שליט"א

ורב שכונת אור החיים בני ברק

RABBI MOSHE SHOUL KLEIN

Dayan in Beth Din

of Hagaon Harav Wzner Shelita

And Rabbi of Or Hachayim are Bnei Brak

בס"ד, יום י"ח בכסלו תשס"ו לפ"ק

הנה זה יותר מחמש שנים שיצא לאור ספר "יסוד הטהרה" ע"י ידידינו הרב הגאון רבי הלל ורטהיימר שליט"א אשר כל ההלכות שבו ע"פ דרך הפסק שבירדנו לפני ת"ח וחברים מקשיבים ע"פ דרך ההוראה שקיבלתי ממו"ר פוסק הדור עמוד ההוראה מרן הגר"ש ואזנר שליט"א בעל "שבט הלוי" וזכינו שנתקבלו הדברים לפני כל יודעי דת ודין הן ת"ח והן להמון העם, ונעשה צורך גדול להעתיק הספר ללשון אנגלית, וכבוד ידידי הגאון רבי שלמה פוזן שליט"א שהוא ת"ח ובקי בהוראה ובקי בלשון הנ"ל מנצח על המלאכה שיהיה **כתוב בדקדוק גדול**, וכבוד הרה"ג רבי הלל ורטהיימר שליט"א השקיע הרבה כוחות שיצא לאור בהידור רב חן חן להם והשי"ת ישלם שכרם בזה ובבא בכל טוב סלה.

ויה"ר שהדברים יתקבלו לרצון לפני אדון כל ולפני קהל עדת ישראל להרבות גבולי הקדושה והטהרה בישראל.

וע"ז באתי עה"ח

משה שאול קליין

משה שאול קליין

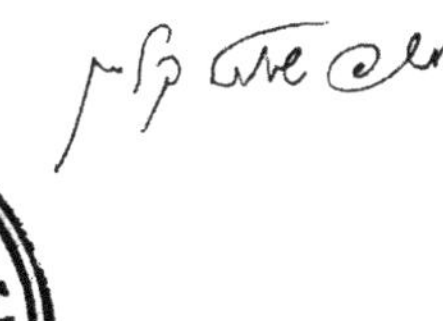

A Blessing from the Author's Father

My heart rejoices to see that you, my dear son, R' Hillel, while constantly toiling in Torah, took the initiative to write the sefer Yesod HaTaharah, and with Heaven's help, this important and needed work is now available to the Jewish People. Your *sefer's* content, style and format are such that the awareness of family purity will certainly increase. All will attain clear understanding of the many laws and will find it much easier to put them into practice.

You have certainly caused great pleasure to your grandfather, my beloved father זצ"ל, after whom you are named. He, along with millions of other pure and holy martyrs, was murdered in the Holocaust, but not before expending unlimited energy and dedicating all his years to strengthening the pillars of Jewish life, particularly in the area that is the subject of your sefer.

In Romania, during the difficult and troubled times after World War I, despite economic hardships and many other sorrows of European Jewry, my father undertook to build a kosher mikveh. He was barely able to scrape together a livelihood for himself, his wife and his family that was blessed with many children. The leaders of his community told him that hardly anyone in town had a penny to spare, and it was certainly not the time for building a mikveh. In the days leading up to World War II, no one knew what the morrow would bring, but your grandfather went ahead anyway and started drawing up plans for the *mikveh*.

I have in my possession a pamphlet that he published in which one reads some of the *halachic* give and take as to how the construction of that mikveh proceeded. The pamphlet contains correspondence between him and many *gedolei* Torah of the era, such as the Gaon Rabbi Shaul Brach זצ"ל, Admor of Kashow, Rabbi

Eliezer Dovid Greenwald זצ"ל, Av Beis Din of Satmar, the Gaon Rabbi Yitzchak Isaac זצ"ל, of Spinka. One sees what great care was taken regarding every detail of the mikveh, for your grandfather saw that our nation's survival depends upon the fulfillment of the laws of family purity.

You have become deeply involved in an area of *halacha* that was very dear to his heart. Therefore, I am certain that in Heaven he will be a *meilitz yosher* for you. He will speak in your favor so that you will be privileged to continue to sit in the tents of Torah, and the wellsprings of your wisdom shall flow out into the world.

בני אם חכם לבך, ישמח לבי גם אני I, as your father, add my blessings that you merit to continue in your Torah studies, enjoying excellent health, great pleasure and complete peace of mind. May you merit to see all your children upright individuals blessed by Hashem, and, so, too, all the generations that shall come forth from them.

Your father,
Eliyahu Wertheimer

Introduction

זה היום עשה ה' נגילה ונשמחה בו

Today is truly a happy day, for it marks a great addition to our many-faceted programs that promote the observance of the laws of family purity. From today onwards, English speaking Jewry will have access to a precise, carefully edited English translation of the Hebrew Yesod HaTaharah, a widely acclaimed, up-to-date reference work on an area of halachah that is vital to the holiness of every Jewish home. Yesod HaTaharah in English will enable the laws of family purity to be more carefully observed and practically applied on a much wider basis.

The English translation of Yesod HaTaharah represents yet another link in the long chain of efforts of Machon Taharas Yisrael, an organization established almost ten years ago with blessings from many of the greatest Torah luminaries of the present generation. Under the leadership and guidance of HaRav HaGaon Rabbi Moshe Shaul Klein שליט"א, disciple of Maran HaRav HaGaon Rav Shmuel HaLevi Wosner שליט"א, Av Beis Din of Zichron Meir in Bnei Brak, the author of the Shevet Halevi, Machon Taharas Yisrael has succeeded in greatly increasing knowledge and observance of these laws. It is our sincere hope and prayer that through this new work, in English, more legions of Jews will join the ranks of those who faithfully keep these halachos in every detail.

One of the first initiatives of Machon Taharas Yisrael was to organize a network of shiurim throughout Israel, so that people from all types of backgrounds could come and learn about family purity. Simultaneously, we began training gifted avreichim to speak about the subject, give classes and make halachic rulings. Rabbi Klein שליט"א presented these specially selected avreichim with an in-depth series of shiurim. So that the avreichim would learn how to apply the knowledge practically to particular cases and special situations, he had them observe poskim and listen while the poskim handled questions that were brought before them. Today, these highly trained avreichim give shiurim throughout the country and provide halachic guidance and other types of assistance to communities that have no Rabbi to be consulted regarding these matters.

With Hashem's help, our training programs have produced true experts who serve communities throughout the country, teaching the public, answering questions and furthering the observance of these vital halachos.

As time went on and we sponsored hundreds of shiurim throughout Israel, it became clear that it would be very beneficial if summaries of the shiurim, along with the practical rulings of Rabbi Klein שליט״א, would be put into writing. To bring this needed material to larger numbers of Jews, and to make it available in writing for those who attend our shiurim, Machon Taharas Yisrael has published three sefarim in Hebrew: Yesod HaTaharah, Yedias HaTaharah and Mishmeres HaTaharah. These widely-acclaimed, brief but comprehensive works are written in clear, concise and simple language, with accompanying charts and tables, so that even the more complicated laws are easily understood.

Last year, to encourage more and more avreichim to embark upon the study of this area of halachah with the aim of mastering it, Machon Taharas Yisrael began to arrange examinations on the subject. Those who excelled in the exams received cash prizes, and through this program hundreds of additional avreichim have become experts in the halachos of family purity. Without question, the success of this endeavor and the great thirst for knowledge of these laws fully justifies the investment and expense that is involved in continuing and expanding the program.

When Jews outside of Israel heard about the great positive effects of Machon Taharas Yisrael programs, and word spread of the high quality of our publications, we received many requests to have our books and shiurim translated into languages other than Hebrew. Our first response to these requests is the book before you, Yesod HaTaharah in English, for English-speaking Jews the world over. G-d willing, we will continue with similar efforts and will make our books and shiurim available in French, Spanish and other languages.

* * *

I hereby give my blessings and thanks to Rabbi Shlomo Posen שליט"א for accepting the task of reviewing the halachic accuracy of the translated manuscript. His thorough work added considerable clarity to the text. Similarly, my blessings and thanks to Rabbi Yisroel Krausz שליט"א for his collaboration and assistance in sifting through the text, revising, questioning, verifying and weighing each and every word. Without his proficiency this sefer would not have been possible. Their tireless, devoted efforts have produced an extremely useful and important sefer. May they merit to continue to dwell in the tents of Torah, enjoying peace of mind and excellent health, and may their wellsprings of Torah flow outwards into the world.

I have no doubt that with Hashem's help, this work will be extremely helpful to all who teach and learn these halachos. It will be an invaluable tool for reference and review. On the other hand, despite all great care and good intentions, errors are always possible, and sometimes points might not be stated clearly. Therefore, we ask readers that if they come across anything of this nature, please bring it to our attention so that we can attend to the matter for future editions.

* * *

Due to the scope of Machon Taharas Yisrael programs, it is no small job to raise the funds that are required for us to continue our efforts, let alone expand them. Anyone who sees our organization from close up, recognizes immediately that our budget demands are very great. It is equally clear that Heaven will send abundant blessing to all those who generously help and join us in our needed and holy work to promote family purity throughout the Jewish People.

* * *

I also express my gratitude to the glorious and renowned Ponevezh Yeshiva, where I merited to learn Torah from great luminaries of our generation, Rabbi Dovid Povarsky זצ"ל, Rabbi Shmuel Rozovsky זצ"ל, and Rabbi Elazar Menachem Mann Shach זצ"ל. May the current Rabbonim there continue to inspire today's youth with love of Torah, and dedication to understanding and fulfilling it in every detail.

Hashem has helped me to be in close contact with leading halachic authorities of our times, particularly the Gaon Maran Rav Shmuel HaLevi Wosner שליט"א, Av Beis Din of Zichron Meir, and the Gaon Maran Rav Nissim Karelitz שליט"א, Rosh Kollel of Kollel Chazon Ish and Av Beis Din of Ramat Aharon. May they merit to continue teaching us Hashem's ways until the coming of the Mashiach.

* * *

My heartfelt thanks to my dear parents, may they live and be well. To my father and teacher, R' Eliyahu שליט"א, son of my martyred grandfather, HaRav HaChassid R' Hillel זצ"ל, may Hashem avenge his blood, and my mother and teacher Maras Penina שתחי', daughter of my other martyred grandfather, HaRav HaChassid R' Ben Zion זצ"ל, may Hashem avenge his blood – may Heaven bless both of you. May you derive great joy and pleasure from all of your children, grandchildren and great grandchildren. May you enjoy excellent health and long, contented lives.

This publication is dedicated to the memory of my father-in-law זצ"ל, who showed great esteem for Torah scholars, ran to do chessed and supported Torah learning all his days, HaRav HaChassid R' Avraham, son of HaRav HaChassid R' Dov HaLevi Kaiserman זצ"ל. He passed away on Cheshvan 17, 5750, leaving a good name behind him. May his soul cleave to the Source of Life.

I would also like to give my blessings to my mother-in-law, Maras Chava Kaiserman שתחי׳. Her home is such a pleasant place, and she is always a help to us in many ways, encouraging us in our learning and our fulfillment of mitzvos. May Hashem amply reward her.

With all my heart I give thanks to my wife, Maras Esther שתחי׳, always at my side with encouragement and support, efficiently running the house, helping the entire family to learn and teach Torah. May it be Hashem's will that together we merit great satisfaction from our children, and may our home always be blessed.

* * *

I praise and thank the Almighty for continuously and mercifully helping me in countless ways. As He has helped me to reach this day, may He continue to show mercy upon me and give me the means and the strength to expand the scope of the many programs of Machon Taharas Yisrael. May His blessing be upon all of our holy efforts, and may our nation soon experience the fulfillment of the prophecy, "And I will sprinkle upon you purifying waters." As our Sages teach, "Happy are you, Israel, for before Whom are you purified and Who purifies you? No one other than your Father in Heaven, may His Name be blessed!"

With thanks to Hashem, the Almighty G-d,
Who has orchestrated events so that this sefer
is now available in English,

Hillel Wertheimer

Director, Machon Taharas Yisrael
Lag Ba'Omer, 5766

TABLE OF CONTENTS

Chapter One

How a Woman Becomes a *Niddah*

1. Any discharge of blood that originated from a woman's uterus and entered her vagina renders her a *niddah*, even if the blood has not yet left her body.[1]

2. A woman becomes a *niddah* irrespective of whether the blood appears at her scheduled menstrual period or at any other time. Accordingly, even a woman who is pregnant, breastfeeding, or after menopause, becomes a *niddah* if blood was discharged from her uterus.

A woman becomes a *niddah* regardless of why the blood was discharged from her uterus. Thus even if the bleeding was caused by strain, panic, medication or an internal medical examination,[2] any discharge of blood from the womb renders her a *niddah*.

3. There is no difference whether the bleeding is profuse, as is common during her menstrual period, or whether the discharge is merely a drop, for example a small dot of blood found on an examination cloth. As long as blood is discharged from the uterus,[3] she becomes a *niddah*.

---

1. See later chapter 2.

2. Even if the discharge was caused by an intrauterine device (IUD) (to be used only with permission of a *Rav*), she becomes *niddah*.

3. Concerning a bloodstain found on her body or clothing, see below paragraphs 11 and 12.

4. A woman is a *niddah* if the discharge[4] is either red or black. This includes different shades of these two colors. Golden or brown shades may sometimes also be regarded as unclean colors, and a competent *Rav* must be consulted in such cases.

A color that appears very different from red or black, such as white, green, blue or light yellow, does not render a woman a *niddah*. A decision concerning doubtful colors can be rendered only by a competent *Rav*.

5. All the prohibitions concerning a *niddah* apply to every woman so classified, whether by Torah or Rabbinic law.[5] The situations as to when a woman is regarded a *niddah* by Torah law and when by Rabbinic law are discussed in this chapter.

Sensations

6. According to Torah law, a woman becomes a *niddah* in the following cases: **a)** She has the kind of sensation usually associated with the onset of her period,[6] and finds blood on her body or clothing following this sensation; **b)** She becomes aware of any kind of sen-

---

4. She becomes a *niddah* whether or not the blood that is discharged from her body is wet or dry.

5. Our Sages state that anyone who transgresses a *Rabbinic* decree is culpable of death by the Heavenly Court.

6. Such as the opening of her uterus, or a stinging sensation as can be felt at the onset of urination, or if she trembles, or if she feels that a wet substance starts seeping from within her. However, a feeling of external wetness at the vagina is not regarded as a sensation. If upon awakening she noticed blood and there was no apparent sensation, a *Rav* should be consulted. If she took sleeping pills and found a stain upon awakening, she must suspect that there was a sensation.

sation usually associated with her period, such as a headache or pain in the abdomen, and finds blood on her body or on her clothing following any of these sensations; **c)** She checks herself with an examination cloth and finds blood on it;[7] **d)** She bled during intercourse or found blood when wiping herself immediately after intercourse.[8]

In addition, if she was not aware of any of the above sensations, but observed a large amount of blood, as is normally seen during menstruation, she is regarded as a *niddah* according to Torah law.

According to Rabbinic law, a woman is a *niddah* if she sees even a drop of blood[9] that could have come from within her uterus even if she did not have one of the above sensations.

Obligation to check

7. A woman who senses that her uterus has opened, in the same manner as at the onset of her period, must check herself immediately to determine whether she discharged any blood. (Checking will be discussed in detail in chapter 4).

If she did not check herself immediately, but checked herself

---

7. Even if she says that she is positive that she did not feel anything, she becomes a *niddah* according to Torah law.

8. If she wiped herself more than ten minutes later, we assume that the blood came after intercourse. If it is less than ten minutes, a *Rav* should be consulted.

9. If she saw blood following urination, see below, paragraph 14. Concerning blood found while wiping herself, see below, paragraph 13. A pregnant woman who sees a stain after the onset of contractions should consult a *Rav*. Likewise, a *Rav* should be consulted concerning all doubts regarding sensations.

within half an hour from the time of the sensation, and found a **clean discharge,**[10] she is not considered a niddah. If she checked herself after half an hour has passed, she should consult with a *Rav.*

If she did not check herself at all, or if she checked and found nothing, then she is regarded as a *niddah,* since we suspect that there was blood present but it got lost.

8. The sensation of a tremor or of a wet substance seeping from within her also obligates her to check well for the possible occurrence of blood. However, in these instances if she checked herself and found nothing, she is not regarded as a *niddah.*[11]

9. If she felt any of the sensations that require checking, but she did not check, and finds a clean discharge (see footnote 10) on tight-fitting underwear, she retains her previous non-*niddah* status. But one can depend on this leniency only *bedi'eved* (post-facto). The

10. This refers to finding a discharge in excess of what she usually experiences. However, if the amount of moisture is similar to that encountered regularly, it is regarded as if she did not find anything. (If she wore closely fitting underwear and found a clean discharge see paragraph 9).

11. If *bedi'eved* she did not check herself at all, one may be lenient in the case of a sensation of a discharge of a wet substance seeping from within her. However, in the case of a body tremor one should be stringent, unless she wore closely-fitted underwear and found on it a clean discharge (see paragraph 9). In a case where she has a physical sensation that is common in women upon the onset of menstruation, see Sources and Explanations. If she found a stain after one of the sensations, even after sensing the discharge of a fluid, and there is some reason to believe that the sensation was indeed connected to the discharge of this stain, she becomes a *niddah* even if the size of the stain is less than a *gris,* and even if it is found on a colored garment or on a material that cannot become *halachically* impure (see later paragraph 12).

correct procedure is to perform the aforementioned check.

10. A woman who frequently has clean discharges and senses a wet substance seeping from within her, should check herself on three occasions after experiencing such a sensation. If she discovers herself clean each time, she is not required to check herself again when she senses a flow of a wet substance, as it can be attributed to the frequent clean discharges.[12]

However, if she feels this sensation on the day of her expected period, she must check herself even though she otherwise would attribute this kind of sensation to a clean discharge.

Staining

11. If a stain of blood *(kesem)* is found on her body, her clothing, on bedding that she used, or on other places that blood originating from her uterus might reach, she could be regarded as a *niddah*, even if she had no prior sensation. The following paragraphs will clarify this further.

12. The finding of a stain does not render a woman a *niddah* in the following three cases: **a)** If the area of the stain is smaller than a *gris.*[13] A *gris* is defined as the area of a circle that is 19 mm in

12. She may rely on this even if the sensation occurred during the first three days of the seven clean days.

13. If she finds several stains, none of which has the area of a *gris*, but combined they do equal a *gris*, then it depends where they are found. If they are found on her body, then they have the status of a stain with an area of a *gris* and she is a *niddah*. However, if they are found on her garments, bedding, etc. she is not a *niddah* unless there is one stain the size of a *gris*.

Some authorities contend that a stain found on the body renders a woman a *niddah* even if it does not have the area of a *gris*. One who is scrupulous in

diameter (the size of a U.S penny); **b)** If the item on which the stain was found is colored and not white; [14] **c)** If the item on which the stain was found is made of a material that cannot become *halachically* impure[15] according to the laws governing such impurity.[16]

In these cases, finding a stain does not render the woman

---

mitzvah observance should be stringent in this matter. When a part of the stain is on her body and another part is on a garment, this has the same status as having been found only on the garment. In the case of a black stain, the *poskim* discuss whether one should be stringent even when its area is less than a *gris*.

When the stained garment was subsequently lost or laundered, and there is a doubt whether the stain had the area of a *gris*, or whether it had a color that renders her a *niddah*, or whether the stain was on the colored part of the garment, one may be lenient. These cases of leniency are only in the case of a stain (*kesem*), but if a woman examined herself and then lost the cloth, and there is a doubt regarding the color on the examination cloth, one must be stringent. A *Rav* should be consulted.

14. Any light colored garment, on which red and black shades are discernable, is regarded as being white.

When a stain the size of a *gris* covers both the white part of a garment and its colored part (and the area of the stain is a *gris* only when the two parts are combined), one should be stringent and regard the woman as a *niddah*. All the more so, if one large stain found on two white parts of a garment is a *gris*, even though a colored part separates them, and the stain is also on the colored part, the woman is regarded as a *niddah*.

15. For the same reason, a woman does not become a *niddah* if she finds the stain on the floor. However, if she found a stain on paper, a sanitary pad, or cotton, she should consult a *Rav*.

16. Even if it becomes *halachically* impure only under Rabbinic law, this leniency will not apply.

a *niddah*[17] unless she had one of the sensations enumerated in paragraph 6 close to finding the stain. (In view of this, when consulting a *Rav*, she should relate to him whether she had a sensation at the time and describe it).

13. A woman who finds a stain of blood on an item[18] that she used to wipe herself on the outside of the vaginal area, becomes a *niddah*[19] even if the stain that is found is minute. This is because we are certain that the blood came from her body (see footnote 18).

14. A woman who noticed even a small amount of blood in her urine, or found a drop of blood when she wiped herself following urination, should consult a *Rav* even if she found the blood on paper or any other material that cannot become *halachically* impure.

Medical examinations

15. A woman who had a foreign object[20] (such as a medical

17. However, even though the stain is of the kind that does not render her a *niddah*, it is fitting that she should check herself with an examination cloth, in order to ensure that she is actually still clean.

18. If the item is of the kind that does not become *halachically* impure, or a garment that is colored, or blood found on toilet paper, see Sources and Explanations.

19. This is by rabbinic law, since she did not have a sensation. It cannot be claimed that she actually had a sensation but was unaware of such an event due to the sensation of the wiping, since the wiping was only external.

20. The woman becomes a *niddah* only if the foreign object was inserted into the cervix. However, if it was inserted only into the vaginal canal, and blood was not observed, she does not become a *niddah*. If the foreign object was very slender (up to 2 mm) and no blood was noticed, she does not become a *niddah* under any circumstances.

instrument, a device that injects a substance for the purpose of an X-ray, etc). inserted into her uterus that caused the cervix to widen, is regarded as a *niddah* even if she did not notice any bleeding.[21]

Therefore, a woman who has been treated with medical instruments should first clarify with the physician which instruments were used and what procedures were performed, and then consult a *Rav*.

Wounds

16. A woman who has a wound in her vagina and sees blood, either on an examination cloth or on an item used for wiping, should consult a *Rav*.

Similarly, a woman who finds a stain on her garment or her skin, and she has a wound on her body that might have bled, or she has passed through an area where blood is found, so that it is possible that the stain did not come from her uterus but from some other source, such a woman should consult a *Rav* to determine if she is a *niddah*.

Conduct in situations of doubt

17. Every case where a woman is uncertain if she became a *niddah*

---

21. When the physician's examination is done using a finger, it is usually impossible to insert it into the cervix, because the area is very narrow. However, close to giving birth, when the area is somewhat wider, a finger could indeed be inserted into the cervix. Hence, if the physician inserted his finger and widened the cervix in order to expedite birth or the like, it renders the woman a *niddah*. This being so, the matter should be clarified and a *Rav* consulted.

The authorities discuss whether a non-Jewish doctor or a doctor who is a non-observant Jew can be believed that the woman has a bleeding wound in the vagina. A *Rav* must be consulted in this matter.

or not requires consulting a *Rav*, and until the *halachah* is clarified the couple should conduct themselves as if she is definitely a *niddah*, observing all the laws and restrictions enumerated in chapter 2. This is so even if the doubt arises after noticing a *kesem*.

18. A woman who told her husband that she is a *niddah* may not later on retract her statement, even if she claims that she was not serious the first time. However, if she retracted immediately,[22] she is believed. If the woman provided a justifiable excuse for making the first statement, she is believed even later. However, since this law has many details, a *Rav* should be consulted in each case. A woman should be careful not to say to her husband that she is a *niddah*, unless this is indeed so.[23]

22. Within the time it takes to say the three words שלום עליך רבי.

23. Also, if she found a stain that requires a *Rav's* decision, she should tell her husband that she is in doubt and not that she is definitely a *niddah*.

Chapter Two

Laws of Restrictions

1. From the time a woman becomes a *niddah* until after she immerses in the *mikvah,* marital relations are prohibited by Torah law.[1] This is a very severe prohibition that carries the penalty of *kores* (spiritual excision) for both of them. In addition, the Torah prohibits embracing, kissing or having bodily contact.

Since *yichud* (remaining together in private quarters), however, is permitted for a married couple when the wife is a *niddah*, the Sages feared that the above prohibitions could be transgressed. For this reason they instituted several restrictions. These restrictions are the subject of the present chapter.

2. The couple is not permitted to interact in a manner that may cause them to sin, such as using words of affection or engaging in frivolous conversation or light-headed conduct. Similarly, they must refrain from actions and behavior that may bring about frivolity. However, they are allowed to give gifts to one another.

3. A husband may not look at those parts of his wife's body that are usually covered[2] (this includes her hair, arms and legs), nor hear her singing. He may not smell her perfume, whether it be on her body,

---

1. It is subject to the law of יהרג ואל יעבור (that requires one to forfeit his life rather then transgress it).

2. The penalty for disregarding this prohibition is having children that act improperly.

held by her, or standing on a shelf. It is prohibited to light a candle or a cigarette from fire held by the spouse. However, the wife may hold the *havdalah* candle for her husband.

4. They may not touch one another at all, even if it is not done in a manner of endearment, and even by means of a long article. Similarly, they may not touch a garment that the spouse is wearing, even the part that does not lie directly on the body.[3]

It is forbidden to remove anything from the spouse's body or garment even a feather or dirt, whether by hand or by blowing. It is prohibited to manually fan one another.

5. They are not permitted to hand or throw anything to one another. This applies both to handing or throwing from hand to hand, and to placing or throwing an item into a basket, purse or anything held by the spouse. The same holds for throwing or placing an article on the spouse's body or clothing. They are also not permitted to place or remove an item from a utensil in the other's hand.[4]

---

3. In view of this, when a baby is placed on the spouse's bed, care should be taken not to place it on the part of the blanket with which the spouse is covered. It is proper to take care that the baby should not be placed even on that part of the blanket that is not actually covering the spouse, rather he should be placed on the bed and not on the blanket.

4. A child should not be handed over to the spouse, even if the child is old enough that he goes by himself from one parent to another. Similarly, it is prohibited to be a *kvater* (carrying the baby to and from the *bris*) when this involves handing the child one to the other.

When a spouse holds a child in his / her hand, the other spouse should not place a pacifier in the child's mouth or feed him. However, under difficult circumstances, for example when drops must be placed in the child's eye and the child resists, one may be lenient and have one spouse hold the baby's eye

Eating together

6. The couple may not eat or drink together from one utensil, even if other people are eating or drinking together with them from that utensil. Nevertheless, one spouse may take food from a serving plate and put it on his / her plate. Similarly, they may each slice pieces from the same loaf of bread and take from the same spread, etc.

7. When the husband and wife sit down to eat or drink at the same table, they must do something to remind them that the wife is now a *niddah*.[5]

This reminder can be done in a number of ways: **a)** They can eat on separate placemats or towels, or only one of them can use a placemat, provided that they do not usually do so when she is not a *niddah*. **b)** They can place a conspicuous item[6] on the table between them that is not usually there during the meal. It can even be an item that is usually placed on the table during a meal, but which is now placed in a different location from the ordinary and they are aware of this change. **c)** If each of them usually sits in a specific place, one of them should now sit in a different place.

If they sit far enough from one another so that one cannot stretch out a hand to the plate of the other, a reminder is not needed. They also do not need a reminder if another person sits

---

open while the other places the drops in the eye.

5. However, they may not eat or drink from the same utensil even with a reminder.

6. A small or low item can be used, as long as it is discernible. It is also possible to use an item that is usually placed on the table during a meal, but is not currently needed, for example, a loaf of bread from which they are not currently eating, or a jug from which they are not currently drinking.

between them.[7]

Leftover food and drink

8. The husband is not permitted to eat or drink his wife's leftover food or drink. Leftovers are defined as anything not usually eaten once another person ate from them. However, a loaf of bread from which the wife cut a slice, or a spread that she used for smearing on her food are not regarded as leftovers. When using a cup from which she drank, there is no need to rinse it beforehand.[8]

Even if additional food or drink was added to her leftovers, he may not eat or drink them. However, if her leftovers were transferred to another vessel, it is permissible for the husband to eat and drink them. This leniency only applies to food that requires a dish. After the leftovers were transferred, they may be returned to the original vessel and eaten.

If another person ate from her leftovers in between, the husband may also eat from them.

If the wife left the room, the husband may eat and drink her leftovers. However, when she comes back, the prohibition returns and the husband must stop eating her leftovers.[9]

If the wife ate or drank before she became a *niddah*, and then she became a *niddah*, the husband may not eat or drink her leftovers.

---

7. Under extenuating circumstances, it is possible to forgo the placing of a reminder when other people sit with them at the table, even if the married couple is sitting next to one another.

8. Still, it is commendable to be stringent and rinse out the cup.

9. Some authorities are lenient in this case.

If the husband is not aware of the fact that the food or drink that he wants to eat or drink are his wife's leftovers, there is no need to inform him. However, if he knows that these are her leftovers, but does not know that she is a *niddah*, he should be informed.[10]

If the wife tasted the food or drink merely to check their taste, they are not regarded as leftovers and the husband may eat them.

The wife may eat her husband's leftover food, and drink his leftover drinks.

Serving food and drinks

9. The husband is prohibited to pour a drink for his wife in front of her. Similarly, the wife is prohibited to pour a drink for her husband in front of him.[11] They are also prohibited to serve food or drink to one another, unless they do so in a manner that they are not accustomed to. For example, the food or drink can be placed somewhat farther away, or placed with the left hand.[12]

10. The husband is prohibited from sending his wife a cup of wine or another important drink (a drink served to honor a guest) via an emissary. This prohibition also applies to a *kos shel bracha*. For this reason the husband may not ask another person to pass his wife the cup of wine on which he made *kiddush*. Similarly, he should not place this cup in front of her as was explained in the previous

---

10. After the wife has immersed herself in a *mikvah* and is permitted to her husband, he may eat and drink the leftovers from which she ate and drank when she was a *niddah*.

11. This also applies to adding milk to coffee that is in front of the spouse.

12. Being that one customarily serves with the right hand, serving with the left hand is a sufficient distinction.

paragraph. He may place the cup at some distance from her, or leave the cup in front of him and let her take it, or she could ask another person to pass it to her.

Sitting together

11. They may not sit on the same bench if this may cause it to sway. However, they may sit on the same bench if it is fastened to the ground or is very heavy and does not have soft upholstery. This is because it will not move due to their sitting on it.

However, they may sit on the same bench, even if it will sway, when another person or a large or tall article is located between them.[13]

12. They may not ride alone in the same car, even on separate seats, if they are going on a pleasure trip. Visiting relatives or friends, or traveling to a festive event is not regarded as a pleasure trip. Hence, they may travel alone in a car for these purposes, provided that they sit on separate seats,[14] or another person or a large or tall article is located between them (as above in paragraph 11).

Sleeping arrangements

13. The husband may not lie or sit on his wife's bed, or lie on her bed linen, even when she is not present.[15] If the wife is out of town for several days, he may lie on her bed and on her bed linen.

The wife is only prohibited from lying on her husband's bed or

---

13. They may also sit on a sofa with soft upholstery, or on the same seat in a car, if another person or a large or tall article is located between them.

14. The couple must be careful not to touch one another.

15. This restriction, however, does not include an easy chair or an armchair.

on his bed linen when he is present,[16] but she may do so when he is not present.

14. They may not lie on the same bed or on two beds that touch one another. If the beds are parallel to one another, they should be moved far enough apart[17] so that the blankets cannot touch one another even accidentally.

15. The wife is prohibited from making her husband's bed in his presence. Similarly, the husband is prohibited from making his wife's bed in her presence. The prohibition holds even if this is performed in an unusual manner.[18]

This prohibition applies only if the bed is being made in order to lie on it. However, it is permitted to make the bed after it was used, to tidy the room.

Preparations for washing and bathing

16. They are prohibited from pouring water on one another, for example, for washing. This applies even if they do not touch one another and even if it is not done in the usual manner.

Similarly, either spouse may not prepare water for washing purposes for the other spouse in his or her presence, even when

16. The majority of *Poskim* permit a wife to sit on her husband's bed even when he is present.

17. The custom among G-d fearing people is to keep their beds separated by a distance of an *amah,* which is approximately 60 cm or 24 in. If the room is narrow, 50 cm is sufficient.

18. Nevertheless, one may bring bed linen and place it on the spouse's bed, and then the spouse can make the bed for himself or herself. It is also permitted to make a bed when it has not yet been decided which spouse will use it.

done in an unusual manner.

They may prepare water for each other for a *mitzvah* purpose, for example to be used for washing one's hands upon awakening in the morning, or before eating bread.

If spouse is sick

17. If, G-d forbid, the husband or wife is sick and there is no one to attend to his or her needs except for the spouse, a *Rav* should be consulted concerning what situations and by what means it is possible to be lenient regarding the laws explained in this chapter.

Additional laws of restrictions

18. Under no circumstances may one be lenient regarding any of the laws in this chapter because they are concerned that someone will discern that the woman is a *niddah*.

19. Since a woman remains a *niddah* until she counts seven clean days and immerses herself in a *kosher mikvah,* as will be explained in the following chapters, all that was mentioned in this chapter must be followed until after her immersion.[19] No leniency is permitted even on the last of the seven clean days. Likewise, if the immersion is delayed, no leniency is permitted until after the immersion.

20. A woman may go to *shul* to *daven* when she is a *niddah*. She should, however, be careful not to look at the *sefer Torah* when it is held up until she actually stops bleeding.

21. A woman should not go to the cemetery when she is a *niddah*.

22. The laws enumerated in this chapter must be followed on *Tisha*

---

19. No leniency is permitted even if she acquired her *niddah* status by rabbinic law, for example, due to a stain.

B'Av night and on *Yom Kippur* (even during the day), even if the woman is not a *niddah*. These restrictions do not apply on *Tisha B'av* during the day, except for touching in an endearing manner.

23. When one of the spouses is, G-d forbid, within the seven days of mourning, the couple is prohibited from having relations and engaging in other acts of intimacy, even if the wife is not a *niddah*. This includes the prohibition of lying in the same bed, but does not include other restrictions.

24. A person is prohibited to be lenient concerning all the above prohibitions. The *Sefer Hachinuch* has the following to say concerning this: A person is not permitted to deviate from the good ethics promulgated by the Sages. Even though he finds that his lust has lessened somewhat, he should not say, "I know that my evil inclination will not overpower me". You, my son, should be very careful concerning the and do not accept the assurances of the *yetzer hora* (evil inclination), even if it presents you with a thousand guarantors.

25. In addition to the matters clarified in this chapter, that were promulgated by our Sages as safeguards and barriers to prevent people from coming to sin, the couple should also refrain from any acts that they know to be conducive to improper actions. To again quote the *Sefer Hachinuch*: The general rule is that a person should not do anything that will cause him to have sinful thoughts. He should not act, speak, or think in a manner that will cause his wife to have intimate relations with him. It is impossible to enumerate all the acts that might cause them to be frivolous. For this reason our Sages mentioned only several cases. Concerning other cases, he should watch himself according to his awareness of his weaknesses and his tendency to sin for the Almighty knows our innermost thoughts. If need be he should restrict even those things which are permitted.

Chapter Three

The Five-Day Waiting Period

A woman who became a *niddah* must go through the following procedures in order to emerge from this status. She must wait at least five days from the day she became a *niddah* and must perform the *hefsek taharah* (a cessation of flow check, see chapter 4). If this check is successful, she must count "seven clean days" during which no blood is encountered. At the end of these days, she must wash herself, shampoo her hair, and immerse in a *mikvah*, whereupon she becomes permitted to her husband. The details of these laws will be clarified in the coming chapters. This chapter is concerned with the laws of the five-day waiting period.

The reason for waiting five days prior to starting the seven clean days is in order to ensure that the seven clean days will be free from any discharge of her husband's semen from her body. However, whether there were relations or not, our Rabbis instituted that these five days must be kept in order not to differentiate between situations. (See Sources and Explanations for elaboration of this point).

1. A woman who became a *niddah* in one of the ways enumerated in the first chapter becomes permitted to her husband by counting seven clean days, during which she does not encounter any blood.[1] (The laws of "the seven clean days" will be detailed in chapter 5).

---

1. For the case of bleeding or a bloodstain caused by the rupturing of the hymen *(dam besulim)*, see chapter 12.

She cannot, however, start counting the seven clean days before the five-day waiting period from the time that she became a *niddah* is complete. This is irrespective of whether she encountered any bleeding during these five days.

2. The obligation to wait five days applies whether she sees blood on all five days or only on a single day.

Similarly, there is no difference whether she became a *niddah* because she actually menstruated, or because she checked herself in the vaginal area and found even a drop of blood, or was checked by a physician in a manner that caused her to acquire the *niddah* status.[2] Likewise, if she became a *niddah* because she saw a bloodstain on her garment or because she wiped herself in a way that rendered her a *niddah* she cannot start counting the seven clean days before the five-day waiting period is up.[3]

3. The five-day waiting period includes the day when she became a *niddah* and four additional days.

---

2. A *Rav* should be consulted to determine whether that specific medical examination caused her to become a *niddah.*

3. Should the five-day waiting period cause the night of immersion to come out on Friday night following *Yom Tov* (that is, when Friday is *Yom Tov*) thereby causing too long an interlude between washing herself thoroughly to immersing in the *mikvah,* then if she ceases bleeding on the fourth day, she should carry out the *hefsek taharah* on that day. The same applies if the night of immersion comes out on the night of a *Yom Tov* that occurs right after *Shabbos* (meaning that the *Yom Tov* occurs on Sunday), or on the second night of *Yom Tov.* She will thereby start counting the seven clean days after four rather than five days, and will thus be able to wash herself (*chafifah*) on the day directly preceding the immersion.

There is no difference at what time during the day she became a *niddah*, whether in the morning or in the late afternoon right before sunset, or on the night before.[4] In all cases, she counts the day on which she becomes a *niddah* as day one and then adds four more days.

For example, if she became a *niddah* on Sunday, then that day is counted as the first day of the five-day waiting period. There is no difference whether she became a *niddah* on *motzei Shabbos* or on Sunday afternoon. Even if this happened close to sunset, Sunday is regarded as the first day of the five-day waiting period.

In this case she performs the *hefsek taharah* on Thursday afternoon before sunset (as shall be explained in the next chapter) and the seven clean days start on Friday (meaning after sunset on Thursday). Her immersion night will be on Thursday night a week later.

4. Some *Sephardim* are accustomed to wait six or seven days from the day when the woman becomes a *niddah* before they start counting the seven clean days.[5] Those who are accustomed to act like this should continue to do so. In the case when there is a difference in custom between husband and wife, the wife should follow her husband's custom.

---

4. Regarding these *halachos*, a day begins with sunset of one day and ends with the sunset of the next day. If for example, she started to menstruate after sunset on *Shabbos* (close to the termination of *Shabbos*), then the five-day waiting period starts on Sunday.

If she encountered bleeding on Friday night before sunset, then Friday is regarded as the first of the five-day waiting period, even if she already lit the *Shabbos* candles and prayed *maariv* before sunset.

5. It is proper before starting this custom for the woman to state that she takes it upon herself without vowing *(bli neder)* to continue doing so.

5. In the case when more than five days have elapsed since she acquired the *niddah* status, for example, after giving birth,[6] she can perform the *hefsek taharah* any day that is practical and then start counting the seven clean days.

Similarly, if in the course of the seven clean days she again saw blood,[7] or if blood was found on her examination cloth, or she found an unclean stain, she must repeat the *hefsek taharah* and restart the seven clean days. In this instance, she may perform the *hefsek taharah* on the same day she became a *niddah* (see chapter 4, paragraph 7) and start counting the seven clean days from the next day, without first waiting five days.

6. Moreover, even if for some reason she did not immerse herself until after she again menstruated, she may perform the *hefsek taharah* immediately and start counting the seven clean days without waiting five days.[8]

---

6. See chapter 13 for laws that apply to a woman after giving birth.

7. If she became a *niddah* again at the night of immersion, before she had relations, she can perform the *hefsek taharah* on the next day and start counting the seven clean days. This applies only if this happened when she immersed herself because she initially became a *niddah* due to menstruation bleeding. However, if she acquired *niddah* status because of a stain, or because of hymen rupture, this leniency does not apply.

8. Similarly, a bride before her wedding may perform the *hefsek taharah* and start counting the seven clean days immediately when she ceases bleeding, even if this is within five days of her period.

This also applies to a woman who acquired her *niddah* status because of the rupturing of her hymen (*dam besulim*), and then menstruated (before she immersed herself). She observes the five-day waiting period from the time of the rupturing of her hymen.

Similarly, a woman who did not immerse herself after giving birth and in the meantime had her period may perform the *hefsek taharah* immediately after she ceases menstruating, without waiting five days.

7. If she found a bloodstain or if she checked herself with an examination cloth and found a questionable stain but did not yet show it to a *Rav*, and the couple, out of doubt,[9] separated as if she were a *niddah*, if a day or more later the woman actually became a *niddah*, she may start counting the five-day waiting period from the day they separated due to the questionable stain.[10]

8. If she mistakenly started counting the seven clean days without the five-day wait, a *Rav* must be consulted.[11]

---

9. This applies only when they in fact suspect that the stain may cause the woman to become a *niddah*. However, if they separated because they chose to be stringent and not because the *halachah* actually so required, or for some other reason and not because of any doubt that she may be a *niddah*, she cannot count the five-day waiting period from the day when they decided to separate. She must, rather, count the five-day waiting period from the day she actually became a *niddah* and then count the seven clean days. Similarly, if they suspend all relations because either the husband or the wife is a mourner, the five days cannot be counted from the day when mourning started. She starts counting only from the day she became a *niddah*.

10. This is so even if it was later verified that the doubtful stain did not render her a *niddah*.

11. See Sources and Explanations.

Chapter Four

Hefsek Taharah

(a cessation of flow check)

A woman who becomes a *niddah* in one of the ways explained in chapter 1 must count seven days (called the seven clean days), during which there is no bleeding or staining, and only afterward can she immerse herself in a *mikveh*. She can begin these seven clean days only after: **a)** She waits five days from the day she became a *niddah*; **b)** She has stopped bleeding; and **c)** She successfully performs the *hefsek taharah*.

Details concerning the laws of the five-day waiting period were elucidated in the previous chapter. In this chapter, we will explain the details concerning the *hefsek taharah*.

1. A woman may begin counting the seven clean days only after she definitely establishes that bleeding has indeed terminated. She does this by checking herself before sunset on the day proceeding the "clean days" using a pre-checked examination cloth (*eid bedikah*). If no trace of blood is found on the cloth after this examination, the *hefsek taharah* is successful and she can begin counting the seven clean days. Without this verification the seven clean days cannot begin.

Preparation for *hefsek taharah*

2. Prior to performing this check,[1] she should wash herself with

---

1. If she checked herself for a reason other than to be able to start counting the seven clean days, and did not recheck herself for the *hefsek taharah*, a *Rav* should be consulted.

water[2] around the vaginal area. It is preferable to also wash all lower parts of the body, and as a *hiddur mitzvah* (enhancement of the *mitzvah*) some are accustomed to wash their entire body.

If in her preparation for the *hefsek taharah* she also washed inside the vaginal area or washed herself while sitting in water, she should wait a few minutes before preceding with this check.[3]

---

2. She may wash either with warm or cold water. See paragraph 11 regarding washing before the *hefsek taharah* on *Shabbos* and *Yom Tov*.

3. If she checked herself immediately without waiting, she can *bedi'eved*, after the fact, be lenient that this check was acceptable. If she washed herself only externally and not inside the vagina, she can carry out the *hefsek taharah* immediately without waiting.

She can also perform the *hefsek taharah* immediately if she is afraid that it will be delayed until after the time when it is permissible to make this examination (see paragraph 5). When she checks herself immediately after washing, however, she should be particular to place a *moch dachuk* in the vaginal canal (see paragraph 7) since this will provide extra clarification as to whether her bleeding has indeed stopped. If, however, she did not perform the *moch dachuk* examination the *hefsek taharah* is valid *bedi'eved*.

A woman who frequently injures herself when examining her vaginal canal should preferably wash a few hours before the *hefsek taharah*, so that the natural mucus that gets washed away will have a chance to return and moisten the area. This will make the examination easier. If it is still difficult for her to carry out this examination, she should smear a little petroleum jelly (Vaseline) in the vaginal canal. She can even smear an abundant amount of this jelly if it is done a few hours before the examination since during that time it is absorbed into the body, thus allowing her to more easily insert the examination cloth. (Creams with a water base instead of an oily base are preferable. This type of non-oily cream can be applied even a few minutes before the *hefsek taharah*. When needed, a small quantity of this non-oily cream can even be put on the examination cloth). If she has no cream, she

If she showered but did not wash within the vaginal area, she may perform the *hefsek taharah* immediately without waiting.

If she performed this check without washing herself at all and the *bedikah* cloth was found clean, it is a valid *hefsek taharah*.

Method of checking

3. After washing, she performs the *hefsek taharah* in the following way: She wraps the examination cloth around her forefinger and inserts it in the vaginal canal as deeply as possible. She then turns it in a manner that will ensure that the complete surface area including any possible folds and crevices are carefully checked.[4] If she did not insert it deeply[5] or did not check all the crevices, the examination is unacceptable.

If she detects any trace of blood during this examination and it is still before sunset, she can re-check herself[6] until she has a clean

---

should wet the examination cloth with a little water, squeeze it out well and then perform the examination. (The examination cloth may not be made wet on *Shabbos* and *Yom Tov,* and even checking with a wet examination cloth prepared beforehand is forbidden on these days. One should, therefore, slightly wet the vaginal area before the examination).

4. The most comfortable way to do this examination is by raising one foot on a chair, etc. while the other foot remains on the floor.

5. Whenever one is doubtful if the examination was done correctly, e.g. whether it was inserted deep enough or other questions, a *Rav* should be consulted.

6. It is proper to wait a few minutes between one examination and the next, just like after washing (see paragraph 2), unless it is getting close to sunset. She does not need to wash herself again before re-checking.
Likewise, a woman whose seven clean days were interrupted, due to traces of

bedikah.

Type of examination cloth

4. The examination should be carried out with a soft,[7] clean,[8] white, laundered cloth made up of densely woven threads.

Checking by inserting a finger without wrapping the examination cloth around the finger is invalid.

Time of checking

5. The *hefsek taharah* **must** be performed before sunset.[9] If it is done

---

blood found on the examination cloth, does not need to wash herself before the new *hefsek taharah*. However, if she detected blood outside of the vaginal canal such as on a garment near her vaginal tract and the like, (rather than upon examination), it is proper to wash herself before the *hefsek taharah*.

7. The ideal cloth to use is that made of cotton or a similar soft, absorbent material on which blood is well discernible. Synthetic fiber cloths tend to spread the blood over a large area making it difficult to discern the blood. Nonetheless, if synthetic fiber cloth was used, the examination is acceptable.
Ideally, one should not check using paper, but if this was already done with white, soft tissue paper and it was not torn, one can be lenient and consider that examination as being valid. It is advisable not to use cotton balls or swabs since remnants of it may remain in the vagina. An examination using a tampon is invalid since it cannot be inserted inside all the skin folds.

8. One should check the examination cloth beforehand to ascertain that it is completely clean.

9. Care must be taken to use a calendar that specifies the precise times for sunset in the location where the examination is carried out.
When a woman travels by airplane, she should perform the examination early and not rely on seeing the sun from the airplane. This is because, even if she sees the sun, if below on the ground at that same place the sun has already set,

after sunset, or even if one is **doubtful** whether it was done before or after sunset, the examination is invalid.

In communities where *ma'ariv* is before sunset, it is preferable that she perform the *hefsek taharah* before the community *davens ma'ariv*. If, however, she performed the check after the prayers and even if she herself also *davened ma'ariv*, one may be lenient, provided that it was done before sunset.

6. The examination should initially be performed no earlier than *minchah ketanah*.[10] Ideally it should be made during the half hour before sunset. (Concerning the time for checking on *erev Shabbos*, see paragraph 10).

If, however, she examined herself before *minchah ketanah* and did not re-examine herself before sunset, she may be lenient *bedi'eved*.[11]

This leniency (that the check performed before *minchah ketanah* is valid *bedi'eved)* only applies when it is not done on a day that she actually began bleeding. However if the *hefsek taharah* is being done on a day that she began bleeding (for example, if during the seven clean days she either menstruated or detected a bloodstain on the *bedikah* cloth, in which case she does not have to observe the

---

her examination is regarded as having been performed after sunset.

10. Since a difference of opinion exists concerning the time of *minchah ketanah,* she should ideally perform the check from an hour and a half before sunset.

11. If she did not encounter bleeding on the day that she wishes to perform the *hefsek taharah*, she may be lenient and perform this check even in the morning if there is some need for doing so. If, however, she encountered bleeding sometime during that day she should not be lenient unless a great need exists.

five-day waiting period, see above chapter 3, paragraph 6), then the examination is invalid even *bedi'eved* if it is done before *minchah ketanah*.[12] (See next paragraph about *moch dachuk)*.

Moch dachuk

7. Following a successful *hefsek taharah*, she should insert a new *bedikah* cloth, cotton or tampon deep into her vagina just before sunset and leave it there until nightfall.[13] (This procedure is known as the *moch dachuk)*. Nevertheless, if she did not do so, her examination is valid *bedi'eved*.

This applies when she performs the *hefsek taharah* on a day that she did not start menstruating. But if done on a day that she began fresh bleeding (as in the preceding paragraph), there is a difference of opinion. Sephardim must be stringent and unconditionally disqualify the examination if a *moch dachuk* was not used.[14] In such

---

12. If she only found a *kesem* (a bloodstain found on a garment or on her body, but not on the examination cloth, occurring without any sensation) in the middle of the seven clean days, even if she made the *hefsek taharah* on that same day before *minchah ketanah* she can be lenient *bedi'eved*.

13. Ideally she should leave the *moch dachuk* inside until nightfall (צאת הכוכבים). If she finds it difficult to leave it in for such a long time, she may remove it 18 min. after sunset, and in Eretz Yisrael even after 13 ½ min. Those who always follow *Rabbeinu Tam's* opinion regarding nightfall, should leave the *moch dachuk* inside for 72 min. after sunset, but those who follow *Rabbeinu Tam's* opinion only in regard to Torah-based laws, need not follow the "72 min. rule" in this matter.

14. Nowadays since it is common to wear tight-fitted, white underwear there is no reason to fear that a drop of blood will fall on the garment and not be noticed. Therefore, when absolutely necessary if her garment was found clean from any signs of blood, Sephardim also can rely on a *hefsek taharah* done on

a case, this check must be redone on the next day (see footnote 14). Ashkenazim[15] may be lenient, *bedi'eved,* if they did not insert the *moch dachuk,* as long as the *hefsek taharah* was performed after *minchah ketanah.* A scrupulous person should be stringent concerning this law.

Checking the cloth

8. The *bedikah* cloth must be checked in daylight on both sides in order to ascertain whether it has on it blood or any stain that has any resemblance to red.[16] The *moch dachuk* should also initially be checked in daylight. However, if they were checked by candlelight or by an electric light and no questionable stains were found, they are valid.

9. She must wear clean, white, laundered underwear before sunset (see chapter 5 paragraph 5).

Hefsek taharah on *erev Shabbos*

10. On *erev Shabbos* the *hefsek taharah* should ideally be performed

---

the same day that menstruation began (e.g. a bloodstain was detected on the examination cloth during the seven clean days), even if they did not insert the *moch dachuk.* They she should check themselves as soon as they can after nightfall.

15. This depends upon the husband's custom.

16. Concerning the *hefsek taharah,* one is more stringent with shades of colors found on the *bedikah* cloth than with other examinations. For this reason when showing the examination cloth to a *Rav,* one must specify that this is a *hefsek taharah.* Likewise, if the woman knows that initially the stain was closer to red than it was when she showed it to the *Rav,* she must tell him this. It is good practice to be prudent and immediately bring a doubtful *bedikah* cloth to a *Rav* rather than wait a day or two.

before candle lighting. If, however, she did not do so, she can still do it after candle lighting, but before sunset. (See the next paragraph detailing how to perform the *hefsek taharah* on *Shabbos).*

In places where people are accustomed to begin *Shabbos* a long time before sunset, she should do a *bedikah* once before candle lighting, and then another before sunset. Afterwards she should insert the *moch dachuk*[17].

Hefsek taharah on *Shabbos* and *Yom Tov*

11. The *hefsek taharah* may be performed on *Shabbos.*[18] Before the examination, she should wash near the vaginal area and between her thighs. She can even use hot water if it was heated on *erev Shabbos,* such as water that was placed on the fire on *erev Shabbos.* (It is forbidden to wash one's entire body or most of it with hot water on Shabbos).

She should take care when washing to use neither a cloth nor a sponge nor soap, irrespective of whether it is hard or paste-like.[19] One must also take care when mixing cold and hot water together to avoid transgressing the forbidden activity of *bishul* (cooking) on *Shabbos.*[20]

---

17. Where there is no *eiruv,* it is forbidden to go out in the street with the *moch dachuk* in place.

18. When performed on *Yom Tov* it is even permissible to heat up water in order to wash the vaginal area and between the thighs.

19. It is permitted to use liquid soap, but some opinions advise not to use it.

20. She should mix the cold water with the hot water when the hot water is in a *kli sheini* (a vessel to which the water was emptied from the vessel that was on the fire).

After washing, she checks herself with a bedikah cloth,[21] in the way explained above in paragraph 3.

Hefsek taharah on *Yom Kippur* and *Tishah B'Av*

12. She may perform the *hefsek taharah* on *Yom Kippur.* Before checking herself, she should wash only the vaginal area, because of the special prohibition of not washing on *Yom Kippur.* She should cleanse only this immediate area even if she only uses cold water. She may use pre-heated water as mentioned in the previous paragraph, but she must be careful to follow the same instructions as one observes on *Shabbos.*

13. She may also perform the *hefsek taharah* on *Tishah B'Av* or when she is in mourning. Before the *bedikah* she should only wash the vaginal area. This can be done with warm water.

After washing, she should check herself with a *bedikah* cloth (as explained above in paragraph 3), and wear previously worn, clean underwear that was not yet laundered. If such a garment is not available, she may wear a freshly laundered undergarment.

Hefsek taharah when the seven clean days are postponed

14. When a woman performed a *hefsek taharah* (after the five-day waiting period), but for some reason did not immediately start counting the seven clean days, she need not redo the *hefsek taharah* on the day before she starts counting; [22] the previous

---

21. On *Shabbos* it is forbidden to wet the *bedikah* cloth in order to make the examination easier, even if she has sensitive skin (see above footnote 3). She should wet the vaginal area as described there, but not use any creams.

22. On condition that she intended to count the seven clean days when she made the *hefsek taharah.*

hefsek taharah is sufficient.[23]

Hefsek taharah before waiting five days

15. Ideally she should not perform the *hefsek taharah* until the five days have passed.[24] Therefore if her menstrual flow stopped before five days passed, or she became a *niddah* because of a *kesem* (stain), or through finding blood on a *bedikah* cloth and did not have any further menstrual flow, she should nontheless perform the *hefsek taharah* on the fifth day (in the late afternoon) and start counting the seven clean days on the next day.

Even when she performed the *hefsek taharah* during the five days after she became a *niddah* and the examination cloth was found clean, she should not initially rely on this examination but should re-check herself just before the end of the fifth day so that the *hefsek taharah* immediately precedes the counting the seven clean days.

When a need arises to perform the *hefsek taharah* during the

23. Likewise, if she performed the *hefsek taharah* and forgot to check herself on the first of the seven clean days, she need not redo the *hefsek taharah* and can begin counting the seven clean days on the next day. Even if seven or more days passed before the beginning of the seven clean days, she may begin counting the seven clean days although they were delayed by many days after the *hefsek taharah.*

24. This is so although, by the letter of the law, the *hefsek taharah* may be performed immediately after she ceases menstruating, as for example when the flow was for only one or two days and then stopped. However, since she can only start counting the seven clean days after the five-day waiting period is over, ideally she should not perform the *hefsek taharah* in the middle of the five-day waiting period. She should rather wait until the end of the fifth day, in order to perform this check right before the seven clean days.

five-day waiting period from the time that she became a *niddah*, she may perform this check even on the same day that she became a *niddah*. For example, if she expects to travel on the fifth day and is afraid that she will not be able to perform the *hefsek taharah*[25] on that day, she may do so before. However, as previously noted, she may not begin to count the seven clean days until the five-day waiting period is over. If it turns out that she is able to re-check while traveling, she should ideally do so.

25. When she is able to perform the *hefsek taharah* on the fifth day, but for some reason cannot wash on that day, she may wash herself as soon as her menstrual flow has stopped, and perform the *hefsek taharah* on the fifth day.

Chapter Five

Counting the Seven Clean Days

1. A woman who has become a *niddah* must count "seven clean days" before immersing herself in the *mikvah* in order to be permitted to her husband.[1] This is to verify that she will not see even a drop of blood during these seven days. In the coming paragraphs we will explain the laws applicable to these days and the manner in which she verifies that the bleeding has stopped completely.

In chapter 3 it was explained that a woman cannot begin the seven clean days until after waiting five days from the time she became a *niddah*, and after performing the *hefsek taharah*.[2]

2. The seven clean days are counted from **the day after** she performed a valid *hefsek taharah*. The day on which she made the *hefsek taharah* does not count as the first day of the seven clean days. Thus if she performed a *hefsek taharah* at the end of the fifth day after becoming a *niddah*, the first of the seven days begins that

---

1. According to some opinions it is a good *minhag* (custom) to say each day: "Today is the 1st day of the clean days. Today is the 2nd, etc". This is, however, not the widespread *minhag*. See Sources and Explanations for laws regarding a woman who mistakenly counted less than seven clean days.

2. Even if more than five days have elapsed from the day that she became a *niddah*, she can start counting only from after the *hefsek taharah*. For example, a woman who performed the *hefsek taharah* on the eighth day after becoming a *niddah* begins counting the seven clean days on the ninth day, which is the day after she performed the *hefsek taharah*.

evening which is the beginning of the sixth day from the time that she became a *niddah*.

Time and method of checking

3. She must check herself twice a day on each of the seven clean days, once in the morning upon getting up, after sunrise,[3] and the second time in the late afternoon after *minchah ketanah* (see chapter 4, footnote 10) but not later than sunset. (A reliable Jewish calendar that specifies these times should be consulted).

This checking is done with a clean, white *bedikah* cloth inserted into the vaginal canal, taking care to check all the folds and crevices as explained in chapter 4, paragraphs 3 and 4.

After the examination, she inspects the cloth to check for any shade of redness (as in chapter 4, paragraph 8). A *Rav* should be consulted about any questionable mark.[4] She should also check her underwear when she removes it.[5]

---

3. If, however, she examined herself after *alos hashachar* (the break of dawn), which is before sunrise, the examination is valid. This is so even on the first or seventh day of the seven clean days.

4. If more than one *bedikah* cloth is involved, it is proper to indicate by some mark or by writing on the end of each cloth the kind of examination that was performed. A distinction should be made between a *hefsek taharah* and an examination during the seven clean days. Which of the seven clean days and the time of the day (i.e. the morning or late afternoon), should also be indicated. It is preferable to consult the *Rav* as soon as possible, as the color may change with time.

5. Nevertheless, *bedi'eved* not checking the garment does not invalidate the seven clean days.

Omission of examinations

4. If she did not check herself daily with a *bedikah* cloth, but at least checked herself once on the first of the seven clean days **and** once on the seventh day, it is valid *bedi'eved*.[6]

If, on the other hand, she did not check herself on the first day or on the seventh day,[7] even if she checked herself on the intermediate

---

6. A woman who has a cut, an abrasion, or an irritation in the vaginal canal should perform only the *hefsek taharah* and not insert a *moch dachuk* (unless it is the first day after renewed bleeding or finding a bloodstain on the *bedikah* cloth, since in these cases some opinions obligate her to use a *moch dachuk*, as in chapter 4, paragraph 7). During the seven clean days, she need check herself only once on the first day and once again on the seventh day. It is correct to do an external wipe on the days in between.

This refers only to a woman who has reason to suspect that she cannot successfully check herself every day because of a cut or abrasion. It does not apply when her concern is that the examination cloth will not come out clean because of uterine bleeding as happens frequently after childbirth, miscarriage, or sometimes in the first months of pregnancy. In these instances the examinations must be performed twice daily since the bleeding originates from the uterus.

7. We will present several examples. 1) A woman checked herself on days one to six, but forgot to do so on the seventh day. After immersing herself in the evening she realized that she failed to check herself on the seventh day. 2) She checked herself on the first and second days of the seven clean days, but did not check herself on the rest of the days, not even on the seventh day. On the immersion night, even after immersing herself, she realized that she forgot to check herself on the seventh day. 3) She checked on the first day and not on the second day but checked again on one of the intermediate days. She then forgot to check on the seventh day, and only remembered on the immersion night. The law in these three cases is that, as long as she did not have marital relations, she is forbidden to her husband. She must check herself

days, a *Rav* should be consulted. (See footnote 7).

White sheets and undergarments

5. During all of the seven clean days a woman should be particular to

---

the next day, which is the eighth day, and re-immerse herself in the *mikvah* at night. 4) She checked herself only on the first of the seven clean days, but did not check herself at all during the other days, and on the night of immersion before she had relations she remembered that she forgot to check herself during these days. She is forbidden to her husband, and must restart counting the seven clean days. 5) She checked on the seventh day, but did not check herself at all during the first six days, not even on the first day. Then she remembered on immersion night that she had forgotten to check all the other days. If the couple did not yet have relations, she is forbidden to her husband. In this case the examination of the seventh day is counted as the first examination of the seven clean days, and she must add six more clean days during which she must continue checking daily.

However, in all the above cases if she already had relations, she is *bedi'eved* permitted to her husband, since she checked herself on the first day or on the seventh day. 6) If she checked herself only on one of the intermediate days and then immersed herself, the immersion is not valid. If she did not yet have relations with her husband, then that check is considered as the check of first day. She should continue checking herself until she completes seven days, and then again immerses in a *mikvah*. If she already had relations with her husband, she must wait four days (and check during those days), complete the missing days of the seven clean days and re-immerse herself.

[In all the *bedi'eved* cases above where she checks herself on the eighth day and then immerses, the above ruling applies if she did not check because she forgot to do so, or she made a mistake. However, if she stopped counting the seven clean days because she thought her husband will be away for a long period of time or for a similar reason, and she deliberately stopped counting the seven clean days, even during the intermediate days, she should consult a *Rav*. (See later paragraph 7 and the footnote).]

wear clean, laundered, white underwear, and put a clean, laundered, white sheet on her bed.

If she does not have laundered underwear, she should at least be careful to wear underwear that is white and free of stains. If, however, she wore underwear with stains, but she can clearly discern what was previously there, and knows with certainty that during the seven clean days there were no additional stains, one can be lenient.

Washing and bathing

6. Women customarily try to avoid sitting in a warm bath during the seven clean days since the water enters the vaginal area and can change the color of blood to white. Nevertheless, for medical needs and the like, one can be lenient. She may, however, shower and swim in a pool during the seven clean days. It is proper for her to perform the examination for that day (as in paragraph 3) before washing and swimming.[8]

Diverting attention

7. During the seven clean days she should be mindful that she is now in the process of the seven clean days. If she diverted[9] her attention completely from keeping these clean days, for example, when she thought that her husband would be away for a long period of time and she will not need to immerse herself in the *mikvah*, or

---

8. If for medical reasons she needs to put ointment or a suppository in the vaginal canal, she should do so after the first *bedikah* of that day. She should be especially careful about this on the first and seventh days of the seven clean days.

9. However, if she diverted her attention after the seven clean days, before she immersed herself, it does not affect her count at all.

when she believed that she saw an unclean stain,[10] but later found out that she was mistaken and then wants to continue counting, she should be stringent and start counting again. On the other hand, if when she diverted her attention from counting, she did not conclusively decide to discontinue counting the seven clean days, she may continue counting.

Whenever a question arises concerning diverting one's attention from keeping the seven clean days, a *Rav* should be consulted, since this law has many details and one case is not similar to another.

8. If she finished counting the seven clean days, but did not immerse herself immediately, she does not need to continue checking. It is, however, proper for her to check[11] once on the day that she immerses herself.

10. Finding a *kesem* or a questionable mark on the *bedikah* cloth and wanting to verify its *halachic* implications with a *Rav* is not considered diverting her attention. If she is doubtful whether or not she completely diverted her attention from counting, but we see that she continued to wear white underwear and check her clothes, this is not regarded as diverting her attention. The time period that is considered diverting one's attention is a whole day or a whole night (*onah*).

11. However, a *kallah* (bride) who completed counting the seven clean days and even immersed herself should ideally continue checking herself every day until the wedding.

Chapter Six
The Laws of Chatzitzah

As explained in the previous chapters, a woman who becomes a *niddah* and wishes to purify herself must first wait five days, perform the *hefsek taharah,* and then count "seven clean days". On the night preceding the eighth day, she immerses herself in a kosher *mikvah* and is permitted to her husband.

This chapter discusses how a woman prepares herself to ensure that she immerses properly.

1. According to *Torah* law, the entire body, including all the hair, must be in the *mikvah* water during immersion. If even a tiny part of her body or a single hair protrudes from the water, the immersion is invalid.

The entire body, including the hair, must be immersed at the same time. Immersing one part of the body first and then the rest of the body is invalid.

Definition of *Chatzitzah* in *Torah* law and rabbinic law

2. As mentioned above, the *mikvah* water must reach every external part[1] of the body and the hair. If most of the body **or** most of the hair is covered by an intervening substance (*chatzitzah)*, and she minds it being there, and it prevents the water[2] from reaching the

1. See below, paragraphs 6-8.

2. According to some opinions, even if a *chatzitzah* does not prevent water from reaching the body, one is not permitted to immerse in the *mikvah* until

hair or the body, the immersion is invalid by *Torah* law.

According to rabbinic law, if even a minute part of her body or hair is covered by a substance that prevents water from reaching it and she minds it being there (she is particular about it), the immersion is invalid. Also, if most of her body or hair[3] is covered by a *chatzitzah*, the immersion is invalid even if she does not mind it being there.

3. What is regarded as a substance or object that she minds? Anything that she finds disturbing at some time or other (not only at the time of immersion or close to it), or under some circumstances. Therefore, a ring that she enjoys wearing, but removes when she kneads dough is considered a *chatzitzah* even though it does not disturb her during immersion.

If she is pleased that the object is on her body or on her hair, but most married women would prefer to remove it, the object is regarded as a *chatzitzah*. And conversely, if most married women are pleased with such an object on their bodies but she does not like it, it is a *chatzitzah*[4].

---

it has been removed, e.g., a loose item. For this reason she should initially remove anything on her body, even if it is very loose.

3. According to some opinions, every area where hair is located is considered as a separate area. Therefore, if most of the pubic area or armpit is covered by a *chatzitzah*, even if she and most other women do not mind it, the covering is still regarded as a *chatzitzah*. Initially the *chatzitzah* should be removed, but if it was not removed, one may be lenient.

4. In summary: A *chatzitzah* according to *Torah* law is something that is found on most of her body or most of her hair. In rabbinic law, something is a *chatzitzah* even if it is found on a small part of her body or hair, as mentioned

4. To reiterate, any substance or object on a woman's body that comes between her and the water is considered a *chatzitzah*. Only under all the following conditions is the interposing substance not considered a *chatzitzah*; **a)** The *chatzitzah* is on a minority of her body or hair; **b)** She does not mind its presence and it does not disturb her if it remains on her; **c)** She never minds its presence, at any time or under any circumstances; **d)** Married women do not ordinarily mind its presence under any circumstances.

If all these conditions are met, the immersion is valid, even if the *chatzitzah* was not removed. This is true despite the fact that the substance or item interposed between her and the water, and thus prevented water from reaching the parts of her body or hair on which it rested. It is subordinate and considered part of the body.

5. Notwithstanding the above, she should initially remove everything found on even a small part of her body or hair, even if she does not mind its presence and married women do not ordinarily mind it.

Hidden places

6. The water must touch all exposed parts of her body. It is not necessary, however, for the water to touch parts of her body that are exposed only occasionally, such as inside her mouth, eyes, nose[5] and

in paragraph 2. See also paragraph 4 which follows.

5. This refers to the part of the nose that widens in such a manner that in the course of certain movements the inner area is visible. However, anything deeper than this, is regarded as a "recessed area" and a *chatzitzah* there is not problematic (see below, paragraph 8). The same applies to ear openings; every place that is visible when one looks into the ear is regarded as a hidden location, which means that it must be free of *chatzitzah*. Deeper

ears. These areas are known as "hidden places", since they are not always exposed.

Although it is not necessary for water to actually reach the hidden places, they must nevertheless be free of any *chatzitzah,* so that water could reach them. That is, if water were to reach these hidden places, the water would touch the body directly and not an intervening substance. If a *chatzitzah* is found in a hidden place, the immersion is invalid. For example, even though water need not enter the mouth during immersion, if a substance was lodged between the teeth that would prevent water from reaching there, the immersion is invalid. Similarly glutinous substances or mucus in the eye, nasal mucus or ear wax are considered a *chatzitzah* (see chapter 7 footnote 4).

7. The same is true of body folds in areas such as armpits, beneath the neck, between the legs and between the toes. Although she need not open them for the water to reach there, and she immerses herself assuming a normal comfortable position (see chapter 8 paragraph 12) these areas must still be free of *chatzitzah.* If they are inaccessible to water due to *chatzitzah*, the immersion is invalid.

Recessed locations

8. Internal areas that are never visible such as the inner cavity of the ear[6] or the upper part of the nasal cavity need not be accessible to

---

parts of the ear, however, that are not visible to someone who looks into the ear, are regarded as recessed and do not have to be accessible to water; a *chatzitzah* in such a place does not present a problem.

6. This refers to the inner part of the ear which is not visible to a person who looks into the ear, as in the previous footnote.

If there is a medical reason why water cannot be allowed to enter into her

water and the laws of *chatzitzah* do not apply there. (These areas are known as "recesses".[7])

Types of *chatzitzahs*

9. A *chatzitzah* that invalidates an immersion is defined as anything that prevents water from reaching any part of the body. This includes dirt, paint, jewelry or any foreign substance, as will be detailed below.

10. A thick, liquid substance, such as thick oil, is regarded as a *chatzitzah* and must be removed before immersion. This also applies to ointments and similar substances. If she immersed herself with a thick oil, ointment or a similar substance on her body, the immersion is invalid.

11. Even a non-dense wet substance on any part of the body must be removed if she minds its presence. If she immersed herself with such a substance on her body, she should consult a *Rav*. (See paragraph 17 below concerning a fresh wound from which blood is oozing which she received near the time of her immersion).

12. Ideally, even a wet substance that she does not mind having on her body should be removed. This is in accord with paragraph 5 above, that initially a *chatzitzah* should be removed even if it covers only a small part of the body and she does not mind it.

13. An effort must be made to remove remnants of paint,[8] iodine,

---

ear, a *Rav* must be consulted.

7. See below paragraph 20, concerning whether a splinter in the body is regarded as being in a recessed location.

8. Even if she uses paint extensively and, unlike other women, does not mind residual paint on her hands, she must still remove the paint before immersion.

makeup and ointment. If they resist removal and no actual substance is perceptible, she may immerse herself. This is true even if they caused a discoloration of the skin. However, if a layer of the substance remains that is perceptible to touch, she may not immerse herself until it is removed.

Similarly, if she handled food that stained her skin without leaving any substance, she should try to remove the color. If the color cannot be completely removed, she may immerse herself since no substance remains on the skin.

Ornaments

14. Jewelry that is for ornamental purposes and covers only a small part of the body is, strictly speaking, not regarded as a *chatzitzah,* even if it fits tightly. This is because its presence is desired for ornamental reasons and it covers only a small part of the body. Nevertheless, it should ideally be removed before immersion, as stated above in paragraph 5.

Jewelry that covers most of the body or most of the hair[9] is regarded as a *chatzitzah.* If she immersed herself with such jewelry pressed tightly to her body,[10] the immersion is invalid.

15. If women sometimes remove the jewelry, it is regarded as a

---

Bedi'eved, if she did not remove the paint and is not in the habit of removing it even in honor of *Shabbos,* she may be lenient.

9. See above paragraph 2 footnote 3, that according to some opinions any area where hair is located is regarded as a separate area; initially, these opinions should be followed.

10. For cases where jewelry is not tightly pressed to the body, see footnotes to paragraph 15.

chatzitzah. For example, ornaments that are removed when she is washing or performing other tasks such as kneading dough are considered a *chatzitzah.* This applies even to women who are not in the habit of removing such jewelry, since most women are. Therefore, chains, bracelets[11] and rings[12] that are usually removed during washing or when performing other tasks are regarded as *chatzitzah.*

Make - up

16. Nail polish, whether clear or colored is not a *chatzitzah,* even if it has substance. It is treated like a substance that covers a small part of the body and does not bother her. Because hair dye is not perceptible to touch, dyed hair, even when it includes all the hair, it is not a *chatzitzah.*[13]

---

11. Initially, even loosely worn chains, bracelets and rings that do not prevent water from reaching the body should be removed. If she immersed herself without removing them and they are very loose, the immersion is valid *bedi'eved.* If they are not very loose, a *Rav* must be consulted.

12. If it is impossible to remove a ring from a finger, she should initially have a goldsmith cut the ring off. Under difficult circumstances, if the ring is somewhat loose and can be turned in its place around the finger, she should turn the ring while she is in the *mikvah* water before completing her immersion and should not stick her hand out of the water until the immersion is completed. If she immersed herself wearing a ring that is so tight that it cannot be turned, a *Rav* should be consulted.

13. According to the strict letter of the law, artificial nails or eyelashes are not considered *chatzitzah.* Hair coloring that is ruined or fading, invalidates the immersion. (If only a minority of the hair coloring is ruined, one may be lenient *bedi'eved*). The same applies also to any substances that are used for beautification.

Makeup that is not water resistant and will therefore be spoiled in the

Some women remove any substance that can be removed, even a substance placed on the body for beauty.[14] This is a commendable practice.

Wounds

17. Congealed blood on a wound is regarded as a *chatzitzah*. This also applies when the blood has not completely congealed, but has stopped flowing and has begun to congeal to the point that a thread-like trail is pulled from it when it is touched. If she immersed herself with this type of wound, the immersion is invalid.

The bleeding from a wound that occurred close to the time of immersion is usually "minded". The blood must be wiped off before immersion.[15] If she immersed herself without wiping off the blood, she must consult a *Rav* whether or not the immersion is valid.

18. If a scab has formed on a wound, she should soften it with warm water. If the scab is easily removed after softening it, she must remove it. If the scab is difficult to remove, this softening is all that is required.

19. A closed wound from which skin has not peeled off is not a *chatzitzah*, even if it contains pus. The same applies to a blister that

---

water must be removed before immersion. If she immersed herself without removing it, the immersion is invalid.

14. Regarding a color stain on the body that is not perceptible to touch and is not wanted, see paragraph 13 above.

15. She should wash the area with water close to the time of immersion. If she fears that the bleeding will resume, she should wet the wound with *mikvah* water. In this case the blood will not be regarded as a *chatzitzah*, even if the wound resumes bleeding.

forms due to a burn or the like (see paragraph 30). As long as no skin has peeled off and the wound is closed, it is not regarded as a *chatzitzah.*

20. A splinter that protrudes from the skin or is level with the skin invalidates immersion. If it is completely lodged inside the flesh, the immersion is valid *bedi'eved* even if the splinter can be seen. Initially she should not immerse herself unless the splinter cannot be seen at all[16] or skin has grown over it.

21. One may not immerse wearing a bandage, cast or band-aid although their presence is desired; they must be removed before immersion.[17]

22. Surgical stitches that require removal are regarded as a *chatzitzah.* One may be lenient and immerse with self-dissolving stitches.

Warts and loose skin

23. Any natural part of the body, even if it is redundant, is not regarded as a *chatzizah* unless it is ready to fall off or be cut off.

24. Opinions differ among the *Rishonim* as to whether a part of the body that is scheduled to be removed, is considered a *chatzitzah* or not. Most *Rishonim* contend that it is not a *chatzitzah.* Others are stringent concerning this matter. The accepted ruling is that according to the letter of the law a part of the body that is scheduled to be removed is not considered a *chatzitzah,* but one should try to

16. For this reason one should be stringent and not immerse with Chinese acupuncture needles.

17. She must be careful to remove all remnants of ointment or adhesive from the area.

accommodate the opinion of those who are stringent and remove it before immersion. (Concerning situations that are *bedi'eved* see the following paragraphs).

25. According to the lenient opinion (that a part of the body that is scheduled to be removed is not regarded as a *chatzitzah)*, many authorities maintain that it is a *chatzitzah* if it has begun to separate from the body.

Even according to the stringent opinion mentioned in paragraph 24, if she and most other women do not mind it, it is not a *chatzitzah*.

26. A wart is not regarded as a *chatzitzah*, since it is a part of the body. Nevertheless, if she intends to remove it, ideally, it should be removed[18] before immersion. If she immersed without removing it, the immersion is valid.

27. A wart that has started to fall off[19] must be removed before immersion. If she did not do so, she should immerse herself again after removing it. If a night has passed, then a *Rav* should be consulted.

28. Hardened or dry skin on the feet or other parts of the body that has not begun to peel off is not regarded as a *chatzitzah* even if it bothers her. This is the case only if she does not usually remove it. If she ordinarily removes it[20] and she minds it being there, initially,

---

18. If she is unable to remove it before immersion, she need not postpone the immersion.

19. If she intends to remove the wart by applying some remover that will cause it to fall off, this should not be done near the time of immersion because it may cause the wart to be considered a *chatzitzah*.

20. If she ordinarily does not mind it, but removes it only because of immer-

she should remove it even if it has not begun to separate from the body. If she did not remove it and immersed herself, the immersion is valid *bedi'eved*.[21]

29. If any area of peeling skin is so large that she is usually particular about it and makes sure to remove it, then she must do so. A small area of peeling skin that she is not usually troubled by, is not regarded as a *chatzitzah*; there is no need to remove it.

If she immersed herself without removing a large area of peeling skin that she would ordinarily remove, she must immerse herself again after she removes it.[22] If a night passed after she immersed herself without removing the skin, a *Rav* should be consulted.

A woman whose skin is peeling due to sunburn need remove only the large areas of peeling skin that people are usually particular about.

Blisters

30. A blister whether it is filled with fluid or pus or not, is not a *chatzitzah* as long as it has not opened. Fluid or pus inside a blister, or the skin that covers it, are not considered *chatzitzah* (as above, in paragraph 19). If the blister opens, forming loose shreds of skin, the rule in paragraph 29 applies. If these shreds are so large that she usually removes them, she must remove them before immersion. If

sion, she is considered to be not particular about it and it is not a *chatzitzah*.

21. If it is not too much bother she should remove the skin and immerse herself again, but should not postpone her immersion if she cannot remove it (for example, on Friday evening when it is forbidden to remove the skin, or if the *mikvah* has already closed).

22. If she discovered peeling skin after immersion, and she is not sure if it was present during immersion, she does not need to immerse again.

they are smaller and she would otherwise not remove them, they are not a *chatzitzah*.

Dandruff

31. Dandruff attached to the scalp is regarded as a part of the body and is not a *chatzitzah*. However if she ordinarily removes it, she should also do so before immersion in the same way that she always does when she washes. Dandruff detached from the scalp must be removed. She should shampoo her hair thoroughly, as is required before immersion, and comb her hair carefully to remove the loose dandruff.

If she immersed herself with dandruff in her hair, since the dandruff is not tightly attached to the flesh or hair, the immersion is valid *bedi'eved*.

Teeth and hair that are to be removed

32. A loose tooth, even one that disturbs her and will eventually be pulled, is not considered a *chatzitzah*. A tooth that aches very much and must be pulled immediately should be pulled before immersion. If she did not do so, she should consult a *Rav*. (For other laws of *chatzitzah* in the teeth, see below paragraphs 38 – 42).

33. Hair that is to be cut because it is too long should be cut before immersion.[23] (See paragraph 10 in the following chapter that discusses the custom of not cutting hair close to the time of immersion). Similarly, women who customarily shave off their hair

23. A bride who intends to shorten her hair before the *chuppah* should preferably do so before, and not after, immersion. If she does not intend to shorten her hair before the *chuppah*, but just to arrange it, even if it will involve cutting some hair, it need not be done before immersion.

before immersion (including those who shave off their pubic hair [24]) should be particular to do so before immersion.[25] (See chapter 7 paragraph 10).

Chatzitzah of the nails

34. The *Rishonim* state, and it is cited in the *Shulchan Aruch,* that it is the established custom of Jewish women to cut their fingernails and toenails[26] before immersion. They should cut them close to the place where they are connected to the flesh.[27]

Fingernails

35. A woman who immersed without cutting all or some of her fingernails, does not need to immerse again if her fingernails are no longer than the end of her fingers, and they are free of dirt. If her nails are longer than the end of her fingers and free of dirt, she

---

24. Some *Ashkenazic* women customarily shave off or shorten the hair on their heads before immersion. *Sephardic* women customarily shave off their pubic hair before immersion.

25. Those whose custom is to shorten their hair before immersion may do so during *sefira* or "the three weeks".

26. Even though one is usually particular not to cut fingernails and toenails on the same day, this does not apply when preparing for immersion.

27. On *Chol Ha'moed* she may cut her nails for immersion in the same way she cuts them during the rest of the year.

During the *shloshim* mourning period, it is preferable to have a non-Jewish woman cut the nails. If this cannot be done, she may cut them herself as usual (with scissors or clippers). The custom is to be lenient.

However it is only necessary to cut the nails until the place where dirt is seen beneath them, and not like those women who mistakenly cut their nails where they are connected to the flesh.

should cut them and immerse again. However, if she already had relations with her husband, or the night has passed even without relations, or the *mikvah* has closed and immersion is no longer possible that night, the immersion is valid.

If her immersion falls on Friday night and she forgot to cut her nails, she may immerse. She should clean thoroughly under the nails, taking care to scrub away only the dirt from the nail, but not any of the nail itself. After she carefully checks that no dirt remains she may immerse herself.

Toenails

If she immersed herself without cutting her toenails, even if there was some dirt under them, she need not immerse again, even on a weekday. This is so only if she does not mind the dirt and most women are not particular about this amount of dirt under their toenails.[28] If the toenails are so long that she intended to cut them and she is particular about it, she must immerse herself again after cutting them. On the other hand, if she already had relations with her husband, or the night passed without relations, or the *mikvah* has closed and immersion is no longer possible that night, the immersion is valid.

Partially detached nails

36. If she began to cut a nail and didn't finish, or banged her fingernail and part of the nail is detached and hanging, she must remove it before immersion. This applies whether a small or large part of the nail is detached and hanging.

---

28. However if she is particular about it, it constitutes a *chatzitzah* even if most women do not mind it, as mentioned above regarding fingernails.

If she immersed herself without removing the detached part of the nail, the following applies: In the case of fingernails, when just a small part of the nail became detached, she must re-immerse after removing the detached part. Even if most of the fingernail was detached, it is appropriate that she immerse again.[29] In the case of toenails, if most of the nail became detached, she need not immerse again, but if only a small part of the toenail became detached, she must immerse again after removing it.[30]

---

29. In all the cases mentioned in this paragraph (where she is required to immerse again if she did not cut off the detached part of a fingernail), if she already had relations with her husband, she need not immerse again. This is so even if a small part of the nail is detached, so long as it is not tightly pressed to the remaining part of the nail so that water can enter.

If the night passed and she did not have relations with her husband or the *mikvah* closed so that immersion was not possible again that night, if most of the nail is detached, one may be lenient and not do another immersion. However, if only a small part of the nail is detached, one should not be lenient and should immerse the following night.

If the immersion fell on a Friday night, and she noticed that most of her fingernail was detached, she can be lenient in a case of pressing need and immerse herself. In this case, before immersing herself completely in the *mikvah*, she should lift the detached part of the nail a little to allow the *mikvah* water to enter and only then completely immerse. However, if only a small part of the nail is detached, the immersion should be postponed until *motzei Shabbos*, after cutting off the detached part.

30. If she discovers on Friday night that most of a toenail is detached, and she does not mind it, she should enter the *mikvah* and before completely immersign herself, make an effort to lift the detached part slightly to allow water to enter, and then completely immerse herself. If only a minority of the toenail is detached, initially, she should not be lenient; but should delay her immersion until *motzei Shabbos*, after cutting off the detached part.

37. Immersion when a nail became separated from the flesh beneath it (for example, due to injury), depends on whether most of the nail became separated or only a small part. If most of the nail became separated and there is enough space for the *mikvah* water to enter between the nail and the flesh, it is not regarded as a *chatzitzah*. If a small part of a nail separated from the flesh beneath it and most of it is still attached to the flesh so that water cannot enter, it is a *chatzitzah*. If she lifts the nail slightly while in the *mikvah* so that water enters between the nail and the flesh, she may immerse.

If she needs the nail to protect the area until it heals, or if she does not want to remove the nail because it will hurt, the nail is not regarded as a *chatzitzah*. Still, she should make every effort to lift the nail while in the water at least a little, in order to separate it from the flesh.

Dental fillings, crowns and bridges

38. As explained in paragraph 6, a *chatzitzah* in the mouth or teeth invalidates immersion. Even though it is not necessary for water to actually enter the mouth, the mouth must be accessible to water. (Concerning preparations for immersion and what must be done to remove a *chatzitzah* from the teeth, see the following chapter, paragraph 8).

39. Permanent fillings (even in most of her teeth) are not a *chatzitzah*. However if she suffers pain in a tooth with a permanent filling and the filling will have to be removed, then it is a *chatzitzah*.

40. A temporary filling placed in a tooth for only several days should initially be regarded as a *chatzitzah*. However if she intends to leave the filling for an entire month,[31] it is not regarded as a *chatzitzah*.

31. This means that it will remain there for a month from the time the tooth

In case of need, if a temporary filling is to remain for only a week one may be lenient and not consider it a *chatzitzah.*[32]

41. A dental crown is not a *chatzitzah*, even if it is temporary,[33] but it is preferable that the crown be in place for at least a month.[34] Care should be taken that the crown is not removed on the day following the immersion (see footnote 31).

42. It is preferable not to use braces (teeth-straightening wires) at all because they may well be regarded as a *chatzitzah*. In case of need, however, braces may be used, provided that they are not removed for at least half a year.

---

was filled. It need not remain there a month from the day of immersion. Nevertheless one should be particular not to have it removed the day after the immersion.

32. All the more so if she prefers the filling for aesthetic reasons, for example, if part of the tooth was broken, or the dentist filed down a part of the tooth and filled it so it now appears intact. In these cases, one may definitely be lenient if the filling is left for only a week.

As mentioned above, if the tooth containing the filling hurts, and therefore the filling will be removed, the filling is a *chatzitzah*.

33. The same holds true for a bridge between two teeth that holds an artificial tooth in place. According to the strict letter of the law, such a bridge is not a *chatzitzah*, but it is preferable that it be in place for at least a month (see footnote 34).

34. A temporary crown or bridge that can be seen is regarded as an ornament (see paragraph 14); one may be lenient even if it will be in place for only a week. In a case of need, one may be lenient even with a crown or bridge that cannot be seen, even if it will be in place for only a week.

Head lice

43. People normally detest the presence of a single head louse or nit. Because they attach themselves tightly to the hair, they are regarded as *chatzitzah.* A woman who suspects there are lice or nits in her hair must remove them[35] by means of preparations available for that purpose, and the use of a lice comb to ensure that none are present during immersion. If she immersed herself with lice or nits in her hair, see Sources and Explanations.

---

35. It is recommended that the treatment of lice or nits with a suitable preparation and a dense comb begin several days before immersion. This should be repeated several times to ensure that all lice and nits are removed prior to immersion.

Chapter Seven

Preparations for Immersion

1. The *Torah* requires a woman to check herself very carefully, before she immerses in the *mikvah*, to ensure that no *chatzitzah* is present on her body, hair or nails. Nothing must adhere to her body that she does not want there, and her hair must be free from any knots or entanglement. (This checking is called *"Iyun"*).

Concerning her hair, *Ezra HaSofer* instituted that a woman should not rely on her inspection alone, but should also wash and clean her hair with warm water and comb it out well. This ordinance was established because knots, sweat, and dirt are more frequently found in the hair than on the rest of the body.

Furthermore, *Chazal* teach us: "A person should always instruct his wife to rinse her body folds and all hidden places with water". The details of this requirement will be explained shortly.

From the time of the *Talmud*, all women are accustomed to wash well and rinse their entire body in warm water before immersion, both the areas with hair and the entire body.

The details of these laws will be explained in the following paragraphs.

Washing and combing of hair

2. As previously mentioned, a woman must wash and clean all of her hair thoroughly[1] with warm water.[2] Afterwards, while the hair is still wet, she should comb all of the hair[3] on her body (for example, head, armpit and pubic) to ensure that no knots or dirt remain.

Preparation of the body

3. She should wash, cleanse, and rub the rest of her body with warm water, including all folds (such as the armpits, the navel, underneath the chin, underneath the breasts, the genital and anal areas, and the ear and nose passages) since it is likely that sweat and dirt accumulated there.[4]

---

1. If she washed and cleaned her hair but did not comb it, or combed her hair but did not wash it, her immersion is totally invalid. Even if she inspected herself after the immersion and did not find any *chatzitzah,* the immersion is invalid.

2. This washing should be done with warm water or at least with lukewarm water. If she washed her hair with cold water, it is proper to wash it again with warm water. Nevertheless if she washed and cleaned her hair with cold water and then inspected her hair before the immersion and did not find any knots, the immersion is valid.

3. She must comb the hair on her head with a comb, and not with a soft brush or her hand. However, other places where hair is found may be combed even by running her fingers through her hair. Some women are accustomed to use a comb for hair even in other places of the body.

4. Any glutinous substance in the corners of her eyes must be removed. Likewise, she must remove nasal mucus and earwax from the external parts of the nose and ear passages (where they are wider and certain movements make them visible from outside). There is, however, no need to clean the more internal parts of the nose and ear passages (see chapter 6 footnote 5 and 6). If she immersed and realized she did not clean her eyes, nose or ears properly and a *chatzitzah* was present during immersion, the ruling

There is an age-old custom of bathing before immersion while sitting. However, if for some reason she is unable to sit in the bath, it does not invalidate her immersion.[5] It is customary to wash with soap or similar cleansers.

4. In order to be done properly, these preparations should be carried out calmly and without hurrying.

Additional preparations

5. Before immersing, a woman must thoroughly brush and clean the surface and between her teeth,[6] so that no food particles will remain there. If she has cavities in her teeth, she must be careful to clean them as well as she can.

After brushing, she should not eat until after the immersion, but she may drink. If she did eat, she must brush her teeth again before immersion.

6. The *Shulchan Aruch* writes that women have an age-old custom of cutting their fingernails and toenails before immersion. They should

---

differs depending as to whether the mucus was dry or moist and where it was found. A *Rav* must be consulted.

Contact lenses must be removed. If she immersed without removing her contact lenses, she must consult a *Rav*.

5. For example, a pregnant woman who needs to immerse herself in a *mikvah,* but is afraid to sit in a bathtub beforehand because of possible harm to the fetus, does not have to take a bath. It is sufficient for her to wash herself thoroughly under a warm shower.

6. It is not advisable to use dental floss for removing food particles, etc. that are lodged between her teeth, since threads of floss may tear off and remain between her teeth.

be cut close to where they are connected to the flesh.[7] (The details of these laws are explained in the previous chapter, paragraphs 34 - 37).

7. Before immersion a woman should relieve herself, if necessary, in order to ensure that she is relaxed and does not hold herself back during immersion.[8]

8. Women have the custom to refrain from eating meat or poultry on the day that they will be immersing[9] since remnants are liable to become lodged between the teeth. This is an old custom and should not be disregarded even if members of her household might thereby discern that she is planning to immerse that night.[10]

It is also proper not to eat other foods that could leave remnants between the teeth and such as corn, oranges, sunflower seeds and mango. It is permissible to eat fish or a meat soup.

9. She should not knead or handle dough[11] on the day of her immersion to avoid c*hatzitzah*. Likewise, she should avoid handling

---

7. It is not necessary to cut the nails shorter then where dirt can be seen (unlike those women who mistakenly cut even part of the nail that is attached to the flesh).

8. Nevertheless, if she immersed herself without going to the bathroom, even if she needed to relieve herself, her immersion is valid *bedi'eved.*

9. She may eat meat at the *Shabbos* and *Yom Tov* meals. Meat may also be eaten at a *bris milah*, *pidyon haben*, *sheva berochos,* etc., but she must take care to thoroughly clean between her teeth.

10. *Bedi'eved,* if she ate meat on the day of her immersion, she can still immerse, but should be extremely careful to clean her teeth well.

11. If the immersion falls out on Friday night and she is accustomed to knead dough on Friday in honor of *Shabbos*, she may be lenient and do so.

things that are liable to adhere to her body or hair such as glue or paint.

10. It is customary not to take a haircut on the day she will be immersing because hair could remain in the body folds.

It is appropriate for women who are accustomed to cut hair from their head or from their body before the immersion, to do so three days before their immersion. If she did not cut her hair until the immersion day, she should cut it on that day, but must wash herself well and inspect her body folds to ascertain that no hair remains.[12]

Time of preparation

11. Ideally a woman should make all preparations while it is still day, before the time of immersion (night-fall). The reason is that at night she might not prepare herself as well, since she may rush to immerse and return home. It is also correct that all the preparations be done as close as possible to the immersion to ensure that no new *chatzitzahs* adhere to her after the preparations. It is an age-old custom for women to occupy themselves with these preparations while it is still day, finish them by nightfall and then immerse immediately afterwards.

12. If she is unable to do the preparations by day, she can do them at night, provided that they are done thoroughly, calmly, and without hurrying. For this reason, the *Acharonim* enacted that a woman who cannot prepare herself by day and instead does so at night, should occupy herself with the washing, cleansing, combing and all other necessary preparations for at least one hour.

---

12. If she is always particular to cut her hair before immersion, but this time she immersed herself without cutting it, a *Rav* should be consulted.

It is preferable to prepare during the day when one is calm and composed, even though it is not right before immersion, than to do all her preparations at night. At night, she should repeat this procedure directly before the immersion, but need not occupy herself for a complete hour with her preparations.

Inspection before immersion - *Iyun*

13. After the thorough washing, cleansing and combing, she must inspect her body carefully to make sure that no dirt, paint or skin peelings are present. This check is called *Iyun.* Furthermore, she should ascertain that she has no wound, scab, etc. on her body. She should try to inspect all places visually to ensure that no *chatzitzah* is present on them. Places that cannot be inspected visually should be touched and felt, or inspected by another woman (i.e. the *mikvah* attendant).

14. This inspection must be carried out at night, immediately before immersion. If time passed from when she completed her preparations and inspection until immersion, she must inspect herself again before immersing.

Immersion on Friday night or *Yom Tov* night

15. If the time of the immersion falls on Friday night or the night of *Yom Tov*, she must make all preparations during the day[13] since

---

13. Ideally, she should make all the preparations within three hours of her immersion. However if she plans to travel to a different city for *Shabbos,* she may make them earlier. She should, however, be careful not to prepare herself too late, in order to ensure that she will not miss the candle lighting time and will not desecrate *Shabbos*.

If she did not wash, clean, and comb herself, as the *halacha* requires, and it is already *Shabbos*, she must postpone her immersion until *Motzei Shabbos*.

they include activities that are forbidden on *Shabbos* and *Yom Tov*. She should be careful that no *chatzitzah* adheres[14] to her after the preparations. Likewise, her hair should remain combed in a way that it will not subsequently become entangled. She should not eat after her preparations until after she immerses.[15]

Before immersion she must inspect her whole body and hair well. She should touch and feel all places that are not visible to her.

16. If the time of her immersion falls on the second night of *Yom Tov* or on Friday night after two days of *Yom Tov*,[16] she must make all of her preparations on the afternoon before the commencement of *Yom Tov* so that she will not come to profane *Shabbos* or *Yom Tov*. She should gather together the hair of her head after combing it, in a way that it will not subsequently become entangled.

During the time that passes from the preparations until the

If after *Shabbos* began she remembered or discovered that she did not cut her nails, or by mistake left one nail uncut, see chapter 6 paragraph 35 and the footnote there, and the footnote to paragraph 36.

14. If she handled items that cause a *chatzitzah*, she should wash her hands thoroughly.

15. Therefore she should not eat the *Shabbos* meal before immersing. If she did eat after the preparations, but it is still before *Shabbos*, she should wash out her mouth again and clean her teeth. If she ate and realized only after accepting *Shabbos*, she should remove any food particles from between her teeth with a toothpick. See also footnote 17.

16. The same applies if the immersion falls on a *motzei Shabbos* which is *Yom Tov* night (i.e. *Yom Tov* is on Sunday). All preparations must be done before *Shabbos*.

immersion, new *chatzitzahs* are liable to adhere to her. Therefore, she must be careful during *Shabbos* or *Yom Tov* that nothing that can be considered a *chatzitzah* will adhere to her body.

Before immersion she must clean her teeth well to remove all food particles that may be lodged between them.[17] Also she must re-wash with warm water all the body folds and hidden places (such as the armpits, under the neck, in the vaginal area, under the breasts, between the toes, and in the ear and nose passages).

She must thoroughly inspect her whole body and hair before immersion, either by seeing or feeling as explained above paragraph 15.

Immersion on *motzei Shabbos* or *motzei Yom Tov*

17. If the time of her immersion falls on *motzei Shabbos* or on *motzei Yom Tov*[18] (or on *motzei Shabbos* that occurs after *Yom Tov* or on *motzei Yom Tov* that occurs after Shabbos), then she should ideally perform her preparations on *erev Shabbos* or *erev Yom Tov*, respectively. After washing and combing her hair, she should gather together all the hair of her head in a way that it will not

---

17. She may use a toothpick or a toothbrush. She should be careful that her gums do not bleed when doing this. If she uses a toothbrush, she should be careful not to brush near the gums since it is probable that it will cause bleeding. She should use a dry toothbrush or one that is only slightly moist so that there will be no question of *sechitah* (squeezing) on *Shabbos* or *Yom Tov*. She may not use toothpaste to brush her teeth on *Shabbos* or *Yom Tov*.

18. If the immersion occurs on *motzei Tishah B'Av*, she should perform the preparations on her immersion night. If she cannot do so, she can perform the preparations on *erev Tishah B'Av* and be careful that a *chatzitzah* does not adhere to her body, as explained in the previous paragraphs. If possible on *motzei Tishah B'Av* she should wash herself a little and comb her hair.

subsequently become entangled. Because a *chatzitzah* might have adhered to her during *Shabbos* or *Yom Tov,* before her immersion she should again thoroughly rinse her whole body, comb her hair, and brush her teeth.

Before immersion, she must thoroughly inspect her whole body and hair, whether by seeing or feeling, as explained above paragraph 13.

If she did not carry out the preparations on *erev Shabbos / Yom Tov*, she may *bedieved* perform them on *motzei Shabbos / Yom Tov*. She must, however, be careful to do them thoroughly and calmly. She should spend at least an hour doing the preparations, as explained above in paragraph 12.

Chapter Eight

The *Mitzvah* of Immersion - *Tevilah*

1. After performing the *hefsek taharah,* counting the "seven clean days", washing and cleaning her body, and combing her hair thoroughly (as explained in the previous chapters), a woman must immerse herself in a *mikvah* in order to be permitted to her husband. If she has not immersed herself (even if she washed her body), even if many years have passed since she last saw blood, she remains forbidden to her husband with all the severity of the Torah prohibitions.

Likewise, if she immersed herself before completing[1] the count of seven clean days, her immersion is invalid (see footnote).[2]

When her husband is away from home

2. When her husband is out of town and will definitely not return

---

1. She should not immerse herself in a *mikvah* during the seven clean days (not even on *erev Yom Kippur*) although she intends to immerse herself again at the end of the seven clean days.

2. She must make up the missing days and then immerse again at the end of seven clean days. If she had relations with her husband before seven clean days passed, see Sources and Explanations at the beginning of chapter 5. If seven clean days passed, but she did not check herself in the intervals prescribed by *halacha,* see chapter 5 paragraph 4 and the footnote there. If she immersed herself, had relations, and only afterward remembered that she did not wait the five-day waiting period, see Sources and Explanations chapter 3 paragraph 8.

that night, the custom is that she does not immerse that night.[3] She should postpone the immersion until he is due to arrive. If, however, her husband is in town, it is a *mitzvah* for her to immerse as soon as she finishes the seven clean days,[4] and she must not postpone the immersion[5] (see paragraph 7).

Time of immersion

3. The time for immersion is after nightfall[6] and

---

3. If it is doubtful whether her husband will return home that night or not, she should immerse that night. Likewise, if he is scheduled to arrive home some time the next day during the day, she should immerse so that she will be permitted to him when he returns. If he plans to arrive the following night, and she will be rushed to complete her preparations on the night of his arrival, she should immerse the previous night. If she immerses herself on a night that her husband is out of town, it is customary to put a knife under the mattress on which she sleeps or to cover herself with her husband's garment when she goes to sleep.

4. It is sinful for a woman to postpone her immersion to spite her husband. Doing so brings calamities upon the world.

5. Should it become necessary to postpone the immersion, a *Rav* should be consulted.

6. Those who follow *Rabbeinu Tam* concerning the time of nightfall in all circumstances (regarding both Torah and Rabbinic laws) should be stringent and immerse only when it is night according to this opinion. When a necessity arises, they may rely on the opinions that it suffices to return home after the time of nightfall, therefore she should be careful not to return home before the nightfall begins according to *Rabbeinu Tam*. Those who are accustomed to adhere to *Rabbeinu Tam's* opinion concerning the time of nightfall only regarding *Torah* laws, may immerse earlier and need not be particular that the immersion be after nightfall according to *Rabbeinu Tam.*

not[7] during the day.[8] Whether the immersion follows the seven clean days immediately, or whether it is delayed to another day she must immerse at night. Similarly, if she already immersed herself in a *mikvah* but a *Rav* instructed her to immerse again, she must immerse herself only at night and not during the day. If it is impossible for her to immerse herself at night, she should consult a *Rav.*

Immersion of a bride

4. A bride whose "seven clean days" terminate on the day of the *chuppah* (meaning that her immersion night falls on the night of her wedding), can immerse herself on the morning of the wedding day after sunrise (*hanetz hachamah*) if the *chuppah* is scheduled to be after nightfall.

---

7. *Chazal* prohibited a woman to immerse during the seventh day out of concern that the couple may have relations on the seventh day after her immersion and she might subsequently see blood before nightfall. This menstrual spotting would invalidate the counting of the seven days retroactively and they would thus have engaged in a forbidden act.

8. *Chazal* forbade this because they feared that her daughter might think that it is permitted to immerse during the day. Even a woman without a daughter is included in this *gezeirah* (rabbinical enactment).

A woman who prepares for immersion at home and only goes to the *mikvah* for the immersion, should not leave her house for the *mikvah* too early. She should leave at a time that she estimates that until she will be able to immerse, it will be after nightfall. If she performs the preparations at the *mikvah,* she can leave her house even earlier in the day. Also, if the *mikvah* is far from her house and she estimates that even if she leaves her house earlier (after making all the necessary preparations) she will arrive at the *mikvah* after nightfall, she may leave her house earlier.

In such a case she must check herself in the morning of the seventh day before the immersion. Since the immersion is invalid, even *bedi'eved,* without this inspection, the *mitzvah* of counting is not finished until this inspection is carried out. Before sunset she should perform the second daily examination.

If the *chuppah* is scheduled to take place during the day, she should consult a *Rav* for guidance.

Immersion on Friday night and *motzei Shabbos*

5. If the seventh day of the "seven clean days" falls on Friday, [9] she immerses herself on Friday night. She should be careful not to squeeze water out of her hair (*sechitah*). It is only permitted to immerse on Friday night if her husband is in town. If the seventh day of the "seven clean days" falls on *Shabbos*, she immerses herself on *motzei Shabbos.*

One may not postpone the beginning of the counting (for reasons of convenience and the like) so that the immersion night will fall out on Friday night or *motzei Shabbos*. Likewise, if the counting of the "seven clean days" finishes beforehand, she may not postpone the immersion for reasons of convenience until Friday night or

9. Although the *Acharonim* discuss the various *halachic* implications of immersing on *Shabbos* in warm water (whether it is included in the *gezeirah* not to bathe on *Shabbos* in warm water), the custom is to be lenient in this matter. In our times one should surely not be stringent since women are not used to immersing themselves in cold water. If they were told to do so they would not be able to immerse themselves with the composure that is needed to ensure that the water reaches all parts of their body.

motzei Shabbos. If she did so,[10] whether intentionally or by default,[11] she should consult a *Rav* if she is allowed to immerse herself.

If she immersed on Thursday night, but a *Rav* instructed her to immerse again, and she could not immerse herself again that night, she can immerse on Friday night[12] or on *motzei Shabbos*.

Immersion on *Yom Kippur, Tisha B'Av* or during *shivah*

6. It is forbidden to immerse on *Yom Kippur*, *Tisha B'Av* and during her seven days of mourning (*shivah*).

When *Tisha B'Av* falls on *Shabbos* it is permissible to immerse on Friday night, but a scrupulous person should be stringent.[13]

---

10. If she postponed her immersion to the night of *Yom Tov*, even out of negligence or intentionally, she is allowed to immerse.

11. It is accepted practice to permit a delayed immersion on Friday night if a woman had a reason for postponing it. If she intentionally postponed the immersion to Friday night or was negligent, some opinions are stringent and do not allow her to immerse, and therefore she should consult a *Rav*. If she postponed the immersion until *motzei Shabbos*, one should not be stringent even if she postponed it without any valid reason.

12. All the more so, if this immersion is performed only because of stringency or a *hiddur* (enhancement of the) *mitzvah* can she immerse.

13. According to the *Shulchan Aruch*, it is permitted to have relations on *Tisha B'Av* that falls on Friday night, but the *Ramo* writes that some are stringent and that is the custom. If that evening is her immersion night, there is a difference of opinion among the *Acharonim* whether or not relations are then permitted. For those who follow the *Ramo*'s rulings, there is a basis for a scrupulous person to be stringent.

Immersion on an *onah*

7. If her immersion night occurs on the *onah* of the expected period (as will be explained in chapter 10),[14] or on the *onah beinonis* (see chapter 9, paragraph 2),[15] she does not immerse but postpones it to a day when she is permitted to have relations with her husband.

On the days that she is permitted to her husband but for some reason (medical or otherwise) she cannot have relations, it is a *mitzvah*[16] to immerse herself. This is in order to permit other acts of intimacy and lift restrictions that were applicable while she was a *niddah*. This rule applies to Friday night and *Motzei Shabbos* as well.

Blessing for immersion

8. A blessing is recited on immersion, just as we recite a blessing on other mitzvos.[17] The text of the bracha is:

ברוך אתה ה׳ אלהינו מלך העולם, אשר קדשנו במצותיו, וצונו על הטבילה.

9. According to the *Shulchan Aruch*, the *bracha* is recited before the immersion, and according to the *Ramo*, the *bracha* is recited

---

14. If the immersion night coincides with the *Ohr Zarua onah* (see chapter 9, paragraph 2) she may be lenient and immerse, but she should do a *bedikah* before relations.

15. Even if the last time that she had her period was during the day, it is better not to be lenient and immerse herself to have relations on the 30th night. When there is a great need one should consult a *Rav*. However, one may be lenient on the 31st night (from the beginning of her last period, which occurred then during the day), but she should do a *bedikah* before relations.

16. She recites a blessing on this immersion.

17. A woman who is a *niddah* out of doubt or stringency should consult a *Rav* about whether she should recite a *bracha* when immersing.

after the immersion.

Some *Sephardic* women follow the opinion of the *Shulchan Aruch* while others follow the *Ramo's* opinion. Each woman should follow her own custom.

Ashkenazic women are accustomed to follow the *Ramo's* opinion and recite the *bracha* after the immersion.

10. *Sephardic* women who recite the *bracha* before immersion should do so while wearing a robe. Some recite the *bracha* outside of the immersion room. However, if she already took off her robe and entered the water, she should recite the *bracha* when in the water, as explained below.

Ashkenazic women, who follow the *Ramo*'s opinion to recite the *bracha* after the immersion should do so immediately after the immersion while still in the water. They should submerge themselves in the water until their neck, and not look at their private parts while reciting the *bracha*.

The *Sheloh* instituted that *Ashkenazic* women should immerse, recite the *bracha* and then immerse again, so that the *bracha* will be before the second immersion.[18]

11. When reciting the *bracha* in the water or while wearing a robe, she should place her arm below her heart to separate between her

---

18. It is proper to immerse three times. A woman who is accustomed to immerse herself more than three times and wishes to cease this practice does not need to perform *hataras nedarim* (a nullification of vows). On the other hand, if she was accustomed to immerse herself three times and now finds it difficult to do so, she needs to perform *hataras nedarim*. No *hataras nedarim* is required if she wants to deviate from this custom only once due to medical or similar reasons.

heart and her lower body.

Posture during immersion

12. She should not immerse while erect or bent over since the water cannot reach all parts of the body in these positions.[19] She should bend down slightly,[20] with her hands[21] and legs in the same position that they are when she walks. They should not press against her body or be too far from it.

To immerse in such a position the water level in the *mikvah* should be approximately 24 to 30 cm (9.4 to 12 in). above her navel. If the water level is low she should immerse herself in a lying position with her hands and legs spread out.

13. A woman does not need to open her mouth to allow the water to enter. She should close her lips the way she normally does and not press them tightly in a way that covers any parts of her lips that are usually revealed. She must be careful that hair does not enter her mouth when immersing. If she shut her lips tightly or hair entered her mouth, the immersion is invalid.[22]

14. She should also not close her eyes tightly since this causes

---

19. She should not immerse herself in a place where she is afraid that people will see her, since this will prevent her from paying attention to immersing herself properly.

20. She should be in the same posture she assumes when she is rolling dough. If she did not immerse herself in this way, but immersed herself more than one time, and moved herself in a manner that allowed water to come into contact with every part of her body, she can be lenient.

21. She should not hold her eyes or her nose during immersion.

22. If she just clenched her teeth her immersion is valid.

folds to form and prevents the entry of water. If she closed her eyes tightly, she should consult a *Rav*.

Supervision during immersion

15. Immersion must be supervised by another woman[23] to ensure[24] that all of the body and hair is covered by *mikvah* water simultaneously.[25] Immersion without supervision is invalid. If no woman is available to supervise her immersion, she must consult a *Rav*.

Not to harbor doubts after immersion

16. The *Ramban* writes: "It is improper for a person to be too stringent and search for doubts to invalidate the immersion since there is no end to doubts. After she washed and cleansed her head thoroughly, combed her hair with a comb, washed and cleansed her whole body thoroughly with warm water, was careful not to touch any substance that could be a *chatzitzah*, and immersed herself while keeping her limbs and all of her body loose, one should not harbor doubts about flaws in the immersion since such doubts are endless. For example, perhaps she closed her eyes too tightly, or pressed her lips too tightly and other such doubts. Who can possibly discern whether these were actually closed too tight or not?"

---

23. The attendant must be a *Torah* observant woman of at least *bas mitzvah* age (12 years old) who has two puberty hairs.

24. The attendant should not hold onto her during the immersion. If a need arises to hold onto her, the woman supervising should first wet her hands in the *mikvah* water and try to hold her loosely, not tightly.

25. When a great need arises, she may gather her hair in a net and immerse, as long as the net is placed loosely on her head.

Immersion while standing on a bench, step etc.

17. She may not stand on a bench, a sheet, or a mat when she immerses. If she did, her immersion is invalid.

Likewise, she may not stand on a narrow step or on anything that may cause her to be afraid that she will fall because this fear prevents her from immersing with composure. If, however, she already immersed in such a way and is sure that everything was done properly, the immersion is valid.

Intention while immersing

18. A woman must immerse herself with the intention to emerge from her *niddah* status. If she immersed herself without this intention, e.g., if she fell into a *mikvah* or was bathing in the sea, she should initially, immerse herself again. However, she should not recite a *bracha* on this second immersion.

The *mikvah*

19. The immersion must be in a kosher *mikvah*. This means it must contain at least forty *so'oh* (approx. 750 liters, 200 US gallons, or 165 UK gallons) of rain water or spring water, or water that became fit for a *mikvah* by its being connected to rain water or spring water according to the requirements of *halacha*. If she did not immerse herself in a kosher *mikvah*, even if she were to wash herself in all the waters of the world, she remains in her *niddah* status.

The laws associated with a *kosher mikvah* are many and complex, therefore immersion should take place only in a *mikvah* that has been authorized and is supervised by a competent *Rav*.

Upon leaving the *mikvah*

20. After immersing herself, a woman must be careful not to encounter a *tamei* animal (a dog or a donkey for example) or a non-

Jew. It is therefore proper[26] to touch the *mikvah* attendant's hand after her immersion so that the attendant will be the first person she meets after immersion.

21. *Ashkenazic* women should not rinse their whole body[27] with water after the immersion,[28] but *Sephardic* women are not stringent with this.

22. A woman must be discreet and not tell others of her immersion.[29]

23. A woman should inform[30] her husband that she has immersed herself according to the *halacha*. Before informing him, it is forbidden for them to be lenient in any of the laws of restraints that are explained in chapter 2, even if the husband knows that she has returned from the *mikvah*.

---

26. It is a worthwhile custom after the immersion for the woman who supervises her to announce: "*Kosher*!"

27. But it is permitted to wash part of her body.

28. If a woman is fastidious in her cleanliness she may be lenient even if she is *Ashkenazic*.

29. About someone who discloses her immersion it is written:

ארור שוכב עם כל בהמה (דברים פרק כ"ז פסוק כ"א).

However, she should not postpone her immersion to avoid it becoming obvious to her close family. This is especially true if the *mitzvah* of פרו ורבו (of having a son and a daughter) has not yet been fulfilled.

30. She can also hint to him that she has immersed herself. However, some opinions are stringent and obligate her to actually inform him.

Chapter Nine

Separating When Anticipating the Period

1. When her period is expected, whether the woman has an established period, *veset kavuah* (i.e. a fixed time for menstruating), or she has a non-established period, *veset she'aina kavuah,* even though bleeding has not yet been observed, the couple is forbidden to have relations[1] since it is possible that she may become a *niddah* while they are having relations. (See below chapters 10 and 11 for the laws as to when bleeding is to be expected).

Poskim commend being stringent and refraining from hugging and kissing at the time when the period is expected.[2] However, other restrictions such as handing an object from one to another, eating from the same plate, pouring a drink, etc., are permitted on the day of the expected period.

Time of separation

2. The obligation to separate applies for the *onah* - the day or night during which the period is expected. *Onah* is defined as either a daytime or a nighttime. Thus, if the next period[3] is expected to

---

1. If the night of her immersion falls at the time that the period is expected, she postpones her immersion (see above chapter 8, paragraph 7).

2. They should also refrain from touching in an endearing manner, and all the more so from sleeping in the same bed, even if both are dressed.

3. If she observed bleeding close to sunrise and did not ascertain whether the

occur during the day, then the above restrictions are applicable

---

bleeding was before or after sunrise, by the strict letter of the law she need only anticipate the onset of her next menstruation in the daytime. However, to be stringent one should also restrict the night. However, in this case she is not required to separate during the "*Ohr Zaruah onah*" that precedes that night.

Similarly, if she observed bleeding close to sunset and did not ascertain whether it was before or after sunset, by the strict letter of the law she only needs to anticipate that her period will begin during the nighttime. However, to be stringent she should also include the preceding day, but need not separate for the *Ohr Zaruah onah* preceding that day.

The same rule applies if she forgot whether she observed bleeding during the day or at night. She is always required to observe the later *onah*. However to be stringent she should also observe the previous *onah*.

If she arose a short time after sunrise however, and observed bleeding, even though it is possible that the bleeding started before sunrise while she was sleeping, she only needs to be concerned about the daytime *onah*. She need not be concerned that she started bleeding at night. If the bleeding is profuse, however, and it is evident that it started before sunrise, she must observe the night *onah* and not the day *onah*. Similarly, if she observed bleeding immediately after sunset, even though it is possible that it started before sunset, she only needs to observe the nighttime *onah*. She need not be concerned that she started bleeding during the daytime. If the bleeding is profuse, as above, she must observe the *onah* of the day and not the *onah* of the following night.

If she forgot entirely when her period occurred, she is permitted at all times.

If she knows when her last period occurred, but does not remember when the period preceding the last one occurred, she only needs to be concerned about *onah beinonis* (days 30 and 31 from her previous period) and about the date of the month of the previous period. (After her next period, she will also have to take into account that menstruation could begin after the time interval (*haflagah*) that occurred between the last two periods).

from sunrise to sunset of that day. If the expected time for the next period is during the night, then the above restrictions are applicable the entire night, from sunset to sunrise. It is commendable to be stringent and separate on the preceding *onah* (the "*Ohr Zarua onah*"), as well. For example, if it is a day *onah,* then the couple should separate during the day and also the night before.

The rules applying to the times when bleeding is likely to begin will be clarified in the following chapters.

In the case of the *onah beinonis*, which is on the 30th and 31st days from the beginning of her previous period (below chapter 10, paragraph 2 and from paragraph 16 onwards), she should anticipate the onset of menstruation for the entire day (both at night and the following day) that the *onah* falls out on. The above restrictions apply during these two 24 hour periods, of day 30 and of day 31. This means that from the sunset after the 29th day until the sunset after the 31st day, separation is required. There is no difference whether the previous period started during the day or during the night.

Obligation to check

3. On the day or the night when she is to be concerned that her period may commence, she must check herself with an examination cloth to determine whether her period has begun. [4] She must do

4. She checks herself twice during that *onah*: once at the beginning of the *onah*, and once at the end of the *onah*. Hence, if the period is expected in the daytime, she checks once after getting up in the morning (after sunrise) and once before sunset. If the period is expected at night, she checks once at the beginning of the night (after sunset) and once before she goes to sleep. It is commendable to be meticulous and check also after getting up in the morning.

In the case of the *onah beinonis*, the following should be done. If the last

this whether she has an established or a non-established period, and also in the course of the *onah beinonis* (see previous paragraph). How to perform this *bedikah* and the kind of examination cloth to be used, are discussed in chapter 4 paragraph 3 and 4.

4. If she checked herself, as explained above, and did not find any blood, the couple may be together as soon as the *onah* has passed. However, within the *onah,* all the above restrictions apply (as explained in paragraph 1) even after she checked herself.

Omission of checking

5. If she did not check herself during the *onah* of her expected period, and the *onah* passed without her noticing any bleeding, if it is a *veset kavuah* or an *onah beinonis*, relations are still prohibited

---

menstruation began during the night, she should check twice (as above) during the night that follows the 29th day and again twice during the night that follows the 30th day. She should also check once close to the end of the 30th day and once close to the end of the 31st day. If last time bleeding began during the day, then she should check twice on the 30th day (as above) and twice on the 31st day. It is commendable to be meticulous and also check once at the start of the night following the 29th day and once at the start of the night following the 30th day.

If she finds it difficult to check twice during a given day or night, she should check at least once, preferably towards the end of the *onah* (day/night). In the case of the *onah beinonis* she should check towards the end of the *onah* (day/night) when bleeding was last observed. This means that if bleeding was observed last during the day, she should check close to the end of the 30th and 31st days. If bleeding was observed last during the night, she should check before going to sleep on the night that follows the 29th day and on the night that follows the 30th day.

It is commendable to perform additional *bedikahs* during the times that the period is expected.

until she performs a *bedikah* and finds no blood.[5] This check is valid even if a long time has passed from the day of her *onah*.[6] In the case of a non-established period,[7] she is permitted immediately after the *onah* (day/night) of the expected period has passed, even if she did not then check herself.[8]

6. In the case of a *veset kavuah* or *onah beinonis*, if she did not check herself on the day of the expected period, initially, she should not wash the inside of the vaginal area before examination. *Bedi'eved*, the check is valid even after washing. Some authorities contend that on the *onah* of an anticipated period she should refrain from taking a bath[9] or washing the inside of the vaginal area before performing the examination. *Bedi'eved* the *bedikah* is valid even if she did wash the area, and the couple may be together after the *onah* has passed.

Traveling at the time of the expected *onah*

7. Before embarking on a trip a husband should show expressions of affection to his wife, even on the *onah* of the anticipated period. According to the *Shulchan Aruch*, this even includes relations. In

---

5. Therefore the husband should verify before relations if she indeed checked herself.

6. It is correct that she checks as soon as she remembers.

7. In the case of an expected period due to *veset haguf* (bodily symptoms), if she failed to check herself the couple may not be together until she checks and finds herself clean. This is even when it was non-established and the *onah* passed with no sign of bleeding.

8. See chapter 12 concerning the obligation of a woman who has no established period to check before relations.

9. However, one may take a shower. If there is a need to take a bath or wash the inside of the vaginal area, she should check herself before doing so.

this case, she should check herself beforehand. The *Ramo* is of the opinion that it is commendable to be stringent and limit this affection to soothing talk.[10] It is recommended that he ask his wife's consent to forgo relations.

Undergarments

8. Colored, close-fitting underwear should not be worn during the *onah* (day/night) of the expected period.

Menstruating with intervals

9. If she started menstruating, stopped, and then started again, there are cases when she counts her period only from the initial bleeding. Whereas, there are other cases when she has to count also from the second time that bleeding was observed.

10. If the second bleeding started more than seven days after the start of the first bleeding, then the second bleeding must also be counted as a period. This applies even if the second bleeding happened only one time, and even if the blood was then found only on a *bedikah* cloth.[11]

11. If the second bleeding started **within** seven days of the beginning

10. One may be lenient when the obligation for separation is based on stringency, for example the "*Ohr Zarua onah*" (see above paragraph 2). Since these laws involve many details, one should consult a *Rav.*

11. According to this, if she carried out the *hefsek taharah* on the seventh day (after the commencement of her menstruation), and on the next day she found blood upon checking herself in the morning, she must expect her next menstruation both from the beginning of the actual period, and also from the day she found blood on the examination cloth. If it was a doubtful color and it is not certain that it is actual blood, a *Rav* should be consulted.

of her menstruation, and this happened three times in a manner that established a fixed period, then also the second bleeding must be included in calculating her expected periods. This applies even if blood was found only on a *bedikah* cloth.

12. If the second bleeding started within seven days of the beginning of the first, but this did not occur three times in a manner that establishes a fixed period, then she needs to include the second bleeding in calculating her periods, only when two conditions are met: **a)** The intermission between the two bleeding events be at least an entire day (night and day). **b)** The second bleeding did not occur during the days that she usually menstruates. In this case if the second bleeding was noticed only on a *bedikah* cloth, she does not include it in her calculations.

13. If the first bleeding was scanty and the second was profuse, as is usual during a period, and at least one day (night and day) passed between the two events, then also the day of the second bleeding must be included in calculating her periods.

Chapter Ten

Days of Separation for a Woman with a Non-Established Period

1. The nature of women is to menstruate from time to time; this is known as the *veset* (period). The *veset* usually lasts several days, and then the bleeding stops until the next *veset*.

Our Sages established *halachic* rules to calculate when a woman should anticipate the occurrence of her next *veset*. These are based on her previous menstrual patterns or on physical sensations that occurred together with the period. During these times she must separate from her husband and check herself as was explained in chapter 9 paragraph 1.

The cycle is counted from the day she starts bleeding, even if the bleeding continues for several days.

2. When calculating to determine these anticipatory days, the cycle is counted from the day she started bleeding. If her previous periods began according to a clear pattern, she is known as "a woman with an established *veset*". If the previous periods were not regular, she is known as "a woman with a non-established *veset*". The term "a woman with an established *veset*" applies to a woman who menstruated three times in a fixed pattern. However, a woman who has not had three menses that followed a fixed pattern (and also a woman who only saw once or twice) is regarded as one with a non-established *veset*. The establishing of the fixed cycle is discussed in the next chapter.

A woman who does not have an established cycle must anticipate the onset of her period at the following three times: **a)** "the day of the interval" (*veset haflagah*), **b)** "the day of the month cycle" (*veset hachodesh),* and **c)** "the average cycle" (*onah beinonis).*

Since she does not know when her next period will take place, she must anticipate the onset of menstruation during all these times, as shall be explained.

If the period was accompanied by bodily sensations (*veset haguf*), she must also anticipate that the reoccurrence of these sensations could cause the onset of her period, as shall be explained.

Veset haflagah

The *veset haflagah* is the day when she expects her period to begin based on the interval between her last two periods. This means that just as a given number of days passed between her last two periods, so too, we anticipate that menstruation may begin again after the same number of days. For example, if there were twenty-eight days between her last two periods, we anticipate that her next period will occur twenty-eight days after the last one. (This concept is explained further in paragraph 3).

Veset hachodesh

The *veset hachodesh* is the day of the month (according to the Jewish calendar) when she had her last period. She anticipates that menstruation will begin the next month on the same date that it occurred the previous month. This means that if her last period occurred on the 20th of *Tishrei*, then she anticipates that the next period will occur on the 20th of *Cheshvan*.

Onah beinonis

The *onah beinonis* (average cycle) means that we anticipate that menstruation will occur at the time that most women menstruate.[1] According to most opinions, it is the 30th day from the beginning of the previous period. (If the month on which her last period occurred had only twenty-nine days, it will coincide with the *veset hachodesh*). This is the accepted ruling. According to other opinions, the *onah beinonis* is to be expected on the 31st day after the onset of the previous period. (If the month of her last period had thirty days, it will coincide with the *veset hachodesh*). Ideally this opinion should also be followed.

Veset haguf

The *veset haguf* is menstruation preceded by unusual physical symptoms. These symptoms include headaches, stomachaches or other physical sensations that are evident that they are associated with the onset of her menstruation. Upon the re-appearance of these physical sensations she must anticipate that menstruation will begin. This applies whether the previous period began with the appearance of these physical sensations, or toward the end of their appearance, or after them. See further on paragraph 26.

Calculating the *veset haflagah*

3. A woman that has not established a *veset* must take into account that her period might begin after the same number of days that elapsed between her last two periods.

The number of interval days is counted from the first day of the first period until the first day of the next period. Even if menstrua-

---

1. This applies to a woman with a non-established cycle, because we cannot know when she will start menstruating again. The question of whether or not a woman with an established cycle anticipates the *onah beinonis* is discussed in chapter 11, paragraph 8.

tion continued for several days, the interval is always counted from the start of one menstruation to the start of the next.

In counting the days of the interval, an additional rule is that the first days of both periods are included in the count. For example, if she had one period on the 1st of *Nissan*, and then another on the 25th of *Nissan*, this is regarded as a twenty-five day interval. This is so because the 1st of *Nissan*, which is the start of the first period, and the 25th of *Nissan*, which is the start of the second period, are both included in the count of the interval. Therefore, when counting the interval from the period of the 25th of *Nissan* to the next expected period, the 25th is counted as one of the days of the interval. This means that the day when menstruation starts serves as the last day of the previous interval as well as the first day of the coming interval.

In this case, the day on which the next period is expected is the 19th of *Iyar*, since there are twenty-five days from the 25th of *Nissan* until and including the 19th of *Iyar*.

4. If the day of an anticipated period passes without menstruation, then there is no further need to expect menstruation after a similar interval.[2] For example, in the above case (when the previous periods were on the 1st and 25th of *Nissan*), where she is required to anticipate menstruation on the 19th of *Iyar* (the 25th day from the previous period), if no menstruation occurs, the 25 day *veset haflagah* is uprooted and need not be taken into account anymore.

However, if she now menstruates after an interval of twenty-eight days from her previous period (in our example, if she

---

2. Even if she forgot and did not check herself during the *onah* (on the 19th of *Iyar* in the above example), the *veset* is cancelled because a cycle has not yet been established (see the end of paragraph 2 in the next chapter).

menstruates on the 22nd of *Iyar*), she has to take into account that the next menstruation will occur after twenty-eight days. She no longer needs to expect her period to come after a twenty-five day interval. This means that in the above example she should expect her next period to occur on the 20th of *Sivan*, which is the twenty-eighth day from the previous period.

Uprooting *veset haflagah*

5. The reoccurrence of a period need no longer be taken into account if the day on which the period was expected passed without menstruation, as explained in the previous paragraph. However, if she menstruates before the day of the expected period, the veset is not considered uprooted. She must now anticipate the possible occurrence of her next period on two interval dates: **a)** the shorter interval between her last and current menstruation date, and, **b)** the previous longer interval that has not yet been uprooted. The need to still anticipate the longer interval stems from the fact that that day has not yet arrived and she may menstruate again after such an interval.

For example, if she menstruated on the 1st of *Nissan* forty days after her previous period, then she anticipates her next period on the 10th of *Iyar* (which is the fortieth day from the 1st of *Nissan*). But, she next menstruated on the 25th of *Nissan*, which is a twenty-five day interval from her last period. She must now anticipate her next period on two different interval dates: on the twenty-fifth day from her present period (which is the interval between it and her last period) and also on the fortieth day from this period, since this possibility still exists. (See the following paragraph for the procedure in this case).

Calculation of *haflagah* from last period

6. The time of anticipated menstruation because of a *veset haflagah* is always counted from the first day of her most recent period.[3] That

---

3. If she bled only slightly (accompanied by sensation), or if she found blood on the examination cloth, the days of the interval are counted from the last full-fledged menstruation. This means that this minor bleeding does not interrupt the interval from the last period. However, if the interval from the last period passed and her period did not arrive, then she must anticipate a reoccurrence after an interval which corresponds to the time between the last period and the day of the minor bleeding. We will explain this rule with several examples.

Her period began on the 1st of *Nissan* and then she menstruated again on the 29th of *Nissan*, (which is an interval of twenty-nine days). In this instance she anticipates that her next period will begin on the 27th of *Iyar*. Then she experienced minor bleeding on the 15th of *Iyar*, which is a seventeen day interval from her last period (the 29th of *Nissan*). Several possible menstruation days will now have to be taken into consideration:

(a) She anticipates the occurrence of her next period on the 27th of *Iyar*, which is the twenty-ninth day from the 29th of *Nissan*. The slight bleeding on the 15th of *Iyar* does not interrupt the interval.

(b) If by the time the 2nd of *Sivan* has arrived (seventeen days after the 15th of *Iyar*) she did not yet menstruate, then that day must be kept as a suspected menstruation day since it is the interval day from the minor bleeding.

(c) If the 14th of *Sivan* arrives (the twenty-ninth day from her minor bleeding on the 15th of *Iyar*), and she did not yet menstruate, she should take into account that menstruation may begin that day, due to the *haflagah* of 29 days from the 1st of *Nissan* until the 29th of *Nissan*.

(d) If she menstruated on the 29th of *Iyar* (a fifteen day interval from the minor bleeding on the 15th of *Iyar* and also the thirty-first day from her last period-the 29th of *Nissan*), then she anticipates that bleeding will occur on the 14th of *Sivan*, which is the fifteen day interval (from the period on the 29th of *Iyar*).

(e) She must also anticipate that bleeding may occur on the 16th of *Sivan*, which is an interval of seventeen days (from the period on the 29th of *Iyar*).

is, if the last period occurred twenty-eight days after the period before it, then the twenty-eighth day from her last period is the day of the anticipated present period.

When a woman anticipates dates from two different intervals, both are counted from the last period. For example, if one period occurred after a long interval and the next after a shorter interval, both of these intervals are counted from the first day of her most recent period.

In the previously mentioned case, when she menstruated on the 1st of *Nissan* after a forty day interval, and then again on the 25th of *Nissan*, which is a shorter, twenty-five day interval, she must

---

(f) She also takes into account the 28th of *Sivan* corresponding to the twenty-nine day interval between the 1st of *Nissan* and the 29th of *Nissan*. This is because the short period that occurred on the 15th of *Iyar* may be considered as proper menstruation. If so, all intervals were less than twenty-nine days, thereby not rescinding the longer interval of twenty-nine days.

(g) The 30th of *Sivan* must also be considered, if her period had not yet arrived by then, since it is the thirty-first day from the period on the 29th of *Iyar*.

(h) In addition she must anticipate the possibility of menstration on the day of the *onah beinonis* and on the same date of the month as she did for her previous period, which fall on the 29th and 30th of *Sivan*. See later par. 29.

Similarly, if she had a period on the 1st and on the 29th of *Nissan* (which is a twenty-nine day interval that requires her to anticipate that her next period will occur on the 27th of *Iyar*), but she observed slight bleeding (as above) on the 10th of *Iyar*, which is a twelve day interval from her last period (the 29th of *Nissan*), then she anticipates that she may menstruate on the 21st of *Iyar*, which is the 12th day interval from the minor bleeding (on the 10th of *Iyar*). However, if she did not detect any bleeding on the 21st of *Iyar*, she must still anticipate a period on the 27th of *Iyar*, which is the twenty-ninth day interval from the period of the 29th of *Nissan*.

anticipate her period both on the twenty-fifth and on the fortieth day from her last period. The two intervals are both counted from the last period (the 25th of *Nissan*) and she no longer needs to take into account that she may begin menstruating on the 10th of *Iyar*, which is the fortieth day after her period of the 1st of *Nissan*. Even though we explained that she had to anticipate her period coming on the 10th of *Iyar* (which is the fortieth day after the 1st of *Nissan*), since she menstruated again on the 25th of *Nissan*, we count her interval *veset* days from this last menstruation on the 25th of *Nissan*. If the 19th of *Iyar* passes (which is the twenty-fifth day from the period of the 25th of *Nissan*) and she has not yet menstruated, she must still anticipate menstruation on the 5th of *Sivan* (which is the fortieth day after the 25th of *Nissan*).

Longer intervals followed by shorter intervals

7. It follows from the above that if she menstruated on the 1st of *Nissan* and then on the 3rd of *Iyar*, which is a thirty-three day interval, and she then menstruated after twenty-nine days (on the 2nd of *Sivan*), and then after twenty-eight days (on the 29th of *Sivan*), and then after twenty-six days (on the 24th of *Tammuz*), then she must anticipate upcoming periods after various time intervals, as shall be explained.

First, she should expect that her next menstruation might occur on the twenty-sixth day from her previous period, which is the 20th of *Av*.

Second, if the 20th of *Av* passed and no menstruation occurred, she should anticipate the possibility of menstruation on the twenty-eighth day (the 22nd of *Av*), which is the second from the last interval. Since it was longer than the last interval, it was not uprooted and therefore, she still must anticipate that menstruation may occur after that interval.

Third, if the 22nd of *Av* passed and no menstruation occurred, she should anticipate that she may menstruate on the twenty-ninth day (the 23rd of *Av*), which is the interval that preceded the two previous periods. Since it was longer than those intervals, she still must anticipate that menstruation will occur after such an interval.

Fourth, if the 23rd of *Av* passed and no menstruation occurred, she should anticipate that she may begin to menstruate on the thirty-third day (the 27th of *Av*), which is the time interval that preceded all the other periods. Since it was longer than all the other intervals, it was not uprooted and she still must anticipate that menstruation will occur after this interval.

Shorter intervals followed by longer intervals

8. On the other hand, if the intervals between her periods occurred in a different pattern, with the shorter intervals first, followed by longer intervals, she need not anticipate menstruation after the short intervals since they were uprooted. For example, if her menstruation began on the 1st of *Nissan*, and then twenty-six days later (on the 26th of *Nissan*), and then twenty-eight days later (on the 23rd of *Iyar*), she no longer needs to anticipate the onset of menstruation on the twenty-sixth day from her last period. This is so because the second interval (of twenty eight days) was longer than the first and the twenty-sixth day had already passed without her having her period.

If her next period occurs on the twenty-ninth day, then she no longer needs to anticipate the onset of menstruation on the twenty-eighth day from her last period. If a subsequent period occurs after thirty-three days, she does not need to anticipate the onset of menstruation on the twenty-ninth day from her last period, and so on.

The general rule is that a later, long interval rescinds the need of anticipating the onset of menstruation after a shorter interval. On the other hand, a later, short interval does not rescind[4] the need to anticipate the onset of menstruation of a previously longer interval.

9. Accordingly, if at times she has her periods after a short interval and at times after a long interval, without any apparent pattern, she must check whether the longer interval has uprooted the shorter interval or whether the longer interval has to be kept in addition to the later, shorter interval.

For example, if the first period began on the 1st of *Nissan* and the second on the 29th (a twenty-nine day interval), and the next period began after twenty-six days (on the 24th of *Iyar*), and the next after twenty-eight days (on the 22nd of *Sivan*), she must anticipate the occurrence of the next period after twenty-eight days (on the 19th of *Tammuz*), which corresponds to the last interval, and also on the twenty-ninth day (on the 20th of *Tammuz*). This is because the last interval was not followed by a longer interval and the need

4. Since a shorter interval between periods does not rescind the need to anticipate the onset of menstruation after a previously longer interval, if between several long equal intervals she menstruated and had several short intervals, then she has an established *veset* for the longer interval. For example, if she menstruated after thirty-five days, and then menstruated several times after shorter intervals, and then again after a thirty-five day interval, and then menstruated after shorter intervals, and her subsequent period was on the thirty-fifth day from the last period, she is regarded as having an "established period" with a thirty-five day interval (see chapter 11). Regarding anticipating the possibility of menstruation on the *onah beinonis* and the *veset hachodesh*, see Sources and Explanations.

for anticipating her period on the twenty-ninth day has not yet been rescinded. Nevertheless, she does not have to anticipate the occurrence of a period on the twenty-sixth day because it was followed by the longer interval of twenty-eight days.

The *onah* in which to expect one's period

10. Sometimes one has to anticipate the appearance of a period during the *onah* of the daytime, whereas at other times one has to anticipate that a period may begin during the *onah* of the night. (The *onah* of day is from sunrise to sunset, and the *onah* of night is from sunset to sunrise, as explained earlier in chapter 9, paragraph 2). It depends on the *onah* of one's last period.[5] For example, if her period occurred during the daytime on the 1st of *Nissan* and then at night on the 25th of *Nissan*[6] (a twenty-five day interval), she is required to anticipate menstruation on night of the 19th of *Iyar*. Since her last period was at night, she must assume that her next period will also occur at night and must therefore separate from her

5. In a case when she has to anticipate the possibility of menstruation at different time intervals, because longer time intervals preceded shorter intervals and therefore the longer intervals have not yet been uprooted, she must anticipate these longer time intervals on the *onah* when those periods originally occurred. For example, she menstruated at night after an interval of thirty-three days, then menstruated during the day after a twenty-nine day interval, then menstruated at night after twenty-eight days and then on the twenty-sixth day in the daytime. She has to anticipate the possibility of menstruation during the daytime *onah* of the twenty- sixth day from her last period, during the night *onah* of the twenty-eighth day, during the day *onah* of the twenty-ninth day and during the night of the thirty-third day.

6. This means on the night preceding the day of the 25th of *Nissan,* not on the night that follows it.

husband on the night of the 19th of *Iyar*.[7] Her period on the 1st of *Nissan* which was during the day, serves only as a starting point for calculating future menstrual intervals.

Similarly, in the opposite case, if her period on the 1st of *Nissan* occurred at night, and the period on the 25th of *Nissan* took place during the daytime, she must anticipate the coming of her next period during the day[8] of the 19th of *Iyar*.

All that has been explained in the previous paragraphs applies to the *veset haflagah*. However, she must also anticipate the possible occurrence of her period on the *veset hachodesh* and the *onah beinonis*, as shall be explained.

The *veset hachodesh* (the day of the month cycle)

11. As stated above in paragraph 2, a woman with a non-established cycle must anticipate menstruation on the same date of the month as her previous period. For example, if her previous period occurred on the 1st of *Nissan*, she anticipates menstruation on the 1st of *Iyar*.

Menstruation is to be expected only during the same *onah* (day or night) as the previous period. For example, if the previous period occurred on the night of the 1st of *Nissan*,[9] then she separates

---

7. The night preceding the day of the 19th of *Iyar* and not the night following it.

8. She must also separate herself from her husband during the preceding *onah* (on the night of the 19th of *Iyar*), because of the *Ohr Zorua onah*. And if her period on the 25th of *Nissan* took place at night, she must also anticipate the onset of menstruation during the daytime of the 18th of *Iyar* because of the *Ohr Zorua onah*, as was explained in the previous chapter, paragraph 2.

9. If, however, her period occurred during the day of the 1st of *Nissan*, she should also anticipate the possibility of a period on the night preceding the

for the *veset hachodesh* on the night of the 1st of *Iyar*. She need not anticipate its appearance during the daytime of this date (see paragraph 17 regarding anticipating a reoccurrence of her period during daytime, but for a different reason).

Rescinding *veset hachodesh*

12. If the date of the month of the expected period passed and she did not menstruate,[10] she no longer needs to anticipate menstruation when that day of the month arrives in the future. For example, her previous period began on the 1st of *Nissan*, requiring her to anticipate that her next period might begin on the 1st of *Iyar*. If the 1st of *Iyar* passed and her period did not come,[11] she no longer needs to anticipate that her period will begin on the 1st of the month. Therefore she does not have to anticipate the possible occurrence of a period on the 1st of *Sivan*.

Additional *veset hachodesh* days

13. As explained in the previous paragraph, the suspicion that a period may occur is rescinded only if the day of the expected period passes and she does not menstruate. If she has her period before

---

1st of *Iyar*, because of the *Ohr Zorua onah*.

10. Similarly, if her period arrived early, and she was no longer menstruating on her *veset hachodesh* date, she no longer needs to be concerned about the possibility of menstruation on that day in subsequent months. For example, if she had her period on the 20th of *Nissan*, and again on the 15th of *Iyar* and the menstruation continued only until the 19th of *Iyar*, she no longer has to anticipate the onset of her period on the 20th of *Sivan*.

11. Even if she forgot and did not check herself on the day of the expected period, the *veset hachodesh* is rescinded because we are not dealing with an established period (see the end of paragraph 2 in the following chapter).

the expected date, however, the suspicion that the next period will occur on the original date of the month remains, and she must anticipate the coming of her next period on two dates.

For example, she had a period on the 1st of *Nissan*, which requires her to anticipate the possible occurrence of her next period on the 1st of *Iyar*, but her next period came early, on the 20th of *Nissan*. She must now take into account, both the 20th of *Iyar* (which is the date of the month of her previous period) and the 1st of *Iyar* (which is the date of the month of the period of the 1st of *Nissan*). This is because her expected period for the 1st of *Iyar* was not rescinded, since her period came prior to that date.[12]

However, if the 1st of *Iyar* passed and she did not menstruate, then she no longer anticipates a period on the 1st of *Sivan*, since the 1st of the month has been rescinded.

14. If she had a period on the 1st of *Nissan*, and again on the 28th of *Nissan*, and the latter period continued through the 1st of *Iyar*, then the expected *veset hachodesh* of the 1st of the month is not rescinded, because she was still menstruating on the 1st of Iyar She must take into account that her period may come both on the 28th of *Iyar*, which is the date of the month of her last period (the 28th of *Nissan*) and on the 1st of *Sivan*, which is the date of the month

12. The *onah* in which she anticipates the *veset* of the earlier non-rescinded period is calculated according to the *onah* in which she menstruated then, and not according to the *onah* of her more recent period (see footnote 5). Therefore, if the menstruation of the 1st of *Nissan* was during the day, and the menstruation of the 20th was during the night, she anticipates her period on the 1st of *Iyar* in the day and on the 20th at night.

of her period on the 1st of *Nissan.* [13]

Veset on *Rosh Chodesh*

15. If she had a period on the 30th of the month (the first day of *Rosh Chodesh)*, she must anticipate the coming of her next period on *Rosh Chodesh* of the following month whether that month has only 29 days or 30 days. This means that if the next *Rosh Chodesh* is only one day, she must anticipate the possibility of her next period on that day (which is the first of that month). If the next *Rosh Chodesh* is two days, she anticipates the possibility of her next period on both days. Therefore, if the first day of *Rosh Chodesh* passes and she does not menstruate, she must still anticipate the possibility of a period on the second day of *Rosh Chodesh.*

The requirement to anticipate her *veset* on both days of *Rosh Chodesh* is only when her period began on the 30th of the month. However, if she had her period on the 1st of the month, even though the next *Rosh Chodesh* is two days, she only anticipates the possible occurrence of her next period on the first of the month and not on the first day of *Rosh Chodesh*, which is the 30th of the month. [14]

---

13. Hence, if she had a period on the 10th of the month, and afterwards several periods occurred before the 10th of the month which continued until the 10th, and then again had a period on the 10th and additional periods before the 10th as above, and a third period on the 10th, she is regarded as having an established cycle for the 10th, even though her periods did not occur consecutively on that date. This is because the need to anticipate the possibility of a period on the 10th of the month has not been rescinded. Regarding anticipating the *veset* on the *onah beinonis,* see Sources and Explanations.

14. However, if she had three periods on *Rosh Chodesh,* even though they were not on the same date, she is regarded as having an established cycle for *Rosh Chodesh*. For example, if one period was on the 1st of the month and the

The *onah beinonis* (the average cycle)

16. As stated above in paragraph 2, a woman who does not have a *veset kavuah* must anticipate the possible occurrence of her next period on an *onah beinonis*, which is thirty days from the onset of her previous period. According to some authorities, this is on the thirty-first day from the onset of her previous period. Initially one should also follow this opinion.

17. According to a number of *Poskim*, the need to anticipate menstruation on the *onah beinonis* applies to the full 24-hrs of that day. It makes no difference whether she had her last period during the day *onah* or the night *onah*. Although with regard to other instances of anticipation for possible periods, if she had her previous period at night, she only needs to anticipate the possible occurrence of her next period at night[15] and not the following day, this is not so in the case of the *onah beinonis*. She anticipates the possible occurrence of her next period on the thirtieth day both during the night and day.

---

other two were on the 30th of the month (or vice-versa), since all three periods occurred on a day that is known as *Rosh Chodesh* she is regarded as having an established cycle on *Rosh Chodesh*. This means that when *Rosh Chodesh* is one day, she anticipates the possible occurrence of her next period on that day, and if it is two days, she anticipates the possible occurrence of her period on both days. The *veset hachodesh* is not rescinded until *Rosh Chodesh* passes three times without her menstruating. See chapter 11 paragraph 21.

15. This is besides the need to anticipate menstruation on the day or night before the expected period, because of the *Ohr Zorua onah*. Hence, if her previous period was in the daytime, she must also anticipate the possible occurrence of her next period on the previous night. If her previous period was at night, she must also anticipate the possible occurrence of her next period on the previous day (as explained in chapter 9, paragraph 2).

Initially[16] one should follow this opinion.[17] Also on the thirty-first day one should be stringent to anticipate the possible oncoming period during both the night and day.

18. Therefore, if she had her period on the 1st of *Nissan*, she must anticipate the possible occurrence of her next period on the 30th of *Nissan*, which should be the thirtieth day from her last period, and on the 1st of *Iyar*, which is the thirty-first day from her last period. She must anyhow anticipate menstruation on the 1st of *Iyar* because of the *veset hachodesh*.[18]

Similarly, if she had her period on the 1st of *Iyar*, she must anticipate the possible occurrence of her next period on the 1st of *Sivan*, which is the thirtieth day from her last period. This is because *Iyar* is a 29 day month. In this case, she must anyhow anticipate the possible occurrence of her next period on the 1st of *Sivan* because of the *veset hachodesh*.[19] In addition she must anticipate the possible occurrence of her next period on the 2nd of *Sivan*, which is the thirty-first day from her last period.

19. The day on which she must anticipate the possible occurrence of

---

16. In the case of necessity, or when the immersion night falls on the evening of the thirtieth day and she had her last period in the daytime, she should consult a *Rav*.

17. Even if her last period was after an interval of 30 days, whether she then saw in the daytime or at night, she must anticipate the possible occurrence of her next period on the thirtieth day, both in the daytime and at night.

18. In a 30 day month, the thirty-first day is always the same day as the *veset hachodesh*.

19. In a 29 day month, the thirtieth day is always the same day as the *veset hachodesh*.

her next period, due to the *onah beinonis*, is counted only from the last period and not from the one preceding it. Therefore, if she had her period on the 1st of *Nissan* and again on the 17th of *Nissan*, she does not need to anticipate that her period will come on the 30th of *Nissan*. The 1st of *Iyar* is prohibited because of the *veset hachodesh* but not because of *onah beinonis*. She must anticipate the possible occurrence of her next period because of *onah beinonis* on the 16th of *Iyar* and the 17th of *Iyar*, which are 30 and 31 days after her last period.

Similarly, if she had a period on the 1st of *Nissan* and again on the 24th of *Nissan*, she does not need to anticipate that she will menstruate again on the 30th of *Nissan* or on the 1st of *Iyar* for the *onah beinonis*. (However, she anticipates menstruation on the 1st of *Iyar* for the *veset hachodesh*[20]). She must anticipate menstruation on the 23rd and 24th of *Iyar* because of the *onah beinonis*.

20. If the thirtieth day passed without bleeding, she does not need to be concerned about her next *onah beinonis*. Therefore, even if an additional thirty days pass without her getting her period, she need not anticipate menstruation on the fifty-ninth day from her last period.

21. Any woman who does not have an established cycle must anticipate menstruation because of the *onah beinonis*. Even if the interval between her periods is always greater than thirty days, she must still anticipate menstruation on the thirtieth and thirty-first days.

Menstruation during a group of days – *Yamim Hanevochim*

22. A woman who does not have an established cycle, but usually

---

20. This means that she has to check herself on that day. However, abstinence is inapplicable in this case, because if she menstruated on the 24th of *Nissan*, there is insufficient time for her to purify herself.

menstruates within a group of three[21] days must separate[22] on all three days because of her anticipated period. Besides this she must separate for the other *veset* days as in paragraph 2 above.

For example, if the usual interval between her periods is between twenty-six and twenty-eight days, but without a set pattern, then she must always anticipate menstruation on days twenty-six, twenty-seven, and twenty-eight. (This is in addition to the need to anticipate the possible occurrence of her next period on the *onah beinonis*,[23] the *veset haflagah*, and the *veset hachodesh*). These days are known as the *yamim hanevochim* (days of confusion).

23. In case of necessity, such as on the immersion night, marital relations on these days are permitted, provided that it is not the very day of the anticipated period. All the more so, if the husband is about to leave on a journey, relations are permitted as above. In these instances, she should do a *bedikah* before they have relations.

---

21. When menstruation occurs within a group of more than three days, she does not have to anticipate a possible period during such a group of days. Others are meticulous and require such a suspicion over a group of seven days, but not more than that.

22. According to some authorities she has to do a *bedikah* daily, whereas others contend that the couple is only required to separate, but she does not need to check herself. One may be lenient in cases of necessity (except for her *veset* days, when she must check herself). According to all opinions, if she has not performed any *bedikos* during these days, then she does not need a subsequent check.

23. Even if the intervals between her periods range between thirty-five and thirty-seven days, and she does not usually have her period earlier than the thirty-fifth day from the onset of menstruation, she must still separate on the *onah beinonis*.

24. If she changed her menstruation pattern three times and her period began a few days before the *yamim hanevochim* or after them,[24] she no longer needs to anticipate menstruation during the *yamim hanevochim*. Even if she subsequently menstruated once during these days, she does not need to anticipate menstruation during the entire *yamim hanevochim*, unless she has reverted back and re-established menstruation during the original set of days.

25. A woman after pregnancy or nursing no longer needs to anticipate that she will menstruate during the *yamim hanevochim* in which she usually menstruated before pregnancy. This applies as long as she does not menstruate again several times during the same days, as clarified above in paragraph 24.

Physical symptoms

26. A woman whose menstruation was preceded by unusual physical symptoms (such as excessive yawning, sneezing, burping, excessive gas in the digestive tract, headaches, stomachaches or similar discomforts), must anticipate menstruation when these symptoms next occur.[25] This is so only if it is obvious that these are associated with the onset of her period. It is irrelevant whether

---

24. This means on days that are not close to this set of days. For example, the intervals between her periods ranged between twenty-six and twenty-eight days and now she started menstruating on the twenty-first and twenty-second day. The same applies if her periods were delayed to thirty-two and thirty-three days from the previous periods in a manner that makes it obvious that the new set of days do not belong to the old set.

25. This law is involved. It depends on the time of the menstruation, and whether it occurs at the beginning of the appearance of these events or at their end, and many other details. For this reason a *Rav* should be consulted concerning menstruation accompanied with physical sensations.

the period occurred simultaneously with these symptoms, on their termination, or came after them.

Staining

27. If a stain was found on her body or garment, even though this causes her to become a *niddah*, it is not regarded as a period and therefore she does not need to anticipate its reoccurrence.[26]

28. If she had one of the sensations described in chapter 1 paragraph 6 and then found a stain, the day when the stain was found should be regarded as the start of her period. This is because such stains are regarded as full-fledged menstruation and the beginning of a period.

29. A small amount of bleeding that occurs together with a sensation (as described above chapter 1, paragraph 6), or upon checking with a *bedikah* cloth, is considered like a period[27] with regard to her *veset* calculations.[28] The manner in which it should be anticipated with regard to the *veset haflagah* is explained above in the footnote to paragraph 6.

---

26. If she found a stain on her body, or on her garment, or on a sanitary pad but did not begin menstruation until the next *onah* (day or night), she should ask a *Rav* when to anticipate her next period.

27. If she performed a *bedikah* (for example, on a *veset* day) and found blood on the examination cloth, but only started bleeding heavily after that *onah* (of day or night) within 24-hours, the time when the blood was found on the cloth should be considered as the first day of the period. If more than 24 hours passed between the two events, a *Rav* should be consulted.

28. In this instance, one may be lenient concerning the *Ohr Zorua onah*.

Chapter Eleven

Days of Separation for a Woman with an Established Period

1. In the previous chapter we discussed the laws regarding the times for anticipating menstruation for a woman whose cycle is not-established. That woman is called "a woman with a non-established cycle". In this chapter we shall discuss the laws for anticipating menstruation of a woman whose monthly period occurs at regular fixed times. Such a woman is called "a woman with an established cycle" (*veset kavuah)*.

2. Various *halachic* distinctions exist between a woman with an established cycle and a woman with a non-established cycle. We will enumerate several of them: **a)** If the day during which menstruation was expected has passed and she did not check herself, a woman with a non-established cycle may be together with her husband without further checking. A woman with an established cycle may not be until she performs a *bedikah*. **b)** Since we do not know when a woman with a non-established cycle might menstruate, she must anticipate menstruation at various times as was explained in the previous chapter. On the other hand, a woman with an established cycle anticipates menstruation only at that fixed time and does not have to be concerned with the possibility that her period may start at a different time (see paragraphs 7, 8 for additional details). **c)** Regarding a woman with a non-established cycle, if the day that she anticipates menstruation passes without menstruation, that day is rescinded and she does not need to anticipate that she will menstruate on that specific day in the future (unless she again menstruates on that date of the month or again has the same interval between periods). For example, a woman with a non-established cycle who menstruated on the 1st of the month, but did not menstruate on that date the following month, does not need to anticipate that her coming menstruation will occur on the 1st, unless she again menstruates on the 1st of the month.

This is not so with a woman who has an established cycle. Even if she did not menstruate on the day that she anticipated menstruation, she must nevertheless anticipate that the next month she will menstruate on her fixed day. For example, if a woman established a cycle for the 1st of the month and did not menstruate on that day, she must still anticipate that the next month she will menstruate on the 1st of the month.[1] If, however, three months have passed in which she did not menstruate on that particular date, she no longer needs to anticipate menstruation on that day.

The same is true in the case of a woman who established a cycle of menstruating at equal intervals between periods (for example, every twenty-eight days). Even if menstruation occurred after thirty-two days, she must continue anticipating the possibility of menstruating after an interval of twenty-eight days.[2] If, however, she did not menstruate on the twenty-eighth day, she must still an-

---

1. Even if she menstruated in the middle of the month, (for example on the 10th or on the 15th) she must still anticipate menstruation on the 1st (besides anticipating possible menstruation on the days of the recent change).

2. The twenty-eight days are counted from the first day of the last menstruation. She does not have to anticipate menstruation after an interval of twenty-eight days from the time she thought that she would menstruate but did not.

ticipate menstruation on the thirty-second day because of the last interval. (She must also anticipate menstruation on the same date of the month as her last menstruation. See later in paragraph 8 that in such a case she also anticipates menstruation on the *onah beinonis).* **d)** An established cycle is rescinded only after she checked herself and saw that she did not menstruate on the day of the anticipated period,[3] whereas a non-established cycle is rescinded even if she did not check herself.

3. Furthermore, a woman with an established cycle that was rescinded because she did not menstruate three times on her fixed day,[4] returns to her original status of a woman with an established *veset* if she menstruates again even just once on the day of her previously fixed *veset* even after several years.[5] This applies only if she has not established a new fixed cycle. If she established a new cycle, and

---

3. If she forgot to check herself on the day that she anticipated menstruation, but checked after the day and did not find blood, she may rely on this inspection with regard to uprooting that *veset.*

4. One rescinds a *veset haflagah* only through menstruating three times after longer intervals. A *veset hachodesh* is rescinded only if she did not menstruate at all on that day.

5. This is the ruling of the *Shulchan Aruch.* She is again considered a woman with an established cycle and therefore she does not have to anticipate possible menstruation on any of her previous irregular times. However, many opinions disagree and maintain that since she did not menstruate three times on the day of her established cycle, she has thereby completely rescinded her established cycle. According to these opinions she does not revert to her previous established cycle by menstruating again one time on that menstruation day. One should, therefore, be stringent and also anticipate the menstruation dates of the irregular cycle.

then menstruated on the day of her previously established cycle, she does not return to her previously established cycle.

This paragraph applies to both a day of the month cycle and an interval cycle.

Veset haflagah (cycle of intervals between periods)

4. A woman who menstruated four times[6] at three equal intervals establishes a cycle of *veset haflagah*. For example, if she menstruated after three intervals of twenty-eight days,[7] she is considered a woman with an established cycle of menstruating every twenty-eight days. Now that an established cycle has been set, she must always anticipate that twenty-eight days following the beginning of her period she will menstruate again, until this *veset* is rescinded three times, as explained in paragraph 2.[8]

---

6. A *veset* is established by menstruating three times following the same pattern. A *veset haflagah* is created by three equal intervals between periods. This means that menstruation occurred four times, since the first interval is comprised of the first and the second menstruation.

7. It was explained in the previous chapter that intervals are calculated by counting the first day of the previous period and the first day of the current period. For instance, if she menstruated on the 1st of *Nissan* and on the 28th of *Nissan*, this is considered a *haflagah* of twenty-eight days. The 1st of *Nissan* and the 28th day of *Nissan* are both included in the *haflagah*. Likewise, in her calculation of anticipating the upcoming twenty-eighth day, she must take into account the day that she last began menstruating and the day that she anticipates that menstruation will begin. Since her second period was on the 28th of *Nissan*, she should anticipate menstruation on the 25th of *Iyar*, which is the twenty-eighth day from the 28th of *Nissan*, since the 28th of *Nissan* and the 25th of *Iyar* are included in the counting.

8. In this case (where there is an established cycle for menstruating at twenty-

5. *Veset haflagah* is established only if the three periods occurred on the same *onah* (i.e. they were all during the day or all during the night). If some of them were during the day and some at night, then she is still regarded as a woman with a non-established cycle.

6. Although it was stated in the previous paragraph that establishing a *veset haflagah* requires that all three periods occur during the same *onah*, nevertheless, the first menstruation preceding these three equal periods can be at a different *onah*. This is because the first menstruation serves only as a starting point for calculating the length of the first interval, but it is not included as one of the times that establish a *veset haflagah*. Therefore, even if the first menstruation was during the day, and the following three periods with equal intervals were during the night, she has established a *veset haflagah* at night.

---

eight day intervals), this cycle is rescinded if the twenty-eighth day passes three times without her then menstruating, and she checked herself on those days and did not observe any blood. (If the checks for rescinding the *veset* were done after the *onah* has passed, they are valid).

If she had an established cycle for long intervals, but later periods occurred at three equal shorter intervals (thus establishing a shorter *veset haflagah*) and her period ended before the time of her previously longer intervals, she anticipates menstruation at the shorter intervals and does not need to anticipate the longer intervals if her period is delayed. However, the established cycle for longer intervals is not altogether rescinded, and if she later menstruates even once at the longer interval, she returns to the established cycle of longer intervals. From then on, she anticipates menstruating after both the longer and shorter intervals.

If an established *veset* for long intervals was followed by menstruation at three equal shorter intervals and the flow continued until the anticipated time of her previously longer interval, then she must anticipate both the shorter and the longer intervals.

The reverse is also true. If her first menstruation was at night, and the three following periods that occurred at equal intervals were during the day, then she has established a *veset haflagah* for menstruating at that interval during the day.

7. The following example demonstrates what we have just explained: If menstruations began on the 1st of *Nissan*, the 28th of *Nissan*, the 25th of *Iyar* and the 23rd of *Sivan*, which are four periods with three equal intervals of twenty-eight days,[9] this will not establish a *ve-*

9. Some *Poskim* contend that if she menstruated twice at twenty-eight day intervals and the third time after twenty-six days, but her flow continued until the twenty-eighth day, that she has established a *veset haflagah* of twenty-eight days.

The following example demonstrates this case: Her periods began on the 11th of *Nissan*, the 8th of *Iyar* and the 6th of *Sivan*, which constitutes three periods with two equal intervals of twenty-eight days. Her next period however, began early on the 1st of *Tammuz*, which is only twenty-six days after the menstruation of the 6th of *Sivan*, but the flow continued until the 3rd of *Tammuz*, which is twenty-eight days from the menstruation on the 6th of *Sivan*. In this situation she is considered to have established a *veset haflagah* of twenty-eight days.

Nevertheless, since this matter is disputed, she must also anticipate menstruation on several other dates. First, she anticipates menstruation on the 26th of *Tammuz*, an interval of twenty-six days from her last menstruation, which occurred after an interval of twenty-six days. Second, she anticipates menstruation on the 28th of *Tammuz*, an interval of twenty-eight days from the beginning of her last menstruation (since in the past she menstruated after intervals of twenty-eight days and a shorter interval does not rescind a longer one). Third, we are stringent and require her to anticipate menstruation on the 1st of *Av* since her continued flow on the 3rd of *Tammuz* may have established a *veset haflagah* of twenty-eight days, and twenty-eight days after the 3rd of *Tammuz* falls on the 1st of *Av*. (She also anticipates the *onah set haflagah* unless the last three periods occurred during the same *onah*, that is, all were either at night or in the daytime.[10] If one of

---

beinonis and the *veset hachodesh* on the 1st and 2nd of *Av*, because she menstruated on the 1st of *Tammuz*).

This rule applies only if there were two twenty-eight day intervals followed by an early menstruation after twenty-six days, with the flow continuing until day twenty-eight as above. However, if she had an interval of twenty-eight days, and then menstruated after twenty-six days with the flow continuing until day twenty-eight, and the third interval was after twenty-eight days, then she is not considered as having established a *veset* for twenty-eight day intervals (unless she menstruates twice at twenty-eight day intervals after the period that occurred after the twenty-six day interval).

If a woman menstruated three times with two equal intervals in between, followed by a fourth menstruation that started earlier, and then menstruated a fifth time after an interval equal to the first two intervals, we are stringent and maintain that she has established a *veset haflagah*. The fourth time that she menstruated, in the middle, does not prevent establishing a regular cycle. For example, a woman menstruated twice after thirty-day intervals, such as on the 2nd of *Nissan*, the 1st of *Iyar* and then the 1st of *Sivan*. Then she menstruated on the 10th of *Sivan*, which is after an interval of ten days, and then on the 30th of *Sivan*, which is after an interval of twenty-one days (from the 10th of *Sivan*). The interval between the 1st of *Sivan* and the 30th of *Sivan* was thirty days (although there was a period in between, on the 10th of *Sivan*). In this case we are stringent and consider her as having established a regular cycle of intervals of thirty days, and she must separate on the 29th of *Tammuz* in accordance with all the stringencies of an established *veset*. Furthermore, she must anticipate menstruation on the 20th of *Tammuz*, an interval of twenty-one days from her last menstruation that was on the 30th of *Sivan*. (In addition, she must anticipate menstruation on her *onah beinonis* and the *veset hachodesh*).

10. This means the night before the day of the 28th of *Nissan*, and the night

these three periods was at night, but the others were during the day (or the opposite), she has not established a *veset haflagah* of twenty-eight days. Only the first menstruation (the 1st of *Nissan*) may be at a different *onah* than the following three periods.

8. A woman with an established cycle of intervals (for example, her period begins every thirty-two days), needs to anticipate menstruation only at the time of this established cycle. She does not need to anticipate menstruation at other times, either on the *veset hachodesh* or on the *onah beinonis*.

However, this only applies when her regular cycle of intervals is greater than thirty days, as above. If she established a *veset haflagah* of less than thirty days, and the day of that interval passed without menstruation, then she must also anticipate menstruation on the *onah beinonis* (the thirtieth day after her last period). Nonetheless, in this case, the *onah beinonis* is to be expected only on the same *onah* (day or night) of her established cycle.[11] In a case of necessity one can be lenient and not take the *onah beinonis* into account.

Deviating from her fixed cycle

9. If the pattern of her established *veset haflagah* was disrupted, and she menstruated after a new interval, then she must anticipate menstruating at the following three times: **a)** On the day of her

---

before the day of the 25 of *Iyar* etc., and not the night after that day.

11. This means that if she established a twenty-eight day *veset haflagah* during the night *onah* and the time of that interval passed without menstruation, then she anticipates only the night of the thirtieth day but not the 30th during the day. If conversely, she had a regular cycle of twenty-eight day intervals during the day *onah* and that interval passed without menstruation, then she anticipates menstruation on the thirtieth during the day but not at night.

regular interval. **b)** On the day of her most recent interval (as a non-established cycle). **c)** On the day of the month of her most recent menstruation.

She need not anticipate menstruation at the time of the *onah beinonis* since she has an established cycle.

An example of the above situation follows: A woman has an established *veset haflagah* with intervals of thirty-two days due to menstruation on the 1st of *Iyar*, the night of the 3rd of *Sivan*, the night of the 4th of *Tammuz* and the night of the 6th of *Av*. If she then menstruates on the night of the 3rd of *Elul*, which is an interval of only twenty-eight days, she must anticipate menstruation on the night of the 1st of *Tishrei*, which is an interval of twenty-eight days from the first day of her last period. She must also anticipate menstruation on the night of the 3rd of *Tishrei*, which is the date of the month of her last menstruation. [12] If these dates pass and her period has not yet begun, she must separate for her established cycle of thirty-two days, which falls on the night of the 5th of *Tishrei*, an interval of thirty-two days from her last menstruation.[13]

---

12. She does not need to anticipate menstruation on the day of the 3rd of *Tishrei* because of her *onah beinonis* or on the 4th of *Tishrei*, since she has an established cycle. (If the flow after the twenty-eight day interval continued for five days until day thirty-two, see above footnote 9).

13. If the following month she also did not menstruate on the day of her regular cycle, but did so after an interval of twenty-nine days (thus her intervals were: 32, 32, 32, 28, 29), then the next month she must separate from her husband on the menstruation date of her regular cycle (of thirty-two days), on the menstruation date of her last interval (twenty-nine days) and on the same date as the date of the period of the last month. She does not have to anticipate an interval of twenty-eight days, since it was rescinded

Another example of a woman whose *veset haflagah* pattern was disrupted follows: A woman established a *veset haflagah* of twenty-eight days during the night *onah* because of menstruation on the 1st of *Iyar*, the night of the 28th of *Iyar*, the night of the 26th of *Sivan* and the night of the 23rd of *Tammuz*. If she then menstruated on the night of the 25th of *Av*, which is after a longer interval of thirty-two days, she must anticipate menstruation on the night of the 22nd of *Elul*, which is when her established *veset haflagah* (of twenty-eight days) falls. She must also anticipate menstruation on the night of the 24th of *Elul*, (which is the thirtieth day from her last menstruation) because of the *onah beinonis*,[14] the night of the 25th of *Elul* (which is the *veset hachodesh*) and the night of the 26th of *Elul* (which is after an interval of thirty-two days from her last menstruation).

If the last time she menstruated (after a new interval) was during the day, her established cycle remains on the night *onah*, see above chapter 10, footnote 5.

Incremental *veset haflagah*

10. A woman can establish a *veset haflagah* of incremental intervals if each time she menstruates it is a day later than her previous in-

---

by her not menstruating on that interval in the month following it. However, if the next month menstruation was after a shorter interval, such as after an interval of twenty-two days (32, 32, 32, 28, 22), the shorter interval of twenty-two days does not rescind the longer interval of twenty-eight days.

14. As explained in paragraph 8, if her *veset haflagah* was shorter than the *onah beinonis*, and the day of her established cycle passed without menstruation, then she only needs to anticipate the *onah beinonis* during the *onah* (day or night) of her established cycle.

terval. In this case she anticipates menstruation by adding one day to her previous interval.[15]

For example, a woman who menstruated after an interval of twenty-five days, and then menstruated after twenty-six days, and then after twenty-seven days (that is, four periods separated by intervals that progressively increased by one day), has established an incremental interval cycle.[16] In such a case, she must anticipate menstruation after an interval of twenty-eight days, and so forth.

Others rule that she need not be concerned about this type of cycle until she has menstruated at least five times with four progressive intervals which follow this pattern. Since both opinions should be taken into account, if she menstruates only four times with three incremental intervals it is regarded as an established cycle only with respect to stringencies,[17] but not with regard to leniencies.[18] Therefore, she must still anticipate possible menstruation dates similar to a woman with a non-established cycle. If the next time she men-

15. She does not anticipate menstruation according to this pattern until a *veset haflagah* of incremental intervals has been established as will be explained.

16. This only refers to cases where all of the last three periods (through which her cycle was established) occurred on the same *onah* (day or night).

17. Therefore the next month she must anticipate menstruation after a twenty-eight day interval.

18. This means that we do not consider this as an established regular cycle that rescinds an irregular cycle. Therefore, because it is possible that she did not establish a regular cycle, she must separate also on: (1) the *onah beinonis*, (2) on the day corresponding to her last interval, and (3) on the day of her *veset hachodesh* according to her menstruation of the last month, in addition to the new anticipated day created by her incremental *veset haflagah*.

struates is after an interval of twenty-eight days, it will then be considered an established cycle of incremental intervals even if it entails leniencies.

11. The same rule applies when a woman begins to menstruate in a pattern where each period begins a day earlier than the previous period. For instance, she menstruates after an interval of thirty days, then after an interval of twenty-nine days, and then after an interval of twenty-eight days. (This means that she menstruated four times and these periods were separated by intervals that decreased progressively by one day). In this case, as above, we are stringent and regard her as having established a *veset haflagah* of incrementally decreasing intervals,[19] and she must now anticipate future dates according to this cycle. But she must also anticipate her period on the days a woman with a non-established cycle does. Therefore, the next month she anticipates her period after twenty-seven days, and so forth. However, she does not follow this regular cycle with regard to leniencies (with respect to not needing to anticipate menstruation on other dates), unless she has her next period after an interval of twenty-seven days. If she has her next period after an interval of twenty-seven days she has now established a fixed cycle according to all opinions and anticipates her next period after an interval of twenty-six days and so forth.

12. A *veset haflagah* of incremental intervals is established only when it is consistent each time. If, however, menstruation once occurred after an increase of one day from the previous interval, and the next time after an increase of two days from the previous in-

19. This applies only if her three last periods, through which her *veset* was established, occurred during the same *onah* (either all during the day or all during the night).

terval, without a set pattern, then a cycle of incremental intervals cannot be established.[20]

13. A cycle of incremental intervals is only established when menstruation occurs in a certain pattern, and each time the interval increases or decreases, as explained in the previous paragraphs. If, however, the intervals follow a pattern of progressive increasing or decreasing days, even if it repeats itself, no cycle is established. For example, if menstruation occurred after an interval of thirty-two days and then after thirty-three days, and this pattern occurred three times (32 33; 32 33; 32 33), then she does not establish a cycle of repeated incremental intervals.[21] Rather, she anticipates menstruation dates like any woman with a non-established cycle.

14. If a cycle of incremental intervals was established, such as menstruation after thirty days, thirty-one days, thirty-two days and thirty-three days, then the next menstruation is expected after thirty-four days. If the thirty-fourth day passes without menstruation, and menstruation occurs instead after a longer interval (such as thirty-six days), she must anticipate her next menstruation after

---

20. If her incremental interval increased each time by an additional day, for example, if she first menstruated one day later than her previous interval and afterward menstruated two days later than her previous interval, and then menstruated three days later than her previous interval, some authorities contend that she establishes a *veset* according to this pattern, since it follows a certain order.

21. In this case she has established a *veset haflagah* for thirty-three days, since the longer interval of thirty-three days rescinds the shorter one of thirty-two, while the interval of thirty-two days does not rescind the interval of thirty-three days (since we rule that a shorter interval does not rescind a longer one). See Sources and Explanations chapter 10 paragraph 8 footnote 4.

thirty-five days, since according to the pattern of her established cycle she was to expect menstruation after such an interval. She does not need to anticipate menstruation after an interval of thirty-four days, however. (If the thirty-fifth day passes and menstruation does not occur, then she anticipates menstruation the following day on the thirty-sixth day as a non-established cycle, since her last menstruation took place after thirty-six days).

15. The previous paragraph only applies to the case when menstruation occurred after a longer interval. If, however, she menstruated after a shorter interval, the *halachah* is different. For example, menstruation occurred after intervals of thirty, thirty-one, thirty-two and thirty-three days (as in the previous paragraph), and now she menstruates after thirty days. She must anticipate her next menstruation after thirty-four days.[22] (She must also anticipate menstruation on the thirtieth day after her last menstruation as a non-established cycle).

Day of the month cycle - *Veset Hachodesh*

16. A woman who began menstruating three times on the same day of the Jewish month (according to the Jewish lunar calendar),[23]

---

22. This applies only if her menstruation did not continue to the anticipated day of the thirty-four day interval, and therefore we consider her last early menstruation as being a change from her normal pattern. If, however, she menstruated after thirty days and her flow continued to the thirty-fourth day, then she anticipates menstruation after an interval of thirty-five days. She calculates the expected thirty-fifth day interval from the thirty-fourth day. This is besides anticipating menstruation on the thirtieth day (which is calculated from the onset of the menstruation).

23. There is no *halachic* significance to fixed menstruation dates that follow the secular calendar which is based on the sun (the Gregorian calendar).

establishes a regular cycle for this day. For example, if she menstruated on the 5th of *Nissan*, the 5th of *Iyar* and the 5th of *Sivan*, she must anticipate menstruation on the 5th of *Tammuz*. If the 5th of *Tammuz* passes and she does not menstruate on that date, she must still anticipate menstruation on the 5th of *Av*, and so forth. She must always take the 5th of the month into account until the 5th of the month passes three consecutive times without menstruation.[24]

17. A cycle of menstruating on the same day of each month is established only when menstruation takes place three times in the same *onah* (day or night). Menstruations which sometimes occur during the day and sometimes at night, do not combine to the three times needed to establish a regular cycle. Her status remains as a woman with a non-established cycle.

Therefore, if menstruation began during the daytime of the 5th of *Nissan*, the 5th of *Iyar* and the 5th of *Sivan*, she establishes a regular cycle for the fifth of each lunar month during the day. If menstruation began each time at night, then she establishes a regular cycle of monthly menstruation on that date at night. On the other hand, if she began menstruating on the 5th of *Nissan* at night and on the 5th of *Iyar* at night, and then on the 5th of *Sivan* in the daytime, she has not established a regular cycle for the fifth of the month.[25]

---

24. An established cycle is rescinded only if the day passes and she checked herself, and did not observe any blood.

25. However, if the first two periods occurred during the day and the third one started at night and continued through to the day, then she must be stringent and consider this as an established cycle. Therefore, if she menstruated on the 5th of *Nissan* during the day, on the 5th of *Iyar* during the day, and on the night of the 5th of *Sivan* and her period continued to the day, she anticipates having established a cycle for the day *onah* the 5th of each month,

In this case she must anticipate possible menstruation on the 5th of *Tammuz* during the day, because of her non-established day of the month cycle.[26] If the day of the 5th of *Tammuz* passed without menstruation, then she need not anticipate any more periods on the 5th of the month.

18. A monthly cycle is established even when there are other periods in between. For example, if she began menstruating on the 1st of *Nissan*, the 20th of *Nissan*, the 1st of *Iyar* and the 1st of *Sivan*, then she has established a monthly cycle for menstruating on the 1st of each month. This is so even though menstruation also occurred between the periods of the 1st of *Nissan* and the 1st of *Iyar*.

Similarly, if menstruations began on the 1st of *Nissan*, the 1st of *Iyar*, the 26th of *Iyar*, and then the bleeding stopped, and started again on the 1st of *Sivan*, a monthly cycle for menstruating on the 1st of each month has been established. She need not anticipate any other menstruation dates, not even the twenty-sixth of the month.

Deviation from an established *veset hachodesh*

19. If a *veset hachodesh* was established and instead of menstruating on that date the next month, menstruation began later on a different date, they must separate the following month both on the date of her established cycle and also on the date of her last menstruation. For example, she began menstruating on the 5th of *Iyar*, the 5th of *Sivan*, and the 5th of *Tammuz* (thus establishing a *veset hachodesh*), but in the month of *Av* she did not menstruate until the 8th of the month. Missing the 5th of *Av* does not rescind the established cycle,

---

as will be explained in par. 20.

26. Besides anticipating menstruation on the 4th of *Tammuz* because of the *onah beinonis* and because of her last interval of thirty days.

and therefore they must separate on the 5th of *Elul* (the date of her established cycle). She also needs to anticipate menstruation on the day of her last menstruation, the 8th of *Elul* (because of the non-established *veset hachodesh*), and on the 10th of *Elul* (because of the non-established *veset haflagah* of thirty-three days). However, she does not need to anticipate menstruation on the day of the *onah beinonis* because she still has an established cycle.

If she missed her established period again in *Elul* and menstruated on the 6th of *Elul*, her regular cycle has not yet been rescinded. They must separate on the 5th of *Tishrei* for two reasons: 1) because of her established *veset hachodesh,* and 2) because that is the day of her most recent (twenty-nine day) interval. They must also separate on the 6th of *Tishrei*, since she must anticipate the date of the non-established *veset hachodesh.*[27] In addition, they must separate after thirty-three days (on the 9th of *Tishrei*) which is the previous longer interval, since a shorter interval does not rescind a longer one (see chapter10, paragraph 5).

20. If menstruation occurred on the 1st of *Nissan*, the 1st of *Iyar*, and the 26th of *Iyar*, and the flow (of the 26th of *Iyar*) continued without interruption until the 1st of *Sivan*, some authorities contend that she is regarded as having established a monthly cycle for the 1st of the month regarding stringencies. This is because she menstruated twice on the 1st of the month, and third time also there was bleeding on the 1st of the month. In this case she also anticipates menstruation on the 26th of *Sivan* because her last menstruation may have

---

27. If the menstruation on the 6th of *Elul* continued on to the 8th of *Elul*, then the menstrual date of the 8th of the month has not yet been rescinded. This is because she menstruated on that day and they must also separate on the 8th of *Tishrei*. See above chapter10, paragraph 14.

been caused by of the 26th of the month (the day that she started menstruating, and not by the 1st of the month on which there was bleeding), on the 22nd of *Sivan* because of the twenty-six day interval from the 1st of *Iyar* to the 26th of *Iyar*, on the 27th of *Sivan*, which is the interval of thirty-one days from the 1st of *Nissan* to the 1st of *Iyar* (which is a longer interval that was not yet rescinded).

Establishing the *Rosh Chodesh veset*

21. If she began menstruating three times on *Rosh Chodesh* even if they are not all on the same date, she has established a fixed cycle for *Rosh Chodesh*. For example, if one of the periods occurred on the 1st of the month (*Rosh Chodesh*) and the other two were on the 30th of the month (the first day of *Rosh Chodesh*), she establishes a cycle for *Rosh Chodesh* and she must anticipate possible menstruation on both days of future *Roshei Chodashim*.[28] Therefore if *Rosh Chodesh* is one day, she anticipates menstruation on that one day, and if it is two days, she anticipates menstruation on both days. Although the three menstruations did not occur on the same date of the month (one was on the 1st of the month and the last two were on the 30th of the month), since the common denominator of these three times of menstruation is that they all occurred on a day called *Rosh Chodesh*, she establishes a cycle for the days of *Rosh Chodesh*.[29]

---

28. If she menstruated three times on the 1st of the month, then we maintain that her menstruation is caused by the date of the month and not by *Rosh Chodesh*. However, it seems that if she menstruated on the 30th of *Tishrei*, the 30th of *Cheshvan*, and the 30th of *Kislev*, then she has established a regular cycle for *Rosh Chodesh*. She then needs to separate on the 1st of *Shevat* even though she did not previously begin menstruation on the 1st of the month.

29. If she began menstruating on the 1st of *Iyar*, the 1st of *Sivan*, and the 30th of *Sivan*, continuing on to the next day, the 1st of *Tammuz*, it is not clear

A cycle for *Rosh Chodesh* is established only when all three periods occurred during the same *onah* (day or night), as explained above in paragraph 17.

The *Rosh Chodesh* cycle is rescinded if *Rosh Chodesh* passes three times without any menstruation. However, if she did not menstruate on the 30th of the month but on the 1st, the established cycle of *Rosh Chodesh* is not rescinded since she menstruated on *Rosh Chodesh*.

Incremental day of *veset hachodesh*

22. A woman can establish a cycle of incremental day of the month menstruation[30] when she menstruates one or two days later each month.[31] However this is only if the progression is consistent (see

---

whether she has established a cycle for *Rosh Chodesh* or a cycle for the 1st of the month, (since a woman can establish a cycle by menstruating twice from a "closed wellspring" and the third time during an "open wellspring", as explained in the previous paragraph). The 30th of the next month must be anticipated in any event as a non-established *veset* because of her menstruation on the 30th of *Sivan*. However this non-established *veset* would be rescinded if she did not menstruate on the 30th. An established *veset* for *Rosh Chodesh* has different *halachos*.

30. When the dates reach the end of the month, there is a doubt how the cycle continues after menstruation on the 30th of the month. Do we anticipate that the next menstruation will occur on the 1st of the next month, or do we say that her regular incremental day-of-the-month cycle is annulled.

31. If she menstruated three times following a certain pattern of the days of the month, then again menstruated another three times in the same pattern, and then again another three times according to that pattern, she establishes a cycle according to this pattern. For example, if she menstruated on the 1st of *Nissan*, the 2nd of *Iyar*, and the 3rd of *Sivan*, and then on the

above paragraph 12).

For example, if menstruation occurred on the 15th of *Nissan*, the 16th of *Iyar* and the 17th of *Sivan* (in the same *onah*), a cycle of menstruating one day later each month has been established.[32] This means that her menstruation is caused by the additional day of each month, and she must continue to anticipate menstruation according to this pattern. Therefore, in the above example she anticipates menstruation on the 18th of *Tammuz*, the 19th of *Av* and the 20th of *Elul* (in the same *onah* as the previous times that she menstruated).[33]

1st of *Tammuz*, the 2nd of *Av* and the 3rd of *Elul*, and later menstruated on the 1st of *Tishrei*, the 2nd of *Cheshvan*, and the 3rd of *Kislev*, she establishes a cycle according to this pattern. She must now anticipate menstruation on the 1st of *Tevet*, the 2nd of *Shevat*, the 3rd of *Adar* and then again on the 1st of *Nissan* etc.

32. But as long as she has not established a cycle of incremental monthly periods, she does not anticipate menstruating according to such a pattern. Consequently, if she menstruated on the 15th of *Nissan* and the 16th of *Iyar*, then she anticipates menstruation on the 16th of *Sivan* because of two reasons: 1) *veset hachodesh* for the 16th of the month, and 2) the 16th of *Sivan* is the date of the *onah beinonis*, since it is thirty days from her menstruation on the 16th of *Iyar* (*Iyar* has only 29 days). Even though she does not need to anticipate the 17th of *Sivan* because of an incremental day of the month cycle, nevertheless she must anticipate that date according to the opinions that the *onah beinonis* is thirty-one days after her last menstruation. She likewise anticipates the 18th of *Sivan* because of the interval of thirty-two days that passed between the 15th of *Nissan* and the 16th of *Iyar*.

33. She anticipates menstruation on these days whether she menstruated on another day or did not menstruate at all, since these are her established times of menstruation calculated according to her regular incremental day of the month cycle.

Some authorities contend that this *veset* is only established after four periods, and her incrementmal *veset* can only be considered established if she menstruates a fourth time on the 18th of *Tammuz*.[34] She would then no longer need to anticipate other menstruation dates that are required of a woman with a non-established cycle. However if she had only three periods, we must comply with both opinions and consider it as an established cycle only regarding stringencies, but not regarding leniencies. She would then continue to anticipate other possible menstruations just as a woman with a non-established cycle would.[35]

23. All of the above also applies if her period begins one day earlier each month than the month before or for a similar consistent pattern. For example, if menstruation began on the 19th of *Nis-*

---

34. In the same *onah* as the previous three times. Even if she did not menstruate on the 19th of *Av* (which is the next date on which we anticipate menstruation for this incremental day of the month cycle), she must still anticipate that her period will begin on the 20th of *Elul*, and so forth.

35. In this case she must anticipate menstruation on the 16th of *Tammuz* since it is the *onah beinonis*, thirty days after the previous menstruation. She also anticipates menstruation on the 17th of *Tammuz* for three reasons: 1) It is the day of the *veset hachodesh* from her menstruation on the 17th of *Sivan*. 2) It is after an interval of thirty-one days corresponding to the last interval that was thirty-one days (from the 16th of *Iyar* to the 17th of *Sivan*). 3) It is the *onah beinonis* according to the opinion that the *onah beinonis* is after thirty-one days. She also anticipates that her period may begin on the 18th of *Tammuz* for two reasons: 1) According to some opinions she established an incremental day of the month cycle. 2) Because it is after an interval of thirty-two days and the earlier interval of 32 days between the period beginning the 15th of *Nissan* and that beginning the 16th of *Iyar* was not yet rescinded.

san, the 18th of *Iyar* and the 17th of *Sivan* (and these three times of menstruation were in the same *onah*), then she has established a *veset hachodesh* of incremental decreasing days according to some authorities. She should now anticipate menstruation according to this pattern in addition to her other *veset* days.

Therefore, in the above case she anticipates menstruation again on the 16th of *Tammuz* in the same *onah* as her previous periods and so forth. However, she does not have the leniencies of an established *veset kavuah*, unless her next period begins on the 16th of *Tammuz*. Then she is regarded as having established a cycle of decreasing incremental monthly periods according to all opinions.

Alternate month cycle

24. If the periods come on the same date of every alternate month in a regular pattern, then a cycle for menstruation on that date of every alternate month is established. For example, if menstruation occurred on the 1st of *Nissan*, the 1st of *Sivan* and the 1st of *Av*, then she has an established cycle and anticipates menstruation again on the 1st of *Tishrei*. If she did not menstruate on the 1st of *Tishrei*, then she anticipates menstruation on the 1st of *Kislev*. If she did not menstruate on the 1st of *Kislev*, then she anticipates it on the 1st of *Shevat*. If she did not menstruate on the 1st of *Shevat*, then her established alternate month cycle is rescinded.

25. If she menstruated at other times in between these periods: for example, if in addition to menstruating on the 1st of *Nissan*, the 1st of *Sivan*, and the 1st of *Av*, she also menstruated on the 28th of *Nissan* and on the 2nd of *Tammuz*, she has not established a regular alternate day of the month cycle. Therefore, she anticipates all potential menstruation dates just like any woman with a non-established cycle, as explained in the previous chapter.

Some authorities contend that even if she has an additional menstruation between the second and third periods, for example on the 28th of *Sivan*, then she still has established a cycle for alternate months.

Day of the week cycle

26. If menstruation took place three times on the same day of the week, with equal intervals between them,[36] then a cycle for the same day of the week at those intervals is established.

For example, if a woman began menstruating on a Sunday, and four weeks later (on the 29th day) she again began menstruating on a Sunday, and again four weeks later she menstruated on a Sunday, then she has established a cycle for every fourth Sunday.[37]

---

36. If she menstruated three times on a certain day of the week, and menstruated an additional time between these three times, she has not established a day of the week cycle. For example, if menstruation occurred on Sunday *parshas Noach* and Sunday *parshas Vayeitzei* (an interval of thirty-six days), on Monday *parshas Vayeishev* (an interval of sixteen days) and Sunday *parshas Vayechi* (an interval of twenty-one days). Although she menstruated three times on Sundays with five week intervals in between, since she also menstruated between the three times, she does not establish a day of the week cycle. Nonetheless she still anticipates menstruation on Sunday *parshas Yisro* because of the interval of thirty-six days that has not yet been rescinded.

If two of her periods began on Sundays after an interval of four weeks and her third menstruation began one day earlier (or even more than one day earlier) and her flow continued through to Sunday, which is the day on which she would have established a cycle for days of the week had the menstruation begun then, she does not establish a cycle for days of the week although she menstruated twice from a "closed wellspring", and the third time from an "open wellspring".

37. One must pay careful attention to the listing of menstruation dates. If she

27. One establishes a day of the week cycle only when all three periods take place on the same *onah* (either all during the day or all at night). If, however, they did not all occur on the same *onah*, then she does not establish a cycle of days of the week.

28. If three periods occurred on Sundays with intervals of four weeks between them, and four weeks later her period comes on a Monday (a thirty day interval), she anticipates the next menstruation on a Sunday, after an interval of four weeks (less one day), because of her established Sunday cycle. If she did not menstruate on that Sunday, then she anticipates menstruation according to her last interval (on Tuesday which is thirty days from the last menstruation).[38] She also anticipates menstruation on the same day of the month as her last period as a woman who has a non-established cycle.

29. If three periods began on Sundays with four week intervals between, and her next menstruation which was expected on a Sunday after four weeks came a day earlier, on *Shabbos* (after an interval of twenty-eight days), she must still anticipate menstruation on Sunday four weeks and one day later. She must also anticipate menstruation after an interval of twenty-eight days from her last period[39]

---

menstruated twice after an interval of twenty-nine days, then she must check if the three times she menstruated were on the same *onah*, since in such a case she establishes a cycle for days of the week.

38. Although she menstruated only one day after her anticipated established cycle (i.e., instead of menstruating on Sunday her fixed day, she menstruated on Monday), she must nevertheless anticipate menstruation on Tuesday after four weeks because the interval is counted from her last actual menstruation.

39. In this instance she must anticipate menstruation on the third coming Friday since we count the days of interval from the beginning of her last menstruation.

and on the same day of the month as her last period, similar to a woman with a non-established cycle.

30. An established day of the week cycle only applies when menstruation occurrs three times on the same day of the week. If, however, she menstruates a fourth time on the same day of the week, since this is also an equal interval cycle we now consider it as an established cycle of equal intervals, and not as a day of the week cycle.

For example, a woman menstruated three times on Sundays with two intervals of four weeks in between, then after four weeks she menstruated again (a fourth time)[40] on Sunday (and all the periods were on the same *onah*). Although after the third time, she established a day of the week cycle and menstruation was to be anticipated every fourth Sunday, after the fourth time, a pattern of equal intervals of twenty-nine days was created, thereby establishing an interval cycle of twenty-nine days and annulling the day of the week cycle. In the future she need only anticipate new periods according to the equal interval cycle and not according to the day of the week cycle.

Therefore, since we count the interval cycle from the last actual menstruation (see above chapter 10 paragraph 6), should she change her pattern and menstruate earlier (e.g., after a twenty-eight

40. If her periods began three times on Sunday after four weeks, and the fourth time it began a day earlier (that is on *Shabbos*) but her flow continued to Sunday, meaning that her periods occurred twice after a twenty-nine day interval and the third time after a twenty-eight day interval and the flow continued to the twenty-ninth day, her established cycle for Sunday has not been rescinded (and she must also anticipate menstruation for both the day of the month and for the interval of twenty-eight days just as she anticipates a non-established cycle).

day interval) or later (e.g., after a thirty day interval), then she must anticipate her established cycle of an interval of twenty-nine days from her last menstruation. She does not need to anticipate the day of the week cycle, since it was annulled after she established a regular equal interval cycle by menstruating four times with equal intervals. She must also anticipate menstruation according to the last interval that was shorter or longer than the established interval, like in the case of a non-established cycle.

Similarly, a woman who menstruated three times on Sundays every fifth week (with all the periods on the same *onah*) establishes a day of the week cycle and anticipates menstruation on Sunday after five weeks. If her fourth menstruation comes on Sunday after five weeks (on the same *onah* as the previous periods), then she has established a cycle of thirty-six day intervals because her periods occurred four times with equal intervals of thirty-six days. She no longer anticipates the day of the week cycle, but instead anticipates the equal interval cycle. Therefore, should she menstruate earlier (such as after an interval of thirty-five days) or later (after an interval of thirty-seven days), rather than according to her previous pattern, then she must anticipate a regular cycle of an interval of thirty-six days from the last menstruation. She does not need to anticipate the day of the week cycle, since it was annulled because her periods occurred at equal intervals. She must, however, anticipate menstruation also according to the last interval that was shorter or longer than the usual, like in the case of a non-established cycle.

31. A day of the week cycle is only established when all menstruation occurs on the same day of the week. Therefore, if menstruation began on Sunday, four weeks later on Monday, and then four weeks later on Tuesday, she does not establish a cycle for days of the week[41] according to this pattern.[42] This is so even though all three periods occurred on incremental days of the week and on the same *onah*. In this instance she anticipates menstruation on the date of the month, the interval, and the *onah beinonis*, like all other instances of a non-established cycle.

Veset hakefizot (jump-induced cycle)

32. Out-of-the-ordinary physical exertion that brings on bleeding and occurs three times is called *veset hakefizot*, as for example; bleeding after jumping or after receiving a blow[43] or after carrying

41. However, if she begins menstruating a fourth time on Wednesday after four weeks, she establishes a *veset kavuah* of thirty day intervals.

42. Likewise any other similar pattern, such as an incremental increase of two days and also an incremental decrease of one day or more.

43. Only when the jumping or blow was out-of-the-ordinary does she attribute the bleeding to that act. However, bleeding after ordinary jumping or a minor blow may be not attributed to that activity, even if it happened three times. She is therefore considered like a woman who bled naturally (not due to jumping) and anticipates all the potential menstruation dates, even if she does not jump on the day that menstruation is expected.

If menstruation occurs three times after she exerted herself with three different activities (e.g., once after jumping, the second time after carrying something heavy and the third time after receiving a blow), then she establishes a cycle for any of these activities, and from then on anticipates menstruation after any one of them. It stands to reason that she must anticipate menstruation following any other unusual physical effort of any kind (see Sources and Explanations). If she bled three times after jumping, there is a doubt as to whether she needs to anticipate menstruation after a other physical exertions, such as carrying a heavy item.

something heavy or after exercising. However, until this phenomenon has occurred three times, she need not anticipate bleeding after such an exertion. When she exerts herself this way a fourth time she must anticipate bleeding and must separate until the end of that *onah*.[44]

She must also anticipate the *onah beinonis* from the time that she bled like a woman with a non-established cycle (see chapter 10, paragraphs 16, 17), even if she does not then jump.

33. This above-mentioned cycle is rescinded even after just one time, even though it required three times to be established. This means that if the same physical activity that caused this *veset* took place again but did not bring on bleeding, the cycle is rescinded.[45] In this aspect this *veset* is different from other established *vestot* that are rescinded only after her three periods did not occur on the day that they were expected.

34. If a woman jumped and only menstruated on the next day, and this occurred three times on no fixed day of the month,[46] when she

---

44. This is unless she has a set time for menstruation during that *onah,* as explained later in paragraph 35.

45. For example, if the regular cycle was established by menstruating after jumping, it is rescinded by a single event of jumping or carrying a heavy item that was not followed by menstruation.

If she menstruated three times after carrying out three diverse activities and thus established a cycle, as above footnote 43, then she rescinds this cycle by a single event of jumping, or carrying a heavy item that was not followed by menstruation.

46. And also not at regular intervals. In any event, three consecutive periods cannot establish a *veset haflagah*, since we have here only two intervals

jumps a fourth time she must anticipate menstruation on the next day. She does not need to anticipate menstruation on the same day that she jumped. (See later paragraph 39).

Similarly, if she jumped three times and each time menstruation began on the fourth day after jumping, then she anticipates menstruation on the fourth day after the next jumping. She does not need to anticipate menstruation in the interval between jumping and the fourth day.

35. If a woman jumped and menstruated two hours later, with the flow continuing for just one hour, and this occurred on three occasions, when she jumps a fourth time, she need only anticipate menstruation two hours after jumping, and only for one hour. From the time she jumped until two hours afterwards, and after the hour of her fixed time to menstruate passes, she is permitted (even before the termination of the *onah*).

If she menstruates after jumping, but not after any fixed time interval, e.g. sometimes she menstruates immediately and sometimes after an hour or more, then she anticipates menstruation from the time she jumped until the end of the *onah* (either day or night).

Veset caused by jumping on a specific day

36. A cycle can be established by out-of-the-ordinary physical exertion that takes place on a specific day. Thus, a woman who menstruated three times on the same day of the month after jumping, (e.g. she menstruated after jumping on *Rosh Chodesh,* for three months), establishes a cycle for both of these causes, (i.e. the day of *Rosh Chodesh,* and jumping during the same *onah*). Therefore, when the fixed time of her menstruation arrives, which is *Rosh Chodesh*, and

---

between the periods.

she jumps on that *onah*, she must anticipate menstruation from the moment of jumping[47] until the end of the *onah*. If, however, she did not jump when the fixed time (*Rosh Chodesh*) came, she does not anticipate menstruation. She also does not anticipate menstruation if she jumps on a different day.

Similarly, if her period comes four times after jumping on days that are separated by equal intervals, then she establishes a complex cycle of equal intervals and jumping. She anticipates menstruation only when these happen together, as stated above regarding a complex cycle of fixed days and jumping. (See footnote to paragraph 57).

Women who establish these types of *vestot* that involve a complex cycle of jumping and days, as above, must also anticipate the *onah beinonis* (even if jumping did not occur), similar to a woman with a non-established cycle,[48] since her periods are not due to a natural cause.

37. This cycle is rescinded when her set date arrives on three occasions and she jumped but did not menstruate. If, however, the day arrived and she did not jump,[49] or she jumped on another day and

---

47. Even if all her periods occurred at a fixed time after jumping, (e.g., if she menstruated all three times two hours after jumping, see paragraph 35), she must anticipate her period until the end of that *onah*, since her cycle is also composed of days.

48. But, she does not have to anticipate that her period will begin on other dates, even if she then jumps, since she has an established cycle.

49. A woman who established a cycle of menstruating on *Rosh Chodesh* after jumping (see paragraph 36), and her cycle was rescinded because *Rosh Chodesh* passed three times during which she jumped and did not menstruate, if in the future she jumps on *Rosh Chodesh* and menstruates, she returns to her

did not menstruate, she has not rescinded her cycle since it was only established if she jumps on a set day.

38. A woman who established a complex cycle of *Rosh Chodesh* and jumping, after jumping three times on *Rosh Chodesh* and then menstruating, if on the fourth month she jumped on the day before *Rosh Chodesh* and did not menstruate, and the next day on *Rosh Chodesh* she menstruated without jumping, has not rescinded her complex established cycle of jumping and days, and it is not considered as an established cycle for *Rosh Chodesh* alone.

Nevertheless, she must anticipate menstruation on *Rosh Chodesh* alone as in a case of a non-established cycle. She rescinds the complex established cycle only in the way explained above in the previous paragraph. The same applies to a complex established cycle of jumping and intervals.

39. If she jumped on a certain day of the month and menstruated the next day, and this occurred three times, she has established a cycle for that day of the month, regardless of whether she jumps or not. When that day of the month passes three times without menstruation, she has rescinded this cycle.

The same is true in regard to a complex cycle of jumping and intervals. If she began menstruating three times after equal intervals, and each of the three times she menstruated only the day after she jumped, then she has established a *veset* of intervals alone, whether or not she jumped on that day.

40. If she jumped on two consecutive months on *Rosh Chodesh*, and menstruated each time, and on the third *Rosh Chodesh* she men-

---

previously established cycle. This is so only as long as she does not establish another cycle.

struated without jumping, then she has established a cycle for *Rosh Chodesh* only, without it being composed also of jumping.

The same is true in regard to a *veset haflagah*. If she menstruated three times after jumping, at two equal intervals of twenty-eight days, and then menstruated after a third interval of twenty-eight days without jumping, she establishes a cycle of twenty-eighty day intervals, whether she jumps or not.

41. If she jumped on *Rosh Chodesh* and menstruated and a month later jumped on *Rosh* Chodesh and menstruated, and then jumped in the middle of the month and menstruated, she has established a cycle for jumping only. The law concerning such a case is as above in paragraph 32. She does not have to anticipate menstruation on *Rosh Chodesh*.

42. If a woman jumped on *Rosh Chodesh* and menstruated, and jumped again the next month on *Rosh Chodesh* and menstruated, and the third month jumped on the day before *Rosh Chodesh* and did not menstruate, but the next day, on *Rosh Chodesh*, she menstruated without jumping, she has established a cycle for *Rosh Chodesh* alone without jumping. Some are of the opinion, however, that she has established a complex cycle of both *Rosh Chodesh* and jumping.

43. A woman who menstruated[50] once or twice because of-out-of-the-ordinary physical exertion (e.g. after jumping, receiving a blow,[51] exercising, etc.), does not need to anticipate its re-occur-

50. This is only when she experiences proper menstruation. A bloodstain on her clothing (without any sensation) is not reason enough to anticipate a *veset*, even if such an event occurs three times.

51. This type of cycle can only be established after unusual jumps or blows. If she menstruates after a minor jump or blow, then she does not have to be

rence after such an act, as long as it has not been established. Even if she repeats this act a third time, she does not need to anticipate that she will menstruate. There are however instances where she has to anticipate menstruation after even one such occurrence, as will be explained in the coming paragraphs. (After this happened three times, see above paragraph 32).

44. A woman who menstruated because of jumping (or other acts) must anticipate menstruation if she repeats that act on the same day the next month. For example, if she jumped on the 1st of *Nissan* and then menstruated, and then jumped on the 1st of *Iyar*, she must anticipate menstruation after jumping[52] until the end of that *onah*. However, before jumping[53] she does not need to anticipate menstruation.[54]

---

concerned that it was caused by the jump or blow. However, she must anticipate all the potential periods that menstruation requires her to anticipate without jumping.

52. It could be that even if she engages in a strenuous activity other than jumping on that day, she should anticipate menstruation because she may be prone to menstruate following any unusual exertion.

53. She checks herself on that day only after jumping, since the examination is meaningless before jumping.

54. If the 1st of *Iyar* passed and she neither jumped nor menstruated, she does not anticipate menstruation on the 1st of *Sivan*, even if she jumps. Some authorities contend that if she jumps on the 1st of *Sivan*, she must anticipate menstruation until the end of that *onah*.

If she menstruated normally on the 1st of *Iyar* without jumping, then she anticipates menstruation on the 1st of *Sivan* because of the *veset hachodesh* even if she does not jump, since on the 1st of *Iyar* she menstruated without jumping. However, in this case, if the 1st of *Sivan* passes and she did not

In the above case, if she did not menstruate from the 1st of *Nissan* until the 30th of *Nissan*, then she anticipates menstruation on the 30th of *Nissan* because of the *onah beinonis* (even if she does not jump on that day). Likewise, she anticipates menstruation on the 1st of *Iyar* according to the opinions that the *onah beinonis* is on the thirty-first day after the previous menstruation (even if she does not jump on that day). However, if she menstruated again in the middle of the month of *Nissan*, then she anticipates the *onah beinonis* from the last menstruation and not from the menstruation of the 1st of *Nissan*. She also anticipates menstruation on the 1st of *Iyar* only if she then jumps.

45. If she menstruated once after jumping (or after another unusual physical exertion, as above in paragraph 43), she does not need to anticipate menstruation after the interval between the last two periods. For example, if she menstruated naturally on the 10th of *Adar*, and then on the 1st of *Nissan* she menstruates after jumping, she does not have to anticipate menstruation on the 21st of *Nissan* (which is based on the interval of twenty-one days from her menstruation on the 10th of *Adar* to the 1st of *Nissan*) even if she jumps.

---

jump and did not menstruate, then a difference of opinion exists whether she continues to anticipate menstruation on the 1st of *Tammuz* after jumping on that day.

If she menstruated on the 1st of *Nissan* after jumping, and again on the 28th of *Nissan* without jumping and her flow continued until the 1st of *Iyar*, according to all opinions she anticipates menstruation on the 1st of *Sivan* if she jumps on that day.

All the more, if she menstruated on the 1st of *Nissan* after jumping, and again on the 28th of *Nissan* after jumping, and her flow continued until the 1st of *Iyar*, then she anticipates menstruation on the 1st of *Sivan* after jumping according to all opinions.

However, when menstruation occurs twice because of jumping, such as when she jumps and menstruates on the 1st of *Nissan*, and jumps on the 20th of *Nissan* and menstruates, she must anticipate menstruation on the 9th of *Iyar* (that is the interval of twenty days from the 20th of *Nissan* based on her last two periods). This means, that if she jumps on the 9th of *Iyar*, she must anticipate menstruation until the end of the *onah* (day or night), as in ordinary cases of anticipating menstruation as is explained in the previous chapter. However, if she does not jump on the 9th of *Iyar*, she does not anticipate menstruation on that day.

In this case, besides her needing to anticipate menstruation after a twenty day interval together with jumping as above, she also anticipates jumping-caused menstruation on the dates of the month of the two past periods (the 1st of *Iyar* and the 20th of *Iyar*). Likewise, she anticipates menstruation on the *onah beinonis* from the last time she menstruated (even if she does not jump), as explained earlier paragraph 44.

Cycles indicated by physical sensations – *Veset Haguf*

46. If a woman menstruated three times independent of any set day,[55] and her periods were accompanied (either in the beginning of the menstruation or before) by unusual physical sensations[56] such as headaches, stomachaches, or other physical sensations. She

55. See paragraph 55 concerning the case of a cycle accompanied by physical sensation that is combined with the day of the month or an equal interval cycle.

56. This applies only if the three periods were accompanied by the same physical sensation. If, however, on two of them she experienced headaches and on one of them she felt a stomachache, she does not have a *veset kavuah* indicated by physical sensations. Nevertheless if these sensations reoccur, she anticipates menstruation as with a non-established *veset*.

establishes a cycle for periods indicated by physical sensations, and must anticipate menstruation each time she experiences the same physical sensation.[57]

47. If after she established a cycle of physical sensations, these sensations reoccurred, and she checked herself and did not find any blood, she still anticipates that she may menstruate the next two times she experiences these sensations. (This follows the rule of an established *veset,* see above paragraph 2). If she experienced these physical sensations three times and each time checked herself, but did not find any blood, then this *veset* of sensations is rescinded. From now on even if these sensations appear again, she does not anticipate[58] menstruation.

48. If she established a cycle for physical sensations and afterwards menstruated three times without experiencing these sensations, she has not rescinded her cycle.[59] A physical sensation cycle is rescinded only when she experiences these sensations and does not menstruate, as mentioned in the previous paragraph.

In this case where she menstruated additional times without experiencing physical sensations, she should anticipate menstruation at the following times: 1) on the same date of the coming month, 2) according to the interval, and also 3) on the day of the *onah beinonis*. Even if she menstruates just once without these sensations,

57. In the following paragraphs (51-54) we will explain how long she should anticipate the onset of menstruation.

58. Nonetheless, if she once again menstruated when experiencing these sensations, this established cycle returns.

59. Even if her periods occur many times without these sensations, she still has not rescinded her established cycle (even if this happens for many years).

she anticipates menstruation at all the above-mentioned times just as in the case of an irregular cycle.

49. In the case of the physical sensations cycle, there is no difference whether the three periods that established the cycle were on the same *onah* (day or night) or not. Accordingly, even if one of the three periods occurred during the day and the other two occurred at night (or vice-versa), she establishes a cycle for physical sensations. Every time she feels the same sensation, she needs to anticipate menstruation. In this respect the physical sensation cycle differs from the day of the month or the interval cycle. (See above paragraph 5 concerning a regular equal-intervals cycle and paragraph 17 concerning a regular day of the month cycle).

50. If all the periods that established the physical sensations cycle occurred on different days in no fixed pattern, then she does not have to anticipate other possible times of menstruation, such as the day of the month cycle or the interval cycle.[60] (See the coming

---

60. Since she has now established a *veset haguf*, the dates on which the periods occurred and the intervals between the periods are irrelevant. Therefore, she only anticipates further menstruation when these physical symptoms reoccur. Also, any previous dates of anticipated menstruation have now been rescinded with the establishing of this *veset*.

However, if in the past she established a day of the month cycle, then she also anticipates menstruation according to that cycle, even though she has now established a cycle for physical sensations. For example, she menstruated on the 1st of *Nissan*, the 1st of *Iyar*, and the 1st of *Sivan*, hence establishing a cycle for the 1st of the month. Then she menstruated on the 1st of *Tammuz* with a physical sensation, on the 1st of *Av* with a physical sensation, and again on the 18th of *Av*, with the same physical sensation. She must still anticipate menstruation on the 1st of *Elul*, the 1st of *Tishrei*, and the 1st of *Cheshvan* because of her previously established day of the month cycle. Although she

paragraphs concerning the *onah beinonis*). The laws concerning three periods of a cycle of physical sensations which occur on the same day of the month or after the same interval, will be explained in paragraphs 55 - 58.

51. Physical sensations may cause menstruation at various times. Some women menstruate immediately at the start of these sensations, others menstruate after the sensations have set in, and yet others only after the sensations cease. We will explain each case.

52. If a woman's established cycle of periods comes immediately at the start of her physical sensations, and the menstruation continues also after these sensations pass,[61] she must anticipate her next menstruation as soon as she experiences these sensations until the end of the *onah* in which these sensations started. (If it was during the day *onah*, she anticipates until the end of the day, and if it was during the night *onah*, until the end of the night). After the *onah* in which these sensations began has passed, she no longer needs to anticipate menstruation.

When menstruation occurs immediately upon the start of physical sensations, she must also anticipate the *onah beinonis.*

53. If a woman established a physical sensations cycle in which menstruation starts two hours after the sensations occur and

---

established a cycle for physical sensations, her established day of the month cycle has not been rescinded, and it is possible that she will continue to menstruate on the 1st of the month without a physical sensation. The same is true concerning an established equal intervals cycle.

61. If her periods only last for the duration of these sensations, then she anticipates menstruation only while she is experiencing these sensations and not until the end of the *onah*. However, such a phenomenon is rare.

continues after the sensations pass, she must anticipate her next menstruation from two hours after the onset of the sensations until the end of the *onah* (day or night) in which she experienced these sensations. Some authorities contend that she is forbidden to her husband immediately[62] upon experiencing these sensations.

In this case when the periods do not occur immediately upon experiencing these sensations, she anticipates only the physical sensations cycle that she established and not the *onah beinonis*.[63]

54. If she established a cycle for menstruating about an hour after the sensations have ended, she anticipates that her future periods will occur about an hour after the sensations end, and continues anticipating until the end of that *onah* (day or night). It is proper for her to anticipate menstruation immediately upon the onset of the sensations and not only an hour after the sensations have ended.

---

62. According to these authorities, only if the sensations and the periods occurred during the same *onah* (day or night) does she need to separate from her husband from the onset of the sensations. However, if she established a cycle of experiencing these sensations during one *onah* but menstruates in the next *onah*, then she anticipates menstruation only from the beginning of the second *onah*. Accordingly, if a cycle is established where menstruation begins two hours after the occurrence of these sensations (as in the above example), and the sensations occurred within the last two hours of the *onah*, she does not have to anticipate menstruation upon the onset of these sensations but only from the beginning of the next *onah*. Likewise, if she usually experiences these sensations for several days e.g. for three days, and only menstruates on the third day, then she does not have to anticipate menstruation from the onset of these sensations but only from the beginning of the *onah* during which she usually menstruates. This is so even though her flow also continues after the sensations have ended.

63. Some opinions rule that she also anticipates the *onah beinonis*.

She does not need to anticipate that her period will begin on the *onah beinonis.*[64]

If she established a cycle of periods where menstruation occurs a day after[65] the physical sensations have ended, then she anticipates future periods a day after these sensations have ended. She does not anticipate menstruation immediately upon the onset of these sensations, nor the *onah beinonis*. Nonetheless, it is proper for her to perform a *bedikah* before relations.

If a woman usually experiences these sensations for several days, but sometimes menstruates after one *onah* from the onset of the sensations, and sometimes after two or three *onos*, but never earlier than one *onah* after the onset of the sensations, in the future when she experiences these sensations she is permitted to her husband during the entire first *onah* after the start of the sensations. This is so even though she is accustomed to continue menstruation after the sensations have stopped.

Complex cycle of veset haguf and days

55. If her periods occurred three times on the same day of the month and were accompanied by physical sensations, then she establishes a complex cycle of sensations on that set day of the month. The same applies to an equal intervals cycle together with physical sensations. The laws concerning these cases will be explained in the coming paragraphs.

---

64. According to some opinions, she also anticipates the *onah beinonis.*

65. If menstruation began more than two days after the sensations ended and this occurred on three occasions, it is proper for her to anticipate such a pattern. However she does not have to anticipate a period after so long a delay if it was less than three times.

56. If menstruation began on the 1st of *Nissan*, the 1st of *Iyar*, and the 1st of *Sivan*, during the day *onah*, and at each of these three times she experienced the same physical sensations, then she must anticipate menstruation on the 1st of *Tammuz* from the beginning of the *onah* of the day, even before the sensations occur. Even if at all the three above-mentioned times she menstruated towards the end of the sensations and not at their onset, she must anticipate menstruation from the beginning of the *onah*[66] since this cycle is composed also of days.

However, if the sensations occurred on a different day, such as on the 25th of *Sivan* (and not on the 1st of the month), she does not have to anticipate menstruation on that day. This is because her cycle is not only established because of sensations, but combines periods on a set day (the 1st of the month) together with the sensations.

57. The same applies to an equal intervals cycle. If three periods accompanied by the same physical sensations occurred after an interval of twenty-eight days each (i.e. four periods separated by twenty-eight day intervals, such as on the 1st of *Nissan*, the 28th of

66. If a cycle was established that occurred three times on the same day of the month, but these did not occur in successive order, for example, she menstruated on the 1st of *Nissan*, and again on the 1st of *Iyar*, both times with sensations. Then she skipped the 1st of *Sivan*, without menstruating and without experiencing physical sensations, and then again menstruated on the 1st of *Tammuz* with physical sensations (all on the same *onah*). Although she established a complex cycle of physical sensations together with menstruation for the 1st of the month, she only anticipates menstruation on the 1st of *Av* from the onset of the sensations and not from the beginning of the *onah*. If she does not experience any sensations, she does not anticipate menstruation.

Nissan, the 25th of *Iyar*, and the 23rd of *Sivan,* on the same *onah*),[67] then she must anticipate her next menstruation after an interval of twenty-eight days on the same *onah* (day or night) even before the sensations occur. Even if the three periods occurred towards the end of the sensations and not at their onset, she must anticipate menstruation from the beginning of the *onah* since it is a complex cycle composed also of days.

If the sensations however occurred on a different day, such as after an interval of twenty-six days, and not at the established time (after an interval of twenty-eight days), she does not need to anticipate menstruation. This is because her established cycle combines intervals of twenty-eight days together with sensations and is not based just on sensations.

58. If a cycle was established composed of both a specific date of the month and physical sensations, then she only anticipates menstruation on her fixed date and not for any other *veset* days, not even the *onah beinonis*.

Similarly, if she established a complex cycle of physical sensations with equal intervals, she need only anticipate her fixed cycle and does not anticipate any other *veset* days, not even the *onah beinonis*. However, if the established cycle of intervals together with physical sensations is less than thirty days, and the day that

---

67. In this case of a complex cycle of equal intervals accompanied by *veset haguf*, the first menstruation must also be accompanied by the same physical sensation. (In the example presented in this paragraph, this refers to the 1st of *Nissan)*. In this point it differs from the ruling explained in paragraph 6, that for a cycle of equal intervals it is sufficient that the last three times of menstruation were on the same *onah* (day or night), because in the cycle of *veset haguf* the first menstruation is part of the building of the cycle.

she anticipated menstruation passed without menstruation, some authorities maintain that she should anticipate that her period may begin on the *onah beinonis*.

Rescinding complex cycle of *veset haguf* and days

59. If she established a complex cycle of physical sensations on a set day of the month (such as three periods on the 1st of the month together with physical sensations), and then she menstruated three different times without physical sensations, her established complex cycle has not been rescinded. Nevertheless she anticipates these additional times of menstruation as well.

60. Similarly, if she established a complex cycle of physical sensations together with the day of the month (such as three periods on the 1st of the month together with physical sensations), and then the 1st of the month passed three times without any of her fixed physical sensations nor menstruation, she has not rescinded her complex cycle of physical sensations together with the day of the month. If in the future she experiences these physical sensations on the 1st of the month, then she must anticipate menstruation.[68]

61. However, if she established a complex cycle of physical sensations on a set day of the month, and when the day of the month arrived she experienced the physical sensations, but her period did not come on that day, it is considered as having rescinded her established cycle once, providing that she checked herself and did not detect any

---

68. However, from now on she only anticipates menstruation on the 1st of the month from the time she experiences these physical sensations and not from the beginning of the *onah*. If she established a cycle of periods occurring after two hours from the onset of these sensations, then she only anticipates menstruation two hours after the onset of these sensations on the 1st of the month.

blood. If this occurs three times, and after checking herself she does not detect any blood, then she has rescinded this cycle. From now on, even if this day arrives and she experiences the same physical sensations, she does not have to anticipate menstruation.

Nonetheless, if after the established cycle was rescinded, and she again menstruated on this set day and experienced the same physical sensations, she returns to her previous complex established cycle.

Cycle caused by eating sharp foods

62. A woman who menstruated after eating a pungent food and associates her menstruation with the eating of this food, must anticipate future menstruation upon eating this food as a non-established cycle. This means that if she eats this sharp-tasting food again, she must anticipate menstruation from the time that she eats the food until the end of that *onah* (day or night). This *veset* is rescinded if she eats the food again and does not bleed afterwards.

63. If her period occurs three times after eating a pugnent food, then she establishes a cycle for eating that sharp food. Nonetheless, she must also anticipate the *onah beinonis* since she has no specific time to menstruate.

This cycle is rescinded when she eats this food three times and does not menstruate.

Menstruation regulated by pills

64. A woman who takes medication or pills[69] that prevent menstruation, and three consecutive times while taking the

---

69. This is after being instructed to do so by an Orthodox *Rav* who is an expert in these laws.

medication or pills she does not menstruate, need not separate from her husband during the times that she would ordinarily anticipate menstruation.[70]

65. Women usually begin menstruating within two days of stopping a series of medication. One must be careful to separate one day after taking the last pill. If it has been proven three times that menstruation does not occur within a set number of days after taking the last pill, then she does not need to anticipate menstruation until after those days pass. However, one should be careful and separate one day earlier. For example, a woman who has established three times that she does not menstruate within three days of taking the last pill, should separate from her husband after two days.

66. If she completely stopped taking the pills and later menstruated, she must separate from her husband the next month on the *onah beinonis* of that menstruation. Likewise, she must anticipate the *veset* days that were relevant before taking these pills and must abstain on those days. This is so even regarding a non-established cycle because missing periods while taking these pills is no indication of rescinding her cycle.

Initially she should also anticipate menstruation according to her *veset haflagah* or the day of the month on which menstruation occurred during the time that she took these pills (whether these times were established or non-established). Even if it is apparent

70. If a *kallah* (bride) is taking pills in order to postpone her period and the night of the *bi'as mitzvah* (first marital act) comes at a time that she would usually anticipate menstruation, one can be lenient even if she has not established three times that these pills prevented her from menstruating. This leniency is based upon the fact that today these pills have been proven to be effective in many women.

that these periods occurred only because she took these pills, nevertheless, it happens frequently that her body continues to menstruate at the same times as when she was taking the pills. However, if the first time she menstruated naturally (after she stopped taking the pills) was not at those same times,[71] then it is obvious that she is not continuing to menstruate in that pattern, and does not need to anticipate those times.

67. If a woman forgets to take even a single pill it is possible that this will cause the same type of bleeding that occurs after she terminates a series of pills. It is therefore proper for her to separate from her husband on the day that she is liable to menstruate. For example, a woman accustomed to menstruate three days after taking the last pill in a series should anticipate menstruation three days after missing a single pill, and should separate from her husband on that day. Although she does not need to abstain from relations if that day passes without menstruation, it is proper for her to check herself before relations. She should continue to check before relations until a week has passed from the time that she forgot to take the pill.

68. Different types of antibiotics[72] are likely to decrease the effectiveness of these pills. Therefore one must anticipate that bleeding may occur if she is on a course of antibiotics. It is proper for one who takes antibiotics in conjunction with pills, to perform a *bedikah* before relations.

---

71. This is so even if she now menstruated after a shorter interval, and has not yet rescinded a previously longer interval that occurred during the time she took the pills.

72. Such as Moxypen, Moxyvit, Hiconcil (that are generally called Amoxycillin trihydrate), Zinnat (generically called Cephalosporin) and others.

Chapter Twelve

Laws of a Bride and Hymenal Blood

1. Before marriage, every woman[1] must perform a *hefsek taharah*,[2] count seven clean days, and immerse herself in a *mikvah* observing all the pertinent laws. She then becomes permitted to her husband when she marries. The wedding should be scheduled at a time that will allow the prospective bride to purify herself before the wedding.

Ideally, the counting of the seven clean days and the immersion in the *mikvah* should be carried out immediately before the day of the wedding. This means that the *mikvah* night should be on the last night before the day of the wedding.[3] If that is not possible and she

1. This applies even to a woman who has never menstruated, to an elderly woman who is many years after menopause, and even to a widow or a divorced woman. This is so even if the divorcee is remarrying her first husband. However, if she never menstruated or did not menstruate after the last time she immersed herself in a *mikvah*, then this immersion is valid *bedi'eved* even if she did not perform a *hefsek taharah*.

2. A virgin, who cannot check herself deeply within her vaginal canal (see above chapter 4 paragraph 3), should check as well as she can. She should be careful that the examination does not cause bleeding.

3. If after she began the seven clean days or after she immersed herself, the wedding was postponed and no new date was decided upon, the counting of the seven clean days and the immersion must be repeated before the wedding.

Likewise, if both sides resolved not to marry at all, and later changed their must immerse herself earlier, then she should make an effort not to immerse earlier than four nights before the wedding. (For example, if the wedding is scheduled to take place on Wednesday during the day or Wednesday night, then she should not immerse herself before Sunday night). If she must immerse herself even earlier, she can do so *bed'ieved.* In any event, she should perform a *bedikah* once daily after the immersion, until the first marital act.[4]

Chupas niddah

2. If the wedding date was set, and later it became apparent that the prospective bride would not be able to purify herself in time for the wedding, the accepted practice is for the wedding to be held at the set time. The groom should be told beforehand that his bride is a *niddah.*

If the *kallah* is a *niddah* at the time of the *chupah,* then the *chasan* should make an effort not to touch her when he places the ring on her finger. It is likewise forbidden for the groom to hand the *kesubah* (marriage contract) or the cup of wine directly to the bride.

In such a case the *chasan* and *kallah* are forbidden to be alone together in a room (*yichud*) until after she has immersed in a *mikvah* (as will be explained in the next paragraph). Therefore, it is forbidden for them to remain alone in the *yichud* room (where they go after the *chupah*) even for a short time.

---

minds, even if they changed their minds immediately, she must count seven clean days again and immerse herself. However, if one of the sides still wants to marry and only the other side wants to cancel, she does not have to count seven clean days again.

4. Even if several days pass after the marriage without marital relations taking place, it is still proper for her to check once every day until the first marital act.

3. If the *chupah* took place when the bride was a *niddah*, or if the bride menstruated after the *chupah* before the first marital act[5] took place, then they cannot be alone until after she immerses in a *mikvah*. Until that time a "guard" (chaperon) must be present with them. It is customary for a boy (a minor) to sleep in the same room as the groom and a girl (a minor) to sleep in the same room as the bride. During the day they also cannot be alone without a minor being present.[6]

The first marital act

4. If the bride immersed, then the first marital act should be performed on the wedding night and not be postponed unless an overriding reason exists.

According to Torah law hymenal bleeding does not render a woman a *niddah*, since it is due to a wound and does not originate from the uterus. However, our Sages decreed that a woman who experiences hymenal bleeding, must follow the same procedure as a woman who experiences natural bleeding of a *niddah*. Only after counting the seven clean days and immersing herself in the *mikvah* is she permitted to her husband. (See later paragraph 7 regarding how many days she waits before starting the seven clean days). Therefore, if the bride is a virgin, they must separate after the first

---

5. If the male and female reproductive organs only made external contact, and afterward she menstruated, one should be stringent and not allow them to be alone. However, if there was partial entry one can be lenient.

6. In case of difficulty, if a "guard" (chaperon) cannot be found, then one can be lenient during the day and rely on the door being slightly open to the public, but not at night.

marital act[7] because of hymenal bleeding. They must then observe all the restrictions that apply to a *niddah.* She is not permitted to him until she performs the *hefsek taharah*, counts the seven clean days, and immerses herself.

Even if she did not notice any hymenal blood, they must separate from each other after the first marital act. This is because it is possible that some hymenal bleeding took place but sperm covered the bleeding or that the blood may have dissolved and become lost.

If there was some contact between the male and female reproductive organs, or if there was minimal penetration (*ha'ar'ah*) and she did not bleed, they do not need to separate. Nonetheless, if most of the male reproductive organ penetrated, they must separate even if she did not notice any bleeding.[7*]

5. After hymenal blood was found, the husband should wash his hands and recite the following *bracha* (without the name of *Hashem* or mentioning His being King over the world):

ברוך אשר צג אגוז בגן עדן, שושנת העמקים בל ימשול זר במעיין חתום, על כן אילת אהבים שמרה בטהרה, וחק לא הפרה, ברוך הבוחר בזרעו של אברהם. [8]

---

7. However, it is permitted to finish the marital act even though hymenal bleeding is taking place.

7*. Many times doubts arise regarding the extent of the penatration. Therefore it is correct for the bride to perform a *bedikah* after the first marital act. If she finds blood she is forbidden to her husband. If there is no blood a *Rav* should be consulted.

8. Blessed is the One who placed a nut in the Garden of Eden, a rose of the valley, not permitting a stranger to rule over the sealed spring, therefore the deer of love was guarded in its purity, and did not violate the law. Blessed is the One who chooses the seed of Avraham.

6. The *chasan* and *kallah* must separate[9] at the time of expected menstruation (day of *veset*) even if the first marital act has not yet taken place. (See above chapter 9 for details concerning the laws of separation due to suspected menstruation, and see above chapter 10 and 11 when these suspected menstruation dates fall). However, they may be lenient concerning the *Ohr Zarua onah*.

Hefsek taharah after hymenal bleeding

7. Even if she did not notice any hymenal blood, or if she noticed and the flow stopped, she cannot perform the *hefsek taharah* until four days[10] after the first marital act. For example, if the first marital act took place on Sunday night, she cannot perform the *hefsek taharah* until Thursday afternoon.

Although it was explained above (chapter 3 paragraph 1) that a *niddah* cannot perform the *hefsek taharah* until five days pass from the beginning of her period, in the case of hymenal bleeding four days are sufficient.[11]

Bleeding encountered again during further marital acts

8. If, after purifying herself, she again noticed blood during relations,

---

9. But *yichud*, being alone together, is permitted.

10. If in the meantime she menstruated routinely, then she becomes a regular *niddah* and must wait five days from the first marital act before she performs the *hefsek taharah*.

11. A woman who experiences hymenal bleeding because the hymen was injured or surgically removed, or while checking herself with an examination cloth, becomes forbidden to her husband as if she had experienced the natural bleeding of a *niddah*. However, in these instances she need wait only four days before counting the seven clean days.

the couple must separate from each other as above in paragraph 4. This applies to any subsequent hymenal bleeding during marital relations.[12]

In a case where blood was not noticed during the first marital act or afterwards, but was noticed at a later marital act, they must consult a *Rav* for guidance.

9. The first marital act may be performed on *leil Shabbos* (Friday night). The bleeding that occurs is not a violation of the laws of *Shabbos*.

Checking before and after relations

10. After the couple have relations without any further hymenal bleeding, they should proceed as follows. If the woman does not have an established cycle[13] (see above chapter 10), then she must check herself with a *bedikah* cloth the next three times[14] before and after relations. This is done to ascertain that the marital act does not cause her to become a *niddah*.[15] Likewise, the husband wipes himself with an examination cloth after these three acts and checks it. They may not engage in relations without inspecting the cloth

---

12. She may perform the *hefsek taharah* after four days whenever she becomes a *niddah* because of hymenal bleeding.

13. A woman who has an established cycle is forbidden to check before or after relations. If, however, her husband instructs her to check, it is permitted for her to check beforehand but not afterward.

14. It is a long-standing custom that these checks be done the first three times after the marriage (after there is no longer any hymenal bleeding). One should be meticulous and also check for possible menstruation when having relations three times after the shortest interval of the last three periods.

15. If these checks are done when she does not naturally menstruate, such as when she is pregnant, they are not considered valid.

with which she checked herself beforehand. If blood was noticed before relations, she is a *niddah* and they must separate.

If after relations blood was found upon inspection, they must separate, and a *Rav* must be consulted for guidance.

11. The examination before relations should be performed within half an hour.[16] An effort should be made to perform the *bedikah* afterwards, as soon as possible.

12. After she checked herself three times as required and did not notice any blood, according to the strict letter of the law she is not required to check herself anymore before or after relations.

However, it is proper for a scrupulous woman to check herself before relations, at a time interval corresponding to the shortest of her last three intervals between periods, after her last menstruation (see above chapter 10, laws of an interval cycle), For example, if her last periods were after twenty-three days, twenty-nine days and twenty-six days (in this or any other order) it is proper for her to check herself before relations after twenty-three days from the beginning of her last menstruation. On the days that they must separate due to an anticipated *veset*, however, they are forbidden to have relations even if she checks herself and does not notice any blood (as explained above in chapter 9, paragraph 4).

13. Women normally stop menstruating from the beginning of pregnancy. Therefore, once it has been verified that she is pregnant, she does not need to be stringent and check herself before relations, even if three months have not yet passed from the onset of her pregnancy.

---

16. As long as she does not sleep after she checks herself.

14. Although according to the letter of the law, she does not need to anticipate menstruation for twenty-four months after giving birth, women often menstruate before twenty-four months have passed. Since menstruation at this stage does not occur at regularly fixed times it is proper that in the first months after the birth she check herself before relations to prevent any possible mishaps.

Chapter Thirteen

Pregnancy, Childbirth, Nursing, and Menopause

1. During the first three months of pregnancy a woman is still considered liable to menstruate. She should therefore anticipate menstruation on the basis of periods that she had before becoming pregnant, even though her *veset* falls on a day that she definitely knows that she is pregnant. She must anticipate menstruation on the day of the month cycle (*veset hachodesh),* the interval cycle *(veset haflagah)* and all other days on which she would normally anticipate menstruation, as explained above in chapters 10 and 11. On these days she must separate from her husband and check herself as was explained above in chapter 9.

There is no difference whether she has an established cycle or non-established cycle.

2. If she saw blood during the first three months of pregnancy, she must separate on all the relevant *veset* days that come as a result of this menstruation. This applies only when these expected *veset* days fall during the first three months of pregnancy. For example, if she menstruated during the second month of her pregnancy, she must anticipate a reoccurrence of menstruation on the day of the month cycle and the day of the interval cycle during the third month of her pregnancy. If she has an established *veset* for the day of the month or interval cycle, she must also anticipate the reoccurrence of her established *veset*.

3. If she has an established cycle for the day of the month that she did not yet rescind, she must separate from her husband and check herself on the day of her anticipated period during the entire first three months, whether she menstruated or not from the beginning of her pregnancy.[1]

However, if she had an established interval cycle, she does not need to anticipate its reoccurrence unless she actually menstruates. For example, if she has a cycle of thirty-two day intervals, she must anticipate menstruation on the thirty-second day from the first day of the last of her menstruations, whether it occurred before or after she became pregnant.[2] Once the day of the anticipated period passes and she checks herself and finds that menstruation did not occur, she no longer has to anticipate its reoccurrence unless she menstruates again. In that case, she must anticipate the possible occurrence of her period thirty-two days from that menstruation.[3]

However, if she did not menstruate again, she does not need to anticipate menstruation after an additional interval of thirty-two days, which is a sixty-three day interval from her last period. (This is because anticipated menstruation for the *veset haflagah* is only following actual menstruation).

1. Even if she did not menstruate three times on the day of her scheduled regular period, it is not rescinded, and when her pregnancy and nursing days finish, she must again anticipate the occurrence of her established period as will be explained in paragraph 10.

2. If this day falls after the first three months of her pregnancy, she does not have to anticipate it, as is explained later in paragraph 4.

3. She must also anticipate menstruation on the day of the interval between her last and present period. This is true unless this date falls after the first three months of pregnancy, as is explained later in paragraph 4.

In the case of the *onah beinonis*, she needs to anticipate the onset of her next period only after the last actual menstruation. In this case, whether the latter occurred before or after she became pregnant, once the day of the *onah beinonis* passes and she does not menstruate, she does not need to anticipate the reoccurrence of this cycle unless she menstruates again.

4. A pregnant woman needs to anticipate menstruation on her *veset* days only if they are anticipated within the first three months of pregnancy. When she begins the fourth month of pregnancy she no longer needs to anticipate menstruation which is based on her periods before pregnancy, or those that occurred during the first three months. This is because from the fourth month of pregnancy a woman is considered free of menstrual blood and we do not anticipate any more menstruation.

Menstruation after the third month of pregnancy

5. A woman who menstruated in the fourth or subsequent months of her pregnancy must anticipate the onset of menstruation on the same day of the next month and on the day of the *onah beinonis,* as is the case with a woman with a non-established cycle. However, she does not need to anticipate menstruation according to the interval of the number of days from her last menstruation from before the fourth month, whether that menstruation was before the beginning of the pregnancy or within the first three months.

If she menstruated twice after the third month, however, she does have to anticipate menstruation according to the interval between these two periods.

6. Even if she menstruates three times from the fourth month onwards following a pattern that would ordinarily create a *veset kavuah*, such as if she menstruated three times on the same day of the month during the same *onah*, she does not establish a cycle on the basis of these menstrations. She must however anticipate menstruation once, as in the case of a non-established cycle. According to this, if the day on which menstruation was anticipated passed without bleeding, she does not have to anticipate menstruation on that day the following month or thereafter.

The same applies regarding *veset haflagah*. Even if she menstruates four times at three equal intervals she does not establish a *veset haflagah,* and anticipates menstruation only once, as in the case of a non-established cycle.[4] Thus, if the day on which menstruation was expected passes without bleeding, she does not need to anticipate menstruation following this time interval anymore.[5]

Veset days for a nursing woman

7. During the Talmudical era, menstruation was regarded as unlikely twenty-four months from giving birth. During this period, there was no need to anticipate menstruation on days that were established in the past as times of expected menstruation. (A woman was given the *halachic* status of "a nursing woman" during the entire twenty-four month period whether or not she actually nursed the child, and was not required to anticipate the occurrence of menstruation).

If she menstruated, however, once during these twenty-four

---

4. In this case of menstruation at three equal intervals, she does not need to anticipate any other *veset* days except for an anticipated period after her time interval.

5. If she did not menstruate again, she anyway does not have to anticipate the interval cycle, as above in paragraph 3. If she menstruates again at a different interval, she needs to anticipate menstruation only after the last interval and not the previous ones.

months,[6] she had to anticipate the *veset hachodesh* and the *onah beinonis* because of this period, just as with a non-established cycle.

If during these twenty-four months she had three periods on the same day of the month during the same *onah*, or four periods at three equal intervals, she did not establish a cycle on the basis of these periods, because she had the status of a woman who does not menstruate and it was not anticipated that she would again have her period until twenty-four months had passed from childbirth. Nevertheless, she still needed to anticipate menstruation once as in a non-established cycle. For example, if her periods began on three consecutive months on the 10th of the month, she would anticipate her period on the 10th of the next month. If this day passed without bleeding, she did not need to anticipate menstruation on 10th day of the coming months, since she had the status of a woman who does not naturally menstruate.

8. Nowadays, the nature of women has changed and they menstruate within twenty-four months after birth. Therefore if she established a fixed cycle during these months, she should keep it as a *veset kavuah* with respect to stringencies.

Thus, if three periods began on the same day of the month, or after equal intervals, she establishes a fixed cycle for that date of the month or for that interval, and must anticipate menstruation on those days until she rescinds these cycles three times by not menstruating on the anticipated days. The same applies if her periods were accompanied three times by physical sensations, in which case she is regarded as having established a *veset haguf.*

6. Whether or not she was nursing.

However, if she had an established cycle before the pregnancy, it is not rescinded by the new cycle established during the twenty-four months after giving birth. In this case, she reverts to her previous *veset* after twenty-four months have passed from childbirth, as will be explained in paragraph 9.

If she menstruates once within these twenty-four months, she anticipates the day of the month and the *onah beinonis*. If she had two periods during these months, she must also anticipate menstruation based on the time interval between the two periods. If she has additional periods, she anticipates further menstruation just as she would if she was not within twenty-four months of childbirth.

However, as long as she does not menstruate after giving birth, she does not need to anticipate any of the cycles enumerated in chapters 10 and 11.

Expected dates after childbirth

9. If she had an established cycle before becoming pregnant, or if she established a cycle within the first three months of pregnancy, she does not need to anticipate the reoccurrence of these cycles from the fourth month of pregnancy until twenty-four months after giving birth. However, immediately after the twenty-four months are over she reverts back to her previous *veset kavuah* as long as she has menstruated at least one time since childbirth.[7]

For example, if she had an established cycle for her periods to begin on the 10th of the month, and twenty-four months passed

---

7. Nowadays, it is unusual for a woman not to have menstruated until twenty-four months following childbirth.

after her giving birth, and she has already menstruated,[8] she must anticipate menstruation on the 10th of the next month, which is the twenty-fifth month after giving birth.

The same is true if she had an established interval cycle of twenty-eight days between periods and twenty-four months from giving birth have passed, she reverts to anticipating the twenty-eight days interval cycle after menstruating.[9]

The same applies if she had an established cycle for the days of the week. For example, if she menstruated three times on Sunday after intervals of twenty-nine days, the first Sunday after she completes pregnancy and nursing, she must anticipate her period if she menstruated once (see footnote 8).

10. If before becoming pregnant she had an established cycle, for example, on the 10th of the month, and she did not menstruate during the first three months of pregnancy, she does not rescind her cycle but rather, reverts to anticipating her established cycle after twenty-four months from giving birth have passed and she menstruated once.

11. If she had a non-established cycle before becoming pregnant (either a *veset hachodesh* or *veset haflagah*), she does not have to anticipate possible menstruation after twenty-four months from giving birth have passed.

Sensations during pregnancy

12. A pregnant woman who experiences a sensation similar to that

---

8. Even if she did not menstruate after the twenty-four months but menstruated during the twenty-four months.

9. This is only if she menstruated after the twenty-four months.

associated with menstruation, even after three months from the start of pregnancy (during which time she is unlikely to menstruate), must check in order to ascertain whether or not she has a blood discharge from the womb, as is the case when she is not pregnant (see above chapter 1 paragraph 7).

If she checked herself however and did not find anything, if the sensation occurred three months after she became pregnant, she remains clean and does not become a *niddah*.

Childbirth

13. Every woman who gives birth acquires a *niddah* status by Torah law and is forbidden to her husband, even if she did not bleed while giving birth.[10] They must follow all the laws of abstention detailed in chapter 2.

14. She acquires this *niddah* status following one of the four occurrences listed below: **a)** She detects blood or experiences copious discharge of placenta fluid; **b)** she has strong and very frequent contractions (every two or three minutes in a steady sequence);[11] **c)** she cannot walk and must lie on the birthing bed (or chair); **d)** she has infrequent contractions, but her cervix is open more than two fingers.

After childbirth

15. A woman who gave birth to a boy, may strictly speaking immerse herself immediately after performing a *hefsek taharah* and counting seven clean days, but after giving birth to a girl, the immersion can

10. The husband should not be present in the delivery room during birth.

11. If the labor pains ceased entirely and she did not give birth, she is permitted to her husband.

only take place two weeks after the birth. The seven clean days can be counted within the week of the birth of a boy and within the two-week's from the birth of a girl.

However, it is worthwhile to wait at least about six weeks[12] before immersion, in order to re-gain strength.

Laws after a miscarriage

16. A woman who miscarried has the status of a *niddah*. If she miscarried after 40 days from the start of pregnancy,[13] she has the same status as a woman who gave birth. Therefore, if the miscarried child was a female, she can immerse herself (after counting the

---

12. A woman who bleeds during the "pure days - *yemei tohar*" (within forty days of the birth of a boy and eighty days of the birth of a girl), even if this occurs after she immersed herself following the birth, must conduct herself as if this is an ordinary menstruation of a *niddah*. No leniencies apply to this blood discharge, and even the immersion must be performed with a blessing.

13. A *Rav* should be consulted concerning the point from which we begin to count these forty days. Even if it is within forty days of her last immersion, she cannot automatically assume that she does not have the status of a woman who gave birth. This is because it is possible that she became pregnant before her previous period.

It is also important to point out that it is sometimes unclear when the miscarriage terminated. One should therefore count two weeks from the day that the miscarriage definitely finished, for example, from the time of the curettage or a similar event. Under no circumstances should the count be commenced from the time she started bleeding.

A dead fetus (after forty days from the start of the pregnancy) has the laws of a dead body. Therefore a male *Kohen* may not enter the building or be present there until the fetus has been removed.

seven clean days) only two weeks after the miscarriage. The same applies when the gender is unrecognizable or in doubt. She now anticipates all her periods in the same manner as after giving birth, as was explained in the previous paragraphs.

Older Women - Menopause

17. As women become older, their periods stop and they no longer see blood. They then acquire the status of women who do not naturally menstruate. A woman attains this status when she reaches old age and three average cycles (that is, ninety days) pass without menstruation. When this happens, she no longer needs to anticipate the re-occurrence of her previous periods, even if they were established cycles.

Nowadays it is difficult to define old age. Nevertheless, if a woman is more than sixty years old and three average cycles passed without menstruation, we assume that her periods will not reoccur. However, at an earlier age, one should be stringent and anticipate all her periods even if three average cycles passed without menstruation.

18. Women do not stop menstruating abruptly upon approaching menopause. Rather, the frequency of a woman's periods gradually diminishes until they stop entirely. During this time, as long as she does not attain the status of a woman who does not menstruate, as explained above, besides having to anticipate her period on *veset* days based on previous periods, it is proper that while her periods are erratic she check herself before relations in order to avoid transgressing the *niddah* prohibition.

19. If after menopause she menstruated once or twice, she need not anticipate future menstruation, even in the same manner as a woman with a non-established cycle (even though it is obvious that she is a *niddah* due to this bleeding). This, however, applies only if the menstruation did not occur on the day of her previously established period that she had before reaching menopause. If it occurred on the same fixed day as her previous established period, she reverts back to it even after one menstruation.[14]

20. If after her periods have completely stopped she menstruates[15] three times, she is no longer regarded as unlikely to menstruate and must anticipate the occurrence of her next menstruation as a woman with a non-established cycle, until a further three average cycles have passed without any menstruation.

---

14. This is only if it was a proper menstruation or she saw blood on the examination cloth. It does not apply if she just experienced staining.

15. Only if she experienced bleeding as in the above footnote 14.

מקורות וביאורים

Sources and Explanations

for both Text and Footnotes

נכתב ונערך ע"י

הרב הגאון משה טובי' דינקל שליט"א

רב שכונת בית ומנוחה בית שמש ובמח"ס דבר חריף

מתוך לימוד עם

הגאון ר' משה שאול קליין שליט"א

מהדורה מורחבת עם הוספות ותיקונים

אייר תשס"ו

The Sources and Explanations beneath the line refer to the **footnotes** in the main text of the *sefer*.

פרק ראשון

1. "Any discharge of blood" — שו"ע סי' קפ"ג סעיף א'.

"uterus" — עיין רמב"ם פ"ה מהל' איסו"ב ה"ג.

"has not yet left her body" — שו"ע סי' קפ"ג סע' א'.

2. "irrespective" — שם ובט"ז ס"ק א'.

3. "There is no difference" — מתני' נדה מ' ע"א ומימרא דר' זירא שם ס"ו ע"א ושו"ע סי' קפ"ג סעיף א'.

4. "Different shades" — שו"ע סי' קפ"ח סעיף א'. ובטור הובא ממשנה וגמ' דף י"ט ע"א דרק ה' מיני דמים טמאים באשה, ד' מיני אדום והשחור (שג"כ אדום הוא אלא שלקה), אלא שהאידנא נתמעטה הבקיאות חזרו לטמא כל שיש בו מראה אדום בין אם הוא כהה הרבה או עמוק, וכן כל מראה שחור (ועיין ברמב"ן שם ע"ב שמטמאים כל מראה שחור ואפילו בהיר מזית, וע"ע לשון הר"ן בפ"ב דשבועות, וכ"פ הגר"ז שם ס"ק ב'). ובב"י הובא מהגמ' שם ע"ב שכבר בזמן האמוראים היו כמה חכמים דלא חזו דמא משום דלא בקיאי.

"Golden" — בבדיקת הפסק טהרה נזהרים המורים יותר משאר בדיקות שלא יהא דומה כלל וכלל למראה האסור מאחר שעדיין לא נסתם מעיינה ואפשר ששיירי דם מעורב במראות טהורות ואינו ניכר כל כך, ובפרט אחרי רחיצה. וע"ע חכמת אדם כלל קי"ז סעיף ט' ומהרש"ם בדעת תורה סי' קפ"ח מה שכתב לענין מראה זהב ושעוה.

"brown shades" — הסדרי טהרה סי' קפ"ח ס"ק א' ושאילת יעב"ץ ח"א סי' מ"ד וחכמ"א כלל קי"א ס"א' מתירים, אולם הבית מאיר והלחו"ש שם והבית שלמה יו"ד ח"ב סי' ד' מחמירים, ומצוי גם מראה אדום שנראה כגוון החום לאחר שנתייבש, וכן מצוי מראה חום הנוטה לאדום או לשחור, ועל כן יש לשאול חכם.

פרק ראשון

4. "wet or dry" — שו"ע סי' קפ"ח סע' ד'.

6. "stinging sensation" — שו"ת חת"ס חיו"ד סי' קס"ז בד"ה נחזור לענינינו ובסוף סי' ק"נ והובא בפת"ש" סי' ק"צ סק"ו, ערוך לנר נדה נ"ז ע"ב ברש"י בד"ה דארגשה וערוך השלחן סי' קפ"ג סעיף ס'.

"light yellow" — עיין בפת"ש סי' קפ"ח ס"ק ב'.

5. "Rabbinic law" — שו"ע סי' קצ"ה סע' י"ד. ועיין שו"ע סי' קצ"ג ס"א, רמ"א סי' ק"צ ס"א וסי' קצ"ו סע' י"א חכמ"א כלל קי"ג ס"ד. ועיין היטב בתוס' שבת י"ג ע"ב בד"ה בימי ליבוניך מש"כ בשם ר"ת ודו"ק.

6. (a) "sensation" — נדה נ"ז ע"ב אמר שמואל וכו' בבשרה עד שתרגיש בבשרה וכו'. בביאור סוגי ההרגשות עיין פת"ש סי' קפ"ג סק"א.

(b) "any kind of sensation" — שו"ת מהר"ם שיק יו"ד סי' קפ"ד וסי' קע"ז, סד"ט סי' ק"צ סק"א בד"ה אמנם במוסגר, לחם חמודות שעל הרא"ש פ"ט אות י"א ובהגהות אמרי ברוך על החוו"ד סי' קפ"ט וע"ע בהגהותיו לנוב"ק סי' נ"ה. וכ"כ בפרדס רמונים בפתיחה להל' נדה כשמבאר מהות ההרגשות וע"ע שם בסי' קפ"ט במ"ז ס"ק ל"ח. וכ"כ בספר נתן פריו להגר"נ גשטטנר שליט"א סי' קפ"ג, ועי' שיעורי הגרמ"ש קליין שליט"א שפסק לחוש לשיטה זו.

(c) "She checks herself with an examination cloth" — דתולים שהרגישה ומה שאומרת שלא הרגישה הוא משום שטעתה ע"י שמרגשת את צער חיכוך העד, נדה נ"ז ע"ב וברש"י. ועי' אחרונים בדעת הרמב"ם רפ"ח מהל' איסו"ב דע"י הרגשה טמאה ודאי מה"ת ומביאה קרבן ודאי.

(d) "She bled during intercourse" — עיין פת"ש סי' קפ"ג סק"א.

"In addition" — דרכי תשובה סי' קפ"ג ס"ק ו' בשם שו"ת שב יעקב ותשורת שי דבזמנינו נחלשו ההרגשות עיי"ש, וע"כ בודאי ברואה כדרך נשים אנו תולין שהיה בהרגשה המטמאת וכמש"כ הרמב"ם דחזקת דמים שבאים בהרגשה. ועיין בפרדס רמונים בסוף הפתיחה שכתב כן מטעם אחר.

"a feeling of external wetness" — עיין חוו"ד סי' ק"צ ס"ק א'.

"If she took sleeping pills" — בלבוש סי' ק"צ סע' מ"ח ובתשו' מהר"ם לובלין סי' ב' הובא בסד"ט סי' קפ"ג סק"ב בד"ה אמנם, כתבו דאם ראתה כתם מיד כשקמה משנתה חוששים שמא הרגישה בשעת שינתה, אולם בתוה"ש סי' ק"צ סק"נ ובסד"ט שם ס"ק ל"ו נקטו דלא חיישינן לכך דאם איתא דארגשה הוה מתערא אגב צערא וכדאיתא בגמ' דף ג' ע"א. ועיין בשיעורי שבה"ל סי' ק"צ סעיף מ"ח אות ה' שחוכך להחמיר ובפרט בזמנינו שנחלשו ההרגשות. וכשלקחה כדורי שינה דעתו דמן הדין יש לחוש דילמא ארגשה ולאו אדעתא.

נדה נ"ז ע"ב אמר רב ירמיה מדיפתי מודה — "According to Rabbinic law" שמואל שהיא טמאה מדרבנן.

עיין תורת השלמים סי' קפ"ג סק"א ושו"ת מעיל — "even a drop of blood" צדקה הובא בסד"ט סי' ק"צ ס"ק ס"א בד"ה עוד ראיתי דס"ל דבפחות מכגריס טהורה אף שודאי מגופה הוא, אולם הסד"ט שם מחמיר וכ"כ הכו"פ והיד אברהם סי' קפ"ג ופרי דעה שם בשפתי לוי סק"ב, וכן הסכמת הפוסקים.

7. "must check herself" — תרוה"ד סי' רמ"ו שו"ע סי' ק"צ סע' א' וסי' קפ"ח סע' א'.

לדעת הכו"פ הובא בפת"ש שם ס"ק ה' ו' אף — "found a clean discharge" אם מצאה אחר שיעור וסת טהורה וכ"ד הסד"ט שם ובתשו' נו"ב שהובא בפת"ש שם ס"ק ז' ודלא כחוו"ד סי' קפ"ח ביאורים ס"ק ב' דס"ל דמצאה מראה טהור אחר שיעור וסת טמאה. ועיין סד"ט סי' ק"צ ס"ק ד' בד"ה ודע שמסתפק מה שיעור הזמן שאפשר לתלות מראה טהור שתמצא — בהרגשתה. ובערוך השלחן שם סע' ח' ובשו"ת מוה"ר ידידיה טיאה ווייל סי' נ"א כתבו דהוא עד מעל"ע, ולמעשה כתב בשיעורי שבה"ל שם סוף אות י"ב להקל אם בדקה עצמה בתוך חצי שעה להרגשתה.

תרוה"ד ושו"ע שם. ועיין תשו' נוב"ת — "she checked and found nothing" סי' קי"ט וחוו"ד סי' קפ"ח ס"ק ב' וסי' ק"צ ס"ק ג' דאפילו בדקה בתוך שיעור וסת ולא מצאה כלום טמאה, ודלא ככו"פ. ועיין בפת"ש שכתב דגם דעת הסד"ט כהכו"פ, ויש לדון.

בהרגשת פתיה"מ כשבדקה ולא מצאה כלום דטמאה, כתב בתשו' נוב"ת סי' קי"ח בד"ה וכיון ובסי' קי"ט שטמאה מספק ולא מתורת ודאי ולכן בהצטרף עוד ספק אם הרגישה יש להתיר מטעם ספק ספיקא.

---

7. "Even if she says" — כ"כ בגר"ז סי' קפ"ג סוס"ק ג' ובהגה"ה שם. וכ"מ בכו"פ סי' קפ"ג ובסד"ט שם סק"ב במש"כ להוכיח מהרמב"ם ומהרשב"א, וכ"מ בבינת אדם כלל קי"ג סי' ז' אות ח'. ואף שהנטע שעשועים רצה לחלוק על האחרונים בזה ודעתו דמהני ברי לי מ"מ עי' שו"ת מהרש"ם ח"ב סי' קפ"ב שנוטה לדברי האחרונים. ועי' בלחו"ש סי' קפ"ג סק"ב וסי' ק"צ סק"ב דהסכים לעצם יסוד דברי הנט"ש אך מסיק להחמיר בזה ע"פ דברי הרמב"ן שכתב דבזה"ז שאין בקיאות בדבר כל שמצאה דם על העד טמאה, וביאר דכונת הרמב"ן לאפוקי שלא נסמוך על ברי לי, ע"ש. וכ"ש בזמנינו שנחלשו החושים ואין

ובעיקר דינו של התרוה"ד, עיין בפתחי תשובה סי' ק"צ ס"ק ז' בשם שו"ת הרדב"ז ח"א סי' קמ"ט ושו"ת שאילת יעב"ץ ח"ב סי' ה' שחלקו על התרוה"ד ומקילים אם בדקה ולא מצאה כלום, [ומ"מ גם לדבריהם צריכה בדיקה אחר הרגשתה וכמפורש ברדב"ז שם וכ"מ קצת בשאילת יעב"ץ שם ולכן אם לא בדקה כלל אף לשיטתם יש להחמיר] אולם להלכה בודאי אין לזוז מהשו"ע שפסק כהתרוה"ד.

8. "**she checked herself and found nothing**" — בהרגשת זעזוע הגוף דעת החכמ"א כלל קי"ג סע' א' הובא בפת"ש סק"ד דיש להקל ולתלות בשאר מקרים וכ"ה במקור מים חיים, ועיין שו"ת חת"ס חיו"ד סי' ק"נ שמחמיר בזה, ומאחר דאף בהרגשת פתיה"מ יש מקילין, ע"כ נקטינן כהחכמ"א, הכרעת הגרמ"ש קליין שליט"א בשיעוריו.

וכן לענין הרגשת זיבת דבר לח יש להקל בבדקה ולא מצאה כלום וכמו"ש החת"ס בתשו' שם דהרגשה זו אינה מוציאה מחזקת טהרה, ובפרט דיש לצרף דעת החת"ס בתשובותיו סי' קמ"ה וקנ"ג ובעוד מקומות דהרגשת זיבת דבר לח איננה הרגשה כלל. אמנם החכמ"א בכלל קי"ג סע' א' החמיר גם בהרגשת זיד"ל, ועיין שו"ת שבה"ל ח"ב סי' פ"ח וח"ה סי' קי"ג.

9. "**finds a clean discharge**" — תפארת צבי סי' א' ס"ק י"ד ושו"ת שבט הלוי ח"ב סי' פ"ח וע"ע ח"ה סי' קי"ג.

עיין ביאורים ומקורות לסעיף ז' דשיטת החוו"ד דאחר שיעור וסת אף במצאה מראה טהור טמאה, ואפשר דבנמצא מראה טהור על הבגד תולין הרגשתה בזה אף אחר זמן, דתלינן דכבר יצאה מיד אחר הרגשתה, ומה"ט מסתבר דבנמצא על הבגד אף אחר חצי שעה תלינן הרגשתה בזה.

10. "**A woman who frequently**" — חכמת אדם כלל קי"ג סע' ג'.

הנשים מבחינות כ"כ בהרגשות על כן אין להתייחס לאמירתה ברי לי ואף הנטע שעשועים יודה לזה.

8. "**more than ten minutes later**" — מן הדין איתא בגמ' נדה ס"ו שהוא תוך שיעור וסת והוא שיעור מועט מאוד, אולם הרמ"א דסי' קפ"ז כתב שאין אנו בקיאין בשיעור זה. ודנו האחרונים מהו שיעור הזמן שבודאי אין חשש ראתה מחמת תשמיש, ועיין שיעורי שבה"ל שם אות י"א שכתב שיעור של עשר דקות ובפחות מזה ישאלו חכם.

"on the day of her expected period" — שיעורי שבט הלוי סי' ק"צ ס"ק י"א בד"ה ובדברי חיים.

---

10. "in excess of what she usually experiences" — תשו' חת"ס סי' קס"ח הובא בפת"ש סי' ק"צ ס"ק ו'.

11. "If *bedi'eved* she did not check herself at all" — בהרגשת זיבת דבר לח סומכים בדיעבד על החת"ס שאינו בגדר הרגשה עכ"פ לענין זה כשאין ריעותא, אבל בזעזוע הגוף דהוי ודאי הרגשה מוכח בחכמ"א ובמקור מים חיים שיש להקל רק אם בדקה ולא מצאה כלום. [ולא שייך לצרף בזה שיטת הרדב"ז והיעב"ץ שהובא במקו"ב לסעיף ז' שחולקים על התרוה"ד, משום דבלא בדקה כלל אף אינהו ס"ל להחמיר וכנ"ל במקו"ב שם].

"physical sensation that is common ... upon the onset of menstruation" אשה שהרגישה אחת מהרגשות וסת הגוף יש בזה ג' חילוקי דינים, א' אם מעולם לא היה אצלה סימן זה קודם הופעת הוסת, והרגישה אחת מהרגשות וסת הגוף, אינה צריכה בדיקה כלל וגם אין חיוב פרישה אלא מותרת לבעלה. ב' אם ראתה פעם אחת דם ע"י הרגשה זו שהרגישה עתה, צריכה בדיקה, ואם עבר הוסת ולא בדקה ולא ראתה אסורה לבעלה עד שתבדוק. ואם בדקה ולא מצאה כלום שוב אי"צ לחשוש לא לוסת [דהיינו כשתרגיש שוב הרגשה זו אינה צריכה בדיקה ולא לפרוש מבעלה] ולא להרגשה [שאם תרגיש הרגשה זו אינה צריכה לחוש שמא ראתה], עיין בכל זה בשו"ע סי' קפ"ט סע' כ"א. ויש מקילים בעבר הוסת ולא בדקה שאינה צריכה בדיקה עוד, עי' ט"ז שם ס"ק ל"ח ושם בנקוה"כ. ג' אשה שיש לה וסת קבוע למיחושי הגוף, לכשתרגיש הרגשה הרגיל וקבוע אצלה צריכה בדיקה, ולכו"ע אם עבר הוסת ולא בדקה צריכה בדיקה ואסורה עד שתבדוק. וראה פרטי דינים אלו בדיני וסתות בעז"ה.

אך צל"ע עד כמה זמן מהני בדיקה, דלגבי וסת קבוע לחודש או להפלגה מהני בדיקה אפילו אחר כמה ימים, אבל בנידו"ד דיש גם חשש הרגשה, כמו"ש הסד"ט שם ס"ק כ"ז ובהגה' אמרי ברוך על החוו"ד רס"י ק"צ ובמע"מ שעל הרא"ש פ"ט דנדה, אפשר דרק אחר זמן מועט מהני בדיקה, והוא תלוי בהבנת הט"ז סי' קפ"ט ס"ק ל"ח בטעם הדבר דבוסת הגוף שאינו קבוע אם עבר הוסת ולא בדקה אסורה עד שתבדוק, אם הבדיקה מטעם וסת מהני הבדיקה אחר זמן, ואי הבדיקה משום הרגשה כמו"ש האמרי ברוך ועוד אחרונים א"כ מהני הבדיקה רק אחר זמן מועט, כמו אחר שאר הרגשות.

"If she found a stain" — אף בזיבת דבר לח, להסוברים דזיד"ל הוי הרגשה, אף אי נימא דאינה הרגשה המטמאה בלא מצאה כלום וכמו"ש בחת"ס סי' ק"נ דאי"ז ריעותא מ"מ במצאה כתם טמאה מה"ת דהא דם לפנינו. ולהחת"ס דזיד"ל לא הוי הרגשה מ"מ כיון

12. (a) "smaller than a *gris*" — הטעם מבואר בגמ׳ נדה נ״ח ע״ב שאין לך מטה ומטה שאין בה כמה טיפי דם מאכולת (כינה), ולכן לא גזרו חז״ל בזה, כיון שאם נגזור אין לך אשה טהורה לבעלה. ואף בזה״ז דלא שכיחי כינים גדולים כאלו טהורה (שו״ת חת״ס יו״ד סי׳ ק״נ וסי׳ קפ״ב), ולכן גם בזמנינו שאין שכיח כינה יש להקל בשיעור זה.

אם הכתם עב וכמות שהוא הריהו פחות מכגריס אך אפשר לרדדו ויהיה יותר מכגריס, מסתפק הסד״ט שם ס״ק ס״א אם טמאה.

"the area of a circle etc." — דרכי תשובה שם סוס״ק מ׳.

(b) "colored" — שו״ע יו״ד שם סע׳ י׳. והטעם עי׳ נדה ס״א ע״ב וברש״י דאין מראה דם ניכר בו ולא גזרו על כך. ואף אם ניכר מראה דם על בגד צבוע טהורה, ואף דבדרכ״ת ס״ק ס״ב הביא בשם פוסקים דיש להחמיר, מ״מ משמע סתימת הפוסקים שלא גזרו כלל בבגד צבוע אפילו ניכר שזה דם, עיין שו״ת שבה״ל ח״ב סי׳ פ״ז ושיעורי שבה״ל שם סע׳ י׳ אות ד׳.

דעת החת״ס בתשו׳ חיו״ד סי׳ קס״א דבבגד פנימי גזרו גם בבגדי צבעונים, אולם המהרש״ם ח״א סי׳ פ״א והחזו״א יו״ד סי׳ פ״ט ס״ק ד׳ חולקים, וכן הוראת הפוסקים, וכמו״ש בשו״ת שבה״ל ח״ב סי׳ פ״ז.

ובבגד פנימי הצמוד לגוף שנמצא עליו דם גמור, אין להקל בסתם אלא כשיש עוד צדדים להקל, דמלבד שהדגו״מ פקפק על קולת בגדי צבעונים [אף ששאר פוסקים הקילו] וגם דעת החת״ס דבבגד פנימי אין להקל וכנ״ל, מ״מ אף להחולקים וסוברים להתיר כתם שעל בגדי צבעונים גם בבגד פנימי, אבל כשאין במה לתלות הכתם שמא בא מעלמא ולובשת הבגד מזמן ארוך י״א דחיישינן לדילמא ארגשה ולאו אדעתה, עי׳ שו״ע הרב סי׳ קפ״ג ויסודו מדברי הראשונים ר״פ הרואה כתם. ובפרט לפמ״ש בשבט הלוי דאם נמצא דם גמור שאין לתלות שבא ממקום אחר בזמנינו שנחלשו ההרגשות יש לחוש יותר לדילמא ארגשה ולאו אדעתה, ע״כ אין להקל אלא כשיש עוד צדדים נוספים וכגון כשאינו ודאי דם או כשיש צד תליה שהכתם בא ממקום אחר, הגרמ״ש קליין שליט״א.

דניכר שהדם בא אחר הרגשה זו, עכ״פ לא גרע מדם שהוא ודאי מגופה דטמאה אפילו בכל שהוא וכמו שנתבאר בסעיף ו׳.

12. "the first three days" — דברי חיים יו״ד ח״א סי׳ ל״ד.

(c) "cannot become *halachially* impure" — שו"ע שם סע' י'. ומבואר בסד"ט ס"ק ל"ו וס"ק נ"ג, בכו"פ ובגר"ז, שאף אם הוא ודאי מגופה טהורה, דלא גזרו בדבר שאינו מקב"ט, עי' תוס' נדה נ"ח ע"א בד"ה כרבי נחמיה ובר"ן שם ובחוו"ד ס"ק ח' ובסד"ט ס"ק צ"ג. [ומש"ך ס"ק ל"ט אין ראיה, עי' דרישה שם ופרדס רמונים על הש"ך שם].

בגד הארוג מניילון או דיאולן וכיו"ב אף שהחומר כשלעצמו הוא דבר שאינו מקב"ט מ"מ כיון שנעשה לבגד נחשב לדבר המקב"ט, שו"ת מנחת יצחק ח"ד סי' קי"ח אות א' ועי' שו"ת אגרות משה יו"ד ח"ג סי' נ"ג.

"unless she had one of the sensations" — כיון דטמאה מה"ת וכמו"ש המחבר בסי' קפ"ג לא שייך לומר דלא גזרו.

13. "becomes a *niddah*" — אף דבודאי מגופה קיי"ל דטמאה מדרבנן בכל שהוא וכנ"ל במקורות לסוף סעיף ו'. ואף דבקינוח מבחוץ שייך גם מאכולת תלינן בשכיחי טפי שהוא מן המקור, עי' סד"ט סי' ק"צ ס"ק נ"ז מש"כ בדעת הרי"ו. ולהסד"ט גופיה דס"ל שם ס"ק צ"ג דהעיקר תלוי אם הוא ודאי מגופה או דאיכא למיתלי בדעלמא, דבודאי מגופה טמאה מה"ת אף בדלא ארגשה א"כ

---

13. "combined they do equal a *gris*" — שו"ע סי' ק"צ סע' ח'. והטעם דכשמוצאת הכתם על גופה חמיר טפי, עיין חוו"ד ס"ק כ"ב.

"Some authorities contend" — רמב"ם פ"ט מהל' איסו"ב ה"ו ובהגה' מיי' שם אות א' בשם רבינו שמחה, ועיין שו"ע סי' ק"צ סע' ו' בשם יש אומרים, ושם בש"ך ס"ק י' שכתב דאין להקל. מאידך דעת הראב"ד בהשג' שם להקל ושם במ"מ כתב דדעת הרמב"ן והרשב"א מסכמת לדעת הראב"ד, וכ"ה דעת עוד ראשונים, וכ"פ הב"ח להקל, וע"ע בתוה"ש סק"ט ט' שהעלה לדינא כהב"ח וכ"ה בסד"ט ס"ק י"ב והובא בפת"ש ס"ק י"ג.

"One who is scrupulous ... should be stringent" — דהמחבר הביא דיעה ראשונה בסתם דצריך שיעור גם בכתם שעל בשרה והביא בשם יש אומרים שעל בשרה טמאה אף בפחות מכשיעור, וכנודע דכשמביא דיעה ראשונה בסתם כונתו דהלכה כדיעה ראשונה אלא שיש לחוש לכתחילה לדיעה שניה, וע"ע שו"ע סי' ס"ט סע' י"ט ושם בש"ך ס"ק ע"ח ובפמ"ג, ועוד מקומות, וה"נ כאן דעת המחבר לחוש לכתחילה לדיעה שניה דאי"צ שיעור, וע"ע בספר יד מלאכי בכללי השו"ע אות י"ז, וגם חזינן דעת כמה פוסקים להחמיר בזה וכמובא לעיל מהש"ך דס"ל דמדינא טמאה בפחות מכשיעור, וכ"ה דעת מהר"א ברודא

ה"נ בקינוח י"ל דלדידיה הוי ודאי מגופה וטמאה מה"ת. ובפרט לפ"מ דמוכח בגמ' לענין רואה מחמת תשמיש דקינחה אח"כ ומצאה דם טמאה מה"ת וחייבין בחטאת, ואי קינוח אינו ודאי מגופה אמאי חייבין בקרבן, ומוכח דקינוח חשיב ודאי מגופה, [ודוחק לומר דאיירי שקינחה רק באו"מ ולא נגע העד כלל מבחוץ], שיעורי הגרמ"ש קליין שליט"א.

14. "a small amount of blood in her urine" — שו"ע סי' קצ"א, ע"ש הרבה פרטים בדין זה.

בשו"ת שב יעקב סוס"י מ"ג שכתב "אני רגיל להחמיר כדברי הרמב"ם" וע"ע בלחו"ש ס"ק י"ג שמוכיח כן מדברי כמה ראשונים, כמ"כ בערוך השלחן שם סע' ל' כתב דאין להקל נגד הרמב"ם.

"part of the stain is on her body etc." — סד"ט ס"ק י"ג. ואף דבחוו"ד ס"ק ו' כתב דטמאה מ"מ עיין בפרי דעה שפ"ל ס"ק י' שהשיג ע"ז מהא דמפורש ברמב"ם דכה"ג צריך שיעור, ועי' שו"ת שבה"ל ח"ד סי' ק"ד.

"the *poskim* discuss" — לשון הראב"ד בבעה"נ סוף שער הכתמים הוא ד"אינה תולה בה (במאכולת) אלא כתם אדום", ובחי' רעק"א סי' ק"צ סע' ה' כתב עפ"ז דבכתם שחור טמאה אף בפחות מכגריס, וכ"ה בסד"ט ס"ק י' ופת"ש ס"ק י"ב, וכ"ה להדיא בספר האשכול סי' מ"א. ועיין מה שדן בזה בשו"ת שבה"ל ח"ג סי' קי"ט אות ח' וח"ה סי' ק"ט אות ג'. אולם יש שהקילו בזה, עיין שו"ת מעיל צדקה סוס"י כ' שהביא מה ששמע מהחכמים להחמיר בזה והקשה עליהם מסתימת הפוסקים, ואף דהסד"ט העיר על המעי"צ דמצינו כן שיטת הראב"ד, מ"מ בטושו"ע לא הביאו שיטה זו כלל, וכן העיר בערוך השלחן סע' כ"ב. וכן מסיק להקל בשו"ת אגרות משה יו"ד ח"ג סי' קמ"ב אות ד' ובדברי יציב ח"ב סי' כ"א. ועיין שיעורי הגרמ"ש קליין שליט"א שיש לדון בראיות האגרו"מ והדברי יציב, ומ"מ הביא סמוכין להקל בדין זה מדברי החת"ס, ולמעשה צ"ע.

"When the stained garment was subsequently lost" — חכמת אדם כלל קי"ג סע' כ"ט.

"one must be stringent" — כיון דהוה חשש דאורייתא וכמבואר לעיל סע' ו'.

14. "red and black shades are discernable" — שיעורי שבה"ל סי' ק"צ סע' י' אות ד' ע"פ רש"י נדה ס"א ע"ב.

"both the white part of a garment and its colored part" — במעיל צדקה סי' ס"ב הובאו דבריו בחי' רעק"א לסע' י' ובפת"ש ס"ק כ', כתב להקל כשאין שיעור אלא בצירוף הכתם שעל החלק הצבוע, אבל החוו"ד ס"ק ט' והלחו"ש מחמירים שאף החלק הצבוע

עיין בגמ' נדה נ"ז — "when she wiped herself following urination" ע"ב דמשמע דיש חשש הרגשה בזה, ועיין פתחי תשובה סי' קפ"ג סוס"ק א' שהביא מהחו"ד שם שהוא חשש דאורייתא, ועיין לבנון נטע סי' ק"צ ס"ק י"ד שחלק ע"ז וע"ע חזו"א סי' צ' סק"א. ואם קנחה יותר מדקה אחר הטלת מי רגלים דהוי ודאי לאחר שיעור וסת אין חשש הרגשה, ובעיקר דין קינוח עיין לעיל סע' י"ג.

15. "foreign object" — בשו"ע סי' קפ"ח סע' ג' מבואר דאי אפשר לפתיחת הקבר בלא דם. וכתב בתשו' נוב"ת יו"ד סי' ק"כ דאין חילוק אם גרם הפתיחה הוא מבפנים או שגרם הפתיחה הוא מבחוץ, ועי' בהגהות ברוך טעם וכן בחזו"א יו"ד סי' פ"ג ס"ק א' שמצדדים להקל בפתיה"ק כשגרם הפתיחה הוא מבחוץ, אולם משמעות המחבר שם סע' ג' וסע' ו' וש"ך שם ס"ק י"ב וכ"מ בביאור הגר"א שם לסע' ו', וכ"ד רוב הפוסקים להחמיר.

16. "wound in her vagina" — לענין בדיקת עד יש הרבה פרטים אימתי תולין במכה, וישנן בדיקות שאין תולין בהן וכגון בבדיקת הפסק טהרה וגי"ר של ז"נ, עיין רמ"א סי' קצ"ו סע' י', וכן צריך שיהא ברור שהמכה מוציאה דם, עיין סי' קפ"ז סע' ה', ולכן בכל אלו צריך הוראת חכם.

"a wound that might have bled" — עיין ש"ך סי' קפ"ז ס"ק כ"ז דבכתמים תולין אף אם אינו ידוע שמוציא דם, ועיין שו"ע סי' ק"צ סע' י"א שתולין כתמים במכה שבגופה אפילו אינו באותו מקום כל שאפשר שהדם בא מהמכה וכתבו

מצטרף לשיעור, וע"ש בפת"ש דכן הוא גם דעת התפארת צבי חי"ד סי' כ"ד והתשובה מאהבה ח"א סוס"י קס"ג להחמיר. וכ"כ בשיעורי שבה"ל סי' ק"צ סעיף י' אות ו'.

"All the more so" — דבהא גם המעי"צ מודה דיש להחמיר.

15. "on the floor" — ע"פ רמ"א שם סע' י'.

"paper" — פתחי תשובה שם ס"ק י"ח.

"cotton" — עי' שיעורי שבה"ל שם ס"ק ג'.

16. "halachically impure only under Rabbinic law etc." — נוב"ת יו"ד סי' ק"ט.

17. "it is fitting that she should check herself" — הוראת מרן הגר"ש ואזנר שליט"א, וטעמו הואיל ואין נשים בקיאות בהרגשה וממילא צריך לברר כשיש ריעותא לפנינו.

אחרונים דה"ה במכה שבגופה תולה אף אם אינו ידוע שמוציא דם. ואם תולין בגי"ר עיין סי' קצ"ו שם ברמ"א, בש"ך ובאחרונים.

"this stain did not come from her uterus" — עיין שו"ע סי' ק"צ סע' י"א.

"to determine if she is a *niddah*" — מתני' נ"ח ע"ב טושו"ע שם סע' י"ח.

18. "told her husband that she is a *niddah*" — עיין שו"ע סי' קפ"ה.

---

18. "**a garment that is colored**" — עיין סד"ט סי' קפ"ג ס"ק ב' סוד"ה האחרונים שכתב דבדקה בקינוח בעלמא אינה טמאה אלא טומאת כתם שהוא מדרבנן וכ"כ הכרו"פ הובא בבינת אדם סי' ח' והחוו"ד סי' ק"צ סוס"ק א', ועפי"ז כתב הפרי דעה בפתיחה שער ג' דאם קינחה בדבר שאמקב"ט ומצאה עליו דם טהורה, ותמה על הסד"ט [הובא בפת"ש ס"ק י"ח] שהחמיר בזה. ולדבריו אפשר דה"ה בקנחה בבגד צבוע טהורה וכ"כ בשו"ע הרב סי' ק"צ ס"ק א', וכ"כ בשיעורי שבה"ל סי' ק"צ סע' ו' דבקינוח ע"י בגד צבוע או אינו מקב"ט טהורה וע"ע שו"ת מהרי"ץ ח"א סי' ע"ה. אולם יש כמה צדדים להחמיר בקינוח, עיין שו"ת חשב האפוד ח"ב סי' ע"ה ובשיעורי הגרמ"ש קליין שליט"א דשמא דם הנמצא על קינוח חשיב כנמצא על גופה, ובפרט דהא לדעת החת"ס אין להקל בכתם שעל בגד צבעוני כשהוא ודאי בא מגופה וכנ"ל, ואף להחולקים אפשר דמודי בקינוח דחמור יותר, וע"ע לעיל בהערות לסע' זה דבזמנינו שנחלשו ההרגשות אין להקל כ"כ בדם גמור הנמצא אא"כ יש צדדים שאינו ודאי דם או שהדם בא ממקו"א. וגם לגבי קינוח בדבר שאינו מקב"ט דעת הסד"ט דאם נמצא הכתם ע"ד שאינו מקבל טומאה והוא מונח על דבר המקב"ט מטמא משום כתם, וא"כ ה"ה בקינוח שהאשה מחזקת הדבר שאינו מקב"ט ומונח על ידיה שמקבלים טומאה, וע"כ אין להקל אא"כ יש צדדים נוספים להקל וכנ"ל.

19. "**since the wiping was only external**" — חוו"ד סי' ק"צ סע' א', ועוד. אמנם הסד"ט סי' ק"צ ס"ק צ"ג ס"ל דהיכא דודאי מגופה אף בלא הרגשה טמאה מה"ת, ועי' בקו"א לשו"ע הרב סי' קפ"ג דיש גם צד לומר דשייך חשש הרגשה אף בקינוח, ומ"מ פשטות רוב הפוסקים כהחוו"ד.

20. "**cervix**" — דנו האחרונים אם פתיה"ק הוא בפתח צואר הרחם או בכניסה שמצואר הרחם לרחם, ועי' שיעורי שבה"ל סי' קפ"ח סע' ג' אות ד' בד"ה ולהלכה שההכרעה באחרונים להחמיר בפתח צואר הרחם.

21. "**The authorities discuss**" — עיין פתחי תשובה סי' קפ"ז ס"ק ל'.

פרק שני

1. "marital relations are prohibited by Torah law etc." — רמב"ם פ"ד מהל' איסו"ב ה"א.

"embracing ... bodily contact" — רמב"ם שם פכ"א ה"א ובסהמ"צ ל"ת שנ"ג, וכ"פ הב"י יו"ד ס"ס קצ"ה ובש"ע אבהע"ז סי' כ', ודלא כרמב"ן בסהמ"צ שם שסובר שאינו אסור אלא מדרבנן. ונגיעה שאיננה דרך חיבה,לדעת הש"ך ביו"ד שם ס"ק כ' לכ"ע איננה אסורה אלא מדרבנן, ולדעת הבית שמואל שם ס"ק א' גם בזה לדעת הרמב"ם יש איסור דאורייתא.

"Since *yichud* ... is permitted etc." — סד"ט סי' קצ"ה ס"ק ט"ו בשם הרא"ש.

2. "words of affection etc." — ש"ע ריש סי' קצ"ה, ע"פ אדר"נ ריש פ"ב. וכן פירשו רש"י ורבינו יונה (אבות פ"א מ"ה) את דברי התנא (שם) "אל תרבה שיחה עם האשה", בשיחה של קלות ראש עם אשתו נדה.

"to give gifts to one another" — כרתי ופלתי סי' קצ"ה סעי' א'.

3. "A husband may not look etc." — ש"ע סי' קצ"ה סעי' ז'. גדר מקום המכוסה נתבאר בש"ע או"ח סי' ע"ה ובשו"ת שבט הלוי ח"א סי' א'.

"nor hear her singing" — פתחי תשובה שם ס"ק י'.

"smell her perfume etc." — פתחי תשובה שם ס"ק א'.

"light a candle" — פתחי תשובה שם ס"ק ג'. ולעניין נר הבדלה כ"כ בשעורי שבה"ל סעי' ב' אות ג'.

4. "They may not touch one another" — ש"ע שם סעי' ב'. ועיין לעיל במקורות לסעי' א' אם נגיעה שאיננה של חיבה אסורה מדאורייתא, או מדרבנן.

פרק שני

1. "**יהרג ואל יעבור**" — משמעות הב"י סי' קצ"ה ורדב"ז המובא בפתחי תשובה שם ס"ק ט"ו לענין מישוש הדופק לאשתו נדה.

2. "The penalty etc." — גמ' נדרים כ' ע"א.

4. "even if the child is old enough etc." — התשב"ץ ח"ג סי' נ"ח, הו"ד בפתחי תשובה שם ס"ק ג', מיקל, אבל בשו"ת שבה"ל ח"ב סי' צ"ב וסי' ק' מחמיר.

"even by means of a long article" — כ"מ מש"ך שם ס"ק ג'.

"a garment etc." — פתחי תשובה סס"ק ג' בשם התשב"ץ.

"It is forbidden to remove ... even a feather" — פתחי תשובה שם ס"ק ד'.

"to manually fan one another" — בן איש חי פר' צו סעי' כ"ב, וע"ע שו"ת מנחת יצחק ח"ז סי' ע'.

5. "to hand or throw" — שחששו שמא יבוא ליגע בה, ש"ע שם.

"placing or throwing an item etc. ... on the spouse's body or clothing" שעורי שבט הלוי שם אות ד', ודלא כתוה"ש שם ס"ק ב' שמיקל.

6. "eat or drink together from one utensil" — ש"ע שם סעי' ג'.

"even if other people etc." — פ"ת שם ס"ק ה'. וטעם האיסור לאכול על שולחן אחד ללא היכר, לדעת הרא"ש בשבת י"ג ע"א, האכילה יחד היא דרך חיבה וקירוב, ולדעת הרשב"א בבית הנשים (משה"ב ריש ש"ב) כדי שלא יבואו לאכול מקערה אחת, שאז הוא דרך קירוב. ועיין בסד"ט ס"ק ז' שהאריך.

"put it on his / her plate etc." — ט"ז ס"ק ב'.

7. "eat or drink at the same table" — בספר המנהיג דין יולדת מפורש דה"ה בשתיה.

(b) "an item that is usually placed ... in a different location" — ט"ז יו"ד סי' פ"ח ס"ק ד'.

(c) "sit in a different place" — ב"י בשם רי"ו, סד"ט סס"ק ח', דרכ"ת ס"ק ט"ו.

"sit far enough from one another" — שעורי שבה"ל שם סוף אות ב'.

"if another person sits between them" — רא"ה בבדק הבית, הו"ד בסד"ט שם ס"ק ו', שו"ת שבה"ל ח"ה סי' קכ"ד אות ג'.

"when drops must be placed in the child's eye" — דרכ"ת סי' קצ"ה ס"ק נ"ו.

6. "A small or low item can be used" — סתימת הפוסקים, וכ"פ בשעורי שבה"ל שם אות ג'.

"It is also possible etc." — ש"ע שם.

7. "Under extenuating circumstances" — ברכ"י על גליון הש"ע, שעורי שבה"ל לש"ך שם ס"ק ז', ד"ה ולמעשה.

8. "eat or drink his wife's leftover food or drink" — ש״ע שם סעי׳ ד׳, רמ״א שם סוף סעי׳ ג׳ וש״ך שם ס״ק ח׳.

"a loaf of bread ... or a spread" — שו״ת אגרות משה יו״ד ח״א סי׳ צ״ב, וכ״כ בשעורי שבה״ל שם אות ח׳.

"no need to rinse it" — ב״י סי׳ קצ״ה, באה״ט סס״ק ו׳. ועיין ש״ך שם ס״ק ט׳.

"additional food or drink etc." — ש״ך שם ס״ק ט׳.

"transferred to another vessel" — רמ״א שם. ובשו״ת מנחת יצחק ח״ז סוף סי׳ ע׳ כתב שפשוט שהמדובר רק בדברים שצריכים כלי.

"returned to the original vessel" — רמ״א שם.

"another person ate etc." — רמ״א שם.

"If the wife left the room" — רמ״א שם.

"when she comes back" — בפ״ת שם מתיר, אבל בברכ״י או״ח סי׳ ע״א אוסר.

"before she became a *niddah*" — פשוט, וכ״מ בפתחי תשובה ס״ק ז׳.

"is not aware etc." — רמ״א שם.

"does not know that she is a *niddah*" — לחם ושמלה שם.

"tasted the food" — טהרת ישראל שם סעי׳ י״ג.

"The wife may eat her husband's leftover food etc." — ב״י ורמ״א שם, והטעם דאיהי לא מרגלא ליה לדבר עבירה.

9. "The husband is prohibited etc." — ש״ע שם סעי׳ י׳ וי״ג וש״ך ס״ק י״ג, ודלא כט״ז ס״ק ג׳ שסובר שאסור רק במשקה ולא במאכל.

10. "a cup of wine" — ש״ע שם סעי׳ י״ג.

"another important drink" — בפס״ד צ״צ כתב דה״ה בכל משקים החשובים.

11. "same bench" — רמ״א שם סעי׳ ה׳, ועיין בשעורי שבה״ל שם אות י״א שיש חשש שיבאו ליגע זה בזה, וגם שע״י שמרגישים בנדנוד הספסל מחמת בן הזוג עלולים לבוא לידי הרהור.

---

10. "After the wife has immersed etc." — פשוט.

11. "adding milk to coffee" — שגם זה בכלל מזיגה.

"a large or tall article" — דרכי משה שם אות ה', וממש"כ "תיבה", משמע שצריך חפץ ניכר.

12. "pleasure trip" — רמ"א שם. ולענין ביקור קרובים וכיו"ב, כ"כ בשו"ת רב פעלים ח"ג יו"ד סי' י"ז.

13. "The husband may not lie or sit etc." — ש"ע שם סעי' ה'.

"If the wife is out of town" — פתחי תשובה שם ס"ק ט', דעת תורה שם, שעורי שבה"ל שם אות ה'.

"The wife is only prohibited from lying etc." — ט"ז ס"ק ו', פתחי תשובה ס"ק ח'.

14. "They may not lie on the same bed" — ש"ע ורמ"א סעי' ו'. ותקנת אסיפת חכמי ישראל בלבוב להרחיק המטות זו מזו אמה אחת. ובטהרת ישראל סעי' כ"ז כתב להרחיק כך שלא יוכלו להגיע בהושטת היד זה לזו.

15. "making her husband's bed etc." — ש"ע שם סעי' י"א. וכתב הערוך השולחן סעי' י"ד דה"ה הבעל אסור להציע לאשתו, ויש להחמיר שלא להניח ציפה ע"ג כרים וכסתות קלים כגון בקיץ, שהוא דרך חיבה ששב"ל שם אות ד'.

16. "pouring water etc." — ש"ע שם סעי' י"ב. וכתב בחכמ"א כלל קט"ז סעי' י' דה"ה לבעל אסור ליצוק לאשתו.

"may not prepare water etc." — ש"ך שם ס"ק ט"ז בשם רבינו יונה, ודלא כט"ז שם ס"ק ח' שמתיר.

"prepare water ... for a *mitzvah* purpose" — שו"ת מנחת יצחק ח"ז סי' ע"ב אות א'.

17. "the husband ... is sick" — עי' ש"ע שם סעי' ט"ו ט"ז וי"ז ובדברי הפוסקים שם.

18. "under no circumstances may one be lenient etc." — ש"ך שם ס"ק י"ז, וכתב שנתקבצו הקהלות ועשו חרם על זה. ועיין בשו"ת אגרות משה יו"ד ח"ב סי' ע"ז שהאריך בזה.

---

12. "Being that etc." — שאם אין דרך להקפיד באיזו יד מגישים, אין זה נחשב לשינוי.

16. "permit a wife to sit etc." — סי' קצ"ה ט"ז ס"ק ו'.

19. "by rabbinic law" — ש"ע סי' קצ"ג לעניין דם בתולים.

19. "even on the last of the seven clean days" — שעורי שבה"ל סי' קצ"ה סוף סעי' י"ד, ודלא כמשמעות הש"ך שם ס"ק י"ז.

20. "should not to look at the *sefer Torah*" — או"ח סי' פ"ח מ"ב שם ס"ק ז'.

21. "should not go to the cemetery" — חיי אדם סוף כלל ג', פתחי תשובה ס"ס קצ"ה, מ"ב סי' פ"ח ס"ק ז'.

22. "on *Tisha B'Av* night" — ש"ע או"ח סי' תקנ"ד סעי' י"ח ומג"א ומ"ב שם.

"on *Yom Kippur*" — ש"ע או"ח סי' תרט"ו סעי' א' ומג"א ומ"ב שם.

"*Tisha B'av* during the day" — מג"א ומ"ב שם, ועיין בשעה"צ שם ס"ק מ"ד בטעמא דמילתא דקיל טפי מיוה"כ.

23. "seven days of mourning" — ש"ע ורמ"א יו"ד סי' שפ"ג סעי' א'.

24. "A person is prohibited to be lenient etc." — עיין ספר החינוך מצוה קפ"ח לענין כל העריות.

פרק שלישי

1. "counting seven clean days" — מימרא דר' זירא נדה ס"ו ע"א בנות ישראל החמירו על עצמן שאפילו רואות טיפת דם כחרדל יושבות עליה שבעה נקיים. ונפסק כן בטושו"ע סי' קפ"ג.

"the five-day waiting period from the time that she became a *niddah*" רמ"א סי' קצ"ו סע' י"א. ויסוד דין זה בראב"ש המובא בב"י שם מטעם דהפולטת שכבת זרע בשבעה נקיים סותרת את ספירת אותו יום, ועד שיעברו ארבעה ימים משנטמאה חוששים שמא תפלוט ותסתור ספירתה. והוסיפו את יום החמישי

פרק שלישי

3. "if she ceases bleeding on the fourth day etc." — כדי שלא להרחיק זמן טבילתה מזמן חפיפתה, פתחי תשובה סי' קצ"ו ס"ק ט"ו בשם השל"ה. וע"ש בשם הסד"ט ס"ק מ"ב דאפילו אם שימשה בימים שקודם ראיתה, דהיינו שלא עברו חמשה ימים מיום שימושה אלא ארבעה ימים, ג"כ יכולה להמתין ארבעה ימים בלבד, וכ"נ מסקנתו לדינא, ודלא כמש"כ בשו"ת וישאל שאול יו"ד סי' כ"ב [להגאון רבי שאול בראך זצ"ל אב"ד קאשוי, שבו תשובות מכתבי תלמידו הגדול, מוהר"ר הלל ורטהיימר זצ"ל].

מחשש טעות ע"י תשמיש בבין השמשות, תרוה"ד סי' רמ"ה. אך הרמ"א מביא עוד חומרא בזה בשם האו"ז ומהרי"ק, דלא רק בשימשה צריכה להמתין ארבעה ימים, אלא אפילו בלא שמשה גוזרים לא שמשה אטו שמשה. ומוסיף התרוה"ד על זה, שהגזירה של לא שימשה אטו שימשה היא לא זו בלבד על עצם חיוב המתנת ד' ארבעה ימים, אלא גם על מה שהוסיפו להחמיר להצריך יום נוסף ולהמתין חמשה ימים מאז ששימשה, גם על זה גזרו לא שימשה אטו שימשה, ולכן אחר כל ראיית דם, צריכה להמתין חמשה ימים מאז שראתה עד שתתחיל מנין שבעה נקיים. וביאר הטעם דכשגזרו לא שמשה אטו שמשה גזרו כן אף על היום הנוסף, "משום דחששא דביה"ש חששא פשוטה היא וחשו בה רבנן טובא בכמה דוכתי". והובא להלכה ברמ"א סי' קצ"ו סע' י"א, וכתב וז"ל "ויש שכתבו שעכשיו אין לחלק בין שמשה עם בעלה ללא שימשה וכל אשה שרואה אפילו כתם צריכה להמתין חמשה ימים עם יום שראתה בו ותפסוק לעת ערב ותספור ז' נקיים, וכן נוהגין במדינות אלו ואין לשנות". ומכאן ההלכה למעשה, דכל ראית דם צריך להמתין חמשה ימים אף בלא שמשה.

2. "Likewise ... bloodstain" — רמ"א שם בשם סה"ת וסמ"ג ומובא גם בב"י רס"י ק"צ. ועי' רמ"א סי' ק"צ סע' א' ובבאר הגולה שם. ומסקנת הש"ך ס"ק כ"א דאף בלא שימשה קודם מציאת הכתם דאין חיוב ההמתנה מדינא אלא משום לא פלוג דנהגו להמתין בלא שימשה גזירה אטו שימשה, ג"כ צריכה המתנת חמשה ימים אחר מציאת כתם. ואף דבחוו"ד בחידושים ס"ק י' מביא בשם הש"ך להקל, והיינו שהבין דמה שצידד הש"ך בריש דבריו דבלא שימשה אי"צ להמתין כן הוא גם מסקנתו לדינא, ומה שסיים הש"ך אחר שהביא דברי הלבוש והחמיר ד"וכן נוהגין" הוא מלשון הלבוש אבל הש"ך גופיה ס"ל דאי"צ להמתין, וכן נראה בבאר היטב ס"ק י"ד, מ"מ בש"ך ס"ק ו' [במש"כ בשם המע"מ] משמע שדעתו להחמיר, וכ"כ בתורת השלמים ס"ק י"ח ובסדרי טהרה ס"ק י' בדעת הש"ך ס"ק כ"ב דמסקנתו להחמיר, וכ"פ בחכמ"א כלל קי"ז סי' א'. וכתב בשיעורי שבה"ל דמנהג העולם להחמיר בכתם ואף בלא שימשה. ואף כשאין בעלה בעיר ולא שימשה צריך המתנת ה' ימים בכתם, ובמקום הצורך תעשה שאלת חכם אם אפשר להקל [עי' פת"ש ס"ק ט"ז בשם תשו' חת"ס חיו"ד סי' קפ"ח ובאר היטב שם בשם תשו' שבות יעקב ח"ב סי' ע"ז].

3. "includes the day when she became a *niddah*" — שם ברמ"א.
"There is no difference" — עיין ש"ך שם ס"ק י"ט.

4. "Some *Sephardim* etc." — עיין שיעורי שבט הלוי סי' קצ"ו סע' י"א אות ז'.
"follow her husband's custom" — עי' אג"מ או"ח ח"א סי' קנ"ח ואהע"ז ח"א סי' נ"ט. [וע"ע בפו' לגבי דברים הנוהגים אצל האשה לחוד, ואכמ"ל].

---

4. "she started to menstruate after sunset" — הוראת הגר"ש ואזנר שליט"א, ומוכיח כן מפשטות דברי מהרש"ל וט"ז ס"ק א' וש"ך ס"ק י"ט, דמש"כ שם דאף בהתפללה ערבית כבר עדיין נחשב ליום הקודם הוא רק משום דעדיין יום הוא, ומשמע דביה"ש הוה חשיב כיום המחרת.

ואף שלכאורה היה מקום לדון, שהרי עיקר הטעם דהוסיפו עוד יום א' ושלא תתחיל מנין ז"נ עד יום שישי לראיתה, כיון דאם תמתין רק ארבעה ימים ותתחיל מנין ז"נ ביום ה' לשימושה, אפשר שתשמש בביה"ש, ותסבור שהוא יום ובאמת הוא כבר לילה, ונמצא ששה העונות כלים בליל חמישי, שהוא כבר יום הראשון לספירתה ושמא תפלוט בתחילת ליל חמישי ונמצאת סותרת ספירתה, ולכן הוסיפו עוד יום אחד שלא תתחיל מנין ז"נ עד יום שישי לשימושה, שאז אפילו תשמש בביה"ש, דאפילו אם הוא לילה ותסבור שהוא יום, אין כאן חשש פולטת, כיון שיום ספירתה יתחיל ביום שישי לשימושה שהוא כבר אחר ששה עונות, ומשום לא פלוג לכן בכל ראיה הצריכו חמשה ימים כמו בראתה ביה"ש, ועכ"פ חזינן דבראתה ביה"ש גופא אי"צ להוסיף עוד יום אחד, שהרי גם אם תטעה להחשיבו יום והוא באמת לילה, נמי יחול יום ראשון של ספירת ז"נ אחר ששה עונות, ומטעם זה באמת יש שמקילים בזה.

מ"מ נראה דאינו מוכרח, דבפשוטו יש לפרש החשש שתשמש בביה"ש דאין הכונה דתשמש בזמן שספק אם הוא יום או לילה, אלא הכונה דשמא תשמש בזמן שאפשר לטעות שהוא יום ובאמת הוא לילה, [וכעין מה שמצינו בב"י סי' קצ"ו בשם הרא"ש שצריכה לבדוק בדיקת הפסק טהרה בין השמשות וביאר הב"י דהכונה סמוך לביה"ש], ומחשש טעות הוסיפו יום אחד, אבל הא אנן איירינן בכה"ג שהוא ביה"ש וספק אם הוא יום או לילה, ובספק כזה יש לדון לב' צדדים, אי נימא דכיון דהוא דרבנן הוי ספק דרבנן ולקולא, או דנימא דלא פלוג ולחומרא וכמו שמצינו הרבה דינים שרבנן החמירו בביה"ש כלילה לגבי תענית ועוד, וה"נ בזה דלא פלוג, וגם כדי שלא יהא בלבול שלגבי דין המתנת חמשה ימים נחשב ליום ולגבי וסתות נחשיב ללילה, ואכן יל"ע בזה, אבל ראיה מעיקר הגזירה דביה"ש אין לנו, דהתם ענין אחר הוא וכמשנ"ת. מהגרמ"ש קליין שליט"א.

5. "more than five days have elapsed etc." — דגול מרבבה בש"ך שם ס"ק כ'. וכל שכן כשלא ראתה שוב דם וסתה מאז שנטמאה. וע"ע לחם ושמלה שם. ושו"ת דובב מישרים סי' ח'.

"if in the course of the seven clean days etc" — ט"ז שם ס"ק ח' וש"ך שם ס"ק כ"ב.

6. "Moreover ... until after she again menstruated etc." — דגו"מ שם.

"similarly ... after giving birth" — פתחי תשובה שם ס"ק ט"ז ע"פ הדגו"מ. ויולדת שטבלה אחר הלידה, ושוב ראתה דם, אף שהוא בימי טוהר, צריכה המתנת חמשה ימים קודם שתתחיל לספור שבעה נקיים. ודין דם טוהר הוא כדם גמור לכל דיניו. עי' תשו' חת"ס חיו"ד סי' קנ"ז הובא בפת"ש סי' קצ"ו ס"ק ט"ז. ובשבה"ל סי' קצ"ד סע' א' אות ו' מסתפק בבני ספרד שנוהגין להמתין בכל ראיה ו' או ז' ימים, אם אפשר להקל להם בדם טוהר בה' ימים בלבד. [וכמ"כ מצינו דאף הנוהגים להמתין ששה ימים הקילו גבי כתם שלא להמתין אלא ה' ימים, עי' בן איש חי שנה ב' פ' צו אות ז' וח' ובשו"ת רב פעלים ח"ד יו"ד סי' כ'].

"even if she already lit the *Shabbos* candles etc." — מהרש"ל, הובאו דבריו בט"ז סי' קצ"ו ס"ק א' ובש"ך ס"ק י"ט.

5. "without vowing" — דמנהג אבותיו שגם הוא התחיל לנהוג כן והיה בדעתו לנהוג כן לעולם או שנהג כן ג"פ הוי קבלת נדר. [אולם לא מצד מנהג אבות הוא דחייב להמשיך מנהגם, דאם הוא מבני אותה קהלה שנהגו חומרא, כל זמן שהוא במקומם הרי בלא"ה צריך לנהוג כמותם ולא מהני התרה, ואף לא מצד מנהג אבות אלא מצד שהוא מבני אותה קהלה שנהגו חומרא, דאף אדם שבא ממקום אחד למקומם לאחר שבלו החומרא צריך לנהוג כחומרתם, ואם אביו מבני קהלה שנהגו חומרא, והוא יצא משם, אין בניו צריכים לנהוג כחומרה שנהגו אבותיהם אא"כ התחילו גם הם לנהוג כן ע"ד לנהוג כן לעולם או שנהגו כן ג"פ, וכהא דאיתא שם בשו"ע סע' א' ובמשנ"ב סי' תקצ"ז ס"ק ו' וכן נראה מתשו' זכרון יוסף שהובא בפת"ש ס"ק ה' שם בקצרה, וזהו ככל דיני קבלת נדרים ולא משום מנהג אבות.

7. "If she became a *niddah* again at the night of immersion" — עיין פת"ש סי' קצ"ו ס"ק ט"ז פלוגתת האחרונים בזה, דדעת המעי"צ ושו"ת פני יהושע להקל, וכן דעת

7. "the couple, out of doubt, separated" — שיעורי שבט הלוי סי׳ קצ״ו סע׳ י״א אות ג׳.

8. "If she mistakenly started counting etc." — ראתה דם וסתה, או שנמצא דם על עד הבדיקה, או שמצאה כתם, וטעתה, והתחילה את ספירת ז׳ נקיים קודם שהמתינה חמשה ימים (ראה למטה הערה אות 11), וכבר טבלה ושמשה עם בעלה, אם לא שמשה לפחות ארבעה ימים קודם שהחלה ספירת ז׳ נקיים, יש להקל בדיעבד (ראה למטה הערה אות 12), אבל אם שימשה תוך ארבעה ימים לתחילת ספירת ז׳ נקיים, תשאל חכם כיצד עליה לנהוג (ראה למטה הערה אות 13).

הסד״ט, וכ״כ בחכמ״א כלל ק״ג דין ג׳, ודעת הנו״ב להחמיר. והחזו״א במכתבו שנדפס בריש ספר טהרת בת ישראל מכריע כדעת המקילים.

"This applies only etc." — דבשו״ת מעיל צדקה מוכח דעיקר טעמו להקל בנטמאה בליל טבילה דאי״צ המתנת חמשה ימים, משום דהוי מילתא דלא שכיחא שתראה שוב מיד אחר וסתה, ועל כן כתב המעי״צ והובא בסד״ט ס״ק ל״ט דאשה שטבלה בליל י״ג מתחילת וסתה, וראתה שוב בליל טבילה, דאז יש פחות מי״ח ימים מראייתה האחרונה ולא שכיח שתראה, דהוה בלא עת נדתה, בזה הוא דיש להקל דבמילתא דלא שכיח לא גזרו וכמבואר בש״ך ס״ק כ״ג, משא״כ בטובלת לאחר מציאת כתם או לאחר דם בתולים ועברו י״ח ימים מראייתה האחרונה שאז שכיח שתראה, אין להקל, הוראת הגרמ״ש קליין שליט״א.

8. "Similarly, a bride etc." — דגו״מ בש״ך ס״ק ב׳.

9. "they chose to be stringent" — עיין בהשמטות ליוסף דעת מהשואל ומשיב [עמ׳ קנ״ב] שכ״כ לגבי אשה שהחזיקה עצמה לטמאה. ובתשו׳ מהר״י שטייף סי׳ קכ״ח הק׳ עליו דסו״ס החזיקה עצמה לטמאה ואסורה לשמש וא״כ למה לא תחשיב ימים אלו במנין חמשה ימים, אולם י״ל דהשו״מ לא כתב כן אלא בנידונו שהחזיקה עצמה בטמאה לחומרא, ולא מחמת ספק, ולכן אינה יכולה להחשיב ימים אלו במנין חמשה ימים. והטעם י״ל בפשיטות הואיל והוא תלוי ברצונם ויכולים גם לשנות החלטתם שאינם מחמירים על עצמם ומותרים, על כן לא חשיב שהיו אסורין מחמת דיני נדה.

אם הגיע עונת הוסת או עונה בינונית [ראה להלן פרק ט׳], ופרשו זה מזה כדין חיוב פרישה בעונת הוסת, [דלא זו בלבד שמותרים בשאר קריבות, אלא גם יש לה היתר בתשמיש ביוצא לדרך וכיו״ב], וכעבור יום או יותר נטמאה, אינה יכולה למנות את חמשת ימי ההמתנה מאותו יום שפרשו זה מזה, אלא מונה את חמשת ימי ההמתנה מאותו יום בו נטמאה, ולאחר מכן סופרת שבעה נקיים.

כמו כן, אם ראתה למחרת יום כיפור או למחרת תשעה באב, אע״פ שהיו אסורים בתשמיש מיום קודם מחמת איסור תשמיש שבימים אלו, אינה מונה את המתנת חמשה ימים מיום כיפור או מתשעה באב, אלא מאותו יום בו נטמאה. ולאחר מכן סופרת שבעה נקיים. דאף דמצד הדין היו אסורין, מ״מ הא לא פירשו מחמת חשש שטמאה היא אלא מחמת איסורי יוכ״פ ות״ב, ודמי לאין בעלה בעיר דג״כ צריכה להמתין חמשה ימים דאף שלא שייך הגזירה של פולטת מ״מ לא פלוג דשמא לא ידעו הטעם דל״ש גזירה זו באין בעלה בעיר וגזרו בכל גוני דמשנטמאה צריכה להמתין חמשה ימים, ולכן גם בכה״ג שהיתה אסורה משום איסורי יו״כ או ת״ב נמי שייך חששא דלעיל, דשמא לא ידעו הטעם שאי״צ להמתין, ולכן גזרו דבכל גווני צריכה להמתין ואף בכה״ג דל״ש הגזירה.

אם הגיע עונת הוסת או עונה בינונית דנתבאר לעיל. למעשה אין נפק״מ בזה אלא באופן שאסורה ב׳ ימים, דהיינו בעונת היום ובעונת הלילה שלאחריו, דאז אם ראתה בעונת הלילה שהוא זמן וסתה, היה שייך לדון האם נחשב הלילה כיום שני, כיון שכבר אסורה ביום הקודם מחמת עונת וסתה ועדיין לא היה זמן היתר, אבל בכה״ג שעונת וסתה ביום בלבד וראתה בלילה שאחריו, לא שייך לדון דמה שהיתה אסורה ביום הקודם בעונת הוסת דיום יגרום להחשיב אותה עונת הוסת כיום ראשון מהמתנת חמשה ימים, דאי משום שהיתה אסורה מחמת עונת הוסת, הרי מאידך היתה מותרת מיד אחר השקיעה קודם תחילת הלילה, וכיון שהיה רגע של היתר ודאי דלא שייך לצרף יום הקודם. ורק אם ראתה ברגע הראשון של השקיעה דלא היה רגע אחד של היתר, בזה הוא דשייך לדון שמא יום הקודם נחשב ליום ראשון מחמשת ימי ההמתנה, ולהמתידים בראתה ביה״ש להחשיב יום הקודם ליום הראשון מימי המתנה, שוב אין נפק״מ גם בזה, דבלא״ה חשיב יום הקודם ליום הראשון מימי ההמתנה גם לולי שהיה יום הוסת. וכן בראתה למחרת יום כיפור או למחרת תשעה באב אין נפק״מ בזה אלא בכה״ג שראתה ממש מיד בתחילת הלילה של מוצאי יוה״כ או ת״ב, דאילו ראתה מעט אחר תחילת הלילה א״כ כבר היה זמן היתר אחר צאה״כ עד שנטמאה ופשיטא דלא נוכל לצרף היום הקודם למנין חמשה ימים.

בפירשו זה מזה מחמת אבילות עיין דרכי תשובה סי׳ קצ״ו ס״ק פ״ו בשם תוספות ירושלם. וכמו כן באם מאיזה סיבה אמרה טמאה אני, ואח״כ ראתה דם, מונה חמשה ימים מעת שנטמאה ולא מעת שאמרה טמאה אני. הואיל ומדינא מותרת לבעלה ע״י אמתלא שתתן למה אמרה טמאה אני.

10. **"even if it was later verified etc."** — הגרמ״ש קליין שליט״א בשם הג׳ מוהר״ן כהנא מספינקא זצ״ל. וכל זה הוא דוקא אם לא נודע להם שהוא טהור כי אם אחר שנטמאה, אבל אם נודע להם שהוא טהור קודם שנטמאה, אף שהיה ממש בסמוך זה אחר זה ולא שימשו בינתיים, אין מונים חמשה ימים אלא מעת שנטמאה ולא מאז שפירשו זמ״ז, הואיל וכבר היה באמצע זמן מה שהיתה מותרת והיה בידיעתם.

אך יש לדון בכה״ג שהלך הבעל לשאול החכם ע״ד הכתם, וטיהרו, ובשובו לביתו הודיעה לו שנטמאה, האם צריך לדקדק לידע אם הרגע שנטמאה היה קודם שהורה המורה להתיר הכתם או אח״כ, שאם הרגע שנטמאה היה לאחר שכבר הורה המורה להתיר תצטרך למנות חמשה ימים מעת שנטמאה, או דילמא אע״פ שהבעל ידע שהכתם טהור, מ״מ כיון שהיא לא ידעה מכך וא״כ לא היה רגע אחד שנהגו שניהם בהיתר, שהרי היא עדיין נהגה פרישה מספק שמא טמאה היא, שפיר תמנה חמשה ימים מעת מציאת הכתם. ולכאורה כיון דנקטינן הלכתא דאף באין בעלה בעיר נמי צריכה להמתין חמשה ימים וכמו״ש במהרי״ק הובא בש״ך סי׳ קצ״ו ס״ק כ׳ וכ״פ הש״ך שם ודלא כהב״ח, ה״נ מה שהיה הבעל אצל המורה לא עדיפא מאין בעלה בעיר דאעפ״כ צריכה המתנת חמשה ימים מעת שנטמאה, ואולם מאידך עדיין יל״ע דכיון דהאשה מחזקת עצמה בספק טמאה ואצלה האיסור קיים, והרי באם יבוא לשכב אצלה צריכה לשואלו על כך, א״כ הוי כמו מוחזקת בטומאה ויכולה להחשיב יום זה במנין חמשה ימים, ומ״מ מסתבר יותר כהצד הראשון דלא עדיפא מאין בעלה בעיר, ויל״ע עוד בכל זה ונכתב רק להעיר. כל סעיף זה מהגרמ״ש קליין שליט״א בשיעוריו.

11. קודם שהמתינה חמשה ימים — ואם טעתה בספירת שבעה נקיים, ראה להלן בפרק ה׳ סע׳ ד׳ ובתוספת טהרה.

12. יש להקל בדיעבד — סדרי טהרה שם ס״ק מ״ב. ולמעשה יש לדון דגם בטבלה ולא שמשה עדיין, יש להקל בדיעבד, דמש״כ הסד״ט ההיתר בטבלה ושמשה וכנ״ל, היינו משום דכולל בזה גם את דין אשה שהקדימה את ספירת ז״נ קודם ד׳ ימים ולא שמשה קודם ראיתה, דבזה ס״ל להסד״ט בפשיטות דרק בטבלה ושמשה כבר הוא דיש להקל, משא״כ בכה״ג שעכ״פ המתינה ד׳ ימים אלא שלא המתינה חמשה ימים, יש לומר דלהסד״ט ה״נ דיש להתיר גם בטבלה ועדיין לא שמשה. שהרי מצינו דבאופנים מיוחדים התירו אף לכתחילה להמתין רק ארבעה ימים, וכהא דכתב השל״ה לגבי אם יחול ליל טבילה בליל שבת שאחר יו״ט או ליל יו״ט שאחר שבת, או בליל יוט״ש, וא״כ לא מסתבר דבאופנים מיוחדים התירו אף לכתחילה להמתין ארבעה ימים, ובאופן של דיעבד שכבר טבלה ולא המתינה ד׳ ימים נאסור אף שהוא דיעבד, ולכן יותר נראה דלהסד״ט אם המתינה ד׳ ימים אכן יש להתיר גם בטבלה ועדיין לא שמשה, הגרמ״ש קליין שליט״א.

13. תשאל חכם כיצד עליה לנהוג — בתשו׳ חת״ס סי׳ קפ״ח הובא בפת״ש סי׳ קצ״ו ס״ק ט״ו כתב דבנטמאה מחמת כתם יש להקל בדיעבד ובנטמאה ע״י בדיקת עד אין להקל. אבל בלחו״ש ס״ק כ״ה מחמיר בזה אף בכתם. ועיין בסד״ט ס״ק מ״ב שבאם כבר טבלה ושימשה יש להקל באם עברו ארבעה ימים מעת שימושה עד שהתחילה ספירת ז״נ, ועי׳ לעיל בסמוך.

פרק רביעי

1. "She does this by checking herself etc." — ראה בטושו"ע סי' קצ"ו.

2. "Prior to performing etc." — רמ"א שם סעיף ג'. וטעם הרחיצה ביאר בתוה"ש שם ס"ק ו' דהוא משום עצה טובה כדי שלא תמצא כתם בג' ימים ראשונים של ספירת ז"נ שבהם הרי אין תולין, וכמבואר שם בסעיף י'. אולם בסדרי טהרה ס"ק י"ב כתב דאדרבה, מצד הדין הוא, ולא מחמת גי"ר דאין תולין, אלא מצד שאר הימים שתולין בהם כתם, דלכתחילה יש לראות שלא תמצא כתם שנקל בו בספק משום "תליה". וע"ע בסדרי טהרה ס"ק י"ג דכשהיא דחוקה ואין לה מים תרחץ במי רגלים, וכ"פ המהרש"ם בח"א סי' קפ"ט, וכ"כ בחכמ"א כלל קי"ז סי' ח' דאם אין לה מים לרחוץ בין ירכותיה עכ"פ צריכה לרחוץ או"מ אפילו ברוק שבפיה או במי רגליה עד שיהיה נקי, ומבואר בזה כמה החשיבו הפוסקים את ענין הרחיצה.

"she should wash herself" — שון הרמ"א שם "ומנהג כשר הוא כשהאשה פוסקת בטהרה שתרחץ ולובשת לבנים", ולא כתב להדיא דרחיצה קודם הבדיקה, ולפי ב' הטעמים שכתבו הפו' למנהג הרחיצה לא משמע דהרחיצה דוקא קודם הבדיקה, ועיין גם לשון הקצושו"ע כלל קנ"ט סע' א' דמשמע דבדיקה קודם לרחיצה, וכ"ה בשו"ת זכר שמחה סי' קי"ז. ואולם יעויין בחכמ"א כלל קי"ז סי' ז' ח' דרחיצה קודם לבדיקה, וכ"ה בחזו"א יו"ד רס"י פ"א. וכן עמא דבר. ואם הזמן דחוק סמוך לבין השמשות תבדוק תחילה ואח"כ תרחץ עצמה.

"around the vaginal area" — דעיקר הרחיצה היא סביב לאותו מקום מבחוץ, ולא בפנים באותו מקום. ולכן גם אין להוכיח מדברי הרמ"א שכתב דתרחץ ותבדוק ולא הזכיר דצריך להמתין מעט בין רחיצה לבדיקה דמוכח דאי"צ להמתין, דהרמ"א לא איירי בכה"ג שרחצה עצמה בפנים או"מ, כיון דמנהג הרחיצה היא על סביב

פרק רביעי

1. "for a reason other than etc." — דכל מילתא דלא רמיא עליה דאיניש לאו אדעתיה, עי' פת"ש סי' קצ"ו ס"ק י'.

2. "either with warm or cold water" — עיין ש"ך סי' קצ"ט ס"ק י"ב דמשמע דבין בחמין ובין בצונן, וכ"ה בקשו"ע כלל קנ"ט סע' ה' ובחכמ"א כלל קי"ז סע' כ'. ועיין בן איש חי פ' צו אות י' דיש לרחוץ בחמין.

לאותו מקום ולא בפנים. ואכן אם רחצה עצמה רק מבחוץ ולא שטפה בפנים, יכולה לעשות את בדיקת ההפסק מיד בלא להמתין. הגרמ"ש קליין שליט"א. אמנם לעיקר הדין יש להקל אף אם בדקה עצמה מיד אחר הרחיצה כמו שיבואר להלן.

"It is preferable etc." — עיין ברמ"א סע' ג'. ועיין ש"ך סי' קצ"ט ס"ק י"ב מש"כ לגבי רחיצת כל הגוף, ומסתבר דרק לרבותא קאמר דבצונן שרי אפילו רחיצת כל הגוף, אבל לא שיהא מנהג הרחיצה קודם הפס"ט ברחיצת כל הגוף. ואף דכמה פוסקים נקטו בלשונם במנהג רחיצה קודם הפס"ט, דהיינו בכל גופה, מסתבר דאין כונתם אלא לחלק התחתון של הגוף, ולדבויי דצריך לרחוץ גם בין ירכותיה ולא רק פניה של מטה, אבל לא שיהא ענין ברחיצה למעלה מהחגור, דהא לפי ב' הטעמים דרחיצה קודם הפס"ט [כנ"ל מהתוה"ש והסד"ט] אין צורך בזה אלא לגבי מקומות שאם תמצא בהם כתם תטמא, ולא בשאר כל הגוף למעלה מהחגור. וכן משמע בסד"ט ס"ק י"ג בשם הד"ח ובחכמ"א כלל קי"ז סי' ח' וכ'. ומ"מ אפשר שנהגו לרחוץ כל הגוף להידור מצוה דהרי אם נזדקרה יש חשש כתם אף למעלה מן החגור, וא"כ אם נזדקרה בימי נדותה ושוב נזדקרה בז"נ תוכל לתלות. הגרמ"ש קליין שליט"א.

"she should wait a few minutes etc." — חזון איש יו"ד דס"י פ"א, אגרות משה יו"ד ח"ב סוס"י ע"א. וסברתם שהאשה אינה שופעת כל הזמן, ואם כן יתכן שמה שאינה מוצאת הוא מפני שעכשיו רחצה ועדיין לא ראתה שוב. ועיין סד"ט סי' קצ"ו ס"ק כ"ג בד"ה ועוד קשה שג"כ כתב כן בטעם מה דבעינן בדיקת חו"ס.

"If she performed this check without washing herself etc." — שם בתוה"ש ס"ק ו', ומכל שכן לטעמו של התוה"ש הנ"ל, דכל שלמעשה לא מצאה כתם בגי"ר אין שום עיכוב ברחיצה, ע"ש. ועיין בסד"ט ס"ק י"ג בשם הד"ח דאף למש"כ הרמ"א דאין רחיצה מעכבת ובאין לה מים תבדוק בלא רחיצה, מ"מ צריכה לקנח פניה של מטה במאי דאפשר ולא סגי בלאו הכי, וכ"ה בקצשו"ע כלל קנ"ט סע' ב'.

3. **"any possible folds and crevices"** — שו"ע שם סע' ו' ופת"ש ס"ק ט'.

---

3. **"If she checked herself immediately etc."** — כ"מ בשו"ת רעק"א סי' ס', וכ"נ מסתימת הפוסקים שלא הזכירו חומרא זו. ונראה שגם המחמירים איירי רק כשעשתה שטיפה פנימית, אבל ברחיצה רגילה אין להחמיר כלל. ואפילו יושבת באמבטיה אינו נכנס

"If she did not insert it deeply etc." — שו"ע סע' ו'. וכל מה שהקיל המחבר בסע' ו' בשאר בדיקות חוץ מהפס"ט ויום ראשון מז"נ, וכן מה שהקיל הרמ"א בדיעבד אף בבדיקת הפס"ט, הוא רק בלא בדקה עד מקום שהשמש דש, אבל כל שלא בדקה בעומק בחו"ס בעומק יפה כפי כוחה, אינו מועיל כלום ולא הוי בדיקה כלל. וכ"כ בחכמ"א כלל קי"ז סי' ט'.

"did not check all the crevices etc." — כנ"ל בשו"ע ופוסקים.

4. "a soft, clean, white, laundered cloth" — שו"ע שם ע"פ נדה י"ד ע"א, ופרש"י שם שהדם ניכר בו יפה.

"Checking by inserting a finger" — סדרי טהרה שם ס"ק כ"ב חכמת אדם כלל קי"ז סי' ט'.

5. "before sunset" — ב"י ושו"ע שם סע' א'.

בעומק כל כך וכדמשמע בתשו' רעק"א קמא סי' ס' בד"ה תו כתב, במש"כ שם בשם בעל החוו"ד לגבי הגדרת מקומות בית הסתרים ובלוע.

"should preferably wash a few hours before the *hefsek taharah*" — דאין צריכה להסמיך הרחיצה להפס"ט, ויכולה לרחוץ עצמה גם בבוקר אם כבר אינה רואה דם, ולפני השקיעה תבדוק וכו'. ובאשה שהיא רגישה לבדיקות עדיף שתקדים הרחיצה, כי ע"י הרחיצה נשטף לחות הטבעי של או"מ ונעשה המקום יבש, וכשיש שהות בין הרחיצה לבדיקה חוזרת הליחה הטבעית ונוח יותר לבדיקה.

"she should smear a little petroleum jelly" — הוראת הגר"ש ואזנר שליט"א. ויש מקור לזה מפ"ק דנדה י' ע"ב דבנות ישראל משהגיעו לפרקן הרי הן בחזקת טומאה ונשים בודקות אותן רבי יהודה אומר אין בודקין אותן ביד מפני שמעוותות אותן אלא סכות אותן בשמן מבפנים ומקנחות אותן מבחוץ והן נבדקות מאליהן, ומוכח שהשמן אינו מקלקל כ"כ את מראה הדם.

"she should wet the examination cloth" — שו"ת מהרש"ם ח"א סי' קמ"ו, הו"ד בדרכ"ת סי' קצ"ו ס"ק נ"ז. ואם נמצא שאלה על עד הבדיקה לאחר שהרטיבה את העד, עליה לומר להחכם שבדקה בעד כשהיה לח, כי פעמים שעל ידי לחותו מתפשט טיפת הדם ונשתנה מראהו קצת, הגרמ"ש קליין שליט"א.

4. "The most comfortable way etc." — טהרת ישראל סי' קצ"ו ס"ק ב' בשם החת"ס. ועיין תשו' חת"ס חיו"ד סי' קמ"ח בד"ה על כן.

"**even if one is doubtful** etc." — עיין ב"י שם במש"כ דלא מהני בדיקה ביה"ש דכיון דהוא ספק לילה לא מהני דצריך שיהא ודאי קודם יום ראשון של ז"נ, ולכן גם אם הוא ספק אם בדקה קודם שקיעה"ח לא מהני.

"**it is preferable ... before the community *davens ma'ariv***" — רמ"א סי' קצ"ו סע' א'.

"**one may be lenient etc.**" — רמ"א שם ועי' דגול מרבבה ע"ד הש"ך ס"ק ד'.

6. "**no earlier than *minchah ketanah***" — עיין ב"י שו"ע ורמ"א שם סע' א'.

"**Ideally it should be made etc.**" — עיין ב"י שם דלכתחילה תבדוק כמה שאפשר סמוך לביה"ש, וחצי שעה קודם שקיעה"ח היינו סמוך לביה"ש. ועי' שו"ע שם.

"**before *minchah ketanah***" — ע"פ ב"י שו"ע ורמ"א שם סעיפים א' וב'.

"**The leniency ... only applies etc.**" — רמ"א סע' ב' ושם בדגול מרבבה.

7. "***moch dachuk***" — רשב"א בתוה"ב, הו"ד בב"י ובשו"ע שם וז"ל: לעולם ילמד אדם בתוך ביתו שתהא האשה בודקת יום הפסק טהרתה במוך דחוק ושיהא שם כל בין השמשות, שזו בדיקה מוציאה מידי כל ספק, עכ"ל.

"**A scrupulous person etc.**" — הרמ"א בסע' ב' מיקל בזה, וכן פסק בלחם ושמלה, אבל החוות דעת ס"ק ב' והגר"א שם אות ח' מחמירים.

---

6. "**She does not need to wash herself again etc.**" — והיינו דוקא באופן זה שכבר רחצה עצמה ולא ראתה דם אח"כ, אלא שהבדיקה לא היתה נקיה מדם, שאז אין חשש שנכתם פניה של מטה מדם ולכן אינה צריכה אלא לחזור על עשית הפס"ט ולא לחזור ולרחוץ עצמה, [ועי' לעיל במקורות לסע' ב' דעיקר הרחיצה היא מסביב לאו"מ ולא באו"מ בפנים], אבל בראתה דם או מצאה כתם אחר הפס"ט, עליה לחזור ולרחוץ עצמה קודם שתבדוק עצמה לצורך הפסק טהרה, פשוט, וכ"ה בדרכ"ת סי' קצ"ו ס"ק ל"ג בשם השואל ומשיב בהשמטות לדברי שאול ויוסף דעת.

"**Likewise, a woman whose seven clean days were interrupted etc.**" — עיין בסדרי טהרה סי' קצ"ט ס"ק כ' בד"ה עו"ק.

7. "**The ideal cloth to use etc.**" — שיעורי שבה"ל שם סע' ו' אות ב' דיש מינים שאינם מקבלים כל כך את הדם, ועל המורה שבא לפניו עד בדיקה מבד סינטטי לעיין היטב ולברר אם לא נשתנה המראה.

"**Ideally, one should not check using paper**" — שו"ת שבט הלוי ח"ב סי' ק'.

8. "checked in daylight" — רמ"א שם סע' ד', ע"פ הרשב"א בתוה"ב והו"ד בב"י שם שכתב "אור היום יפה לבדיקה".

"they are valid" — ואם ודאי אין שום חשש אי"צ להשאירו לראותו באור יום, שיעורי שבה"ל.

9. "before sunset" — עיין לשון הסמ"ג שהובא בב"י סי' קצ"ו וז"ל: הלכה למעשה הוא שהאשה ביום שפוסקת מלראות תלבש בגדים לבנים נקיים מכתמים "קודם שיהיה לילה" ותתחיל לספור למחרת ז' ספירתה, עכ"ל. ומבואר מדבריו דגם בזמן ביה"ש צריכה ללבוש לבנים. והנה, אף דאפשר דהסמ"ג לא ס"ל להצריך לכתחילה מוך דחוק כל ביה"ש, אבל לדידן דמקפידים על כך לכתחילה א"כ לכאורה לא תצטרך ללבוש לבנים סמוך לאו"מ, מ"מ יש מעלה בלבישת בגד לבן מהודק לגוף בשעת מוך דחוק דבזה הבירור של בדיקת מוך דחוק מעליא טפי, דמוך דחוק שאנו עושים אינו ממלא כל אותו מקום כראוי.

10. "should ideally be performed before candle lighting etc." — רמ"א סע' א' ועיין ש"ך שם ס"ק ד' ה' ובס"ק י"ט, ובדגו"מ בש"ך ס"ק ד'.

"a long time before sunset etc." — עיין ב"ח בד"ה ומ"ש ובדיקה זו, ועי' חכמ"א כלל קי"ז סי' ה'.

11. "may be performed on *Shabbos*" — עיין ש"ך סי' קצ"ט ס"ק י"ב ומשנ"ב סי' שכ"ו ס"ק ו', ושו"ת שבה"ל ח"ה סי' קי"ב.

"she should wash etc." — עי' שו"ע או"ח סי' שכ"ו סע' א' דאפילו הוחמו מע"ש אסור לרחוץ בהם כל גופו. והא דיכולה לרחוץ כל חלק גופה התחתון במים, דכיון דאינה רחיצת כל הגוף או רובו שרי, וכל שכן כשרוחצת עצמה רק סמוך לאותו מקום ובין ירכותיה דשרי בחמין, עיין ש"ך שם בשם המשאת בנימין, וכ"ה במשנ"ב סי' שכ"ו ס"ק ו' דמותרת לרחוץ במקומות המטונפים בחמין וכו'. ובצונן

---

10. "Since a difference of opinion exists ... *minchah ketanah*" — עיין סיכום שיטות הפוסקים בזה במ"ב סי' רל"ג.

11. "If, however, she encountered bleeding etc." — הסד"ט סי' קצ"ו ס"ק ט' מחמיר כשעשתה בדיקה קודם זמן מנחה קטנה, אם ראתה דם באותו יום. והחוו"ד שם ס"ק

מותר מדינא אפילו רחיצת כל הגוף, עי' או"ח סי' שכ"ו סע' א'. וע"ש במשנ"ב ס"ק כ"א דאף בצונן נהגו שלא לרחוץ כל גופו בנהר וכו', ע"ש.

"**water that was placed on the fire on *erev Shabbos***" — וכגון שמשתמש במים אלו עצמם [לאחר שיופשרו מעט] דלא עשה שום מעשה במים, אבל להוסיף מים צוננים אף באופן שאין בו איסור בישול מ"מ אפשר דאסור לרחוץ בהם, עי' חי' רעק"א באו"ח שם ע"ד המג"א ס"ק ד', ובתהלה לדוד שם ס"ק י' מתיר, וצ"ע.

"**neither a cloth nor a sponge**" — והעיר בזה במשאת בנימין המובא בש"ך שם ובמג"א סי' שכ"ו ס"ק ג'.

"**nor soap etc.**" — עיין או"ח סי' שכ"ו סע' י' ובמשנ"ב ס"ק ל'.

12. "**She may perform the *hefsek taharah* on *Yom Kippur***" — משנ"ב סי' תרי"ג ס"ק ל"א.

"**She may use pre-heated water**" — עיין ש"ך סי' קצ"ט ס"ק י"ב.

13. "**On *Tishah B'Av***" — רמ"א סי' תקנ"א סע' ט"ז, ואפילו בט"ב עצמו וכמבואר שם בשעה"צ אות ל"ה.

"**or when she is in mourning**" — מסקנת הט"ז ביו"ד סי' שפ"א ס"ק ב'.

"**she should only wash the vaginal area**" — ש"ך סי' קצ"ט ס"ק י"ב בשם המשאת בנימין, ט"ז סי' שפ"א ס"ק ב' ושעה"צ סי' תקנ"א אות ל"ה.

"**with warm water**" — עיין ביאור הלכה סי' תקנ"א סע' ט"ז בד"ה ולצורך מצוה, ומשמע דאף בט"ב עצמו שרי.

"**wear previously worn etc.**" — עיין כיו"ב ברמ"א או"ח סי' תקנ"א סע' ג' במש"כ דבט"ב עצמו "לא תלבש לבנים רק לובשת חלוק בדוק ויפה", ואי אפשר לפרשו כפשוטו דתלבש בגד שאינו לבן, דאין איסור ללבוש בת"ב בגד לבן אלא האיסור הוא ללבוש בגד מכובס, וע"ז כתב הרמ"א דבת"ב תלבש בגד נקי שאינו מכובס.

א' מחמיר עוד יותר שאף מוך דחוק מעכב. ולהלכה דעת האחרונים לחוש לכתחילה לדעת הסד"ט, ולא חששו להחמיר כהחוו"ד, עיין פת"ז.

12. "**If she only found a *kesem***" — ש"ך שם ס"ק ו' בשם מע"מ. ובכה"ג שהכתם בודאי בא מגופה ובלא הרגשה, יש להחמיר ע"פ מ"ש החינוך דדוקא כתם דאינה מוחזקת בראיה, והיינו דאינו בודאי מגופה, הגרמ"ש קליין שליט"א.

14. "she need not redo the *hefsek taharah* etc." — עיין סד"ט סי' קצ"ו ריש ס"ק י"ח וכ"ה בתפאל"מ כמובא בסד"ט שם.

15. "Ideally she should not perform etc." — עיין תשו' חת"ס חיו"ד סי' קצ"ז, וכן כתבו במלבושי טהרה וטהרת ישראל סי' קצ"ו סעיף י' ושם בבאר יצחק אות קס"ז. ועיין היטב במכתבו של החזו"א הנדפס בראש ספר טהרת בת ישראל דלא נחית ליישב הערת המשיג שם על מה שסתם שם בספר הנ"ל להתיר להקדים ההפס"ט בכל גווני, אלא כתב שם רק דביוצאה לדרך או כשיום חמישי חל בת"ב ודאי יש להתיר להפסיק בטהרה ביום שפסקה, ומשמע דעת החזו"א דאכן חוץ מהמקרים המיוחדים שציין שם, אכן לכתחילה לא תקדים לבדוק תוך חמשת ימי ההמתנה, ואפשר דגם טעמו של החזו"א הוא כדלהלן מדברי הבל"י.

"Even when she performed the *hefsek taharah* etc." — כן מבואר בתשו' חת"ס שם, וכנראה טעמו דאין ראוי להנהיג כן לבדוק תוך חמשה ימים כי היכי דלא תבוא לטעות ולהתחיל ספירת שבעה נקיים מעשיית ההפסק טהרה הראשון, וע"י שיורו לה לעשות שוב הפס"ט תזכור שאין להתחיל ספירת שבעה נקיים אלא מהיום החמישי לראיה. וכן כתב בבית לחם יהודה ס"ק ב' הנדפס בגליון השו"ע שם סע' י' על מש"כ התוה"ש להקל באשה שיש לה חבורות ופצעים ומחמת זה רגילה בכתמים בגי"ר של ז"נ, דיש לה תקנה שתפסיק בטהרה אחר יום א' או ב' לראיתה ותתחיל לספור ז"נ אחר יום ה' לראיתה, דאז תוכל לתלות הכתמים בחבורות דהוי לאחר גי"ר הואיל וכבר פסקה בטהרה אחר יום א' או ב' לראיתה, וחלק ע"ז הבל"י דאף דמן הדין יפה כתב התוה"ש, אבל יש חשש תקלה לכמה דברים אם תבדוק קודם יום ה' לשימושה דהא חכמים השוו

---

13. "18 min. after sunset" — שיעורי שבה"ל שם סע' ב' אות ג'.

"even after 13 ½ min." — שזהו השיעור המיקל ביותר לענין צאת הכוכבים, דצאה"כ הוא שלושת רבעי מיל אחר שקיעה"ח, כדאיתא באו"ח סי' רס"א סע' ב', ולהסוברים ששיעור המיל הוא ח"י דקות, א"כ שלושת רבעי מיל הם שלש עשרה וחצי דקות, כמ"ש המג"א שם ס"ק ט' שהוא רבע שעה בקירוב, ועיין בבה"ל שם שיש סוברים ששיעור זה שוה בכל השנה. ויש אומרים שהשעות והדקות שבכאן הן שעות ודקות זמניות.

14. "Nowadays etc." — וקצת מקור לזה מדברי החוו"ד סי' קצ"א ס"ק ח'.

לא שימשה כמו שימשה ואפילו כתם משום תקלה וכו'. ועפ"ד הבל"י כתב בטהרת ישראל סי' קצ"ו בבא"י אות קס"ז דע"י שתוסיף לעשות הפס"ט שנית בכלות חמשה ימים תו ליכא החשש שכתב בבל"י. ולקושטא דמילתא י"ל דגם

---

16. "Concerning the *hefsek taharah* etc." — כמת אדם כלל קי"ז ס"ק ט' ע"פ מש"כ הפת"ש סי' קפ"ח ס"ק ב' בשם שלה"ק בשם מהר"ם מינץ דאין לטהר במהירות במראה שעוה וכל שכן במראה זהב, ולכן בבדיקה זו שהיא עדיין בחזקת רואה יש להחמיר.

17. "Where there is no *eiruv*" —שו"ת מנחת יצחק ח"ד סי' כ"ח, שו"ת אגרות משה ח"ג סי' מ"ז.

18. "on *Yom Tov* it is even permissible etc." — עיין ש"ך סי' קצ"ט ס"ק י"ב, ועיין שו"ע או"ח סי' תקי"א סע' ב' וביאור הלכה שם בד"ה אבל.

19. "It is permitted to use liquid soap, but some opinions advise etc." — מאחר שעושה בועות והוי כנולד, אבל מדינא שרי. ועי' אגרו"מ או"ח ח"א סי' קי"ג שמחמיר מטעם אחר.

22. "On condition that she intended etc." — משום שבימים אלו שבין עשיית ההפסק טהרה ועד תחילת ספירת שבעה נקיים, לכתחילה עליה לתת את הדעת ולשים לב שאינה רואה דם, ואע"פ שאינה צריכה לבדוק עצמה בעד בימים אלו, מכל מקום לא תסיח דעתה מנקיותה. דעי' בחכמ"א כלל קי"ז סי' י"ב שכתב דאשה שהסיחה דעתה באמצע ספירת ז"נ לא זו בלבד שהימים שספרה אינם עולים לה אלא מוסיף עוד דצריכה לעשות בדיקת הפס"ט מחדש, ומזה שכתב דצריכה גם הפס"ט מחדש משמע דלא זו בלבד דהיסח הדעת מקלקל את ספירת ז"נ והספירה שכבר ספרה אינה עולה לה, אלא גם יש חשש שמא ראתה, דאל"כ לא היתה צריכה הפס"ט מחדש, ולגבי החשש דשמא ראתה אין חילוק בין תוך ז"נ או קודם לכן, ולכתחילה יש$ לחוש לזה שלא להסיח דעת בימים אלו.

23. "Likewise ... and forgot to check herself etc." — שיעורי שבה"ל סי' קצ"ו סע' ד' אות ו'.

24. "ideally she should not perform etc." — ראה במקורות לסעיף זה.

25. "she may wash herself as soon as her menstrual flow has stopped" — כ"נ פשוט. והנה, במכתבו של החזו"א שהובא בראש ספר טהרת בת ישראל מתייחס אל הערת המשיג שם שהעיר למה סתם בספר הנ"ל דמותר להקדים הפס"ט מיד כשפסקה

התוה״ש מודה לזה, אלא דבנידונו איירי באשה שאינה יכולה ליטהר מחמת חבורות ופצעים שיש לה דהוא מצב של בדיעבד, ולכן הקיל, אבל לעולם בסתם אשה שכבר פסק דמה ביום הראשון או השני לראיתה, גם התוה״ש מודה דלא תקדים עשיית ההפס״ט אלא תמתין ליום החמישי ואז תעשה ההפס״ט ולמחרת תתחיל ספירת ז״נ, ואפשר דגם התוה״ש יסבור שאם הקדימה ובדקה עצמה לפני יום החמישי לראיתה, תוסיף לבדוק שוב ביום החמישי לראיתה, כ״ז שמעתי מהגרמ״ש קליין שליט״א.

"**When a need arises etc.**" — מכתבו של החזו״א הנדפס בראש ספר טהרת בת ישראל, וע״פ דברי התוה״ש סי׳ קצ״ו ס״ק י״ג והחוו״ד שם ס״ק ו׳ לענין גי״ר.

"**If it turns out etc.**" — כנ״ל מדברי החת״ס והטהרת ישראל.

לראות והרי צריך להסמיך את עשיית ההפס״ט לז״נ והביא ראיה מזה שכמה יגיעות נתייגעו רבותינו בענין לבישת לבנים והפסקת טהרה בתשעה באב ולא מצאנו חד מנייהו שיכתוב שאם פסקה לראות שתפסיק בטהרה, ש״מ שהקפידו רבותינו על כך לכתחילה, ע״כ, וע״ז באה תשובת החזו״א להתיר ביוצאה לדרך או באם חל חמישי שלה בט״ב וע״פ התוה״ש שמתיר כיו״ב באשה שיש לה חבורות ופצעים. ויל״ע דהרי כל מה שיש למנוע מלעשות הפס״ט בת״ב הוא רק משום הרחיצה, דאילו הבדיקה יכולה לעשות גם בת״ב וביוה״כ, וכיון דבלא״ה כבר פסקה ראיתה למה לא נימא לה דתקדים הרחיצה בלבד, ואת בדיקת ההפס״ט תסמיך לז״נ, ובמה שהזכיר החזו״א יוצאה לדרך, אולי איירי באמת בגוונא שלא תוכל גם לבדוק את בדיקת ההפס״ט בהיותה בדרך, אבל מש״כ כן גם באופן שיום חמישי שלה חל בת״ב צל״ע למה התיר להקדים גם את הבדיקה ולא חילק בין רחיצה לבדיקה, דרחיצה תקדים ואילו הבדיקה תסמיך לז״נ, וכנראה דעתו דהרחיצה וההפס״ט ראוי שיהיו סמוכים זאח״ז, וכשיש צורך להקדים הרחיצה ה״ה שיש להקדים את בדיקת ההפס״ט, וצל״ע.

ומ״מ גם מש״כ החזו״א לענין ת״ב, אין מפורש בדבריו דכן יש להורות לנהוג לכתחילה, אלא דכתב עצם הדין אם מותר להקדים, וכדכתב ד״יש להתיר״, ועל כן נראה דאף בחל חמישי שלה להיות בת״ב, אין לנהוג כן להקדים בדיקת הפס״ט תוך חמשה ימי ההמתנה, אלא תרחץ בת״ב פניה של מטה בלבד דהוי רחיצה שאינה של תענוג אלא רחיצה של מצוה דשרי בת״ב. משיעורי הגרמ״ש קליין שליט״א.

פרק חמישי

1. "must count seven clean days" — מימרא דר' זירא נדה ס"ו ע"א בנות ישראל החמירו על עצמן שאפילו רואות טיפת דם כחרדל יושבות עליה שבעה נקיים, ונפסק כן בשו"ע יו"ד סי' קפ"ג.

אם טעתה וספרה רק ששה ימים, וטבלה ושמשה ח"ו, ונזכרה למחרת, תמתין ארבעה ימים ואח"כ תספור יום אחד נקי ותבדוק בו כדין, [שו"ע ורמ"א סי' קצ"ו סע' י"ב וי"ג. ולמתבאר בתשובת רע"א ח"א — ע"ב בעינן שתדע שלא הרגישה פליטת ש"ז. ואם נודע טעותה רק כעבור שני ימים ויותר, ושמשה כמה ימים, תעשה שאלת חכם, דכיון שהיא פולטת יותר מה' ימים א"כ שמא מיקרי שיש יותר מה' ימים בין בדיקה לבדיקה, והבדיקה שעושה תוך זמן שהיא בחשש פולטת לא מהני לספירה, ועי' חכמ"א]. ויש להחמיר לבדוק ג"כ בכל יום מארבעה ימים אלו, ותחזור ותטבול. [דשמא יום אחד מהם אינה פולטת ואז צריכה בדיקה. ואם לא בדקה באחד מהימים שיש בהם חשש פולטת צ"ע בדיעבד, דהרי אם אכן לא פלטה בימים אלו הרי נמצא שאחד מימים אלו היה זה יום השביעי שלה, ונמצא שחסר לה בדיקת יום השביעי. ואולי אפשר להקל משום ס"ס, ספק דמהני בדיקת יום ראשון בלא שביעי כדעת הרבה ראשונים, ואת"ל דלא מהני שמא אין חסר כאן יום שביעי כיון שהיתה פולטת. אך גם אפשר דכיון דספק הוא אם היא פולטת א"כ אין כאן ספירה ודאית וע"כ אין אחד מימים אלו יכול להיות אף ספק יום השביעי, דספירה הוי דוקא בירור ודאי, (ולגבי ספק ראית דם פשיטא דבכי האי גוונא דלא מהני אלא ספירה ודאית, אך להנ"ל אפשר דכן הוא ג"כ במקום שיש חשש פולטת). אבל למעשה מטעם אחר צ"ע, דהרי יש ראשונים דלא ס"ל דין פולטת אלא לטהרות וכ"ד הרמב"ן שכשהיא הולכת פולטת הכל, ולהרמב"ם פולטת רק ג' ימים, וא"כ אפשר שיש לחוש לשיטות הנ"ל אי לאו דיש להקל משום ס"ס. [והטעם שכתב בחכמ"א שצריכה לבדוק בימים אלו כיון שהיא תוך ספירת ז"נ, צ"ע, דכיון דאינו עולה אי"צ בדיקה וכ"כ בשו"ת תפארת צבי מהגה"ק ר' צדוק הכהן מלובלין סי' י"ח]. אמנם בני עדות המזרח יכולים להקל שבאותו יום תשטוף היטב במים חמים באותו

פרק חמישי

1. "According to some opinions it is a good *minhag*" — השלה"ק בשער האותיות [הו"ד בפת"ש סי' קצ"ו ס"ק ד'] הצריך שתספור בפה, אך בפת"ש שם הביא בשם אחרונים דאין צריך, וכן מפורש בספר החינוך מצוה ש"ל [הו"ד בסד"ט שם ס"ק י"ח].

מקום לנקותו מש"ז, ותספור עוד יום אחד מלבד היום ששימשה בו, ותחזור ותטבול. ובלבד שיודעת בודאות שלא הרגישה פליטת ש"ז. והיות ובימינו קשה להבחין בהרגשות אלו, בני עדות המזרח המחמירין להמתין ארבעה ימים תבוא עליהם ברכה.

3. "She must check herself etc." — שו"ע סי' קצ"ו סע' ד'.

"after *minchah ketanah* etc." — כן הוא בלשונות הראשונים שהובאו בב"י סי' קצ"ו.

"She should also check etc." — הגהות רעק"א שם.

"her underwear" — שו"ע ורמ"א שם סע' ג', וחלוק היינו בגד הסמוך לגוף.

"when she removes it" — דסגי בכך לבדיקת החלוק, ואי"צ בדיקה ב"פ ביום כ"א על עצמה ולא על חלוקה, דבדיקת החלוק היינו כמו בדיקת העד לראות אם נמצא טהור, וא"כ כמו שאם תבדוק כל בדיקות ז"נ, ותעיין בהם רק ביום השביעי ותמצא אותם טהורים דפשיטא דטהורה וטובלת בו ביום, כך בדיקת החלוק יכול מן הדין להיות בסוף ז"נ, שאם נמצא נקי מכתמים טהורה, ורק אם פושטת החלוק ולובשת חלוק אחר אז צריכה לעיין ולראות אם אין כתם בבגד הראשון. הגרמ"ש קליין שליט"א בשיעוריו.

4. "If she did not etc." — שו"ע שם.

"she did not check herself on the first day etc." — עי' דגו"מ שם ופת"ש ס"ק ו' ז'.

5. "white sheet on her bed" — שם, ובחכמ"א כלל קי"ז סי' ח' הזכיר גם כרים וכסתות. ועיין מש"כ בזה בשיעורי שבה"ל שם אות ג'.

"she should at least be careful to wear etc." — כדעת המחבר שם.

"If, however etc." — תורת השלמים שם ס"ק ו'.

---

2. "Even if more than five days have elapsed" — טושו"ע סי' קצ"ו סע' ה' ובש"ך ס"ק ט'.

3. "If, however, she examined herself after *alos hashachar*" — עיין משנה מגילה כ' ע"ב, שיעורי שבט הלוי סי' קצ"ו סע' ד' אות ג'.

5. "Nevertheless, *bedi'eved* etc." — טהרת ישראל סע' כ"ד.

6. "for medical needs and the like etc." — הסכמת האחרונים, דלא כב״ח סי׳ קפ״ח שחושש שמראה הדם משתנה. ואפשר שגם הב״ח מיקל בשעת הדחק.
"swim in a pool" — כי עיקר החשש הוא במים חמים, וכן כיון שהולכת בבגד מהודק סמוך לגופה, אין המים נכנסים בכח.

7. "If she diverted her attention completely" — בשו״ת מעיל צדקה סי׳ ס״ג [הו״ד בסד״ט ס״ק י״ח ובפת״ש שם ס״ק ג׳] החמיר שסותרת לגמרי מנינה, ובשו״ת אמרי יושר ח״ס סי׳ ל״ד כתב שסותרת הימים שהסיחה דעתה, והמהרש״ם ח״ג סי׳ קי״ד היקל בזה לגמרי, ועיין בזה בשו״ת שבה״ל ח״ג סי׳ קכ״ג. ובשיעור הזמן שנחשב להיסח הדעת, בשבה״ל שם כתב דאין לחשוש אלא בעונה שלימה, ומכל מקום נראה שאף אם נחמיר בזה, איננה צריכה לעשות שוב הפסק טהרה, כיון שאין חשש מן הדין שראתה דם, אלא שהיסח הדעת הוא קלקול בדיני הספירה של ז״נ, וע״כ מהני ללא הפס״ט שנית. ועיין חכמ״א מש״כ בזה.
"she did not conclusively decide etc." — שו״ת שבה״ל שם.

---

6. "This refers only to a woman etc." — עיין סד״ט סי׳ קצ״ו ס״ק ט״ו ובדרכ״ת שם ס״ק ל״ט בשם שו״ת שם אריה.

7. "A woman checked herself on days one to six ... She checked herself on the first and second days etc." — שמאחר ובשני המקרים, בדקה את עצמה ביום השני של ז״נ, יכולה להחשיבו כיום הראשון, ואז כשבודקת ביום השמיני נחשב לבדיקת ראשון ושביעי המועילה בדיעבד.
אם בדקה בשביעי ביה״ש יש להקל שתטבול משום ס״ס, דשמא סגי בבדיקת ראשון לחוד וכדעת הרבה ראשונים ושמא אכן בדקה ביום השביעי, וכן הדין בבדיקה של ביה״ש של יום ראשון וביום השביעי בדקה ביום, דיש להקל. והרוצה להחמיר יחמיר לעצמו ולא לאחרים.
"She checked on the first day ... but checked again on one of the intermediate days ... she is forbidden to her husband" — תשו׳ נודע ביהודה יו״ד סי׳ קכ״ח שהובא בפת״ש סי׳ קצ״ו ס״ק ו׳ שכל שאין חמשה ימים בין בדיקה לבדיקה מהני, ולכן אם בדקה ביום הראשון, ובשלישי ובשמיני מהני. וכן אם בדקה ביום הראשון והרביעי וכיו״ב.
"but did not check herself at all during the other days ... She is forbidden to her husband, and must restart etc." — ותתחיל מחדש את ספירת ז״נ עי׳ שו״ע שם סע׳ ד׳ ובפת״ש ס״ק ו׳ וז׳ מש״כ בשם תשו׳ נו״ב וחת״ס.

8. "It is, however, proper etc." — מי נדה קו"א סי' קצ"ז.

פרק שישי

1. "According to *Torah* law etc." — רמב"ם הל' מקוואות פ"א ה"ב ושו"ע סי' קצ"ח סע' א'.

"or a single hair" — עירובין ד' ע"ב ורמב"ם שם ה"ז ושו"ע שם סע' א' וסע' מ'. שנאמר [ויקרא טו, טז] "ורחץ את כל בשרו במים" ודרשינן "את" הטפל לבשרו, דהיינו שערו.

"at the same time" — רמב"ם שם ה"ז ושו"ע שם סע' א', ומקורו מתו"כ הובא בב"י ובט"ז שם.

2. "If most of the body" — עירובין שם ורמב"ם שם סופ"א, והוא מהלכה למשה מסיני.

"or most of the hair" — הרמב"ם בפ"ב מהל' מקוואות הט"ו הביא ש"כזה

"if she already had relations" — שו"ת חת"ס יו"ד סי' קע"ח.

"(and check during those days)" — חכמת אדם כלל קי"ז דין י"ח.

8. "If for medical reasons etc." — אג"מ יו"ד ח"א סי' צ"ד וח"ג סי' נ"ז בד"ה ובזה.

10. "but we see that she continued to wear white underwear" — שיעורי שבה"ל סי' קצ"ו סע' ד' סוף אות ד'.

11. "However a *kallah* etc." — משום חשש דם חימוד. ואולי מסברא תצטרך גם ללבוש לבנים עד בעילת מצוה, אך צ"ע אם יש מקור לזה.

פרק שישי

2. "According to some opinions ... a loose item" — ואף באופן שהוא כל כך רפוי, וכגון שרשרת שעל ידה שהוא רפוי כל כך עד שמתגלגל על ידה מכאן לכאן שבזה אין חשש שמא הוא בגדר מהודק ומן הדין אינו חוצץ ואין חוששין לרפוי אטו שאינו רפוי, עי' תשו' דבר משה שציין הגרעק"א בסי' קצ"ח סע' כ"ג [הובא בגליון שו"ע רעק"א השלם שם], אפ"ה משום שיטת רבותיו של רש"י דס"ל דאף כשאינו מונע ביאת מים חוצץ, יש להחמיר להסירה קודם הטבילה, עי' רש"י שבת נ"ז ע"א, רמ"א סי' קצ"ח סע' ד', וע"ש שם בפת"ש.

הורו הגאונים" דהשיער חשוב כמקום בפנ"ע לענין חציצה, וכל שיש חציצה על רוב השיער והוא מקפיד הוי חציצה מדאורייתא, וברוב שיער ואינו מקפיד, או מיעוט שיער ומקפיד, הוי חציצה מדרבנן, דשיער נידון לעצמו. אבל הרמב"ם גופיה שם חולק ע"ז וכתב "ויראה לי ששערו של אדם כגופו הוא חשוב לענין טבילה ואינו כגוף בפני עצמו כדי שנאמר רוב השיער וכו'". ובר"ן בסוף פ"ב דשבועות כתב לבאר שיטת הגאונים "משמע דס"ל דכיון דאית לן תרי קראי חד לשערו וחד לבשרו, כל חד וחד באפי נפשיה הוא, רוב בשרו ואע"פ שאינו רוב שערו, או רוב שערו ואע"פ שאינו רוב גופו חוצץ", ובשיטת הרמב"ם כתב שם הר"ן "והוא ז"ל סובר שם דשערו ובשרו חד גופא הוא, ואפילו כל שערו קשור נימא נימא אינו חוצץ אא"כ יש בגופו דבר חוצץ שהוא משלים לרוב גופו". והראב"ד בהשג' שם מסכים עם הגאונים. וע"ע בריטב"א עירובין דף ד' שכתב דשיטת רש"י כהגאונים, וכ"כ בקרן אורה עירובין ופנ"י סוכה דף ו'. ועיין ב"י שהביא דכ"ה גם שיטת רבינו ירוחם כהגאונים, וכתב שגם הרא"ש סובר כהגאונים, וחזינן דעת רבים מהראשונים דס"ל כהגאונים, ועל כן פסק בשו"ע סי' קצ"ח סע' ה' כהגאונים. וע"ע בביאור הגר"א שם. - ובפרישה מסתפק אם כל מקום של כינוס שיער נידון לעצמו או כל שיער הגוף נדונים יחד כמקום בפנ"ע, ובתפארת למשה פשיטא ליה לדינא דלשיטת הגאונים לא זו בלבד ששיער הראש חשוב מקום בפנ"ע אלא ה"ה כל מקום של כינוס שיער חשיב כמקום בפנ"ע, [וביותר חידש שם דכמו כן צפרנים נידונים לעצמם, שג"כ נלמד מאותו פסוק דילפינן לדין חציצה בשיער, מאת בשרו ודדשינן את הטפל לשערו, וה"ה צפרנים, ולא עוד אלא שאף כל צפורן נדון בפנ"ע], אלא דבסד"ט ס"ק י"ז כתב דאין הכרע לזה אם כל מקום כינוס שיער נידון לעצמו. — ולכאורה יש לחלק בין הנידונים, דלענין שיער הראש אכן יש לחוש דנידון בפני עצמו הואיל ויש הרבה ראיות מהפוסקים כן, עיין ביאוה"ג בשו"ע סע' ה' ובסד"ט ס"ק י"ט בנידון דהפנ"מ באשה שחלתה ורפואתה ע"י פיזור סמים גורמים סיבוך השערות, דכתב שם הסד"ט דצריכה שעכ"פ רוב שערותיה לא יהיו קלועין דאז לא חייצי אלא מדרבנן, ומבואר דעתו דתליא ברוב שערות הראש בפנ"ע. ואף דהיה אפשר לפי"ז דה"ה שאר מקומות כינוס שיער נידונים בפנ"ע, מ"מ אין ראיה מפורשת מדבריהם אלא לגבי שיער הראש, וגם יעויין בגולות עיליות על מקוואות פ"ט מ"ב פסקא א' שהאריך להוכיח דהא דשיער נידון בפנ"ע הוא רק בשיער הראש. — והנה, בחכמת

אדם כלל קי"ט סוס"י ה' כתב דצ"ע אם לצרף שיטת הרמב"ם לספק ספיקא, ע"ש, ולענין דינא נראה דיותר יש להחמיר בזה בשיער הראש מבשאר מקומות כינוס שיער, שהרי כאמור לגבי שיער הראש יש כמה וכמה ראיות מהפוסקים דנקטו דנידון כמקום בפני עצמו, משא"כ בשאר מקומות כינוס שיער.

"According to rabbinic law" — עירובין שם, ורמב"ם שם פ"א הל' י"ב ושו"ע שם סע' א'.

3. "at some time or other ... or under some circumstances etc." — שו"ע סי' קצ"ח סע' א' וב"ח הו"ד בש"ך שם ס"ק א'. והמקור לזה הוא מטבעת שעליה דחוצצת וביאר הראב"ד הטעם משום דמסירתו לפעמים בשעת לישה, ומבואר דכל שמקפדת על הדבר לפעמים חשיב מקפיד וחוצץ.

ובדין זה דמקפדת לפעמים, יש כמה דרכים באחרונים, דהנה, בפתחי תשובה שם ס"ק א' הביא משו"ת זכרון יוסף חיו"ד סי' י' שכתב דדוקא דבר שיכולה ההקפדה להיות גם עכשיו, אבל אם לא שייך שתהא ההקפדה עכשיו, אינו חוצץ. ובזה ביאר הזכרו"י הא דכתב הראב"ד הטעם דטבעת חוצצת הואיל ומסירתו בשעת לישה דאין כונת הראב"ד דמחמת שמסירתו בזמן מן הזמנים ומקפדת על הדבר מיקרי גם עתה דבר המקפיד, דא"כ אמאי פסק המחבר שם בסע' י"ז דצבע שידיו

---

3. "According to some opinions every area where hair is located" — תפארת למשה הובא בסד"ט ס"ק י"ז, ועי' בפרישה שמסתפק בזה, ובסד"ט שם מסיים ולא ידעתי הכרע לזה, אבל בחכמ"א כלל קי"ט סי' ג' חושש לזה.

"it was not removed, one may be lenient" — עי' לעיל בשם הפרישה וסד"ט, ומהשו"ע סע' ו' מוכח דלא חיישינן לזה, דהא כתב דשער בית השחי הנדבק זב"ז מחמת זיעה אינו חוצץ וכן שער או"מ באיש ובפנויה אינו חוצץ, והטעם ע"ש בש"ך ס"ק ט' לפי שאין אדם מקפיד עליו, ולכאורה הא דין זה דשער בית השחי וכו' איירי אפילו כשיש חציצה ברוב או בכל שער מקום זה, ואפ"ה אינו חוצץ ולא אמרינן דכיון דבמקום כינוס שער זה הוי רובו או כולו שפיר חוצץ אף באינו מקפיד, ומוכח דאין כל מקום כינוס שער נידון לעצמו. ואף דלדעת התפאל"מ נוכל ליישב דהשו"ע איירי כשהחציצה היא רק על מיעוט שיער בית השחי ולכן תליא במקפיד ואינו מקפיד, אבל סתמא דהשו"ע דלא קאמר דאם הוא על רוב אחד מהמקומות הנ"ל חוצץ, משמע דבכל ענין אינו חוצץ ואפילו כשיש חציצה ברובו או בכולו. הגרמ"ש קליין שליט"א.

צבועות אינו חוצץ הואיל ודרך אומנותו בכך אינו מקפיד והרי בזמן מסויים הוא מקפיד עליו להסיר את זה כגון בער"ש ובערב יו"ט וא"כ אמאי לא חשיב מקפיד גם עתה, ועל כרחך דאין כונת הראב"ד לומר דכל שמסירתו ומקפדת עליו לפעמים חשיב מקפיד גם עתה, אלא כונתו דכל דבר שמקפדת עליו לפעמים וכגון טבעת שמסירתו בשעת לישה דסיבת ההקפדה יכולה להיות גם עתה שהרי אם תבוא ללוש עתה תסירנו, בזה הוא דאמרינן דאע"פ שאין בדעתה ללוש עתה מ"מ כיון שסיבת ההקפדה יכולה להיות עתה, חשיב מקפיד וחוצץ. משא"כ דבר שמקפדת רק לזמן מסויים ואין סיבת ההקפדה יכולה להיות עתה, לא חשיב מקפיד. וע"ע אג"מ יו"ד ח"א סי' צ"ז ענף א'. - אמנם בתשו' נו"ב קמא חיו"ד סי' ס"ד ובתשו' חת"ס חיו"ד סי' קצ"ב כתבו לגבי אשה שיש לה טבעת ברחמה דאם צריכה להוציאה בספירת ז"נ חשיב מקפיד דלא גרע מטבעת דחשיב מקפיד הואיל ומקפדת להסירה בשעת לישה, [וע"ש בדבריהם מש"כ בנידון בטבעת ואכ"מ], ומשמע מדבריהם דאף באופן שסיבת ההקפדה היא רק למחר נמי חשיב מקפיד, ואילו להזכרו"י יש לדון דההקפדה בעת ספירת ז"נ ובעת הטבילה לא חשיב מקפיד דאין סיבת ההקפדה שייכא עתה. וראה משנ"ת בזה עוד להלן במקורות וביאורים לסע' כ"א בדין תחבושת וגבס ורטיה שעל המכה, ובמקורות וביאורים לסע' ל"ט בדין חציצה בסתימות שבשיניים.

"**but most married women**" — שו"ע שם סע' א' שדרך רוב בנ"א קובע, ומסע' ו' מוכח שנקבע ע"פ רוב נשים נשואות, וכן מוכח לשון הב"י בענין זה שרוב הנשים הנשואות קובע.

"**And conversely etc.**" — ט"ז שם ס"ק ג' וש"ך שם ס"ק ב'.

.5 "**Notwithstanding the above etc.**" — רמ"א שם סע' א', גזירה אטו דברים החוצצים.

.5 "**the part ... that widens**" — ע"פ מש"כ בתשו' ר' מנחם עזרי' שהובא ברעק"א לסע' ז' דביהס"ת בחוטם וכו' היינו במקום שדרכו להיות מתגלה לפעמים, שיעורי שבה"ל לסי' קצ"ח סע' ז' אות ב'.

.6 "**If there is a medical reason etc.**" — ולפמשנ"ת דחלל הפנימי של האוזן דינו כמקום בלוע שאי"צ אפילו להיות ראוי לביאת מים, על כן בכה"ג שמסיבות רפואיות אסור שיכנסו מים באזנה, יכולה לטבול על ידי שתכניס בעומק האוזן צמר גפן טבול בשמן או

6. "It is not necessary, however etc." — קידושין כ"ה ע"א שנאמר ורחץ בשרו במים, מה בשרו מאבראי אף כל מאבראי.

"that are exposed only occasionally" — שו"ת ר' מנחם עזריה הו"ד בחי' רעק"א לסע' ז' שם, ועיין פתחי תשובה ס"ק ט"ז בשם הנו"ב.

"so that water could reach them" — נדה ס"ו ע"ב וקידושין שם, שו"ע סי' קצ"ח סע' כ"ד וכ"ה, ועי' מתני' מקוואות פ"ט מ"ג. ונחלקו הריטב"א עם התוס' שם אם הוא דין דאורייתא או דרבנן.

7. "body folds etc." — עיין לשון הגמ' בנדה שם ולשון הטור רס"י קצ"ט ושם בט"ז ס"ק א'.

"she immerses herself assuming a normal comfortable position" — עיין שו"ע סי' קצ"ח סע' ל"ה.

8. "Internal areas etc." — כנ"ל בסע' ו', ושו"ת ר' מנחם עזריה ופת"ש שם.

10. "A thick, liquid substance etc." — ראה להלן בסעיף הבא שדבר לח אינו חוצץ, והמקור לזה מהשו"ע סי' קצ"ח סע' י"ד וט"ו שלח אינו חוצץ. ובטעם הדבר נחלקו הראשונים, תוס' פירשו משום שהמים מחלחלים דרך הדבר הלח ובאים על הגוף, והמרדכי פירש משום שעל דבר לח אינה מקפדת. ולשני הטעמים, דבר לח שיש בו סמיכות חוצץ, לתוס', מחמת שהוא סמיך ואין המים מחלחלים, ולהמרדכי מחמת שעל דבר לח שיש בו סמיכות מקפדת שלא יהא

בטיפות אוזן שומניות, ועצה טובה שתכרוך חוט סביב הצמר גפן וימשך כלפי חוץ כדי שתוכל להוציאו אח"כ. שבה"ל ח"ב סי' ק"א ושיעורי שבה"ל לסע' ז' אות ב'.

8. "Even if she uses paint extensively etc." — דאף שאכן פחות רגילות להקפיד משאר נשים, מכל מקום כיון שבדרך כלל מקפדת על כך להסיר הצבע קודם שבת או כשהולכת לחתונה וכיו"ב, יש לחוש דנחשב כמקפיד לפעמים וכמו בטבעת שמסירה בשעת לישה דחשיב מקפיד.

"*Bedi'eved* etc." — דאף שרגילה להסיר הצבע כשהולכת לחתונה וכיו"ב, לא חשיב כמקפדת לפעמים, הואיל ואינו דבר הרגיל. אבל אם מקפדת להסיר הצבע לפני שבת, חשיב מקפדת לפעמים וחוצץ, ואף שעתה הוא יום חול, וכמשמעות הגרעק"א והחת"ס בדין טבעת שבאו"מ ודלא כהזכרון יוסף, וכנ"ל במקורות לסע' ב'.

עליה, וכשמקפדת חוצץ. ועיין רמ"א סע' י"ד דבמקפדת חוצץ אפילו בדבר לח, וכשיש בו סמיכות ודאי שמקפדת.

"This also applies to ointments" — ועיין ערוך השלחן שם סע' ל"ב דאף משחה שע"ג פצע חוצץ.

.11 "Even a non-dense wet substance ... if she minds its presence" רמ"א סע' י"ד דאפילו דבר לח אם מקפדת עליו חוצץ.

"If she immersed etc." — והספק הוא האם אפשר לסמוך על שיטת תוס' שדבר לח אינו חוצץ מחמת שהמים מחלחלים ועוברים דרכו ואין כאן חציצה, ולשיטתם אף שמקפדת על זה אינו מהווה חציצה. ומאחר דהוא תלוי לפי הענין אם החציצה היא על מיעוט גופה ותלוי גם במהות החציצה על כן תעשה שאלת חכם.

.13 "An effort must be made etc." — עיין שו"ע סי' קצ"ח סע' ט"ו וי"ז, ובימינו הכל מקפידים ע"ז.

"no actual substance is perceptible" — דבשו"ע סי' קצ"ח סע' י"ז איתא דצבע שצובעות הנשים על פניהן וידיהן ושער ראשן אינו חוצץ, ובראה"ש וכן ברשב"א בתוה"ב שהובאו בב"י איתא ב' טעמים בהא דאינו חוצץ, א' דהוא עשוי לנוי והוי כגוף האשה או כגוף השער, ב' שאין בו ממשות אלא חזותא בעלמא, ועי' ט"ז ס"ק י"ז וש"ך ס"ק כ"א. והנפק"מ בין הטעמים הוא א' בדבר שאין בו ממשות אלא חזותא בעלמא, אבל אינו עשוי לנוי, וב' בדבר שעשוי לנוי אבל יש בו ממשות. ובנידון דידן בסעיף זה לגבי חציצה בלכלוך של שאריות צבע וכדו',

---

.11 "even loosely worn chains, bracelets etc." — רמ"א סע' א' ופתחי תשובה שם ס"ק י"ג. וכנ"ל במקורות וביאורים להערה 2.

"the immersion is valid *bedi'eved*" — תוספתא הובא בר"ש מקואות פ"ט וטושו"ע שם סע' כ"ג ופת"ש שם ס"ק ד' וי"ג. ועיין חי' רעק"א בשם רמ"א באו"ח דאין אנו בקיאין לחלק בין רפוי לאינו רפוי.

.12 "If it is impossible to remove a ring etc." — שיעורי שבט הלוי לסע' כ"ג אות ו', ועיין פת"ש ס"ק י"ד בטבעת שאין מסירה לעולם אם חוצץ.

.13 "Hair coloring that is ruined etc." — ואף דהוה רק חזותא מ"מ אין מקילים מטעם זה ברוב השערות, ומיהו במיעוט השערות בדיעבד יש להקל.

הרי לא שייך הטעם שעשוי לנוי, אבל בכה״ג שהסירה הממשות ונשאר מראה צבוע מהם, שייך הטעם השני דחזותא בעלמא אינו חוצץ, וצל״ע אם סומכים על טעם זה בלבד להתיר חציצה בדבר שאינו עשוי לנוי והוא חזותא בעלמא. והנה, באמת טעמא דחזותא צריך ביאור, דלעולם גם דבר שיש בו חזותא הרי יש איזה שהוא מראה החוצץ בין הגוף למים ומעכב את המים מלבוא אל הגוף, וא״כ אמאי חזותא אינו חוצץ, וביותר, דבסדרי טהרה [בשיו״ט] ס״ק ל״ג מדייק מהשו״ע דאין סומכים להתיר משום חזותא בלבד, מדכתב בשו״ע שם ״וכן מי שהוא צובע וידיו צבועות אינו חוצץ״ וע״ש עוד ברמ״א, ומשמע דרק לגבי בעלי אומנות אלו הוא דלא הוי חציצה אבל אדם אחר שאינו צבע שפיר חוצץ ואע״פ דהוא רק חזותא, ומבואר בזה דלא סמכינן אטעמא דחזותא בלבד אלא בצירוף הטעם דהוא עשוי לנוי או בכה״ג שאינו מקפיד, ע״ש, ולכן הדעת נוטה דבכה״ג שההקפדה היא ודאית, יש לחוש יותר לחציצה, ואפשר דגם בטבלה ראוי שתסיר החציצה ותטבול שנית אם לא שמשה עדיין, אבל היכא דאין ההקפדה ודאית ואינו אלא חזותא בלבד, יש להקל, ועי׳ בינת אדם סי׳ י״ב (כ״א) שמוכיח דטעמא דחזותא סגי דלא ליהוי חציצה ואף שאינו עשוי לנוי, ועי׳ עוד שיעורי שבה״ל סי׳ קצ״ח סע׳ י״ז שתפס טעמא דחזותא לעיקר.

14. **"covers only a small part of the body ... even if it fits tightly etc."**
וכדין מיעוט שאינו מקפיד שאינו חוצץ אף מדרבנן, וכמבואר בשו״ע סי׳ קצ״ח סע׳ א׳. ותכשיטים כיון שעשויים לנוי, הרי אינה מקפדת עליהם. ואולם אין הטעם שאינו חוצץ מחמת שהוא עשוי לנוי וכדלהלן בסע׳ ט״ז, משום שההיתר של דבר העשוי לנוי שייך רק בדבר שמחמת שעשוי לנוי הרי הוא בטל לגוף, ונחשב כגופה או כשערה, וכמבואר ברשב״א שהובא בב״י [בדין של צבע שצובעות הנשים על פניהן וידיהן ושער ראשן], ש״הרי הוא כאילו הוא מגופו של שער וכבגד צבוע שאין הצבע כדבר נוסף וחוצץ אלא כעיקרו של בגד ואינו חוצץ״ ע״ש, וזה שייך רק בצבע וכיו״ב שעל הגוף ששייך לומר בהם שבטלים לגוף, משא״כ בתכשיטים שעל הגוף, אף שלנוי הם עשויים, מ״מ לא שייך בהם גדר של בטל לגוף. אלא שמכל מקום מאחר ולנוי הם עשויים הרי אינו מקפיד עליהם, וכאשר התכשיטים הם על מיעוט הגוף דינו כמיעוט שאינו מקפיד שמן הדין אינו חוצץ.

וכדין מיעוט שאינו — "Nevertheless, it should ideally be removed etc." מקפיד שמן הדין אינו חוצץ, ואעפ״כ לכתחילה יש להסירם קודם טבילה וכמו״ש הרמ״א שם בסע׳ א׳.

וכדין רובו שאינו מקפיד — "Jewelry that covers most of the body etc." שחוצץ מדרבנן, ולא מהני כאן טעם דעשוי לנוי וכמו שנתבאר לעיל בסמוך, ועל כן מדרבנן הוי חציצה גמורה ואם טבלה עם התכשיט לא עלתה לה טבילה, אלא אם כן התכשיט אינו מהודק וכדלהלן בתוספת טהרה בסע׳ הבא.

15. "sometimes remove the jewelry" — שו״ע שם סע׳ כ״ג ומקורו בתוספתא, והטעם איתא בראב״ד הו״ד בב״י שם ובט״ז ס״ק כ״ג.

"it is regarded as a *chatzitzah*" — וכמבואר לעיל בסעיף הקודם, דלגבי תכשיטים לא מהני הטעם דעשוי לנוי וכדלהלן בסע׳ הבא, דלא שייך בזה ביטול לגוף.

16. "Because hair dye etc." — שו״ע שם סע׳ י״ז, וכבר נתבאר לעיל במקורות לסע׳ י״ד, דבראשונים הובאו ב׳ טעמים בהא דצבע שצובעות הנשים אינו חוצץ, אי משום דעשוי לנוי ואי משום דאין בו ממשות אלא חזותא בעלמא. והנפק״מ בין הטעמים א׳ בדבר שאינו עשוי לנוי והוא חזותא בעלמא, ב׳ בדבר העשוי לנוי ויש בו ממשות. ולעיל שם נתבאר לענין הנפק״מ הא׳ בכה״ג שאינו עשוי לנוי והוא חזותא בעלמא שאם ההקפדה היא ודאית אין להקל ואע״פ דהוי חזותא בלבד, אבל לגבי הנפק״מ הב׳ בדבר שהוא עשוי לנוי ויש בו ממשות דלא שייך טעמא דחזותא,

---

15. "she should wet the wound with *mikvah* water etc." — דהדם שיצא חוץ למקום הפצע אינו חוצץ, די״ל דהדמים מקדמים, עיין סי׳ קצ״ח סע׳ כ״ח וסע׳ ל׳. ופנים מקום הפצע עצמו הרי הוא מקום בלוע, שאין הדם חוצץ, וכמבואר בכעי״ז בתשו׳ בית שלמה יו״ד ח״ב סי׳ י״ב דנקב הנעשה בבשר אדם ונכנס לתוך הנקב איזה דבר אם אינו נראה הוי בלוע ועפ״ז הקיל בנידונו בחור שבשיניים ע״ש, ואע״פ דגבי חץ התחוב בבשר צריך עכ״פ שלא יהא שוה לבשר [דבזה מסקנת הש״ך בס״ק ט״ז להקל אף אם הוא נראה מונח בבשר הפנימי אינו נראה מיקרי הואיל ואינו נראה בשוה לבשר ע״ש, וכן מסיק הסד״ט סוס״ק כ״ה], ועפ״ז באמת החמיר גם בתשו׳ בי״ש שם דצריך שעכ״פ בשוה לשיניים לא יהא נראה שום דבר, מ״מ כאן דמקום הפצע עתיד להתאחות ולא נשאר גלוי לאויר ולא יהא נראה לעין, אף שעתה הוא פתוח מחמת המכה עדיין דינו כבלוע, מהגרמ״ש קליין שליט״א. [וראה עוד אג״מ יו״ד ח״א סי׳ צ״ז ענף ד׳ בד״ה וצריך לתרץ].

אין מצוי נפקא מינה למעשה בזה, דמאחר שהוא עשוי לנוי הרי א"כ אינו מקפיד, וא"כ אם הוא על מיעוט גופה או על מיעוט שערה הא הוי מיעוט שאינו מקפיד דמן הדין אינו חוצץ, [ומסתבר דבזה ליכא החומרא של הרמ"א בסע' א' דלכתחילה יש להסיר אף מיעוט שאינו מקפיד, דלענין זה יש לסמוך על טעם דעשוי לנוי בלבד אף שיש בו ממשות], והנפק"מ למעשה היא רק בכה"ג שיש על רוב גופה או על רוב שערה דבר העשוי לנוי ויש בו ממשות, שהוא דבר שאינו שכיח כ"כ, ויל"ע. ועכ"פ אם הוא דבר העשוי לנוי ואין בו ממשות, אינו חוצץ אף אם הוא על כל גופה או על כל שערותיה.

17. "**Congealed blood etc.**" — שו"ע סי' קצ"ח סע' ט'.

"**This also applies ... has not completely congealed**" — שו"ע שם סע' ט"ז.

"**The bleeding ... close to the time of immersion etc.**" — עי' שו"ע שם סע' ט"ו דדם לח אינו חוצץ. ועיין לעיל ביסוד הטהרה סע' י' וי"א בענין חציצה בדבר לח, דכשמקפדת על זה חוצץ ואפילו אם אינו סמיך ועב, וה"נ בדם לח דבדרך כלל מקפדת על זה.

18. "**If a scab has formed etc.**" — עי' שו"ע סי' קצ"ח סע' ט', ושם בב"ח דלענין הלכה למעשה בכל ענין צריכה לחוף במים עד שיתרככו, דאין אנו בקיאין בין נתפשט חוץ לכנגד פי המכה ובין כנגד פי המכה, וכן אין לחלק בין מכה ממש לבין שרטה שריטות או יש לה חטטין בראשה ובגופה, וכן אין לחלק בין תוך ג' ימים לאחר ג' ימים אלא בריבדי דכוסילתא ממש.

---

18. "**she need not postpone the immersion**" — עיין כיו"ב בחכמ"א דבכלל קי"ט סע' י"ד כתב לענין שכחה ליטול צפורן אחת וטבלה כבר דבאפשר בקל לטבול שנית, תטבול שוב אף אם עבר הלילה, ע"ש, ואעפ"כ הקיל לגבי אם חל ליל טבילה בשבת ושכחה ליטול ציפורן אחת, שיכולה לטבול, ולא הצריך לדחות הטבילה למו"ש. ומבואר דעתו דאין דוחים הטבילה משום כך, ומה שהצריך טבילה אחרת [באם אפשר בקל] גם בכה"ג שעבר הלילה היינו כשבאה בשאלה לאחר שעבר הלילה, אבל אם עי"ז תצטרך לדחות הטבילה לא דחינן, ודו"ק. וא"כ ה"נ לענין יבלת י"ל כן. ולפ"ז ביבלת, אם נזכרה סמוך לטבילה, כיון דאינו בנקל להסירה ולטבול באותה לילה, על כן יש להקל.

"she must remove it" — הגה"ה בב"ח שם, שכן נהגו כמה מן הראשונים. ועיין ט"ז ס"ק י"ד.

"If the scab is difficult to remove etc." — עיין סד"ט ס"ק כ"ג בד"ה גם, דהעיקר כהמחבר דסגי בריכוך ואי"צ להסירו.

19. "A closed wound etc." — לא העור חוצץ דמחובר לגוף הוא, וגם אינו במצב שנחשב לדבר העומד ליקצוץ שחוצץ וכדלהלן בסעיפים הבאים, דאדרבה, בדרך כלל רצונה בדוקא שיהא שם העור דמיגן על הפצע או על מקום הכויה, [וכה"ג שרצונה שיהא שם בדוקא, אף בעומד לקצוץ אינו חוצץ, וכדמוכח בר"ן חולין ע"ג בדין של ידות הכלים, וכן מוכח בתשו׳ חת"ס חיו"ד סי׳ קצ"ה, ונתבארו הדברים בקונטרס בעניני חציצה מהגרמ"ש קליין שליט"א], והמוגלא או המים שבבועה נמי אינם חוצצים, דהוי בלוע.

---

19. "this should not be done etc." — כן צידד הגר"ש ואזנר שליט"א ע"פ תשו׳ חת"ס חיו"ד סי׳ רנ"ו בנדונו ע"ד ס"ת שנשתנה מראה הדיו לאחר הכתיבה ונהפך לאדמדם, אי כשרה או לא. וכתב שם דיש לחלק בין דיו שחור שנתקלקל, לבין דיו שיש חסרון בעיקר הדיו ומחמת כן סופו להתאדם, דבכה"ג שיש חסרון בעיקר הדיו אף אם תחלתו שחור ורק לבסוף נתאדם, מ"מ ס"ת כזה פסול מעיקרו אפילו מה שקראו בו בשחרוריתו, כי לא נכתב בדיו. ומוסיף שם דאין טעם הפסול משום כל העתיד להעשות כעשוי דמי [וכפי שהוא דעת הגר"ש קלוגר זצ"ל במכתבו אל החת"ס] דהתם פליגי בכל העומד לזרוק, לשרוף או לקצוץ, דהני כולהו מחוסרי מעשה ופליגי ביה תנאי, אבל הכא הענין בטבע הוא כך, ודומה לטריפות דהעומד ליטרף כטרוף דמי משום שכבר החל הנגף המכה שסוער והולך עד שעתיד להטרף ע"י נקב במקום שמטריף את הבהמה וכדו׳, וה"נ בנדון הדיו דמתחלה נעשה הצבע באופן זה, ולא מפני שעתיד אלא שכבר הוא כן, ואינו מחוסר שום מעשה ועל כן הוא פסול, עכתו"ד החת"ס. מעתה גם בנידון דידן דסופו של היבלת ליפול מאליה ע"י החומר ולא צריך לשום מעשה קציצה, על כן חמיר טפי משאר עומד לקצוץ, וחשיב כקצוץ כבר, [ואין לחלק בין אם עומד ליפול מחמת טבע דגוף או מחמת גורם אחר, דכן מוכח מדריסה שמחמת הארס גורם לנקוב בטבע ומטריף, ואף שהוא גורם חיצוני]. ומיהו יש לדון, דהא אין נידון הפוסקים בדין עומד לקצוץ האם חשיב באמת כקצוץ או לא, אלא פלוגתתם היא אפילו אי עומד לקצוץ חשיב כקצוץ, האם הוא חוצץ בטבילה או לא, וא"כ מה גריעותא יש בזה שעומד לקצוץ בטבע ותפול היבלת מאליה, וכל כי האי לכו"ע כקצוץ דמי, סו"ס עדיין לא נקצץ ומחובר לגוף, א"כ תליא בנידון הפו׳ אי עומד לקצוץ חוצץ בטבילה. אלא דמאידך יש לומר, דכי היכי

.20 "A splinter etc." — שו"ע שם סע' י"א וש"ך ס"ק ט"ז, ע"פ משנה סוף מקוואות. ובב"י מסתפק בפירוש נראה, והש"ך הכריע לקולא [כפי גירסת הסד"ט] ונראה דלכתחילה יש להחמיר, שכן הוא דעת כמה ראשונים שהובאו בב"י. וכ"ד התפארת למשה.

דבהחל לפרוש הוי חציצה שכבר נעשה מעשה של תחלת הקציצה, כך גם כאן דנתינת החומר הוי תחלת מעשה. ואפשר גם דגרע מהחל לפרוש, דבהחל לפרוש הא מצינו לרבוותא דס"ל דאינו חוצץ דסו"ס מחוסר מעשה קציצה, משא"כ כאן דאינו מחוסר מעשה קציצה כלל, ואפשר דכו"ע יודי דחוצץ. ועל כן עדיף שתטבול עם יבלת שעומדת ליקצץ דבזה הרי מעיקר הדין נקטינן דעומד לקצוץ אינו חוצץ [אף דלכתחילה חיישינן להראב"ן], דזה עדיף טפי מלטבול עם יבלת שכבר נתנה עליה חומר שגורם שתפול דבזה יש צד בהלכה לחוש דעומד לקצוץ שכזה חוצץ וכנ"ל. איברא דמלשון הט"ז משמע דגם זה אינו חוצץ דהא כתב דכל שלא נפרש עדיין כיון שלא נתגלה מעולם אינו חוצץ, ועדיין צל"ע. מהגרמ"ש קליין שליט"א.

.20 "If she ordinarily does not mind it etc." — כן מוכח בפוסקים. דאי לא תימא הכי נמצא דכל מיעוט שאינו מקפיד נמי חוצץ דלעולם חשיב מקפיד דהא מקפדת להסירה קודם טבילה וכמו"ש הרמ"א סי' קצ"ח סע' א' דלכתחילה יש להסיר גם מיעוט שאינו מקפיד, ועל כרחך דכל שמקפדת על כך משום ההנהגה לכתחילה שיש להסיר קודם הטבילה, לא חשיב מקפיד. ובלא"ה כל כי האי שההקפדה היא רק מחמת הטבילה אין נראה דחשיב מחמת זה לדבר המקפיד, וכיו"ב צידד בקובץ הערות מהג"ר אלחנן ווסרמן זצ"ל ליבמות ע"ח, ע"ש. ומצאתי כעין זה בברכי יוסף שנדפס בגליון השו"ע סי' קצ"ח סע' ו' לגבי מה שנוהגות נשים מעדות הספרדים לגלח שער בית הערוה קודם הטבילה, דבאדמת קודש ח"ב סי' י' כתב דאם לא הסירה השערות וטבלה צריכה טבילה אחרת, כיון דרגילות הנשים להקפיד על כך ובפרט שגם היא מקפדת ורגילה להסירן קודם הטבילה, ע"כ מיקרי מקפיד וחוצץ. ותמה ע"ז הברכ"י דאי"ז מיקרי מקפיד שהרי כל ימי טהרתה ובימי עיבורה אינה מקפדת ע"ז, ועל כן פסק להקל בדיעבד אם טבלה ולא הסירה, ע"ש. ומבואר מדבריו דכל שההקפדה היא רק לצורך הטבילה אינו חשיב מקפיד, דזהו שכתב שהרי כל ימי טהרתה ועיבורה אינן רגילות להסיר, דהיינו דמזה שאינן מקפידות להסיר השערות בשאר זמנים כי אם לפני הטבילה מוכח דההקפדה היא רק משום הטבילה וזה לא חשיב מקפיד, ודו"ק. ואפשר שגם האדמת קודש ס"ל הכי דכל שההקפדה היא רק משום הטבילה לא חשיב מקפיד, אלא דיעו"ש שכתב ב' טעמים למנהג זה להסיר שיער ביה"ע קודם הטבילה, אי משום שלא תתגנה על בעלה ואי משום הגמ' בגיטין ו' ע"ב נימא מצא באו"מ וכו' וע"ש ברש"י נימא מצא באו"מ ודרכן היה להשיר את השער ולא ליסכן את בועלה ליעשות כרות שפכה וכו' יעו"ש, ולב' טעמים אלו נמצא דההקפדה

21. "One may not immerse wearing a bandage etc." — וכדאיתא בשו"ע סי' קצ"ח סע' י' "רטיה שעל המכה חוצצת", וע"ש עוד בסע' כ"ג. ונתקשו הפו' בדין זה דרטיה, דלכאורה הא רוצה ברטיה וחפצה בה כדי לרפאות את המכה, ולמה לא יחשב כדבר שאינה מקפדת על זה. ואין לומר דכיון דרוב העולם מקפיד על זה וכללא הוא בדיני חציצה דכל שרוב העולם מקפידים אף שהיא אינה מקפדת חשיב מקפיד, דזה אינו, חדא, דהא לדעת הרמב"ם הגדרת מקפיד ואינו מקפיד תלוי בהקפדת האדם עצמו, וא"כ איך יתפרש לדידיה דין המשנה דרטיה שעל המכה חוצצת, הרי היא אינה מקפדת על כך, ואף לפ"מ דקיי"ל הלכתא דתליא גם בהקפדת רוב העולם והרי רוב העולם מקפידים על רטיה שעל המכה, אכתי תיקשי אמאי רטיה שעל המכה חוצצת, דהא כיו"ב מצינו בשו"ע שם סע' י"ז דצבע שידיו צבועות אינו חוצץ, דכיון שמלאכתו בכך אינו מקפיד על זה, וכיו"ב כתב שם הרמ"א דמי שאומנותו להיות שוחט או קצב וידיו תמיד מלוכלכות בדם אינו חוצץ, ומטעם הנ"ל דכיון שאומנותם בכך אינם מקפידים על זה ואינו חוצץ, ואע"פ דגם התם הא רוב העולם מקפידים על הצבע או על הדם, מ"מ חשיב אינו מקפיד הואיל ורוב בני אומנות זו אינם מקפידים וכ"ה ברמ"א שם, וא"כ ה"נ ברטיה שעל המכה

היא תמידית ולא רק משום הטבילה, ולכן שפיר חשיב מקפיד, משא"כ הברכי יוסף שהקשה על האדמת קודש דהא לא חשיב מקפיד מדחזינן דאינן רגילות להסיר בשאר זמנים בימי טהרתה ובימי עיבורה, משמע דס"ל דבאמת אין כאן הקפדה בעצם, וא"כ משמע דס"ל להברכ"י דאין טעם המנהג משום הטעמים שכתב האדמת קודש, ואפשר דס"ל להברכי יוסף דטעם המנהג הוא עפמש"כ הזוהר בכמה מקומות דצריכה אשה לאעברא שערא כד אתיא לאתדכאה ולאתחברא בבעלה, וכמובא בס' חופת חתנים בדיני חציצה הובא בדרכי תשובה סי' קצ"ח ס"ק צ"א, ולפי זה באמת הוי ההקפדה רק משום הטבילה כשבאה ליטהר לבעלה, ולכן לא חשיב מקפיד, ולעולם גם האדמת קודש מודה דהיכא דההקפדה היא רק משום הטבילה לא חשיב מקפיד. ועי' עוד בקונטרס בדין חציצה בדבר העומד לקצוץ מאת הגרמ"ש קליין שליט"א מה שביאר בדברי הרמ"א סי' קצ"ח סע' כ' בדין מנהג הנשים להסיר הצפרניים קודם טבילה אי חשיב מקפיד מחמת המנהג לקצוץ, ואכמ"ל. וראה עוד במנחת שלמה ח"ב סי' ע"ד מה שהאריך בשאלה זו. וראה עוד להלן במקורות וביאורים השייך להערה 24.

21. "If it is not too much bother etc." — עיין במקורות וביאורים להערה 18 משנ"ת לענין יבלת, ובעור קשה דיותר קל להסיר, יש לנהוג לכתחילה כדעת הפוסקים המחמירים בזה. אלא אם כן אי אפשר.

אי אפשר לומר הטעם דחוצץ משום דרוב העולם מקפידים על זה, דיש לומר דכל מי שיש לו מכה וצריך לרטיה אינו מקפיד על זה. וכדי ליישב זה יש באחרונים כמה דרכים. הדרך האחד, דמאחר דכל מה שרצונה בכך הוא מסיבת רפואה, לא נפיק מגדר של מקפיד, כיון דבאמת אין רצונה בכך אלא דמחמת הכרח סיבת הרפואה הוא דצריכה לכך. ודרך זה מבואר בחכמת אדם [בבינת אדם שער בית הנשים סי' י"ב (כא)], דהביא מש"כ הש"ך סי' קצ"ח ס"ק י"ד דכוחלת לרפואה חוצץ, ולמד משם החכמ"א דכל מה שהוא לרפואה וכגון רטיה וכדו' חשיב מקפיד דרצונה להסיר והסיבה שרוצה בכך היא סיבה צדדית דצריכה לרפואה אבל למעשה אינה רוצה בכך על כן חשיב מקפיד. הדרך השני, דמאחר שמסירתו לכשתתרפא המכה חשיב מקפיד, ואף שעתה אינה מקפדת על כך מ"מ הוי דומיא דטבעת שעליה שחוצצת וחשיב מקפיד הואיל ומקפדת להסירה בשעת לישה, וה"נ ברטיה שעתידה להסירה לכשתתרפא המכה, והיא דעת האבני נזר חיו"ד סי' רנ"ג, וס"ל להאבנ"ז דכיון דטעמא דדבר שאינו מקפיד אינו חוצץ משום דבטל לגוף א"כ כל דמסירתו לפעמים אין שייך לומר בזה דבטל לגוף ועל כן חוצץ. ומ"מ צידד שם להתיר בשעת הדחק דכיון דמיעוט המקפיד אינו אלא מדרבנן כל שאינה מסירתו אלא אחר חצי שנה, יש להקל דחשיב שבטל לגוף ואינו חוצץ, וכהא דכתב רבינו ירוחם לענין קשר של קיימא בשבת דכל שהוא לחצי שנה מיקרי קשר של קיימא.

וברטיה שעל המכה שהיא לזמן קצוב עד שתתרפא המכה, לכאורה היה מקום לדון להקל ע"פ מש"כ בשו"ע הרב או"ח הל' נט"י סי' קס"א סע' ו' בדין ריר היוצא מן המכה ומתייבש ונעשה גליד, שאם אינו מקפיד עליו להסירו או שמצטער להסירו קרוי אינו מקפיד ואינו חוצץ וכדביאר שם הטעם "שמעתה אין דעתו להסירו כל זמן שיהיה בענין זה" ע"ש, ומבואר דס"ל דמעיקר הדין כל כי האי שאין דעתו להסירו אלא לאחר שתתרפא המכה, לא חשיב מקפיד, ומשמע דסברתו היא, דזה שמקפדת להסירו לאחר שתתרפא המכה אי אפשר להחשיבו כהקפדה, דלכשתתרפא המכה הוא מצב חדש, וכיון שכל זמן שיש לה מכה אינה מקפדת, חשיב אינו מקפיד, והוא דלא כדעת האבנ"ז הנ"ל דס"ל דאף אם מסירתו רק לאחר שתתרפא המכה חשיב מקפיד. ועיין לעיל במקורות לסע' ג' שהובא דעת הנו"ב והחת"ס בדין אשה שיש לה טבעת באו"מ שמסירתו בז"נ ובשעת טבילה דחשיב מקפיד לפעמים וחוצצת, ומ"מ אין להוכיח מדבריהם דפליגי על סברת השו"ע הרב הנ"ל, דהנו"ב והחת"ס איירי

בהקפדה שבתוך הזמן שעדיין צריכה להטבעת אלא שצריכה להסירה משום ספירת ז"נ ומשום הטבילה, אבל בכה"ג כנידון השו"ע הרב דכל ההקפדה היא רק לאחר שתתרפא המכה, י"ל דגם הנו"ב והחת"ס יודו דכל כי האי לא חשיב מקפיד, דההקפדה שלאחר שתתרפא המכה היא לאחר שנשתנה מצב מסויים, אבל כל זמן שנשאר המצב של המכה אינה מקפדת כלל, וי"ל דגם להנו"ב והחת"ס לא חשיב מקפיד.

ולענין דינא אין להקל בזה, דבתשו' כתב סופר חיו"ד סי' צ"א האריך לצדד להקל בדין רטיה שהיא לג' חדשים וכואב לה כשמסירתו, דכל שאינה מסירתו לזמן מרובה לא חשיב מקפיד ובפרט מחמת דמצטערת בנטילתו, מ"מ במסקנתו לא סמך להקל על זה מחמת דבספר תשובה מאהבה ח"ג בגליון בסי' קצ"ח הורה בכיו"ב לאסור ע"פ הדין דרטיה שע"ג המכה חוצצת, ומביא שכן הורו שלשה מגאוני דורו ועל כן מסיק שם דכיון שכבר הורו זקנים אלו זצ"ל להחמיר חס לי להקל בהוראה שהחמירו בה גאוני קמאי וכו' יעו"ש, וגם השו"ע הרב דס"ל דמעיקר הדין כל שאינה מסירתו כל זמן שהמכה צריכה להגלד, חשיב אינו מקפיד, נמי לא סמך להקל בזה אלא בנט"י, וכתב "אף על פי שלטבילה מחמירין", ויש לזה יסוד בדברי הראשונים שהובאו בסד"ט סי' קצ"ח ס"ק כ"ג בד"ה ותו קשה לי ועע"ש ס"ק כ"ד שלטבילה מחמירים, ועוע"ש סוס"ק כ"ו, ומה גם דבדבר שהחציצה היא מחוץ לגופו חמיר טפי וכמו"ש הסד"ט, ואפשר דגם השו"ע הרב יסבור להחמיר בזה, על כן יש להחמיר שלא תטבול ברטיה שעל המכה אף שהוא לזמן ארוך. [ומיהו במקום שיש לחוש שיבוא לידי מכשול או בשאר אופני שעת הדחק גדול, יש צדדים להקל בזה וכנ"ל, ותשאל חכם].

22. "**self-dissolving stitches etc.**" — עיין שיעורי שבט הלוי סי' קצ"ח סע' י"א אות ג'.

---

22. "**and she is not sure if etc.**" — דסו"ס להט"ז סי' קצ"ח ס"ק כ"ב כל שלא נפרש ומחובר עדיין לגוף אינו חוצץ כי לא היה מגולה מעולם, ואף שעומד לקצוץ אינו חוצץ, ותו דלגי' כמה מהראשונים אבר ובשר המדולדלין אינו חוצצין, וגם דמאחר דעיינה בעצמה ולא מצאתו קודם טבילה ושכיח שע"י הרחיצה נעשה העור רך ומתקלף בנקל, קרוב לתלות שנעשה לאחר הטבילה ע"י הניגוב וכיו"ב, ועל כן אין להחמיר.

23. "**A bride who intends to shorten her hair etc.**" — עיין תשו' חת"ס חיו"ד סי' קצ"ה דאף דהוי אינו מקפיד מ"מ חושש לחציצה משום דהוי עומד ליקצוץ (ברוב שערות), ובנידונו התיר משום דהמנהג לקצוץ רק לאחר בעילת מצוה, והוי מחוסר מעשה דלא חשיב

.24 "Opinions differ etc." — עי' מתני' מקוואות פ"י מ"ה כל ידות הכלים שהן ארוכים ועתיד לקצוץ מטבילם עד מקום המדה וכו'. והקשו כל הראשונים דמ"מ ליהוי חציצה על מקום החתך דהא עומד ליקצוץ את היד, עי' ר"ש ורא"ש במתני' שם, תוס' חולין ע"ג ע"א, ר"ן רשב"א ומאירי חולין שם, ובעל התרומות הובא בב"י סי' ר"ב, ועיין בדבריהם מה שטרחו ליישב הטעם דבידות הכלים ל"ה חציצה על מקום

עומד לקצוץ, אבל כאשר יש בדעתה לקצר השערות קודם הטבילה לא שייך ההיתר הנ"ל.
"If she does not intend to shorten her hair etc." — דהוי מיעוט שאינו מקפיד.

.24 "Some *Ashkenazic* women etc." — עיין דרכי תשובה סי' קצ"ח סוף ס"ק צ"א. ונוהגים בגילוח או בקציצת השערות כדי שלא יראה שום שיער שלהם מחוץ לכיסוי הראש, וקובעים הזמן לזה קודם הטבילה, כ"נ בדרכ"ת שם.

"*Sephardic* women etc." — עיין בברכי יוסף שנדפס בגליון השו"ע סי' קצ"ח סע' ו' שהביא דבאדמת קודש ח"ב סי' י' כתב דאם לא הסירה השערות וטבלה צריכה טבילה אחרת, כיון דרגילות הנשים להקפיד על כך ובפרט שגם היא מקפדת ורגילה להסירן קודם הטבילה, ע"כ מיקרי מקפיד וחוצץ. ותמה ע"ז הברכ"י דאי"ז מיקרי מקפיד שהרי כל ימי טהרתה ובימי עיבורה אינה מקפדת ע"ז, ועל כן פסק להקל בדיעבד אם טבלה ולא הסירה, ע"ש. ויעויין שם באדמת קודש דבריש דבריו כתב לדון אי חוצץ משום דבר העומד לקצוץ, ולבסוף מסיק דמצד מה שעומד לקצוץ הוא שנוי במחלוקת אם חוצץ או לא, אבל מטעם אחר חוצץ משום דהוי דבר המקפיד. וכן העתיק הברכ"י בשמו דטעם הדבר שחוצץ משום דמקפיד. וצ"ב כוונתו, דמה שייך דין מקפיד שחוצץ בדבר שהוא מחובר לגוף, תינח אי הוה קאי עלה משום עומד לקצוץ, אבל האדמ"ק כתב דחוצץ משום מקפיד גרידא וזה צ"ב. ואף מטעם עומד לקצוץ נמי אינו חוצץ, והוא רק דין לכתחילה ואינו מעכב בדיעבד כי היכי דנימא דתחזור ותטבול [אף בעבר הלילה]. ותו, דאי הוי אמרינן דחוצץ משום שהוא דבר העומד לקצוץ, הא להפרישה דכל מקום כינוס שיער נידון לעצמו, א"כ אף באינו מקפיד נמי חוצץ, וכדין רובו שאינו מקפיד. ובעיקר מה שחלק עליו הברכ"י וכתב דבדיעבד אינו חוצץ ראה לעיל בתוספת טהרה לסע' כ"ח מש"כ בביאור דבריו, ובמה נחלקו האדמת קודש והברכ"י. והנה, יעו"ש בסוף דברי הברכי יוסף שמוכיח גם מהש"ך סי' קצ"ט ס"ק א' שכתב בדין חפיפה, דרק שער ראשה צריכה לסרק ואילו שער בית הערוה ושאר שיער שבגופה תפספס בידיה וסגי בהכי, ע"ש, הרי דאף שלא הסירה השערות עלתה לה הטבילה. וצ"ע ראיתו דהא בני אשכנז לא נהגו כלל להסיר שיער או"מ ושפיר כתב הש"ך דתפספס בידיה, וגם באדמת קודש בתשובתו שם הזכיר דמנהג הסרת שיער בני אשכנז לא נהגו בזה, ומה ראיה היא לנידונו לענין אותן שנוהגות להסיר.

החתך. ומדברי כולם שמעינן עכ״פ דדבר העומד לקצוץ הוי חציצה. ובאמת הראב״ן והסה״ת בשם התוס׳ כתבו דצפורן העומדת לקוץ חוצץ, על פי מתני׳ דידות הכלים.

אלא דיש מקום לדון ולחלק, דרק בידות הכלים שאינן מגוף הכלי אלא שמשמש לכלי ועל כן מה שאינו צריך לכלי ורוצה לקוץ אינו נקרא יד הכלי ומשו״ה הוי כקצוץ וחוצץ, משא״כ בדבר שהוא מחובר לגוף האדם אע״פ שרוצה לקוץ אותו מ״מ א״א לומר דכבר אינו כחלק מהגוף וחוצץ, ועי׳ במהרש״ם ח״ב סי׳ ע״ר שחילק כן.

והנפק״מ לדינא בזה הוא לגבי הדברים המחוברים לגוף האדם ועומדים ליקצוץ אם הם חוצצין בטבילה או לא, וכגון לענין צפורן ושיער וכן יבלת שעומד לקצוץ, דלהחילוק הנ״ל אין ראיה מידות הכלים דהוי חציצה. ובאמת אם נחלק כן יבואר היטב הא דכתבו הראשונים [ספר התרומה, הרא״ש, רבינו ירוחם, רשב״א בתוה״ב הר״ן הסמ״ג הובאו בב״י] בטעם המנהג של קציצת צפרנים קודם הטבילה משום חשש של טיט וצואה שתחת הציפורן ולא כתבו בטעם המנהג משום חשש של צפורן העומדת ליקצץ שחוצץ, די״ל דלדידהו עומד ליקצוץ אינו חוצץ, ואף דבידות הכלים העומדים ליקצוץ שפיר חוצץ אי לאו מהטעמים שכתבו הראשונים הנ״ל [אי משום דבביה״ס דכלים ל״ח לחציצה או משום אינו מקפיד וכו׳ כל חד מטעמא דילי׳], מ״מ בדברים המחוברים לגוף האדם אף שעומד לקצוץ אינו חוצץ.

וכן יש לבאר לפי פירוש השני בב״י בדין צפורן שפירשה מיעוטה ובדין אבר ובשר המדולדלין דחוצצין, דהב״י מפרש בפי׳ הב׳ דעומד ליקצוץ אינו חוצץ, והא דקתני חוצצת ואינה חוצצת היינו באם נמצא על הצפורן או על האבר והבשר המדולדלין דבר החוצץ, אבל הן עצמן אינן חוצצין, וכמ״כ צפורן גדולה העומדת לקצוץ ג״כ אינה חציצה לדרך זו, והיינו כנ״ל, דדבר שהוא מחובר לגוף אינו חוצץ אף שעומד לקצוץ.

אכן להדרך הראשון בב״י שם, כל העומד לקצוץ שפיר חוצץ, ומשו״ה אבר ובשר המדולדלין חוצצין, ורק בצפורן שפירשה רובה או צפורן גדולה שעומדת ליקצץ אינן חוצצין, משום דאינה מקפדת עליהם, ואה״נ אם נשאר בידה צפורן גדולה שמקפדת להסירה הר״ז חוצצת. ועל כרחך צ״ל דגם הראב״ן והסה״ת בשם התוס׳ דס״ל דעומד לקצוץ חוצץ היינו נמי בכה״ג שמקפדת על זה, אבל בלא זה הא מפורש במתני׳ גבי צפורן שפירשה דאינו חוצץ, וע״כ דרק באינה מקפדת אינו חוצץ, אבל במקפדת חוצץ, והיינו מה שהחמיר הראב״ן, דבעומד לקצוץ ומקפדת

חוצץ. ועי"ע בש"ך ס"ק כ"ז מש"כ בסו"ד, וע"כ כונתו כנ"ל ואכמ"ל.

אלא דמצינו עוד שיטה בזה, והיא שיטת המרדכי, דדבר המחובר לגוף והחל לפרוש מהגוף, שפיר אמרינן דדבר העומד ליקצוץ חוצץ. דגבי צפורן המדולדלת שפירשה מיעוטה דחוצצת וכן גבי אבר ובשר המדולדלין דחוצצים, פירש המרדכי הטעם משום שהצפורן החלה לפרוש וגם עומד לקצוץ לכן חוצץ. ועיין דרכי משה וב"ח שהסכימו עם המרדכי בזה. ומ"מ גם להמרדכי נמצא דבעלמא לא אמרינן דעומד לקצוץ חוצץ, ומשמע דהיינו אפילו במקפדת, וע"כ הטעם כנ"ל, דבמחובר לגוף כ"ז שלא קצצו הוי חלק מהגוף ואינו חוצץ אף שעומד לקצוץ, ורק בהחל לפרוש אמרינן דדבר העומד לקצוץ חוצץ.

והט"ז בס"ק כ"ב חולק על המרדכי בזה, ע"ש, ומבואר שם דעת הט"ז דעומד לקצוץ לא הוי חציצה ולכן בצפורן שפירשה מיעוטה אין שאר הצפורן המחוברת לגוף חוצצת מטעמא דעומד ליקצוץ, אלא טעמא דצפורן שפירשה מיעוטה חוצצת משום דבמקום שפירשה יש סדק דק שאין המים נכנסים לשם משא"כ פירשה רובה דהסדק רחב ע"כ אינו חוצץ, ובאבר ובשר המדולדלין היינו טעמא דחוצצין כיון דהאדם מקרב את האבר הקטוע על המקום המגולה כדי שלא יכאב לו, והוי חציצה במקום מגולה, וכעי"ז כתב הלבוש, ועי' סד"ט.

אמנם הב"ח והש"ך סי' קצ"ח ס"ק כ"ה חששו להחמיר בצפורן גדולה העומדת ליקצץ דהוי חציצה וע"פ שיטת הראב"ן וסה"ת בשם התוס' דס"ל דעומד ליקצוץ אף בדבר שהוא מגוף האדם הוי חציצה.

ונמצינו למידים מכל הנ"ל, ג' דרגות. א' דבר המחובר לגוף ועומד לקצוץ ואינה מקפדת על כך, דלא הוי חציצה, וכנ"ל מדברי הב"י בדרך הראשון, וכן צריך לומר גם לדעת הראב"ן דאל"כ הא מתני' מפורש דלא כותיה. וכ"כ בתשו' חת"ס חיו"ד סי' קצ"ה ע"ש היטב. ב' דבר המחובר לגוף ועומד לקצוץ, ומקפדת על כך, ולא החל לפרוש, דלדעת המחבר סע' כ' אינו חוצץ, ולהש"ך בשם הראב"ן כיון שמקפדת על כך ועומד לקצוץ, חוצץ. ג' דבר המחובר לגוף ועומד לקצוץ וכבר החל לפרוש [דבסתמא גם מקפדת על כך], דבזה מצינו שיטת המרדכי הדרכ"מ והב"ח דהוי חציצה.

[כל הנ"ל וכן מה שיתבאר בסעיפים הבאים ובמקורות, הוא ע"פ קונטרס בעניני חציצה בדבר העומד לקצוץ מאת הגרמ"ש קליין שליט"א, וע"ש עוד באריכות].

.25 "According to the lenient opinion etc. ... even according to the stringent opinion etc." — כנ"ל במקורות לסעיף הקודם.

"and most other women do not mind it etc." — ונראה פשוט, דרק לגבי אם נחשב למקפיד או לא הוא שתלוי הדבר הן בהקפדה דידה או בהקפדת רוב נשים, אבל לגבי דבר העומד לקצוץ, אין הדבר תלוי ברוב נשים, אלא בדידה, שכל שעומד לקצוץ אצלה הוי דבר העומד לקצוץ ותלוי בהדינים דלהלן, וכל שאצלה אינו עומד לקצוץ אף שאצל רוב נשים הוא עומד לקצוץ, נחשב לדבר שאינו עומד לקצוץ.

.26 "A wart ... since it is a part of the body" — רמ"א סי' קצ"ח סע' כ"ב.

"if she intends to remove it etc." — הנה, לכאורה היה מקום לדון דאע"פ שכתב הרמ"א גבי יבלת או יתרת שעל גופה דאינו חוצץ, מ"מ הא ברמ"א שם לא נתפרש להדיא דגם בעומד לקצוץ את היבלת אינו חוצץ, והיה אפשר לפרש דאה"נ בעומד לקצוץ שפיר חוצץ. אלא דשיטת הרמ"א דעומד לקצוץ כ"ז שלא פירש אינו חוצץ וכדעת המרדכי. אבל עכ"פ להש"ך וסייעתו בדין עומד לקצוץ דמן הדין אינו חוצץ אבל לכתחילה יש לחוש להראב"ן שחוצץ, א"כ ה"נ ביבלת העומדת ליקצץ יש לחוש דחוצץ. ואף דבלחו"ש פסק דיבלת או יתרת אף בכה"ג שעומדת ליקצץ אינה חוצצת, ולכאורה מקורו מהסמ"ג שהוא המקור לדין זה וכנ"ל, מ"מ להב"ח ולהש"ך ס"ק כ"ה [וע"ע בש"ך ס"ק כ"ז] והחת"ס בתשו' סי' קצ"ה דס"ל דיש לחוש לשיטת הראב"ן דעומד לקצוץ חוצץ א"כ ה"נ יבלת העומדת ליקצץ חוצצת. ואף דהש"ך בסע' כ"ב לא העיר כלום על דברי הרמ"א דאם היבלת עומדת ליקצוץ חוצץ, י"ל דהוא מכיון דהרמ"א לא כתב להדיא את דינו גם בעומד ליקצוץ, וביותר דהא הש"ך רצה לפרש גם בדברי הרמ"א גופיה דס"ל דבעומד לקצוץ חוצץ וכמו"ש הש"ך ס"ק כ"ה לענין צפורן דיש לחוש להראב"ן וכו' וכתב שם דזהו כעין מה שכתב הר"ב בהג"ה וכו', ע"ש.

אמנם בדיעבד אם כבר טבלה אינו חוצץ, דהא מעיקר הדין נקטינן דעומד לקצוץ אינו חוצץ, ועוד דיבלת קיל טפי משכחה ליטול צפורן, דבשכחה ליטול צפורן החמירו עליה לטבול שנית משום טיט ובצק שתחת הצפורן וכמו"ש הגש"ד ודרכ"מ, וזה לא שייך הכא. וכ"ה בשו"ת שבה"ל ח"ג סי' קכ"ז להקל בדיעבד.

.25 "may do so during *sefira* etc." — שיעורי שבה"ל סי' קצ"ח סע' כ' בט"ז ס"ק כ"א.

27. "A wart that has started to fall off" — דיש לחוש להמרדכי, ולהדרכ"מ והב"ח שהסכימו עם המרדכי, דבהחל לפרוש אמרינן דעומד לקצוץ חוצץ. ובפרט דהמקור לדין יבלת שכתב הרמ"א בסע' כ"א דאינו חוצץ, צויין ברמ"א שהוא מדברי הסמ"ג שהובא בב"י, ועי' ביאור הגר"א שכתב דמקור הסמ"ג הוא מאבר ובשר המדולדלין ש"אין חוצצין" והוא כגירסת הסמ"ג בתוספתא שם דאינו חוצץ ודלא כמחבר בסע' כ"א דאבר ובשר המדולדלין חוצצין, וא"כ לדידן דאבר ובשר המדולדלין חוצץ ה"ה די"ל דיבלת או יתרת שהחל ליפרד [דהיינו מדולדלין] דעומדים ליקצץ, שפיר חוצץ.

"she should immerse herself again etc." — שו"ע סי' קצ"ח סע' כ"א.

"If a night has passed etc." — ויש כמה צדדים להקל בזה, חדא דלדעת הט"ז סי' קצ"ח ס"ק כ"ב אין חציצה בדבר שעדיין מחובר לגוף ואף שעתיד לינטל מהגוף, ולכן בציפורן שפירשה כתב הט"ז דאין חציצה במה שנדבק עדיין כי לא היה מגולה מעולם, ומה שעומד לקצוץ לא משוי ליה לחציצה, ופירש הטעם דציפורן המדולדלת ואבר הבשר המדולדלין שחוצצין משום אותו חלק שכבר החל לידלדל דמקום הסדק הוא צר ואין המים נכנסים בו ע"ש בט"ז, וכעי"ז איתא בלבוש שהובא בסד"ט, ולשיטתם כל שנכנס מים במקום שנפרש, אינו חוצץ, וא"כ ה"ה בנדו"ד דאם נכנס מים במקום שהחל ליפרד להט"ז ולבוש אינו חוצץ. ותו, דבתוספתא דאבר ובשר המדולדלין [שהוא המקור לדין המחבר] מצינו גירסת הסמ"ג ועוד ראשונים שהובאו בב"י ובביאור הגר"א דאינו חוצץ, ולדידהו יבלת שהחל ליפרד מהגוף ג"כ אינו חוצץ. ואף דנקטינן הלכתא כהמחבר דחוצץ, מ"מ הא גבי צפורן שפירשה מיעוטה כתב בלחם ושמלה ס"ק כ"ב דבעבר הלילה יש להקל, ועל כן בשעת הדחק יש לצדד להקל בזה לפי ראות עיני המורה.

---

27. "On *Chol Ha'moed* etc." — שו"ע ורמ"א או"ח סי' תקל"ב סע' א'.

"During the *shloshim* etc." — מחלוקת השו"ע ורמ"א עם הט"ז יו"ד סוס"י ש"צ, וכתב הט"ז שהמנהג להקל. (ויש עוד אפשרות שתקצוץ עד קרוב לסוף באמצעות מספריים וכיו"ב, ואת הסוף תתלוש בידיה או בשיניה, ומ"מ כיון שעלולה לקלקל בכך דשמא כשתתלוש תפצע עצמה ויגרום חציצה נוספת של דם וכיו"ב, על כן אין לייעץ לעשות כן).

"However it is only necessary etc." — חכמת אדם כלל קי"ט סי' י"ב.

28. "Hardened or dry skin etc. If she did not etc." — שו"ת שבט הלוי ח"ג סי' קכ"ז.

29. "peeling skin etc." — וכדאיתא בשו"ע סי' קצ"ח סע' כ"ב דאבר ובשר המדולדלין חוצצין, וה"נ בקילופי עור אלו שנדלדלו דחוצצין. ועיין לעיל דדבר העומד לקצוץ והחל לפרוש יש לחוש משום חציצה וכמו"ש המרדכי ודעימיה. וע"ע שו"ת פני יהושע ח"ב סי' ל"ב שהחמיר בזה.

"A small area of peeling skin etc." — כנ"ל דבשו"ע סתם גבי אבר ובשר המדולדלין דחוצצין, ועל כן תחזור ותטבול.

---

29. "In all the cases mentioned etc." — כללו של דבר בכל הנך אופנים של דיעבד שיבוארו להלן, ע"פ כמה צדדי היתר שמצינו בפוסקים בדין צפורן שפירשה. (א) דבפירשה רובה דעת השו"ע דאינה חוצצת. וכ"ה לשיטת המרדכי דבפירשה רובה אמרינן רובו ככולו ואין חציצה במה שנשאר מחובר דהוי כמאן דליתא. (ב) אף דלהש"ך ס"ק כ"ז מחמרינן גם בפירשה רובה להצריך טבילה אחרת וע"פ הרמ"א בדין שכחה ליטול צפורן אחת שמצריך טבילה אחרת ובצירוף שיטת הראב"ן דהושש לעומד לקצוץ שחוצץ, מ"מ כשאי אפשר לטבול שנית אלא ע"י שדוחים הטבילה למחר, דעת החכמ"א להקל דכל שהעיכוב הוא רק מחמת מה שכתב הרמ"א בשכחה ליטול צפורן דמאחר שנהגו ליטול הצפרנים וכו' צריכה טבילה אחרת, או מטעם לכלוך שתחת הצפורן או מטעם דעומד לקצוץ ע"ש בש"ך ס"ק כ"ה, בכה"ג יש להקל שלא לדחות הטבילה משום כך, וה"נ כוותיה בצפורן שפירשה רובה בכה"ג שכל מה שיש להחמיר הוא ע"פ הרמ"א והראב"ן. (ג) דעת הט"ז דכל היכא דמיא עיילי ביה אינו חוצץ, וכעי"ז כתב הלבוש וכן נוטה החכמ"א, דזה צירוף גדול להקל בצפורן שפירשה כל שהוא רחב במקום החתך והמים נכנסים שם. (ד) ועוד יש צד היתר אחד גם בצפורן שפירשה מיעוטה, דאף דדעת השו"ע דחוצצת, מ"מ דעת הלחו"ש להקל בעבר הלילה שלא להצריך טבילה אחרת וע"פ שיטות ראשונים דצפורן המדולדלת שפירשה מיעוטה אינה חוצצת, אלא דקשה לסמוך על זה גרידא נגד דעת השו"ע, אבל בהצטרף שיטת הט"ז דלדידיה כן הוא גם שיטת השו"ע דבכה"ג שמקום החתך רחב ומיא עיילי ביה אינה חוצצת, יש לצרף גם שיטת הלחו"ש ולהתיר. וע"פ זה יבוארו פרטי הדינים שבסעיפים הבאים.

"If she already had relations etc ... If the night passed and she did not have relations with her husband etc." — דבפירשה רובה הא מדינא אינה חוצצת וכמבואר בשו"ע, וכדביארנו לעיל בסמוך, ואף לדעת הש"ך שחשש להחמיר בזה להצריכה טבילה אחרת, מ"מ אין להחמיר בזה יותר מבדין שכחה ליטול צפורן אחת,

“If she immersed herself etc.” — עיין חכמ״א שם שכתב לגבי חציצה בקילופי עור, דכיון שידוע שאין אדם מקפיד על קליפות אלו ואין דרך כלל לחתכן כי נושרין מאליהן, הוי מיעוט שאינו מקפיד דלכו״ע אינו חוצץ, ע״ש. ועל כן בקילופי עור קטנים שאינה מקפדת עליהם אינו חוצץ.

דבעבר הלילה מותרת, וה״נ כן. ואף בלא שמשה אלא שעבר הלילה או שהמקוה סגור ולא ניתן לטבול שוב באותה הלילה, נמי מותרת, וכן בליל שבת, דכאמור כיון דכל מאי מחמרינן גם בפירשה רובה הוא רק לחוש לדעת הש״ך שמחמיר בזה וכמו בשכחה ליטול צפורן, ומאחר דגם בשכחה צפורן נקטינן להקל שלא לדחות הטבילה וכמו שהקיל החכמ״א כיו״ב לענין ליל שבת וכנ״ל בסעיפים הקודמים, ולדעת המרדכי פירשה רובה אינה חוצצת דכמאן דליתא דמי, וכמ״כ לדעת הט״ז בפירשה רובה ומיא עיילי במקום החתך ליכא חציצה, על כן בעבר הלילה או שא״א לטבול שוב באותה הלילה יש לסמוך להקל שלא לדחות הטבילה, ובפרט שדעת הלחו״ש להקל בעבר הלילה אף בפירשה מיעוטה דסמכינן אשיטות הראשונים דאף פירשה מיעוטה אינה חוצצת, ועל כן בכה״ג יש לסמוך להקל שלא תצטרך טבילה אחרת ואי״צ לדחות הטבילה.

“This is so even if a small part of the nail is detached etc.” — דבזה הרי דעת השו״ע דחוצצת, מ״מ הא כאמור דעת הלחם ושמלה דבעבר הלילה יש לסמוך על שיטות הראשונים דצפורן המדולדלת אינה חוצצת בכל גווני, וכאמור, אף דקשה לסמוך על זה גרידא נגד השו״ע, ומ״מ בכה״ג שהוא רחב במקום החתך דאז לשיטת הט״ז ס״ק כ״ב אף דעת השו״ע להקל, על כן בכה״ג הוא דיש לסמוך להקל אף בפירשה מיעוטה.

“However, if only a small part of the nail is detached etc.” — וכמשנ״ת לעיל דאף דבפירשה רובה יש כמה צדדים להקל, דסו״ס דעת השו״ע שפירשה רובה אינה חוצצת, מ״מ בפירשה מיעוטה דדעת השו״ע דחוצצת, אין להקל וצריכה טבילה אחרת. ואף דלעיל גבי אשה ששכחה ליטול צפרניה סמכינן להקל בעבר הלילה אף שלא שמשה או בכה״ג שא״א לטבול שוב באותה הלילה, היינו דוקא התם דמדין השו״ע אינה חוצצת אלא דחיישינן לשיטת הראב״ן שמחמיר משום שעומד לקצוץ, ובזה מקילינן בדיעבד שלא לדחות הטבילה, אבל הכא דדעת השו״ע דחוצצת, אין להקל. [אמנם בשעת הדחק גדול, וכגון באשה שיש חשש מכשול אם תצטרך לדחות הטבילה, אפשר שיש להקל בזה דכאמור דעת הלחו״ש להקל בזה בעבר הלילה וע״פ דעת ראשונים דאף פירשה מיעוטה אינה חוצצת].

“If the immersion fell on Friday night ... she can be lenient in a case of pressing need etc.” — וכמשנ״ת לעיל, דבכה״ג שפירשה רובה דמפורש בשו״ע דאינה חוצצת, אלא דחיישינן למש״כ הש״ך וכנ״ל, וכי היכי דבשכחה ליטול צפורן דחיישינן

"**If a night passed etc.**" — דהא שיטת הט"ז סי' קצ"ח ס"ק כ"ב דטעמא דצפורן שפירשה מיעוטה ואבר ובשר המדולדלין חוצצין, משום מקום החתך של הצפורן או מקום שנפרדו האבר והבשר, דאילו המקום שעדיין מחובר כיון שלא היה מעולם מגולה אינו חוצץ, ורק המקום שנפרד חוצץ מחמת שב' חלקי הצפורן מהודקין או באבר ובשר המדולדלין דמהדקת האבר והבשר אליה כדי שלא יהיו תלויים ומופרדין מהגוף שאז יכאב לה הרבה, ואין המים יכולים לבוא למקום זה, ורק בצפורן שפירשה רובה דמתרחב מקום החתך הרבה הוא דליכא חציצה דמיא עיילי ביה, ע"ש בט"ז,

---

להראב"ן דצריכה טבילה אחרת ואפ"ה נקטינן דאין דוחים את הטבילה משום כך, וכנ"ל, א"כ ה"נ בפירשה רובה דחיישינן להחמיר וכנ"ל נמי יש להקל שלא לדחות הטבילה, ותטבול. ומ"מ אע"פ דלעיל לגבי שכחה ליטול צפורן נתבאר דיש להתיר גם שלא בשעת הדחק שלא תדחה הטבילה, מ"מ הכא גרע טפי, דהא להמהלך שמבואר בב"י בטעם דפירשה רובה אינה חוצצת משום דאין רגילות להקפיד, וכהיום הרגילות להקפיד על צפורן מדולדלת, דמפריע ומקפדת להסירה, ועל כן רק בשעת הדחק אפשר לסמוך להקל בזה ע"פ שיטת שאר הפוסקים.

"**she should lift etc.**" — ע"פ מש"כ הט"ז דהיינו טעמא דפירשה רובה אינה חוצצת, משום דמיא עיילי ביה, על כן תגביה מעט את הצפורן באצבעותיה כדי שיהיו המים נכנסים במקום החתך, דבזה לשיטת הט"ז אינו חוצץ.

"**However, if only a small part of the nail is detached etc.**" — דאף דלדעת הט"ז הא אפשר שתטבול ע"י שתגביה הצפורן מעט באצבעותיה, מ"מ יש להחמיר בזה הואיל ובפשטות שיטת השו"ע דפירשה מיעוטה חוצצת, [וגם לא מצינו לשום אחד מהפוסקים להקל גם בפירשה מיעוטה ע"י שתגביה מעט מהצפורן במקום החתך, ואפשר שהוא משום דאף להט"ז אין לסמוך על מה שתגביה מעט את הצפורן באצבעותיה, דהט"ז רק קאמר דבפירשה רובה סתמא דמילתא דאינו מהודק במקום החתך ואין לחוש שיהא מהודק ואילו בפירשה מיעוטה סתמא דמילתא דמהודק במקום החתך, אבל הא לא ס"ל להט"ז להתיר בפירשה מיעוטה שיועיל להגביה ולגרום שלא יהא מהודק, דיש סברא לומר דכל כי האי לא שרינן לסמוך על כך שתעשה היפך מהרגילות שהוא מהודק, ומצינו דגזרו שלא לטבול בדבר רפוי שעליה אטו אינו רפוי וק"ו בזה שהרגילות היא שיהא מהודק, ובפרט בכה"ג דהטבע הוא להיות מהודק דיותר יש מקום לחוש שמא לא תגביה כראוי וכדו', (וכעין מה דמצינו דאוחז באדם ובכלים ומטבילן טמאין ועי' בט"ז סי' קצ"ח ס"ק כ"ז בשם הרא"ה דה"ט משום דבאלו הוי הטבע לאחוז בכח ועל כן יש לחוש שתאחוז בכח והוי חציצה, ויש

וכעי"ז בלבוש. מעתה בקילופי עור גדולים נמי הוי כצפורן שפירשה רובה דמרוחקים מהגוף והמים יכולים לבוא שם, ונמצא דלהט"ז והלבוש ליכא חציצה בזה. ועיין גם בחכמת אדם כלל קי"ט סי' ט"ז שהקיל בזה וע"פ הט"ז. ותו, דדעת כמה ראשונים והובאו בביאור הגר"א, דאבר ובשר המדולדלין אינן חוצצין וגרסו כן בתוספתא, ע"ש, ועל כן לענין דיעבד בעבר הלילה יש להקל ואף בכה"ג שמקפדת על כך.

30. **"A blister etc."** — כנ"ל בסע' י"ט ובמקורות שם.

"or the skin etc." — ואף שהיה מקום לדון לפמש"כ הלבוש וכ"ה בסד"ט סי' קצ"ח ס"ק מ"א דצפורן עצמה שנפרדה מהבשר כיון שעומדת ליחתך חשיב מקום גלוי

לחלק), ואף דיש לומר דטעמא מאי לא נזכר היתר זה משום דהשו"ע והט"ז איירו לענין להתיר היכא דטבלה עם צפורן שפירשה מיעוטה ולא איירי בכה"ג שאנו צריכין לטבול לכתחילה כך, מ"מ הו"ל לאחד מהפו' להזכיר עצה זו דנפק"מ עכ"פ לענין ליל שבת שהוא דבר המצוי שאשה באה לטבילה בליל שבת ומצאה בידה צפורן שפירשה מיעוטה], ועל כן בצפורן שפירשה מיעוטה אין לסמוך להקל על מה שתגביה הצפורן מעט באצבעותיה. ואף דהלחו"ש הקיל בעבר הלילה אף בפירשה מיעוטה, מ"מ אין להקל לטבול כך לכתחילה, ואף שהוא ליל שבת וא"א בענין אחר, ותדחה הטבילה למו"ש. [אכן בשעת הדחק גדול, וכגון באשה שיש חשש מכשול אם תדחה הטבילה, יש להקל שתטבול ואף בפירשה מיעוטה, ותגביה מעט את הצפורן באצבעותיה וכמבואר כאן בסע' זה, דבזה יש לצרף גם את שיטות הראשונים דאף פירשה מיעוטה אינה חוצצת דמה"ט הקיל הלחו"ש בעבר הלילה אף בפירשה מיעוטה, וכך גם במקום שהוא שעת הדחק כזה, יש לצרף שיטות אלו להקל לטבול אף לכתחילה].

30. **"If she discovers on Friday night that most etc."** — דבפירשה רובה יש להקל שלא לדחות הטבילה וכמשנ"ת לעיל בסמוך ע"פ החכמ"א, ובפרט דבצפרני רגליה הא דעת החמו"ד להקל מחמת דאינה מקפדת, עיין במקורות לסעיף זה, ולכן יש להקל ע"י שתגביה את הצפורן התלויה באופן שמי המקוה יכנסו לשם, דבזה אתאן גם לדעת הט"ז דכל היכי דמיא עיילי ביה אינה חוצצת.

"If only a minority of the toenail is detached etc." — דבפירשה מיעוטה הא דעת השו"ע דחוצצת, על כן אין להקל אף על ידי שתגביה הצפורן באופן שהמים יכנסו לשם, דאף דהט"ז מפרש כן בשו"ע דהיינו טעמא דפירשה מיעוטה חוצצת משום דאין המים נכנסים לשם וא"כ באופן שתגביה כדי שהמים יכנסו לשם היה מקום לדון להקל, מ"מ הא נתבאר לעיל בסמוך דגם לדעת הט"ז צ"ע אם להקל בזה בפירשה מיעוטה, ותו, דהפשטות

וצריך ביאת מים שם, וכשחוזרת ומתהדקת על הבשר חוצצת, וה"ה הכא דהעור נפרד מהבשר וע"פ רוב עומד ליחתך לאחר זמן וא"כ ייחשב הבשר שתחתיו מקום גלוי וצריך שם ביאת מים, מ"מ י"ל דהיינו דוקא כשהיה כבר גלוי זמן מה וכנידון הלבוש, דבזה אף ששוב נדבק מ"מ דינו כגלוי, משא"כ הכא דמעולם לא היה מגולה לאויר העולם נשאר דינו כמקום בלוע. ובפרט שבדרך כלל חפיצה בעור זה שיהא לה לשמירה על מקום זה, משא"כ בנידון דהלבוש שכתב שם שהיתה חותכת את הצפורן מיד אילולי שממתנת לראות אם נתנוונן. ותו דלהגרעק"א בדו"ח כל שהוא לצורך רפואה אינו חוצץ, וע"ע בסד"ט בדין רטיה שעל המכה דאף להסוברים דכל לרפואה חוצץ מ"מ כשהדבר שהוא לרפואה הוא מגוף האשה מודו דאינו חוצץ. [ואה"נ גם בנידון דהלבוש אם יתברר ע"י רופא שיש תועלת להשאיר הציפורן לרפואה יש מקום להקל בזה].

31. "**Dandruff attached to the scalp etc.**" — דקשקשים המחוברים לעור הראש, הוי כגופה, ודבר שהוא מגוף האשה ואינו עומד לקצוץ אינו חוצץ בטבילה וכדלעיל בסע' כ"ג.

"**However if she ordinarily removes it etc.**" — וכדין דבר העומד לקצוץ וכנ"ל בסע' הקודמים.

בשיטת השו"ע הוא דלא כט"ז, עיין ב"י ובדברי המרדכי שהובא בב"י, ועי' דרכ"מ וב"ח שהסכימו עם המרדכי, ולדידהו פירשה מיעוטה חוצצת מחמת עצם הצפורן ולא מחמת דאין המים נכנסים במקום החתך. ואף שבלחו"ש הקיל בעבר הלילה אף בפירשה מיעוטה, מ"מ בנידו"ד בליל שבת דהנידון הוא לגבי להתיר לטבול לכתחילה אין לצרף שיטה זו להקל. [ובמקום צורך, יש לצדד להקל ע"פ שיטת הט"ז הנ"ל וע"פ הלחו"ש שהובא לעיל, ולהתיר לטבול גם בפירשה מיעוטה, ע"י שתגביה מעט הצפורן כדי שהמים יכנסו במקום החתך, ובפרט דבצפרני רגליה יש לדון דאינה מקפדת וכנ"ל ע"פ החמו"ד, והרי להדרך הראשון בב"י כל עיקר הטעם דפירשה מיעוטה חוצצת הוא משום דמקפדת, ואין שייך זה כל כך בצפרני רגליה, ועכ"פ יש לצרף סברא זו לשיטת הט"ז והלחו"ש ולהקל לטבול במקום צורך].

31. "**for a month from the time the tooth was filled**" — עיין לעיל מה שהשוו הפוסקים ביטול לגוף שבכאן לדין קשר של קיימא, וגם התם הרי הזמן מתחיל משעת עשית הקשר, ועיין שערי טבילה סי' ל"ד מו"מ בדין זה.

"**Nevertheless one should be particular etc.**" — דאף אי נידון כגופה מ"מ לא גרע מעומד לקצוץ שחוצץ. ובפרט דהכא גרע טפי דהוא דבר שמחוץ לגופה. ואף דמאידך הא הכא

"comb her hair carefully etc." — דאע"פ שבדרך כלל אינם דבוקים בשערות דלכן אף בכה"ג שמקפיד אינו חוצץ, מ"מ הא לכתחילה גזרינן אף רפוי אטו אינו רפוי וכדלעיל בסע' ב', אך בדיעבד אינו חוצץ וכדין דבר הרפוי שלכתחילה יש להסירו ובדיעבד אינו חוצץ. חכמ"א כלל קי"ט סוס"י ט"ז לענין דילדולי עור.

32. "A loose tooth etc." — עיין שו"ת אבני נזר חיו"ד סי' ר"ס שכתב דשן המתנדנדת אינה חוצצת, ודחה מה שרצה השואל לדון לדמותו לצפורן שפירשה מיעוטה שחוצצת דמי יוכל להבחין אם פירשה ברובה במקום חיבורה או מיעוטה דשמא פירשה מיעוטה וחוצצת וכו', ודעת האבנ"ז דאינו דומה לשם דשן תחוב בעומק תוך בית מושב השיניים ואף שמתנדנד מ"מ תחוב הוא בעומק וא"כ אין לחוש לביאת מים במקום החיבור דחשיב בלוע דאי"צ להיות אף ראוי לביאת מים. וע"ש עוד מש"כ להקל ע"פ הט"ז.

"A tooth ... must be pulled immediately etc." — דבאבנ"ז שם לא דן כלל מצד שהשן עומד לקצוץ, ובפשטות לא איירי בכה"ג שמחמת כאב וכיו"ב עומד לקצוץ מיד, ולכן אף דבאם אין דעתו להסירו באופן מידי אין לחוש משום חציצה ולא חשיב עומד לקצוץ, מ"מ בכה"ג שעומד לעקרה מיד יש לחוש לחציצה לדעת הפוסקים דעומד לקצוץ חוצץ. ומכיון דלאחר שיעקרו את השן נשאר מקומו גלוי, שוב אין כאן ההיתר של האבני נזר משום בלוע. משא"כ בעוד השן בפנים בטבע שפיר כתב האבנ"ז דהשקע הפנימי מיקרי מקום בלוע.

33. "Hair that is to be cut etc." — דיש לחוש להשיטות דעומד לקצוץ חוצץ. ואם מקפדת חוצץ אף במיעוט שערות שעומדת לקוצצן. ואם אינה מקפדת על זה, עכ"פ ברוב השערות יש לחוש דחוצץ, וכדמוכח בשו"ת חת"ס חיו"ד סי' קצ"ה. [ועיין באחרונים מה שכתבו לדון בפירוש "רוב ומיעוט" לגבי חציצה בשערות

עדיפא דגם עתה עדיין רוצה בכך ולפמ"ש הר"ן בחולין ע"ג בדין ידות הכלים העומד לקצצן דכל שרוצה בכך עד הקציצה לא חשיב מקפיד ואף שאח"כ מקפיד וה"נ נימא הכי דלעת עתה אינה מקפדת, מ"מ למעשה יש להחמיר בזה, ואם עומד להוציא אחרי יומיים או יותר, יש להקל.

33. "The same holds true for a bridge etc." — דבכל אלו כיון שהוא משמש לנוי אינו חוצץ. אלא דלכתחילה עדיף שיהא מונח למשך שבוע ימים וכנ"ל במקורות לסע' מ' דבזה אף בלא הסברא של נוי לדעת החלקת יואב הוי גדר של ביטול לגוף.

שקשורות זב"ז, דלכאורה החציצה היא רק במקום הקשר שהוא חלק קטן ביותר, והאיך יצוייר חציצה ברוב שיער. וכן יש לדון כיו"ב בנידו"ד לגבי חציצה בשיער מחמת שעומד לקצוץ, דהיכן הוא מקום החציצה, דאי במקום החתך הא הוי חלק קטן ביותר לגבי כל השיער, והאיך יצוייר חציצה ברוב שערות מחמת דינא דעומד לקצוץ. והנה, לענין קשר בשערות כתב באבנ"ז חיו"ד סי' רס"ג דאיירי שיש הרבה קשרים על כל שיער ושיער, וצל"ע דכיון דצד החיצוני שבקשר אין בו חציצה א"כ אכתי אין חציצה על רוב השיער, וגם לא שייך זה אלא לגבי חציצה של שערות קשורות ולא לנידו"ד בעומד לקצוץ. ובשפ"א סוכה ו' ע"ב כתב לגבי שערות קשורות דהחציצה היא כלפי הראש ולא כלפי השערות וכעי"ז כתב בתשו' משיבת נפש סי' י"ב, וגם זה צ"ב וכדהעיר בשיעורי שבה"ל סי' קצ"ח סע' ה' דהא ילפינן מאת הטפל לבשרו דהחציצה היא בגוף השערות ולא רק מצד הראש. ואכמ"ל].

ולענין דיעבד יל"ע, דלכאורה הא כאמור אם מקפדת על קציצת רוב שערות, א"כ להצד שחוצץ משום שעומד לקצוץ אתאן לחשש חציצה דאורייתא, דהא רובו ומקפיד חוצץ מה"ת. והנה, לענין צפרנים הא חזינן דמעיקר הדין נקטינן דעומד לקצוץ אינו חוצץ, ולכאורה יל"ע להאבנ"ז בסי' רנ"ט דס"ל דצפרנים נידון כמקום בפנ"ע לענין חציצה, וברובו המקפיד הוי מה"ת אף שלגבי שאר כל הגוף הוי מיעוט, ואפ"ה מעיקר הדין לא חיישינן לזה שדבר העומד לקצוץ חוצץ משום ספק דאורייתא, ורק לכתחילה חיישינן להכי, [ועיין עוד בסד"ט ס"ק ל"ט שכתב להקל בדין אשה ששכחה צפורן אחת וטבלה ושמשה, שאין להצריכה טבילה אחרת ודלא כש"ך שהחמיר בזה ע"פ הראב"ן, משום דהראב"ן יחיד נגד כל הפו', ומוסיף עוד דכל עיקרו אינו אלא מדרבנן דהא ליכא אלא במיעוט הגוף], וא"כ לכאורה ה"נ בנידו"ד אף אי רוב השערות עומדות ליקצץ נמי אינו חוצץ, ואע"פ דהוי רובו המקפיד, ולא חיישינן בזה לספק דאורייתא, דהעיקר לדינא דעומד ליקצוץ אינו חוצץ, ורק לכתחילה חיישינן לזה.

"Similarly, women who shave off their hair before immersion" — שיעורי שבה"ל סי' קצ"ח סע' כ' בט"ז ס"ק כ"א, וטעמו ע"פ מש"כ בתשו' חת"ס שם בטעם דשער כלות העומדות ליקצוץ דאינו חוצץ הואיל והמנהג לקצוץ רק לאחר בעי"מ ומחוסר מעשה הוא, ע"ש, ומבואר דכל שאינו מחוסר מעשה ועומד לקצוץ וכגון שרגילה לעשות כן בקביעות, שפיר חוצץ. ועיין שו"ת שבה"ל ח"ד סי' ק"ט. אמנם

לענין דיעבד יש לדון דאינו חוצץ הואיל דכל ההקפדה היא רק מחמת הטבילה, וזה לא חשיב מקפיד, וכדלעיל במקורות וביאורים להערה 20 עיין שם.

"their hair ... pubic hair" — ראה מקורות וביאורים השייך להערה 24 וכן לעיל בהערה 20.

34. "to cut their fingernails and toenails" — מנהג זה הובא בראשונים ובטושו"ע סי' קצ"ח סע' י"ח וסע' כ' וברמ"א שם. וכמה טעמים מצינו בזה. דמלשון הטור סי' קצ"ח, הרשב"א, הרא"ש, הר"ן ורבינו ירוחם משמע דהחשש הוא מחמת צואה שתחת הצפורן דבזה יש חילוק דשלא כנגד הבשר חוצץ וכנגד הבשר אינו חוצץ, ולכן כתבו דמחמת שאינן יכולות לכוון מה נקרא כנגד הבשר או שלא כנגדו, על כן נהגו ליטול הצפרנים בשעת טבילה, ע"ש בדבריהם, ומדכתבו הטעם משום שאינן יכולות לכוון מה נקרא כנגד הבשר וכו', משמע דהחשש הוא משום צואה שתחת הצפורן, דאילו הוי החשש משום טיט ובצק שתחת הצפורן הרי בזה אין נפק"מ בין אם הוא כנגד הבשר או שלא כנגדו דבכל ענין חוצץ. — אך לא כן מפורש בדברי הסמ"ג וספר התרומה והמרדכי בסי' תשמ"ז דכתבו להדיא דהטעם שנהגו הנשים ליטול צפרניהן קודם טבילה הוא מפני חששא של טיט ובצק שתחת הצפורן, ע"כ. והיינו דהחשש הוא משום טיט ובצק שתחת הצפורן שחוצץ גם בחלק שכנגד הבשר כמבואר בשו"ע סי' קצ"ח סע' י"ח, משו"ה נהגו לחתוך הצפורן. ועיין לעיל במקורות וביאורים לסע' כ"ד דכמה ראשונים ס"ל דעומד לקצוץ חוצץ, ועיין מש"כ בב"ח [וכ"מ בש"ך ס"ק כ"ה במש"כ בפירוש דברי הרמ"א] דלהני ראשונים דס"ל דעומד לקצוץ חוצץ, לדידהו הוי טעם מנהג קציצת צפרנים משום חשש של דבר העומד לקצוץ. וראה להלן בסע' הבא הנפק"מ בין הטעמים.

35. "if her fingernails are no longer than the end of her fingers etc." הנה, מעיקר הדין לא היתה צריכה טבילה שנית, אלא דבהגש"ד כתב דהמנהג לחזור ולטבול מחשש לכלוך תחת הצפורן, דא"א לנקר יפה, והיינו אף באופן שכבר טבלה ולא נטלה הצפורן, ועל כן בנידון דידן לכתחילה תחזור ותטבול. והנה, יעויין לעיל בסע' הקודם משנ"ת דמצינו כמה טעמים במנהג נטילת הצפרנים, והנפק"מ בין הטעמים הוא במשנ"ת כאן בסע' זה בשכחה ליטול הצפרנים. דלטעם הרשב"א הטור ודעימיה, אע"פ דלמעשה נהגו לחתוך כל הצפורן גם מה שכנגד הבשר, מ"מ

מחמת עיקר טעם המנהג הי' סגי שתחתוך הצפורן רק באופן שלא יהא ספק אם הנשאר הוא מהעודף על הבשר או לא, וכל שבודאי חתך כל מה שעודף מכנגד הבשר, סגי. משא"כ לטעם המרדכי ודעימיה, אכן משום עיקר המנהג צריכה לחתוך כל הצפורן אף מה שכנגד הבשר, כיון דהחשש הוא משום טיט ובצק שתחת הצפורן, והרי טיט ובצק שתחת הצפורן אף מה שכנגד הבשר חוצץ. ונמצא דנפק"מ לדינא לענין דיעבד אם שכחה ליטול צפורן ואינו ארוך יותר מכנגד הבשר, דלטעם הטור ודעימיה דטעם המנהג הוא מפני שאינן יכולות לכוין וכו', בכה"ג ודאי שלפי עיקר יסוד המנהג אין צריך לחוש יותר, אבל לטעם המרדכי דהחשש הוא משום בצק שנשאר תחת הצפורן, עדיין צריכה לקצוץ גם החלק הנשאר עד מקום חיבורו לבשר ובלא"ה לא יצאה יד"ח עיקר המנהג. וכיון דמשמע בשו"ע סע' י"ח דעיקר המנהג לחתוך צפרנים הוא משום לכלוך הנמצא שלא כנגד הבשר, וכדעת הטור הרשב"א ודעימיה, לכן כשהדבר הוא ודאי שאינן ארוכות אלא כנגד בשר האצבע ואין שום לכלוך תחת החלק הנשאר, בדיעבד יש להקל, דאף שכתב בשע"ד דטוב לטבול שנית, מ"מ בכה"ג שאינה ארוכה יותר מכנגד הבשר, אפשר לסמוך על דעת הטור ודעימיה דבכה"ג אינו בכלל המנהג ואי"צ לטבול שנית. ולהטעם שכתב הב"ח משום חשש של עומד לקצוץ, נמי י"ל דבכה"ג אין הרגילות אצל הנשים להיות עומד לקצוץ, ועל כן אינה חוזרת לטבול שנית.

"**and they are free of dirt**" — ז"ל החכמת אדם (שם סוף סע' י"ד) ואם מסופקת אם היה נקי ועכשיו הוא נקי גם בזה סמכינן לקולא.

"**she should cut them and immerse again**" — רמ"א סי' קצ"ח סע' כ' וז"ל "דמאחר דכבר נהגו ליטול הצפרנים אפילו אם צפורן אחת נשאר בידה וטבלה צריכה טבילה אחרת וכן נוהגים".

"**or the *mikvah* has closed etc.**" — עיין חכמת אדם דבכלל קי"ט סע' י"ד כתב לענין שכחה ליטול צפורן אחת וטבלה כבר דבאפשר בקל לטבול שנית, תטבול שוב אף אם עבר הלילה, ע"ש, ואעפ"כ הקיל לגבי אם חל ליל טבילה בשבת ושכחה ליטול ציפורן אחת, שיכולה לטבול, ולא הצריך לדחות הטבילה למו"ש. ומבואר דעתו דאין דוחים הטבילה משום כך, ומה שהצריך טבילה אחרת [באם אפשר בקל] גם בכה"ג שעבר הלילה היינו כשבאה בשאלה לאחר שעבר הלילה, אבל אם עי"ז תצטרך לדחות הטבילה לא דחינן, ודו"ק. ועל כן כשהמקוה סגור אין

דוחים הטבילה ומותרת.]ואולי כוונת החכ"א דדוקא בליל שבת דקודם הטבילה בודקת צפרניה יפה ע"כ יכולה לטבול, אבל אם שכחה ליטול צפרניה שלא בדקה יפה ואפשר שהיה שם לכלוך ע"כ אם אפשר בקל תטבול שנית, ולפ"ז י"ל שאין להתיר אם שכחה ליטול צפרניה כשלא בדקה יפה קודם הטבילה, מ"מ מסתברא דכיון דלהלכה פוסקים כשיטת הט"ז וסייעתו להתיר אם שכחה ליטול צפרניה בעבר הלילה אף שלא בדקה יפה, א"כ אם אינה יכולה לטבול שנית ויעבור הלילה, הרי מותרת, יש להתירה גם קודם עבר הלילה, ובפרט בנשי דידן שאינן מתעסקות בטיט או בבצק יש להקל יותר[.

"**If her immersion falls on Friday night etc.**" — ע"פ חכמ"א כלל קי"ט סע' ט"ו.

"**she forgot to cut her nails**" — בין אם שכחה צפורן אחת ובין אם שכחה ליטול כל צפרניה, כן משמע בפוסקים ומשנ"ב סי' ש"מ ס"ק ג'. ומה שכתב החכמ"א צפורן אחת או שתים [והוא ע"פ סד"ט סי' קצ"ח ס"ק ל"ט בד"ה ומה שהשיג] אפשר משום דחששו דאם שכחה ליטול כל צפרניה א"א שלא יהא באחת מהן טיט או צואה, ונראה דבמקומות שאין רגילות לעסוק בעבודות של טיט וצואה וכו' [כגון הדרים בעיר] אין לחשוש כל כך לטיט וצואה.

"**toenails**" — פתחי תשובה שם ס"ק י' בשם חמודי דניאל.

"**if she already had relations ... or the night passed**" — דבמש"כ הרמ"א דצריכה טבילה אחרת וכנ"ל פירש בשו"ת מהר"ם לובלין הובא בש"ך שם ס"ק כ"ה וט"ז שם ס"ק כ"א דהיינו בלא עבר הלילה. והש"ך שם ס"ק כ"ה כתב להחמיר לטבול שנית אף בעבר הלילה ושמשה, היכא דאפשר. אמנם בסד"ט ס"ק ל"ט פסק כהט"ז, וכן מצדד להלכה בשיעורי שבה"ל.

36. "**part of the nail is detached and hanging etc.**" — הנה, בשו"ע סי' קצ"ח סע' כ"א פסק דצפורן המדולדלת שפירשה מיעוטה חוצצת פירשה רובה אינה חוצצת. ומצינו כמה דרכים בביאור החילוק שבין פירשה מיעוטה לבין פירשה רובה. **הדרך האחד כתב הב"י**, דבפירשה מיעוטה מקפדת על זה ואתאן לדינא דכל העומד לקצוץ חוצץ, משא"כ בפירשה רובה אינה מקפדת על זה וגם רוב הנשים אינן מקפידות ע"ז לכן אף שעומד לקצוץ אינו חוצץ. **הדרך השני כתב הב"י**, דפירשה מיעוטה חשיבה מחוברת לגוף ועל כן אם יש עליה דבר החוצץ הוי חציצה, משא"כ

בפירשה רובה כבר אינה נחשבת מהגוף ועל כן אם נמצא עליה דבר החוצץ לא הוי חציצה. ולעולם כל העומד לקצוץ אינו חוצץ במקום החיבור. **הדרך השלישי**, הוא מה שכתב המרדכי והובא בב"י, דפירשה רובה אינה חוצצת משום דרובה ככולה, והוי כמאן דליתא, אבל בפירשה מיעוטה ועומדת לפרוש חוצצת, וס"ל להמרדכי דבעלמא בלא החל לפרוש אף אם עומד לקצוץ אינו חוצץ, הואיל והוא מחובר לגוף האדם וכחלק ממנו לא משוי ליה חציצה, אבל בהחל לפרוש שפיר חוצץ, דבזה שפיר אמרינן כל העומד לקצוץ כקצוץ וחוצץ, ולזה הסכימו הדרכי משה והב"ח. **הדרך הרביעי**, הוא דעת הט"ז בס"ק כ"ב דלעולם כל העומד לקצוץ אינו חוצץ במקום החיבור, ורק בהחל לפרוש הוי חציצה במקום החתך, דהצפורן שנפרדה אם היא מהודקת במקום החתך לחלק הצפורן המחוברת, הוי חציצה במקום זה, וזהו החילוק שבין פירשה מיעוטה לפירשה רובה, דבפירשה מיעוטה איכא סדק דק שאין המים נכנסים שם וחוצץ, משא"כ פירשה רובה דהסדק הוא רחב ומים נכנסים שם, וכעי"ז כתב הלבוש וכן נוטה דעת החכמ"א.

"**she must remove it before immersion**" — דבפירשה מיעוטה מפורש בשו"ע דחוצצת וכנ"ל ופשיטא דצריכה להסיר חלק הצפורן שנפרדה, ואף אם פירשה רובה דמבואר בשו"ע דאינה חוצצת וכנ"ל, מ"מ לענין לכתחילה שפיר צריכה לקצוץ ולהסיר את החלק שהוא תלוי, וכמו"ש הש"ך בס"ק כ"ז דלדידן דבשכחה ליטול צפורן צריכה לטבול שנית ה"נ בזה, וכ"ש להטעם דעומד לקצוץ חוצץ, ע"ש. ובפרט דלהדרך הראשון בב"י דפירשה מיעוטה חוצצת משום דמקפדת משא"כ בפירשה רובה דאינה מקפדת, ולפי זה הרי נמצא דכל שמקפדת שפיר חוצץ גם בפירשה רובה. [ובאמת יל"ע בדברי הב"י במש"כ דפירשה רובה אינה מקפדת, דבגמ' שבת צ"ד ע"ב מבואר דצפורן שפירשה וקרובה לינתק התירו ליטלה ביד משום שמצער אותו, וחזינן דבסתמא הוי גדר של מקפיד, וצל"ע. ואף דגבי שבת לא מחלקינן בין רוב ומיעוט, אלא אף בפירשה רובה לא הוי צער אלא בכה"ג שקרוב לינתק וכמבואר שם ברש"י, אבל מ"מ חזינן מיהא דבפירשה רובה וקרובה לינתק הוי דבר שמצערה ובודאי חשיב מקפיד, וכאן לא מחלקינן בזה כלל, וצ"ע]. ואפשר דלזה נתכוין הש"ך במש"כ בצפורן שפירשה רובה דלדידן דנוהגים להצריכה טבילה אחרת אם לא חתכה הצפורן ה"ה הכא וכו' ומסיים ד"כ"ש להטעם דהצפורן גופיה מעכב", דבפשוטו צ"ב בדבריו, דמשמעות דבריו דלהראב"ן יהא הדין דצפורן שפירשה

רובה חוצצת משום דעומד לקצוץ, והרי משנה מפורשת היא דצפורן המדולדלת שפירשה רובה אינה חוצצת, ולכאורה כונת הש"ך מתפרשת רק לפי הדרך הראשון בב"י דפירשה רובה אינה חוצצת משום דאינה מקפדת, ולזה כתב הש"ך דמאחר דלדידן נוהגים להסיר הצפורן קודם הטבילה, והיינו דחיישינן לחציצה מחמת שעומד לקצוץ ושמא מקפדת על כך וחוצץ ולכן הקפידו תמיד לקצוץ הצפורן דחיישינן דהצפורן עצמה חוצצת, על כן גם בפירשה רובה יש לחתכה דשמא מקפדת ע"ז, ועל כן אף בפירשה רובה צריכה קודם הטבילה להסיר את הצפורן שפירשה.

"**If she immersed herself without removing ... she must re-immerse etc.**" לא מיבעיא בפירשה מיעוטה דמפורש בשו"ע דחוצצת ודאי שצריכה לחזור ולטבול, אלא אפילו בפירשה רובה נמי הא כתב הש"ך דלדידן צריכה טבילה שנית, וכנ"ל, וכ"כ בלחו"ש.

"**In the case of toenails etc.**" — דבצפרני רגליה אם פירשה רובה יש להקל שלא להצריך טבילה אחרת, דהא מפורש בשו"ע דפירשה רובה אינה חוצצת, וכל מה שיש להחמיר בזה הוא ע"פ מש"כ הש"ך ס"ק כ"ז להחמיר גם בפירשה רובה דיש לחוש דעומד לקצוץ חוצץ, וע"פ הרמ"א בסע' כ' דמצריך טבילה אחרת, ולכן לענין צפרני רגליה יש להקל דהרי הרמ"א דייק וכתב בזה"ל: ומאחר דכבר נהגו ליטול הצפרנים אפילו אם צפורן אחת נשאר "בידה" וטבלה צריכה טבילה אחרת וכן נוהגין ע"כ, ומדדייק וכתב דין זה לענין צפרני ידיה, משמע דבצפרני רגליה לא נהגו כלל חומרא זו. ותו, דאדברי הרמ"א הנ"ל כתב בפת"ש ס"ק י' בשם חמודי דניאל שאם שכחה ליטול צפורן רגלה אפילו אם יודעת שלא היה נקי אינה צריכה טבילה אחרת, דברגלים אין דרכן של נשים להקפיד, ע"ש, ואף דהחמו"ד כתב כן לענין צפורן ארוכה שלא חתכה או לגבי לכלוך שתחת הצפורן מ"מ חזינן דברגליה אינה מקפדת כל כך כמו בידיה. וכנראה דלזה רמז בלחו"ש [בלחם ס"ק נ"ג, וע"ש בשמלה ס"ק כ']. וכן הוא להדרך הראשון בב"י שהובא לעיל, דאין לחוש לחציצה משום כל העומד לקצוץ בצפרני רגליה הואיל ואינה מקפדת. ואף להמרדכי שהובא לעיל דבהחל לפרוש יש לחוש לחציצה כשעומד לפרוש, מ"מ הא דעת המרדכי דבפירשה רובה הוי כמאן דליתא דרובו ככולו. וכ"ש להט"ז שהובא לעיל דבפירשה רובה מיא עיילי ביה וליכא חציצה במקום החתך דפשיטא דאינו חוצץ.

"**if most of the nail etc.**" — ודוקא נפרדה רוב הצפורן, אבל אם פירשה רק

מיעוטה דמפורש בשו"ע דחוצצת, צריכה טבילה אחרת.

37. "When a nail became separated from the flesh beneath it etc." — על פי דברי הלבוש בסי' קצ"ח סע' כ"א בדין צפורן המדולדלת שפירשה, דאחר שהביא את ב' הפירושים שכתב הב"י בדין זה, כתב הלבוש דאינו נראה בעיניו פירושים אלו וכתב פירוש שלישי בזה, דאיירי שהצפורן נפרדה מהבשר שתחתיה, דחוצצת. וטעמא דמילתא כתב הלבוש, משום דאותו מקצת שפירש אינו חוזר ומתדבק בבשר שתחתיה כבראשונה אלא הולך ומתנונן עד שיפרוש כולו, ואף אם אינו מתנונן מ"מ עכ"פ צריכים לחתכו, והבשר שתחתיה נעשה עתה כבשר עור החיצון של כל הגוף וצריך ביאת מים כשאר מקומות הגלויים שבגופה, ולפיכך כשפירשה מיעוטה חוצצת מפני שאין הדלדול מתרווח ונפתח הרבה ונשאר הצפורן מונח על הבשר שתחתיה ולא יוכלו המים לבא תחתיה על אותו הבשר שהוא נחשב עתה כעור החיצון ואין לך חציצה גדולה מזו וכו' ע"ש.

"If most of the nail became separated etc." — עיין שם בלבוש דזהו הפירוש פירשה רובה אינה חוצצת, דבנפרדה רוב הצפורן בודאי שנתרחב הרבה בין הצפורן לבשר שתחתיה והמים נכנסים שם, על כן אינה חוצצת.

"If a small part of a nail separated etc." — דאם לא נפתח כל כך, וכגון שפירשה מיעוטה ונשארה הצפורן מהודקת לבשר שתחתיה, לפמש"כ הלבוש חוצצת. ומ"מ מטעמים אחרים יש לדון להקל לפי המציאות המשתנית וכדלהלן.

"If she needs the nail to protect the area etc." — וכדעת הפוסקים דכל שהוא לרפואה אינו חוצץ, וטעמא מאי רטיה שעל המכה חוצצת וכמבואר בשו"ע סי' קצ"ח סע' י', משום דפעמים שמסירה את הרטיה לראות אם כבר עלה רפואה למכתו או שמסירתו כדי לתקנו, וזהו דעת הכתב סופר בתשו' יו"ד סי' צ"א וע"ש שכתב דכ"ה דעת הפנים מאירות ח"ב סי' קמ"ו שהובא בסדרי טהרה שם סוס"ק י"ט, והסד"ט גופיה מפקפק על זה, ומ"מ י"ל דכל שהוא לרפואה והחציצה באה מגופה אינה חוצצת, וכעין מש"כ הסד"ט סוס"ק כ"ו והגרעק"א בתשו' מהדו"ק סי' ס' בשם הגאון ר' יעקב מליסא [החוו"ד].

"she does not want to remove the nail because it will hurt etc." — וכמו שכתב בסדרי טהרה שם ס"ק כ"ג בד"ה ותו קשה לי וכו' ובסוס"ק כ"ו, דכל

שמצטערת בנטילתה מיקרי אינו מקפיד על זה.

"she should make every effort etc." — וכמו שכתב שם הלבוש דאם מתרחב באופן שהמים נכנסים שם אינו חוצץ. וכ"ה לפירושו של הט"ז בדין צפורן שפירשה דהחציצה היא במקום החתך מחמת שב' חלקי החתך מהודקים זב"ז ואין המים נכנסים שם, ואין החציצה במקום שעדיין מחובר, וה"נ בנידונינו.

39. "Permanent fillings ... are not a *chatzitzah*" — כן נוקטים כל האחרונים, חוץ מהחכמת אדם [בבינת אדם שער בית הנשים סי' י"ב (כא)] שהחמיר בזה, ומקורו מהא דאיתא בשו"ע סי' קצ"ח סע' י' "רטיה שעל המכה חוצצת" ושם בשו"ע סע' מ"ג איתא דרטיה שעל בית הסתרים חוצצת, דהחכמ"א נוקט דהיינו טעמא דחוצץ דכל שאינה רוצה בכך אלא משום רפואה ואילולי סיבת הרפואה היתה מקפדת על זה, חשיב מקפיד וחוצץ. ולדעת האבני נזר ודעימיה, טעמא דרטיה דחוצצת משום שעתידה להסירו, וכמובא לעיל בסע' כ"א. ונפק"מ בין הטעמים הוא בכה"ג שהרטיה היא על דעת שלא להסירו לעולם, וכמו כן בסתימות הקבועות בשיניים, דלהחכמ"א חוצץ דהואיל ונעשה לרפואה חשיב מקפיד, משא"כ להאבנ"ז ודעימיה כל שאינה עתידה להסירו משם לעולם לא הוי בכלל הדין של רטיה שעל המכה, הואיל ואינה מקפדת על כך ובטל לגוף. - אבל באמת אף להבנת החכמ"א בדין רטיה שעל המכה יש לחלק בין נידו"ד לבין רטיה שע"ג המכה, דברטיה שע"ג המכה, ע"י הרטיה עושים מצב משונה בגוף ובזה הוא דנחלקו אי חשיב שמקפדת או לא, וכנ"ל, משא"כ בסתימות שבשיניים שע"י הסתימה חוזר השן להיות כדרכו הטבעי, ונעשה עי"ז כחלק מהשן, וא"כ לא רק שאינה מקפדת, אלא אדרבה גם הוי הקפדה שיהא שם, וכעין מה שמצינו דכל לנאותו אינו חוצץ וכמבואר בשו"ע סי' קצ"ח סע' י"ז לגבי צבע שצובעות הנשים על פניהן וידיהן ושער ראשן אינו חוצץ, ומשמע דאף אם צבעה את כל השיער אינו חוצץ, דלא רק משום אינו מקפיד הוא דאינו חוצץ, אלא משום דכיון שנעשה לנוי הוי כגופה וכדביאר הרשב"א, והתם אין הכונה רק שאינה מקפדת, אלא דחשיב ממש כגופה, [וכיו"ב נראה דאם צבעה את שערה ורוצה אותו לשבוע או שבועיים, דמסתבר דאינו חוצץ, כיון דאין דנים להקל רק משום אינו מקפיד אלא טפי מכן אנו דנים להקל משום שנעשה כגופה וכמו"ש הרשב"א, ואף שהוא לזמן, וכיו"ב יעויין בכת"ס סי' צ"א שכתב כעין סברא זו], וא"כ ה"ה בסתימות שמחזירים מצב השן

למצבו הטבעי, דנעשה כגופו, דאין זה רק לרפואה שאלמלא לרפואה לא היתה רוצה בכך, אלא אדרבה רוצה שיהא כחלק אחד מהשן וחשיב כגופו, ומחמת סברא זו יש לדון להקל אף כשעתיד ליטלה, וכ"ש כשנעשה כן בקביעות ואין דעתה להסירה די"ל דאינו חוצץ. וסברא זו איתא בתשו' אמרי יושר ח"ב סי' קי"ב לענין סתימות שבשיניים דכיון שמחובר ונעשה כשן ממש שאוכל עמו לא הוי חציצה והביא דסברות אלו כתב בס' תשורת שי סי' ס"ט, אלא דהאמרי יושר כתב שם בנידונו שהסתימה היא לב' שבועות בלבד ולכן כתב שם דלזמן מועט כזה אין להקל, ומינה נשמע דעכ"פ לזמן ארוך וכ"ש אם הוא ע"ד לישאר שם לעולם, יש סברא להקל מחמת שנעשה כחלק מהשן או כתחליף לשן, ולכן אינו חוצץ. - ומאחר דגם ברטיה שעל המכה לדעת רוב האחרונים אם הוא על דעת לישאר שם לעולם אינו חוצץ, ה"ה הכא דכל שהוא ע"ד שתשאר הסתימה בשן לעולם אינו חוצץ, וק"ו שיש להקל בזה בנידו"ד בבית הסתרים דלדעת הריטב"א בקידושין כ"ה כל עיקר הדין דבעינן ראוי לביאת מים בביהס"ת הוא מדרבנן. עוד נראה להוסיף, דאף לפי הבנת החכמ"א דכל שאינה מקפדת על זה רק מחמת סיבת רפואה ואילולי סיבת הרפואה היתה מקפדת על זה חשיב מקפיד, מ"מ לא דמי לאגד שעל המכה וכו' דמיד שלא תצטרך לאגד או לקשקשים לצורך רפואה תסירנו מעליה, דההקפדה היא בכל עת, [ובפרט בסתימות של שעוה או עופרת דאיירי ביה החכמ"א, וכפי שהיה בזמנו, דבעופרת קשה לומר הסברא של נוי, וכן בסתימות של שעוה מסתבר שהוא מורגש בפה כדבר זר], ובזה מובן דרכו של החכמ"א דכל שאינה מקפדת רק משום רפואה עדיין חשיב מקפיד, משא"כ בנידו"ד דגם אם יגיע זמן שכבר לא יהא צורך בסתימה לצורך רפואתה, לא תסירנו, דכבר מסחת דעתה מזה ובטל לגוף, ואף דבתחילת הנחת הסתימה היה זה רק מחמת סיבת רפואתה, מ"מ אין נפק"מ בסיבת הנחת הסתימה, סו"ס לאחר ההנחה הוא בגדר של ביטול לגוף וכמשנ"ת.

"(even in most of her teeth)" — עיין לעיל במקורות וביאורים לסע' ב' משנ"ת בשם הגאונים דהשיער חשוב כמקום בפני עצמו, ומשום דיש ילפותא מיוחדת לדין חציצה בשיער וכדביארו הראשונים בשי' הגאונים, ושכן פסק בשו"ע סי' קצ"ח סע' ה'. וכיו"ב כתב בתפאל"מ לענין צפרנים דנידונים לעצמם ואף כל צפורן נידון לעצמו. ובאבני נזר יו"ד סי' רנ"ט אות ח' הוסיף עוד, די"ל דגם שינים נידון לעצמו, דכיון דטעמם של הגאונים דשיער נידון בפנ"ע הוא משום דיש לחציצה בשיער ילפותא בפנ"ע מאת בשרו את הטפל לבשרו, א"כ בכלל זה כל מה שטפל לבשרו, הן שיער

הן צפרנים והן שינים, ועפ״ז כתב דגם שיניים נידונים לעצמם, ודעתו להחמיר בדאיכא חציצה ברוב שינים אף שאינו מקפיד כיון דמדרבנן רובו חוצץ אף שאינו מקפיד וכ״ש במקפיד דהוי דאורייתא. ועפ״ז כתב עוד באבני נזר שם סי׳ רס״ג אות ג׳ דאם לא נסבור כהתפאל״מ דכל מקום כינוס שיער נידון בפנ״ע, אלא כל שער הגוף כחדא נינהו, אם יש חציצה בשינים לבד, והשינים בצירוף השיער אין רוב, אינו חוצץ, כיון דשינים ושיער מחד קרא נפקא. [ומ״מ כתב דכשיש חציצה ברוב שיער וביחד עם השינים אין כאן רוב, אין השינים מצטרפין להכשיר, כיון דהוא בית הסתרים ושאני משיער דבעי ביאת מים ממש. והוא חידוש]. — ומ״מ למעשה בסתימות קבועות, אפילו אם הם על רוב השיניים, יש להקל, חדא, דאף לפ״מ דקיי״ל להחמיר כשיטת הגאונים דשיער נדון כמקום לעצמו מ״מ לענין כל מקום כינוס שיער אם נדון בפנ״ע יש לצדד קצת להקל, דהא הסד״ט כתב דאין הכרע בזה, וגם משמע קצת בדין שיער בית השחי הנדבק זב״ז דאינו חוצץ ע׳ שו״ע סי׳ קצ״ח סע׳ ו׳, דאף אם נדבק ברובו אינו חוצץ, ואף דהוי רוב מקום כינוס שיער, וגם יעוי׳ בגלות עיליות שכתב דאף אי נחמיר בשיער הראש דנידון בפנ״ע אבל לא בשאר מקומות שיער, ועוד דכיון דהוא ביהס״ת דלהריטב״א קידושין כ״ה אי״צ להיות ראוי לביאת מים אלא מדרבנן, א״כ פשיטא דאינו נדון למקום בפנ״ע, [שהרי כל מה שהחמיר התפאל״מ בצפרנים דנדון כמקום לעצמו הוא רק משום דגם צפרנים נלמד מפסוק מיוחד מאת בשרו, אבל להריטב״א ביהס״ת מדרבנן, וא״כ כיון שאין לימוד מיוחד מפסוק תו אין לנו לומר דהוא נדון כמקום בפנ״ע], וסו״ס הרי אף ברובו הא הוי אינו מקפיד ואין כאן אלא חשש דרבנן, וגם נתבאר לעיל דכל שרצונה בכך ומשתמשת בו כאחד משאר השיניים, הוי דומיא דלנוי, דלא רק דלא חשיב מקפיד, אלא הוי ממש כגופה, הלכך אין לחוש לחציצה אף בסתימות שהן על רוב השיניים.

"However if she suffers pain etc." — דאף דמתחילה היה בטל לגוף, מ״מ הא לא נעשה כגופה ממש כי היכי דנימא דתו לא שייך לומר ע״ז דמקפדת מחמת דהוי חלק מגופה, דרק כל זמן שרוצה בכך הוא דהוי בגדר של ביטול לגוף, וכהא דלנוי אינו חוצץ דמיד כשבטל יופיו ונויו שפיר חוצץ ולא אמרינן דכיון דמעיקרא היה בטל לגוף תו אף במקפדת אינו חוצץ, וכך גם בזה דמחמת הכאב מקפדת על כך אף דמתחילה היה בטל לגוף מ״מ כיון דעתה מקפדת על כך חוצץ.

40. "**A temporary filling etc.**" — הנה, כבר הובא לעיל במקורות לסע׳ כ״א בדין רטיה שעל המכה, מש״כ האבני נזר חיו״ד סי׳ רנ״ג להתיר בשעת הדחק דכיון דמיעוט המקפיד אינו אלא מדרבנן כל שאינה מסירתו אלא אחר חצי שנה, יש להקל דחשיב שבטל לגוף ואינו חוצץ, וכהא דכתב רבינו ירוחם לענין קשר של קיימא בשבת דכל שהוא לחצי שנה מיקרי קשר של קיימא, ע״ש. ולפי זה אין להקל בפחות מחצי שנה, וכל שהוא לימים ספורים ואפילו למשך חודש אין להקל.

"**However ... for an entire month etc.**" — עיין לעיל מש״כ בשם האבני נזר, והנה, אם אכן נשווה גדר ביטול לגוף לענין חציצה לדין קשר של קיימא בשבת וכמו״ש האבנ״ז, א״כ יש לדון דגם סתימה זמנית למשך חודש ימים ג״כ הוי גדר של ביטול לגוף ואינו חוצץ, דהא מצינו שיטות ראשונים לגבי קשר של קיימא דעד חודש חשיב אינו קיימא, ועי׳ בזה בב״י סי׳ שי״ז וע״ע לשון רש״י בשבת דף קי״ב ע״א בד״ה בדחומרתא דקטרי אינהו. - ויש עוד טעם להקל בזה על פי סברת המהרש״ם ח״א סי׳ ז׳ דכל שאינו מקפיד על חציצה במקום זה ולא איכפת לה אם היא חציצה זו או אחרת, חשיב אינו מקפיד אפילו אם תחליפנו כל שבוע, דסו״ס אינה מקפדת על המקום שיהא שם חציצה. אמנם להאבנ״ז לא מהני שאינה מקפדת על המקום, אלא צריך שיהא בטל לגוף וכפשטות דברי רש״י בטעם שאינו מקפיד אינו חוצץ מה״ת משום דבטל לגוף [ויל״ע בהא דלא סגי בהלמ״מ דחוצץ רק בדבר המקפיד ולמה הוצרך להוסיף טעם של ביטול לגוף], וגדר של ביטול שייך רק אם אינה מסירתו לזמן הרבה וכדס״ל להאבנ״ז דרק אם אינה מסירתו חצי שנה חשיב אינו מקפיד דאז הוי גדר של ביטול לגוף ולא אם מחליפה את הרטיה או את הסתימה, ולא סגי במה שאינה מקפדת על חציצה במקום זה. (וכנראה המהרש״ם ס״ל דגם במסירתו שייך גדר של ביטול הואיל ואינה מקפדת על חציצה במקום זה, היות דכיום רוצה בכך ובטל, ומה שאח״כ תניח רטיה אחרת הוא ג״כ אינו מקפיד, ואף לפמש״כ הראב״ד דמקפדת לפעמים חשיב מקפיד, היינו באופן שלפעמים אינה רוצה בכך ומקפדת על חציצה במקום זה, אבל כאן לעולם רוצה בביטול הרטיה לגוף, פעם בזה ופעם באחרת, ויל״ע). - ועוד צד היתר יש בזה, ע״פ מש״כ בתשו׳ בית שלמה יו״ד ח״ב סי׳ י״ב בנידונו באשה שיש לה כאב שיניים מחמת שיירי אוכל בנקבי השן, שכתב שם לדון להקל עפ״מ שמבואר בר״ש במתני׳ דקוץ או חץ התחוב באדם דטעמא מאי אם אינו נראה אינו חוצץ משום דהוי בלוע, ומבואר דאם נעשה נקב בבשר אדם ונכנס לתוך הנקב

איזה דבר, אם אינו נראה הוי בלוע ואינו חוצץ, ולהסכמת הש"ך ס"ק ט"ז כל שאינו שוה לבשר אף שנראה מונח בבשר הפנימי מיקרי אינו נראה, כיון שאינו נראה שוה לבשר, וכתב הסד"ט סוס"ק כ"ה דיש לסמוך ע"ז לדינא כיון דהוא מילתא דרבנן ודלא כב"ח שהחמיר בזה, ע"ש, ועפ"ז מסיק בבית שלמה שם דאם ע"י משמוש למעלה על שיניים אלו תראה שעכ"פ בשוה לשיניים אינו מונח שם שום דבר אף שיש להסתפק שמא מונח בחור בעומק איזה דבר אינו חוצץ, יעו"ש, ולפ"ז יש לדון דבסתימות שאינם עולים למעלה מהשן אלא סותמים את נקבי השן הוי הסתימה גדר של בלוע ואינו חוצץ. [אכן לא בכל מקרה יש לדון דהוי בלוע, ובפרט בכתרים דאין שייך סברת הבית שלמה כיון דעולים מעל השן, אבל בסתימות בדרך כלל הוי בלוע וא"כ י"ל כהבית שלמה דאינו חוצץ]. - ויש עוד סברא להקל, והובאה לעיל בדין סתימות הקבועות, דכיון שע"י הסתימה חוזר השן להיות כדרכו הטבעי ונעשה עי"ז כחלק מהשן, א"כ לא רק שאינו מקפיד, אלא גם הוי הקפדה שיהא שם, וכמו דכל לנאותו דחשיב כגופו ולא רק גדר של אינו מקפיד, וא"כ אף שעתידה להסירו חשיב כחלק מגופה, דהא לעת עתה משתמשת עם סתימה זו. וע"ע להלן בסמוך מסקנת הדברים.

"In case of need etc." — בחלקת יואב סי' ל' דן באשה שיש לה רטיה שעל המכה שצריכה להחליפה כל שבוע, וכתב לדון דחשיב קבוע ובטל לגוף וע"פ דברי האבנ"ז הנ"ל שכתב כן לגבי אם הוא מונח לחצי שנה וס"ל להחלקת יואב דסגי אם הוא מונח למשך שבוע בלבד, דהא קשר של קיימא מדרבנן הוא אפילו לשבוע, וכיון דנידונינו הוא בדבר שהוא חציצה מדרבנן במיעוט המקפיד, א"כ שמא סגי בביטול כזה שמדרבנן הוא ביטול. אבל האבנ"ז בסי' רס"ב [ובסי' רנ"ג אות כ"ג] דחה את דברי החלקת יואב, דכיון דהגזירה של מיעוט המקפיד הוא דגזרינן מיעוט המקפיד אטו רובו המקפיד שחוצץ מדאורייתא, על כן אנו צריכים לדון על מצב של מיעוט האיך יהא דינו כשהוא רוב, וכיון דברוב א"א לדון דבטיל שהרי כל סברות האבנ"ז והחלק"י הוא רק לגבי חציצה שהיא מדרבנן אבל בחציצה שהיא מדאורייתא לא סמכו לומר דבטל לגוף, א"כ ה"ה לענין מיעוט דגזרינן אטו רוב א"א לסמוך דלשבוע חשיב כגדר של ביטול לגוף, דהא יש לחוש שיבואו להתיר כן גם ברובו המקפיד, ועל כן נשאר האבנ"ז לדינא דכל לחצי שנה הוי ביטול ולא בפחות, וגם בזה לא סמך להתיר כי אם בשעת הדחק. אמנם להחלקת יואב אף אם אינה מסירתו לשבוע חשיב אינו מקפיד. - מעתה בנידונינו בסתימות שאינן קבועות,

אתאן לכמה וכמה טעמים להקל, (א) דלהחלקת יואב אפילו אם הוא לשבוע הוי גדר של ביטול לגוף ואינו חוצץ. ואף דהאבנ"ז חולק אעיקר דבריו דכיון שהגזירה היא מיעוט אטו רוב וברוב א"א לסמוך דהוי קבוע תו לא שייך להקל במיעוט דיש לגזור אטו רוב, מ"מ הא הכא הוי חציצה בבית הסתרים דלהריטב"א הוא מדרבנן, והגרעק"א בתשו' סי' ס' מסתמך על הריטב"א, א"כ בביהס"ת א"א להיות מצב של דאורייתא, ולא שייך כ"כ טענת האבני נזר, וא"כ שפיר י"ל דשבוע הוי גדר של ביטול לגוף. (ב) להמהרש"ם כיון שאינה מקפדת על חציצה במקום זה חשיב אינו מקפיד, וכנ"ל. (ג) להשיטות דכל שרצונה בכך אף שהוא לרפואה חשיב אינו מקפיד וכנ"ל במקורות לסע' כ"א בדין רטיה שעל המכה ולעיל בדין סתימות הקבועות, וה"נ בסתימות שאינן קבועות דכיון שרצונה בכך אף שהוא לרפואה לא חשיב מקפיד. (ד) ויש עוד סברא כאן, והובאה לעיל בדין סתימות הקבועות, דכיון שע"י הסתימה חוזר השן להיות כדרכו הטבעי ונעשה עי"ז כחלק מהשן, א"כ לא רק שאינו מקפיד, אלא גם הוי הקפדה שיהא שם, וכמו דכל לנאותו דחשיב כגופו ולא רק גדר של אינו מקפיד, וא"כ אף שעתידה להסירו חשיב כחלק מגופה, דהא לעת עתה משתמשת עם סתימה זו. (ה) ועוד שייך כאן סברת הבית שלמה דחשיב בלוע ואף במקפדת אינו חוצץ. - ולכן אף דאם אפשר שיהא מונח למשך חודש ימים עדיף טפי, דבזה הרי לרש"י בשבת חשיב קשר של קיימא ולהאבנ"ז דגדר קשר של קיימא זהו הקובע להגדרת ביטול לגוף א"כ הא חזינן דאם הוא למשך חודש חשיב קיימא, ומ"מ במקום צורך יש להקל כהחלקת יואב דכל שהוא מונח למשך שבוע חשיב קשר של קיימא ושייך לומר בזה דבטל לגוף, ואף דהאבנ"ז דוחה מ"מ עכ"פ בביהס"ת דהוא דרבנן יש להקל. ומכל שכן דלהבית שלמה הנ"ל בדרך כלל הוי גדר של בלוע, ובפרט למשנ"ת לעיל בשם האמרי יושר דכל שנעשה לחלק מהשן ומשלים את השן, נעשה כחלק ממנו ואינו חוצץ, ולכן עכ"פ בצירוף הסברות הנ"ל יש להקל מדינא גם אם תוציאנו אחר שבוע.

41. **"A dental crown etc."** — עיין לעיל בסעיפים הקודמים. ואף להחכמ"א שמחמיר בסתימות ואפילו בסתימות קבועות, מ"מ בכתר י"ל דמודה להקל, דכן מבואר בדברי החכמת אדם בבינת אדם סי' י"ב (כא) במש"כ שם דשן תותבת אינו חוצץ כיון שהוא לנוי וחילק בין זה לבין סתימות שבנקבי השיניים דחוצצים, דמה"ט

בשן של כסף מותר לצאת בשבת ואף דמה שחוצץ בטבילה אין יוצאין בו, וע"כ דאינו חוצץ, והיינו משום דהוא מונח לנוי, יעו"ש. ומבואר דאף שן כזו שיכולה להוציא נמי אינו חוצץ. [ולא דמי לשיניים תותבות דשם הרגילות להוציא תדיר ולנקותו משיירי מאכל וכדו']. וה"נ בכתר שעל השן, דלאחר שהרופא משייף את השן כדי להניח הכתר שם, במצב זה הכתר משמש גם לנוי. וכל שהוא לנוי אינו חוצץ אפילו שהוא לזמן, דדק לגבי הגדרת מקפיד הוא דאמרינן דמקפדת לפעמים חשיב מקפיד, אבל לגבי הדין של כל לנאותו אינו חוצץ, כבר נתבאר לעיל דכל זמן שהוא מונח לנוי בטל לגוף ואינו חוצץ. ולא דמי לטבעת שמסירה בשעת לישה ולא אמרינן דנעשה כחלק מהגוף, דהכא דנעשה לנוי דמי למש"כ הרשב"א לגבי צבע שנעשה לנוי דבטל לגוף, וא"כ בזה אין דין של מקפיד לפעמים, ותו, דבר"ן חולין ע"ג בדין של ידות הכלים כתב דכל שבדוקא רוצה בכך שיהא עליה בשעת טבילה, אינו חוצץ, וה"נ כן.

"even if it is temporary" — עי' לעיל משנ"ת בדין סתימות וכ"ש כאן.

42. "It is preferable not to use braces etc." — דאינו לנוי אלא לרפואה וכבר נתבאר לעיל במקורות בדין סתימות דבזה יש להחמיר. ועי' גם בשו"ת מנחת יצחק ח"ו סי' פ"ו מה שנדחק להקל בדין חציצה בברזל לישור שיניים, וע"ש בסו"ד דהוא דוקא אחר שנעשה מעשה. ובפרט שיש לדון דאף שלגבי רפואה יש סוברים דלא חשיב מקפיד מטעם דכל אלו שצריכים לזה אינן מקפידים, מ"מ כאן א"א לומר כן, מאחר דלא כל מי שיש לו עקמימות בשיניים עושה פעולות אלו ליישרם ע"י ברזלים אלו. [וגם בעובדא דדן בזה בשו"ת מנחת יצחק נראה שם בלשון השאלה דהוא במקרה מיוחד של חשש נפילת שיניים, ע"ש].

"In case of need etc." — עיין באבני נזר סי' רנ"ג דמדמה לקושר בשבת ומצריך שיהא מונח לחצי שנה. ובאלו הטבעות שהן פנימיות ואינן נראים מבחוץ, אפשר להקל יותר.

43. "Head lice" — מדברי הפוסקים בדין חציצה בכינים נראה שדנו על ג' מיני כינים. הא' הוא מה שמבואר בשו"ע סי' קצ"ח סע' מ"ז מין כינים שדבוקים בבשר ונושכים בעור במקום שיער ונדבקים בחוזק בבשר, ובזה מחלק המחבר בין אם יכול להסירן דחוצצין ואפילו בדיעבד מבואר בש"ך דאם לא הסירתן לא עלתה לה טבילה, לבין אינו יכול להסירן דאינו חוצץ. הב' עוד מין כינים יש והם שאר כינים ופרעושים, דבהגהות שערי דורא הובא בסד"ט ס"ק פ"ח כתב דשאר כינים

ופרעושים אינם נדבקים בגוף והמים נכנסים בהם ולא חייצי כמו טבעות שהן רפויין ולא חייצי, ע"כ, ועפ"ז כתב הסד"ט דשאני כינים המבואר בשו"ע שהם דבוקים בבשר בחוזק. ומשמע מלשון הגש"ד דכינים ופרעושים אלו הם מאותן המצויים בבגדים שאלו אינם נדבקים בגוף ומיא עיילי בהו, וכן הוא להדיא בלשון השע"ד שהובא בדרכי משה סוס"י קצ"ט ע"ש, [וזהו גם טעמו של הרמב"ם בהא דבכתם שעל בשרה אין שיעור גריס, משום דאין שכיח כינה בגוף וכמו"ש בהגה' מיי' פ"ט מהל' איסו"ב, דהיינו דהכינה שבבגדים אינם מצויים בגוף]. **הג'** ועוד מין כינים יש והם הכינים וביצי כינים המצויים כיום, והם אינם דבוקים "בבשר" וכנידון השו"ע, ולא באים מהבגדים ורפויין ומיא עיילי ביה וכמבואר בשערי דורא, אלא ביצי הכינים דבוקים בחוזק על השיער ואף הכינים אפשר שדבוקים בשיער.

"People normally detest etc." — דכינים אלו פשיטא דמיקרי מקפיד וחוצצים. ואף אם תעשה במסרק, כל עוד נשאר כינים בשערותיה הר"ז חוצץ, שהרי אותן שנשארו אינן במצב של אינו מקפיד שמעתה לא תסידם עוד, אלא שכעת אינה מרגשת בהם אבל כעבור יום או יומיים כשתרגיש בהם תחזור על פעולת הסירוק כדי להסירם, וגרע טפי מטבעת דמקפדת לפעמים בשעת לישה דאף שעתה אינה מקפדת ע"ז כלל ואף רצונה שיהא עליה, אפ"ה חשיב מקפיד, ומכל שכן כינים או ביצי כינים שבשיער שבשום פעם אינה רוצה בהם ומקפדת עליהם.

ולכאורה יש להקשות על זה דהא גם בנידון דהמחבר במין כינים וכו' דאם אינה יכולה להסירן אינו חוצץ, הא אפשר דכעבור יום או יומיים תוכל להסירן, וכי נימא דחוצץ, הא משמע במחבר דכיון דגירדה ולא יכלה להסיר אינו חוצץ, וא"כ ה"נ בנידו"ד כיון דעשתה כפי יכלתה על ידי סירוק אולי לא איכפ"ל דאחר יום או יומיים שוב תסרק להסיר מה שנשאר ולא יצא קודם הטבילה ולא משוי לה למקפיד, מיהו זה אינו, דהמחבר איירי בכה"ג שעשתה כל מה שיכולה לעשות להסיר הכינים, אבל כאן בנידונינו דיכולה להסיר על ידי תכשיר המיוחד לכך או ע"י מי חומץ וכדומה, לא חשיב אינה יכולה להסיר, כיון דיש דרך להסיר הכל גם מה שלא יצא על ידי הסירוק. ותו דלענין ביצי הכינים המצויים אף על ידי מסרק קשה להסיר כי אם ע"י החומר המיוחד לכך, [ובאמת יל"ע בהא דבשו"ע ופו' לא נזכר כ"א דין חציצה בכינים ולא לגבי ביצי הכינים, ומ"מ א"א ללמוד מזה לנידו"ד דסו"ס מין אחר של כינים הוא].

וזה אין לומר דלאחר שסירקה כמה פעמים ועשתה כפי יכלתה ויותר אינה

מרגשת בהם ואינה יודעת שיש לה עוד כינים, יחשב כדבר שאינה מקפדת, דזה אינו דוכי מחמת שאינה יודעת על כך חשיב אינה מקפדת, הרי גם אשה שטבלה ולאחר טבילה מצאה עצם בין שיניה דמפורש בגמ׳ שצריכה טבילה אחרת ג״כ ודאי לא ידעה בשעת הטבילה שיש לה עצם בין שיניה, וכי חוסר ידיעה משוי לה לאינה מקפדת. - ואף דבשו״ע סע׳ מ״ז איתא דמה שאינה יכולה להסיר אינו חוצץ, ומבואר בלשון הרוקח וכ״ה בלבוש דהטעם שאינו חוצץ משום דאינה מקפדת, היינו דוקא התם שאע״פ שיודעת בבירור שיש לה כינה, כיון שאינה יכולה להסירו תו חשיב דבר שדרכו בכך והיינו רביתייהו ואינה מקפדת, עי׳ ביאור הגר״א, אבל בכינים המצויים דלא איירי בכה״ג שאינה יכולה להסירו, דאילו היתה יודעת על מקום הימצאו של כינה, היתה טורחת ומסירתו, כי מקפדת שלא יתרבו וכו׳, אלא דאינה מוסיפה לסרק משום שיותר אינה יודעת על כך שיש עוד כינה בשיער, ולמחר תחזור ותסרק כדי להסירו, וא״כ מהיכ״ת שיחשב לדבר שאינה מקפדת. ועל כן קשה לסמוך על כך שתעשה כפי יכולתה בסירוק. אך בזה יש לסמוך להקל, שאם עשתה גם עם תכשיר המיוחד לכך וכו׳, באופן שיש להניח שהכינים אינם פעילות יותר וכן ביצי הכינים התקלקלו או שעכ״פ אינם דביקות יותר, בזה הוא דיש להקל שאם למחרת מצאה כינה בשערה לא תצטרך טבילה אחרת.

"must remove them etc." — שו״ת בית שלמה יו״ד ח״ב סי׳ ל׳. ויל״ע קצת במש״כ שם דכיון שאפשר שתוכל להסירן ע״י חמין לא חשיב אינו יכול ועל כן יש לעשות במשיחה, הרי אם אפשר שעל ידי חמין יכולה להסיר א״כ נצריכנה לעשות על ידי חמין, ולמה הצריכה לעשות ע״י המשיחה, ועכ״פ חזינן מדברי הבי״ש דכל שיש איזה דרך להסיר, כגון ע״י משיחה, לא מהני סירוק הרבה פעמים בכדי להחשיבו אינו יכול להסירן, דהא יכולה להסירן ע״י המשיחה.

והנה, בפת״ש ס״ק י״ח כתב בשם חמודי דניאל דאותן כינים קטנים מתים הדבוקים בשיער צריך להסירן דהוי חציצה. ובלחו״ש השמיט תיבת מתים, ואפשר שהוא בדוקא. וי״ל דטעמו של החמו״ד לחלק בין כינה חיה לכינה מתה ע״פ האיבעיא בגמ׳ זבחים י״ט ע״א לענין חציצה בבגדי כהונה, האם כינה חוצצת או לא, וקאמר התם מתה ודאי לא תיבעי לך דודאי חייצא חיה מאי מי אמרינן כיון דאתא ואזלא רביתא היא ולא חייצא או דילמא כיון דקפיד עלה חייצא, ע״ש. ועפ״ז כתב החמו״ד דדוקא כינה מתה חוצצת כיון דלא שייך לומר בה היינו רביתא. - ועיין

בפתחא זוטא סי׳ קצ״ח סע׳ מ״ז שנתקשה במ״ש הבית שלמה להסיר הכינים ע״י משיחה דהרי עי״ז יהיו כינים מתים דחמיר טפי, ונראה דאף דבמתים לא שייך היינו רביתייהו ועל כן אם יש הרבה כינים ורואים אותם מבחוץ אז יש חשש חציצה, מ״מ אם אין הרבה מהם ואינו נראה מבחוץ, אין מקפידים כיון שאינם חיים, משא״כ באותן שהן חיים אף אם אין רואים מקפידים כיון שהם גורמים לריבוי, וגם הם מטרידים את האדם ע״י שמוצצות את דמו.

ומכל מקום מדברי הפוסקים נראה דלא סמכו על מה שבגמ׳ בזבחים מספק״ל אי אמרינן היינו רביתייהו, והיינו דכתב המחבר דביכול להסירן חוצץ, והרי מבואר בש״ך דאפילו בדיעבד חוצץ. [וכיו״ב יעויין בבאר היטב סי׳ קצ״ח ס״ק י״ט שכתב בשם ס׳ בית הלל דאם אדם אחד יש לו שני אומנויות דהיינו שהוא צובע וסופר ונדבק על ידו צבע ודיו, אזלינן לחומרא. ובסדרי טהרה ס״ק ל״ד מביא דבריו וביאר דמקור הדין הוא מזבחים צ״ח ע״ב בעי רבא דם ורבב על בגדו מהו וכו׳, וכ״כ הרמב״ם בפ״ג מהל׳ מקוואות דהוא ספק אם חוצץ או לא, ועי׳ מג״א סי׳ קס״א ס״ק ד׳ דבטבילה מחמירים, ומוכח כהרמב״ם, ועי׳ פמ״ג שם, וע״ע ש״ך יו״ד סי׳ ק״ד ס״ק ו׳ ופמ״ג שם לענין צירוף איבעי׳ דש״ס לאשוויי ספק, ומכל דבריהם הנ״ל נראה דעכ״פ לענין טבילה מחמרינן ולא מצרפינן ספיקא דהש״ס לספק ספיקא, וה״נ בנידו״ד]. ומה שכתב בביאור הגר״א סע׳ מ״ז בדין כינים דהיינו טעמא דבאינו יכול להסירם היינו רביתייהו ואינה מקפדת, נראה דאין כונתו להגמ׳ בזבחים דאם היה כונתו להגמ׳ היה מציין לגמ׳ מפורשת וכדרכו בכל מקום, אלא י״ל דכיוון בזה להדין בעלמא דבאינו יכול להסיר אמרינן דהיינו רביתייהו, וכהא דאיתא במרדכי לגבי קליעת שערות דבוקות דכיון שסכנה להסירן אינו חוצץ והובא ברמ״א סע׳ ו׳, וע״ש בביאור הגר״א דכיון שא״א להסירן היינו רביתייהו וכהא דיבמות ע״ח לגבי עובר, ע״ש, והכי נמי כן דכיון דא״א להסירן היינו רביתייהו. אבל אין כונתו להגמ׳ בזבחים הנ״ל. וע״ע בשו״ת חת״ס שהובא בפת״ש שם ס״ק ה׳, במש״כ לחלק בין דבר הבא מגופו לבא מבחוץ, ונראה דכינים שאינו יכול להסירן הוה כמו דבר הבא מגופו דאמרינן ביה היינו רביתייהו.

והנה, לכאורה יל״ע בהא דהוצרך בביאוה״ג להוסיף טעמא דהיינו רביתייהו, הא במקור הדין דהשו״ע ברוקח שהובא בב״י כתב הטעם דבאינה יכולה להסיר אינו חוצץ, משום דאינה מקפדת, וכ״ה בלבוש, ולמה הוסיף טעמא דהיינו רביתייהו.

אמנם י"ל עפ"מ שנתבאר לעיל, דבכינים המצויים אף אם תסרק הרבה פעמים מ"מ כיון שלמחר אם תרגיש בכינה שנשארה הרי תקפיד להסיר, על כן קשה להחשיבו עתה כדבר שאינו מקפיד, וגרע ממקפיד לפעמים. ולכאורה יל"ע דלסברא זו הא א"כ גם בנידון דהמחבר באינה יכולה להסיר אמאי אינו חוצץ, הא אפשר דרק עתה אינה יכולה לגרד ולהסיר ואילו למחר שפיר תוכל לגרד ולהסיר, וא"כ לא גרע ממקפיד לפעמים שחוצץ, ואמאי פסק המחבר שאינו חוצץ, [ועי' לעיל], ואפשר דבאמת משום זה הוסיף בביאור הגר"א טעמא דהיינו רביתייהו, דכל שעושה מה שביכלתה להסיר והשאר אינה יכולה להסיר, אינו חוצץ משום דהיינו רביתייהו.

"If she immersed etc." — דלהמבואר לעיל דביצי כינים המצויים דבוקים בחוזק בשיער, ואף הכינים יש להסתפק דאפשר שגם הם דבוקים בשיער, ומאחר דמקפדת עליהם להסירם, א"כ הרי הם חוצצים בטבילה. וכבר נתבאר לעיל דאף שסירקה הרבה ולא מצאה עוד כינה, מ"מ חוסר ידיעה לא משוי לה לאינה מקפדת. ואף דבאינה יכולה להסיר כתב בשו"ע דאינו חוצץ, מ"מ הא מבואר בבית שלמה דכל שיכולה להסיר ע"י תכשיר מיוחד לכך או מי חומץ וכדומה, חשיב יכולה להסיר וחוצץ. ולכן לא מהני מה שתסרק הרבה פעמים ולא תמצא כלום, דאף לאחר שתעשה כן עדיין יש לדון שאם למחר תמצא כינה שנשארה בשערותיה, הוי חציצה הואיל ויכולה להסיר ע"י תכשיר מיוחד לכך וכנ"ל. ותו, דאף אי סירוק הרבה היה מועיל להחשיב שעשתה מה שביכלתה להסיר הכינים, אבל מ"מ לגבי ביצי הכינים אין מועיל הסירוק. ומה שהוזכר בביאור הגר"א טעמא דהיינו רביתייהו נמי לא שייך בנידו"ד, דכבר נתבאר דבפשטות אין כונתו בזה למה שהוזכר בגמ' בזבחים, חדא, דהא איבעיא היא התם, וחזינן דלא מצרפינן ספק דאיבעי' דש"ס לגבי טבילה, ומחמרינן וכנ"ל. ותו, דסברת היינו רביתייהו שייכא רק באם אינה יכולה להסיר בשום אופן, אבל כל שיכולה להסיר ע"י תכשיר וכדו', חשיב יכול, ולא שייך סברת היינו רביתייהו.

ועל כן אם יש לה כינים בשיער אף אם סירקה כמה פעמים, מ"מ אם תמצא כינה בשערותיה למחרת הטבילה באופן שאין להניח שבא מבחוץ, כל שלא עשתה עם חומר מיוחד לכך או עם מי חומץ וכדומה, יש בזה שאלה של חציצה. ורק אם עשתה עם החומר או עם מי חומץ וכדומה, אז יש להניח שהכינים מתו וביצי הכינים נתקלקלו ועכ"פ רפויים הם, ואינם חוצצים. ואז אף אם יש צד שנשאר כינה חיה, יש כמה צדדים להקל, חדא, דבזה תו שייך סברת היינו רביתייהו, ותו דהא אפשר שרפויה היא.

איברא, דבמצאה כינה למחרת הטבילה, ולא עשתה עם התכשיר המיוחד, אף אי נצריכנה טבילה אחרת, מ"מ אפשר דלענין ברכה יש לחוש לספיקת הש"ס דשמא אמרינן לגבי כינה דהיינו רביתייהו, ולא רק מחמת שא"א להסיר. כל מה שנתבאר בסעיף זה שמעתי מהגרמ"ש קליין שליט"א.

פרק שביעי

1. "The *Torah* requires etc." — ב"ק פ"ב ע"א ושו"ע סי' קצ"ט סע' א'.

"*Ezra HaSofer* instituted etc." — ב"ק שם ושו"ע שם. ועיין בסד"ט שם ס"ק ט' שהתקנה כוללת גם רחיצת השיער במים חמין וגם סירוקו.

"to wash well and rinse their entire body" — תוס' שם ובנדה ס"ו ע"ב ורא"ש בנדה שם, ודלא כשיטת הר"ר שמעיה בשם רש"י, הו"ד בתוס' וברא"ש שם, שגם זה בכלל תקנת עזרא, ש"ך שם ס"ק ב'.

2. "with warm water" — נדה ס"ו ע"ב ושו"ע שם סע' ב', מפני שמים קרים מסבכים השיער.

"while the hair is still wet" — סד"ט ס"ק ט'.

"she should comb" — רש"י ב"ק שם ריש עמוד ב', ועיין בסד"ט ס"ק ט'.

"all of the hair on her body" — ש"ך שם ס"ק א'.

3. "the rest of her body" — רמב"ן נדה שם, חינוך מצוה קע"ה, וכתבו שכל המשנה מנהג זה ימתח על העמוד.

"including all folds" — נדה ס"ו ע"ב.

פרק שביעי

1. "If she washed ... but did not comb ... did not wash ... totally invalid" שו"ע סי' קצ"ט סע' ח'.

"Even if she inspected herself etc." — שו"ע סי' קצ"ח סע' כ"ה.

2. "If she washed ... with cold water" — שיעורי שבה"ל סי' קצ"ט סע' ב' אות ב' ואות י' (ד"ה ש"ך ס"ק ד').

"and then inspected her hair before the immersion etc." — משמעות הרמ"א סי' קצ"ט סע' ב' ואות י' (ד"ה ש"ך ס"ק ד').

"bathing before immersion" — שו"ת מהרי"ל החדשות סי' צ"ג ס"ק ד', עפ"י רש"י נדה ס"ח ריש ע"א בד"ה טשטקי, ועי' בדרכי תשובה ס"ק י"ג שכ"ה המנהג.

"It is customary etc." — ש"ך שם ס"ק ג'.

4. "calmly and without hurrying" — שהרי זהו הטעם לשיטת רש"י נדה ס"ח ע"א שצריכה לחוף מבעוד יום, כדי שלא תמהר לטבילתה.

5. "brush and clean ... her teeth" — שו"ע סי' קצ"ח סע' כ"ד.

"If she has cavities in her teeth etc." — ואם נשאר שיירי מאכל בשן שאינה יכולה להסיר מחמת שהוא עמוק בשן, יכולה לטבול, דמקום זה נחשב לבלוע, שאין חציצה במקום בלוע פוסלת את הטבילה, עיין שו"ת בית שלמה יו"ב ח"ב סי' י"ב.

"she should not eat until after the immersion" — רמ"א שם.

"but she may drink" — שיעורי שבט הלוי שם אות ו'.

6. "The *Shulchan Aruch* writes" — סי' קצ"ח סע' י"ח.

7. "a woman should relieve herself" — רמ"א סי' קצ"ח סע' מ"ג.

8. "to refrain from eating meat etc." — שו"ע שם סע' כ"ד.

9. "knead or handle dough" — רמ"א שם סע' כ"ד.

10. "It is customary etc." — דרכי תשובה סי' קצ"ט ס"ק י' בשם בל"י.

"because hair could remain etc." — שם בשם אמרות טהורות להגה"ק מבוטשאטש זצ"ל.

---

3. "the hair on her head" — ש"ך שם סוס"ק א'.

4. "glutinous substance in the corners of her eyes" — שו"ע סי' קצ"ח סע' ז'.

"nasal mucus and earwax" — רמ"א שם סע' מ"ג.

"from the external parts ... There is, however, no need etc." — שו"ת מנחם עזריה הו"ד בחי' רעק"א לשו"ע שם סע' ז', שלא ניתנה תורה למלאכי השרת, וגם שנחשב מקום בלוע [ראה לעיל בפרק הקודם].

7. "It is not necessary etc." — חכמ"א כלל קי"ט סע' י"ב.

8. "Nevertheless, if she immersed etc." — ש"ך סי' קצ"ח ס"ק נ"ה.

9. "She may eat meat etc." — עיין ט"ז ס"ק כ"ה ושיעורי שבה"ל.

10. "*Bedi'eved,* etc." — ט"ז שם.

שם. — "If she did not cut her hair ... but must wash herself well etc."

11. "Ideally ... while it is still day" — לצאת ידי פירש״י, שו״ע סי׳ קצ״ט סע׳ ג׳ וש״ך שם ס״ק ו׳.

"It is also correct etc." — פירוש השאילתות בנדה ס״ח ע״א, הו״ד בתוס׳ שם, שו״ע סע׳ ג׳.

"It is an age-old custom etc." — עי׳ שו״ע שם.

12. "she can do them at night" — רמ״א שם.

"the *Acharonim* enacted etc." — ש״ך שם סוס״ק ו׳ בשם מהרש״ל.

"It is preferable to prepare during the day etc." — דלא גרע מטבילה במו״ש דכתב הרמ״א שתעשה חפיפה ע״ש ומו״ש, וכ״ש בכה״ג.

13. "After the thorough washing ... she must inspect her body etc." כנ״ל בסע׳ א׳, ועי׳ ט״ז סי׳ קצ״ט ס״ק ד׳ וסד״ט שם.

14. "If time passed etc." — ט״ז סי׳ קצ״ט ס״ק ו׳.

15. "Friday night or *Yom Tov*" — שו״ע סי׳ קצ״ט סע׳ ה׳.

"since they include activities that are forbidden on *Shabbos* and *Yom Tov*" שהרי במים חמים אסור מחשש חילול שבת כדאיתא באו״ח סי׳ שכ״ו ומים קרים מסבכים השערות כדאיתא בשו״ע סי׳ קצ״ט סע׳ ב׳, וכן בסירוק יש חילול שבת כדאיתא באו״ח סוס״י ש״ג. וכמ״כ יש איסור בסחיטת אלונטית, וכמ״כ יש איסור שבת בתלישת דברים המחוברים לגוף וכיו״ב כמה מדיני החפיפה הקשורים עם חילול שבת.

"She should be careful etc." — ט״ז שם ס״ק ח׳ ועיין רמ״א סע׳ ו׳, ועיין רמ״א סי׳ קצ״ח סע׳ כ״ד.

---

11. "she may be lenient and do so" — חכמ״א כלל קכ״א סי׳ א׳ התיר אם אין אחר שיכול ללוש.

12. "If she is always particular to cut her hair etc." — עי׳ שו״ת שבט הלוי ח״ד סי׳ ק״ט.

13. "Ideally etc." — ע״פ היראים מצוה קצ״ב שכתב דבתוך שלש שעות נחשב סמוך לטבילתה.

15. "Therefore she should not eat the *Shabbos* meal before immersing" — סד״ט סי׳ קצ״ח ס״ק מ״ט.

“her hair should remain combed etc.” — עיין סי׳ קצ״ט סע׳ ו׳.

“She should not eat etc.” — רמ״א סי׳ קצ״ח סע׳ כ״ד, וסד״ט שם ס״ק מ״ט.

“Before immersion she must inspect her whole body and hair well”

שו״ע שם וש״ך ס״ק י״א, והטעם עיין בר״ן וברשב״א הו״ד בב״י שם, דכיון דעיון דאורייתא אין מקילים להרחיקו מן הטבילה. והנה, בחכמת אדם כלל ק״כ סע׳ י׳ משמע דגם החופפת בע״ש וטובלת בליל שבת, צריכה לחזור ולהדיח ביהס״ת בלילה, ואולי כונתו בזה כביאור הגר״א אות י״ט שכתב דהדחת ביהס״ת בכלל העיון, וצל״ע, אבל לאחר העיון כנראה כונתו כהמשך למש״כ שם בסע׳ ז׳ בנידון שמרחקת הטבילה מהחפיפה ביום או יותר, דאל״ה הי׳ לו להביא מש״כ בט״ז ס״ק ו׳ ועיין ג״כ סוס״ק ט׳.

16. “or on Friday night after two days *Yom Tov*” — שו״ע סי׳ קצ״ט סע׳ ו׳.

“she must be careful during etc.” — רמ״א שם.

“Before immersion she must clean her teeth well etc.” — שו״ע שם.

“She must thoroughly inspect her whole body etc.” — כנ״ל בסעיף הקודם.

17. “she should ideally perform her preparations etc.” — רמ״א שם סע׳ ד׳ וש״ך שם ס״ק ט׳.

“Before immersion, she must thoroughly inspect” — כנ״ל בסעיף ט״ו.

“If she did not carry out the preparations etc.” — שו״ע שם.

פרק שמיני

1. “must immerse herself in a *mikvah*” — עיין ב״י רס״י קצ״ז מקורות

---

18. “If the immersion occurs on *motzei Tishah B'Av*” — עיין ברמ״א סי׳ תקנ״א סע׳ ט״ז ובביאור הלכה, ובהגהות אמרי ברוך שם. ואף דבסי׳ תקנ״ד במ״ב ס״ק י״ח כתב לחפוף בערב תשעה באב, מ״מ מסיום דבריו שכתב ועין רמ״א סי׳ תקנ״א סי״ז מוכח שכונתו רק באופן שא״א לעשות במוצאי ת״ב וכמו שכתב בשע״ת שם וכן נהוג להורות.

פרק שמיני

1. “She should not immerse ... during the seven clean days” — משמעות שו״ת

מגמ׳ ומראשונים בחיוב הטבילה מן התורה.

"she remains forbidden to her husband etc." — רמב"ם בפ"ד מהל׳ איסו"ב ה"ג, ועיין ב"י רס"י קצ"ז, שו"ע שם סע׳ א׳.

"her immersion is invalid" — טור וב"י שם.

2. "When her husband is out of town" — תשו׳ שבות יעקב ח"ג סי׳ ע"ז ושו"ת מהרש"ם ח"ד סי׳ צ"ה.

"it is a *mitzvah* for her to immerse etc." — משום פריה ורביה, מסקנת הב"י שם ושו"ע שם סע׳ ב׳, וכן משום מצות עונה, וכמבואר בדרכ"מ שם אות א׳ בשם תרוה"ד וע"ע תוה"ש שם ס"ק א׳, וכ"כ בשיעורי שבה"ל שם אות ג׳. וחזינן נמי דאף בימים שבהם אין לשמש ע"פ הסוד מ"מ בליל טבילה שרי, וכן בשני רעבון דאסור לשמש וכמבואר באו"ח סי׳ ר"מ סע׳ י"ב ואעפ"כ איתא בב"י דשרי בליל טבילה, וחזינן דמצוה לטבול בליל טבילה ולא לדחות הטבילה ליום אחר.

3. "The time for immersion is after nightfall etc." — נדה ס"ז ע"ב, טושו"ע סי׳ קצ"ז סע׳ ג׳. ואף שמקצת היום ככולו וא"כ היה אפשר מעיקר הדין לטבול מיד לאחר הנץ החמה של יום השביעי, גזרו חכמים שמא לאחר שתטבול תשמש מיד עם בעלה ותראה דם אח"כ בהמשך היום, שאז סתרה מנינה למפרע, ונמצא ששימשו באיסור.

"after nightfall" — ש"ך שם ס"ק ו׳.

"or whether it is delayed" — שם בגמ׳ ובטושו"ע. והטעם משום סרך בתה, שמא תראה בתה שטובלת ביום ותחשוב שהוא יום השביעי, ותבוא לטבול ביום השביעי.

הריב"ש סוס"י תכ"ה, שו"ת רב פעלים ח"ד סי׳ ט"ז. ושבט הלוי. ומהריב"ש אין ראיה דשם איירי בבתולות, וקצת ראיה מהמרדכי שבטלו ב׳ טבילות שנהגו בזמן הקדמונים [עי׳ תוס׳ שבת י"ג ע"ב].

"(not even on erev *Yom Kippur*)" — דכמה גדולים מנעו מנשים בז"נ לטבול אף בעיוה"כ כדי שלא יבואו לידי מכשול. שיעורי שבה"ל.

2. "and then immerse again etc." — עי׳ בטושו"ע סוס"י קצ"ו, ועי׳ ב"י רס"י קצ"ז.

3. "If it is doubtful etc." — שיעורי שבה"ל שם ריש סע׳ ב׳.

4. "A bride" — רמ"א שם ודגול מרבבה בש"ך ס"ק ט' ופתחי תשובה שם ס"ק י' בשם אחרונים, ודלא כש"ך ס"ק ט' שמחמיר.

5. "Falls on Friday etc." — רמ"א סי' קצ"ז סע' ב'.

"she immerses herself on *motzei Shabbos*" — שם. אולם באין בעלה בעיר במו"ש, אפשר דאף עדיף שתטבול במו"ש, ואין לחוש להרחקת חפיפה מהטבילה, דכיון שאין בעלה בעיר, תחפוף בליל מו"ש במתינות ולא תהא מהומה לביתה.

"One may not postpone etc." — רמ"א שם.

"to immerse again" — ש"ך שם ס"ק א'.

6. "It is forbidden to immerse on *Yom Kippur*" — שו"ע או"ח סי' תרי"ג סע' י"ב.

"*Tisha B'Av*" — שו"ע או"ח סי' תקנ"ד סע' ח'.

"seven days of mourning" — שו"ע יו"ד סי' שפ"א סע' ה'.

"her seven days of mourning" — ובשבעת ימי אבילות של בעלה עי' שו"ת אבן השהם שהובא בפת"ש סי' קצ"ז ס"ק ח' שמשמע דס"ל דמותר לטבול, ועיין היטב בשו"ת מהר"ם שיק יו"ד סי' שס"ד שחשש בזה כדי שלא יביא עצמו לידי נסיון [ומה שהביא המהר"ם שיק ראיה מט"ב צ"ע דהרי אבילות חמירא ליה ולכן אין חשש נגיעה באבילות משא"כ בט"ב דהחמירו בהרחקות משום דקילא ליה, עי' שו"ע הרב בקו"א סי' קפ"ד ס"ק ב'].

"When *Tisha B'Av* falls on *Shabbos*" — במשנה ברורה סי' תקנ"ד ס"ק מ' הביא דיעות הפוסקים בזה, ומסקנתו להקל עכ"פ בליל טבילה, ומ"מ דעת הרבה אחרונים להחמיר בזה הלא המה הא"ר שם, תוה"ש סי' קצ"ז ס"ק א' בשם כמה גדולים, סד"ט שם, הגהות חת"ס באו"ח שם, ועוד, וע"כ נכתב דבע"נ יחמיר. ובברור דכ"ז להנוהגין כהרמ"א אבל להנוהגין כדעת המחבר אין מקום להחמיר.

7. "on the *onah* of the expected period" — בשו"ת אבן השוהם הובאו דבריו בפת"ש סי' קפ"ד ס"ק כ"ב מתיר לטבול, אך הערוך השלחן שם סע' מ"ג כתב

"to put a knife etc." — שו"ת שבות יעקב ח"ג סי' ע"ז.

"or to cover herself etc." — כף החיים או"ח סי' ר"מ שתיקח אצלה בגד אחד מבעלה לשמירה.

4. "It is sinful etc." — ב"י שם בשם הזוה"ק.

שחלילה להתיר בזה, כי עלול לבוא לידי מכשול.

"it is a *mitzvah* to immerse" — חת"ס אהע"ז סי׳ קכ"ט שו"ת שבט הלוי ח"ב ריש סי׳ ק"א.

"This rule applies to Friday night etc." — כן משמע בשו"ת מהר"ם לובלין שהובא בש"ך סי׳ קצ"ז ס"ק ג׳.

8. "A blessing is recited etc." — שו"ע סי׳ ר׳.

9. "According to the *Shulchan Aruch* etc." — עיין שו"ע ורמ"א סי׳ ר׳.

10. "*Sephardic* women etc." — שו"ע יו"ד סי׳ ר׳, ועי׳ שו"ע או"ח סי׳ ע"ד סע׳ ד׳.

"Some recite the *bracha* outside etc." — עיין פת"ש סי׳ ר׳ ס"ק ג׳ וראה שיעורי שבה"ל סי׳ ר׳ אות ח׳ מש"כ מדברי הפוסקים בזה, ומסיק דאצלינו אין המרחצאות מזוהמות יותר ממרחץ קר, וע"כ נהגו לברך במקום הטבילה.

"However etc." — שם בשו"ע.

---

6. "Those who follow *Rabbeinu Tam* etc." — שו"ת שבט הלוי ח"ד סי׳ ק"ז ועיין מנחת יצחק ח"ג סי׳ פ"ו.

8. "a woman without a daughter" — ש"ך סי׳ קצ"ז ס"ק ח׳.

"should not leave her house etc." — ב"ח שם והו"ד בקיצור בש"ך ס"ק ו׳. והטעם הוא משום סרך בתה, שתחשוב שמותר לטבול מבעו"י. ולכן אם יש לתלות שיוצאת מביתה מבעוד יום לצורך חפיפה או מחמת ריחוק המקוה מביתה, אין חשש לסרך בתה. וכיום שמצוי רחיצה במקוואות יכולה בכל גווני לצאת מביתה מבעו"י, כיון שהבת תתלה שרוחצת במקוה. ברם יש להעיר לפ"ד הב"ח, דבליל שבת לא תצא מביתה אלא כשיעור זמן שמשערת שעד שתוכל לטבול בבית הטבילה יהיה לילה, דהא לא שייך לתלות שמקדמת לצאת לצורך חפיפה, אלא אם כן המקוה רחוק מביתה דיש לתלות סיבת הקדמת יציאתה משום ההליכה למקוה, כל הנ"ל משיעורי הגרמ"ש קליין שליט"א.

9. "In our times etc." — בפתחי תשובה שם ס"ק ב׳ הביא דעת המחמירים, אבל הסדרי טהרה ס"ק ט"ז הביא שבספר דברי יוסף סי׳ ס"ד היקל בזה והסכים עמו, דבזה"ז ירדה חולשה לעולם, וכ"כ בשו"ת בנין ציון קמא סי׳ ע"ו הו"ד בדרכ"ת שם ס"ק ז׳, והוסיף שאין לערער בדבר שנהגו היתר מדורות הקדמונים לטבול בחמין בליל שבת.

10. "If she postponed her immersion etc." — תורת השלמים שם ס"ק ג׳, ודלא כשו"ת חוט השני שהביא שם, וכ"פ בסד"ט שם ס"ק ה׳.

"*Ashkenazic* women etc." — ע"ש ברמ"א ובט"ז ס"ק ג' וש"ך ס"ק א'.

"The *Sheloh* instituted etc." — באר היטב סי' ר' בשם השל"ה. והטעם שעי"ז יוצאת גם דעת המחבר לברך קודם הטבילה. ועוד מעלה יש בזה שטובלת כמה פעמים, שאף אם בטבילה אחת תשחה ביותר, עלתה לה טבילה מפני שהמים מקדמים לקמטיה לשיטת הט"ז סי' קצ"ח ס"ק ל"ח.

11. "she should place her arm etc." — ע"ש בט"ז ס"ק ג'.

12. "She should not immerse etc." — שו"ע סי' קצ"ח סע' ל"ה.

"To immerse in such a position etc." — שו"ע שם סע' ל"ו ובפת"ש ס"ק כ"א.

"If the water level is low" — שם סע' ל"ז.

13. "and not press them tightly" — שו"ע שם סע' כ"ז וסע' ל"ח.

"If she shut her lips tightly etc." — שו"ע שם.

14. "She should also not close her eyes tightly" — שו"ע שם סע' ל"ט.

15. "by another woman" — שו"ע סי' קצ"ח סע' מ'.

"Immersion without supervision" — שו"ת רעק"א סי' ק"ד מובא בפת"ש שם.

---

11. "If she intentionally postponed etc." — סדרי טהרה ס"ק ד' בד"ה עוד נ"ל, דאף שהרמ"א כתב דמקום שלא נהגו החומרא של ליל שבת אין להחמיר, מ"מ אם דחתה בזדון יש להחמיר. ואם התחילה במזיד לספור ז"נ באיחור כך שטבילתה תחול בליל שבת דינה שוה לאשה שספרה ז"נ ודחתה טבילתה, נו"ב הובא בפת"ש סי' קצ"ז ס"ק ג'. [אבל האבני נזר יו"ד סי' רמ"ז כתב שאם דחתה תחילת ספירתה אין להחמיר, וצ"ע].

"If she postponed ... until *motzei Shabbos*" — פת"ש ס"ק ח' בשם תשו' מקום שמואל. וסד"ט סוס"ק ו'.

12. "stringency or a *hiddur mitzvah*" — שו"ת שבט הלוי ח"ג סי' קכ"ח סוס"ק א'.

15. "However, one may be lenient on the 31st night etc." — שהעיקר לחשוש לעו"ב הוא ביום השלושים, אלא שחוששים לחומרא גם ביום השלושים ואחד כשיטת החוו"ד. ומה שצריכה לחוש בעו"ב כל המעל"ע היא חומרת הכו"פ ושו"ע הרב, וא"כ בליל טבילה אפשר להקל שלא להחמיר ב' בחומרות כאחת. ובשעה"ד יש להקל לגמרי ביום השלושים ואחד.

16. "She recites a blessing" — שו"ת קנאת סופרים בהשמטות סי' ס"ד.

16. "The *Ramban* writes etc." — עי' סוף הל' נדה להרמב"ן.

17. "a sheet, or a mat" — טושו"ע סי' קצ"ח סע' ל"א.

"a narrow step" — שם. רוחב המדרגה יהיה לפחות ארבעה טפחים (32—40 ס"מ) שאז לא תפחד ליפול תוך כדי הטבילה.

18. "with the intention to emerge etc." — עיין חולין ל"א ע"א מחלוקת רב ורב יוחנן אם צריך כונה לטבילה, והמחבר בסוס"י קצ"ח פסק דאם טבלה בלא כונה מותרת לבעלה, אלא שהרמ"א שם חשש לדעת המחמירים, וכתב דיש להחמיר לכתחילה להצריכה טבילה אחרת.

"However, she should not recite a *bracha* etc." — עש"ך שם ס"ק נ"ט.

19. "a kosher *mikvah*" — טושו"ע יו"ד סי' ר"א סע' א'. שיעור 750 ליטר הוא ע"פ שיטת החזו"א וכ"כ בספר שיעורים של תורה בקונטרס שיעורי המצוות סע' ט'. וכתב שם שבשעת הדחק לא יפחות מ-648 ליטר.

"being connected to rain water etc." — עיין כת"י למו"ה ר' הלל ורטהיימר זצ"ל בסוף הספר.

20. "*tamei* animal" — רמ"א סי' קצ"ח סע' מ"ח.

---

18. "It is proper to immerse three times" — ספר חסידים סי' שצ"ד. ורמז לזה ממש"כ [יחזקאל ל"ו כ"ה] "וזרקתי עליכם מים טהורים וטהרתם וגו' אטהר אתכם", שמוזכר שלש פעמים לשון טהרה.

"if she was accustomed to immerse herself three time etc." — שיעורי שבט הלוי סי' ר' אות ו'. ואפשר דגם חומרת הספר חסידים מכיון שיש לזה מקור אין להקל ללא התרת נדרים.

"*No hataras nedarim* is required etc." — עי' דגו"מ יו"ד סי' רי"ד ושיעורי שבה"ל.

19. "in a place where she is afraid that people will see her" — שו"ע סי' קצ"ח סע' ל"ד.

20. " but immersed herself more than one time ... she can be lenient" — שיעורי שבט הלוי סי' קצ"ח סע' ל"ה ע"פ הט"ז שם ס"ק ל"ח. והטעם שבאופן כזה מן הסתם נכנסו המים לקמטים.

21. "She should not hold her eyes or her nose etc." — פת"ש סי' קצ"ח ס"ק ט"ו, מפני שבאופן זה יש מקומות שאין המים מגיעים אליהם.

21. "should not rinse etc." — רמ"א סוס"י ר"א. והטעם כתב שם בש"ך שלא יאמרו שהמרחץ מטהר ולא המקוה. ועיין דרישה סי' קצ"ט ס"ק ד' שהחמיר שלא תרחץ כל אותו היום, ובשו"ת שבט הלוי ח"ה סי' קכ"ה כתב להקל אחר שנהגה קורבה עם בעלה.

22. "A woman must be discreet" — רמ"א סוס"י קצ"ח.

23. "A woman should inform etc." — שו"ע דס"י קפ"ה. וכשבאה ושוכבת אצלה אי מהני, דעת החוו"ד שם הובא בפת"ש ס"ק א' להחמיר, והלחו"ש מיקל בזה. ונראה שאם רומזת שטבלה מהני לכו"ע דאין צריך לומר דוקא בפה, ועי' טהרת ישראל סי' קפ"ה סע' ד'. והמחלוקת היא רק בבאה ושוכבת אצלו שאינו רמז שטבלה אלא רמז שרצונה במעשה ואפשר שיצרה תקפה.

פרק תשיעי

1. "whether the woman has an established period" — שבועות י"ח ע"ב נדה ס"ג ע"ב טושו"ע סי' קפ"ד סע' ב'. ולדעת רוב הפוסקים, אף דבגמ' יליף מפסוק "והזרתם את בני ישראל מטומאתם" אין זה אלא אסמכתא ואיסורו רק

---

22. "If she just clenched her teeth etc." — פת"ש סי' קצ"ח ס"ק י"ז בשם חמודי דניאל.

23. "*bas mitzvah* age etc." — שו"ע שם סע' מ'.

24. "should not hold onto her etc." — שו"ע שם סע' כ"ח וש"ך ס"ק ל"ו ול"ז.
"If a need arises etc." — עי' שו"ע שם סע' מ'.

26. "It is a worthwhile custom etc." — טהרת ישראל סוס"י קצ"ח.

28. "If a woman is fastidious etc." — שו"ת אגרות משה יו"ד ח"ב סי' צ"ו.

29. "However, she should not postpone her immersion etc." — שו"ת שבט הלוי ח"ה סי' קי"ח ס"ק ב'.

30. "some opinions are stringent etc." — עי' שיעורי שבט הלוי סי' קפ"ה אות ב'.

פרק תשיעי

1. "If the night of her immersion etc." — פת"ש סי' קפ"ד ס"ק כ"ב בשם אחרונים ועיין לעיל פרק ח' סע' ז' משנ"ת.

מדרבנן כיון דקיי״ל וסתות דרבנן, וכ״ה דעת הרא״ש הרשב״א בתוה״ב והר״ן בפ״ב דשבועות וכמובא בב״י ע״ש. אולם דעת הנודע ביהודה בתשו׳ מהדו״ק יו״ד סי׳ נ״ה נ״ו שאסור מדאורייתא, הובאו דבריו בפת״ש שם ס״ק ג׳, ובשו״ת חת״ס חיו״ד סי׳ ק״ע כתב כן בשם רבו רנ״א זצ״ל, ושם בסי׳ קס״ו הביא עוד שיטה בזה בשם הרא״ה, עיין כ״ז בפת״ש שם וע״ע בתשו׳ חת״ס סי׳ קמ״ב ובחי׳ חת״ס למס׳ שבועות די״ח ע״ב. אולם דעת השו״ע והאחרונים דאף פרישה סמוך לוסת הוא מדרבנן. ועיין פרדס רמונים בפתיחה מה שהאריך בדברי הנו״ב.

"or she has a non-established period" — משנה נדה ס״ג ע״ב שינתה ליום כ׳ זה וזה אסורים, ושם בגמ׳ ״למיחש לה בחדא זימנא חיישא״, וע״ש בפרש״י ותוס׳ דזהו לענין פרישה מתשמיש, וכ״כ הרמב״ן בהל׳ נדה פ״ה דין י״ח והרשב״א בתוה״ב ב״ז ריש ש״ב וריש ש״ג וכ״פ בשו״ע סי׳ קפ״ד סע׳ ב׳, [ודלא כהרז״ה בהשג׳ לבעלי הנפש שער תיקון הוסתות סי׳ ג׳ אות ט״ז והרא״ה בבדה״ב ב״ז ש״ב שמפרש הא דאי׳ במתני׳ דחוששת בשינתה ליום אחר, דהוא רק היכא דיש לה וסת אלא שינתה, ע״ש].

בוסת שאינו קבוע לכו״ע חיוב פרישה הוא מדרבנן, עיין תשו׳ נוב״ק חיו״ד רס״י מ״ו ותשו׳ חת״ס חיו״ד סוס״י קע״ט.

"*Poskim* commend" — ש״ך סי׳ קפ״ד ס״ק ו׳ בשם הב״ח, חכמ״א כלל ק״ח סע׳ א׳, ועי׳ פת״ש שם סק״ה בשם הרדב״ז, ודלא כהט״ז שם ס״ק ג׳ שאסר מדינא. ובעונת אור זרוע יש להקל כיון דחו״נ אף בעונת הוסת עצמו לדעת הרבה ראשונים מותר וכן הוא דעת השו״ע, וגם עונת אור זרוע אינו מוסכם בפוסקים, לכן יש

---

2. **"from touching in an endearing manner"** — דלתרוה״ד סי׳ ר״נ שאוסר בעונת הוסת כל מה שאסור מה״ת בנדה, ה״ה דנגיעה דרך חיבה אסור, דכיון דעובר על לא תקרבו, גזרו ביה רבנן לאסור בעונת הוסת דשמא תראה ויעבור על לא תקרבו, ואף להב״ח דלא אסרו אלא תשמיש, וחו״נ אינו אסור מן הדין אלא משום המחמיר תע״ב, מ״מ יש לדון דכמו כן בקירבה של נגיעה דרך חיבה אף שאינו אסור מן הדין מ״מ יש גם בזה משום המחמיר תע״ב.

"and all the more so etc." — שו״ע הרב סי׳ קפ״ד ס״ק ו׳. וכדמצינו לענין אבילות ביו״ד סי׳ שפ״ג דחו״נ מותר לדעת המחבר שם, ואעפ״כ שינה במטה אחת יש להחמיר משום לך לך אמרינן לנזירא וכו׳. ומוכח עוד שם דשינה במטה אחת בלא בגדים אסור מן הדין דבכלל איסור תשמיש הוא.

להקל. וביותר, דכיון דיסוד חומרת האו"ז אינו סתם מחשש שמא תראה שהרי אינו יום וסתה ולמה נחוש שתראה, אלא הוא מחשש שמא תקדים לראות בגרמת התשמיש וזה אין שייך בחו"נ וכמו"ש החת"ס סי' ק"ע לגבי חו"נ ביום הוסת, וא"כ לא שייך בזה מש"כ התרוה"ד דמה לי איסור לאו או כרת, ודו"ק, ואף דאולי נכנס בכלל קדושים תהיו וכדברי הרמב"ן ר"פ קדושים, אבל אינו חומרא מן הדין, שיעורי הגרמ"ש קליין שליט"א.

"**However, other restrictions etc.**" — דבזה אף התרוה"ד מתיר וכמפורש בדבריו בסי' ר"נ ומקורו ע"פ הגה' מיי' פ"ד מהל' איסו"ב בשם הרמב"ן. וה"ה דדברי הרגל מותר, דהתרוה"ד לא אסר בעונת הוסת אלא מה שאסור מה"ת בנדה, משא"כ דברי הרגל דאינו אסור בנדה אלא מדרבנן ומשום הרחקה, יש להתיר בעונת הוסת. ומש"כ במלבושי טהרה ס"ק ו' והעתיקו בטהרת ישראל סע' י"ב דגם בזה המחמיר תע"ב כמו בחו"נ ומשום דבאדר"נ השווה דברי הרגל לחו"נ, צל"ע, דחו"נ הא אסור מה"ת להרמב"ם משום לא תקרבו משא"כ דברי הרגל, ומש"כ באדר"נ אסמכתא הוא, ולא דדמי מדינא לחו"נ. ואם כי העושה גדרים לקדש עצמו גם בזה, קדוש יאמר לו ועי' רמב"ן ר"פ קדושים, מ"מ אינו בכלל מה שכתבו הפו' דהמחמיר תע"ב.

2. "**applies for the *onah* etc.**" — שו"ע שם. ועיי"ש בחוו"ד סק"ה ובגר"ז שם ס"ק י"ב ופרי דעה בפתיחה שער השביעי בד"ה ומעתה, דתלוי בהנץ החמה ושקיעתה, [ועיין פרד"ר סי' קפ"ד בש"ח ס"ק י"ג].

"**the *Ohr Zarua onah***" — ש"ך שם ס"ק ז', וכתב שם הב"ח דהירא את דבר ד' נוהג כהאור זרוע, ודעת החת"ס בתשו' חיו"ד סוס"י קע"ט לחוש לחומרת האור זרוע מדינא ואף בוסת שאינו קבוע, וע"ש שיטתו בזה. ומש"כ בשו"ת תשורת שי ח"א סי' ער"ה דבוסת שאינו קבוע אין צריך לחוש לעונת או"ז, יעויין בשו"ת שבט הלוי ח"ב סי' ע' וח"ד סי' צ"ח סק"ה דלהלכה נקטינן לחוש לעונת או"ז אף בוסת שאינו קבוע. ובטעם החומרא עיין שבה"ל ח"ב שם. ואולם הב"י שם ובחוו"ד שם ס"ק ג' וברעק"א בהגה' לש"ך שם ועוד הרבה אחרונים מקילים שלא לחוש לעונת או"ז אף בוסת קבוע, וכ"כ החזו"א במכתבו שבראש ספר טהרת בת ישראל אות ו'. ועל כן במקום צורך יש להקל אף בוסת קבוע. וכמ"כ בליל טבילה יש להקל, שבה"ל שם. ומ"מ תבדוק קודם תשמיש, שיעורי שבה"ל סי' קפ"ד סע' ב' בט"ז ס"ק ב'.

"which is on the 30th and 31st days etc." — ראה במקורות להלן פרק הבא סע' ט"ו.

"The above restrictions apply etc." — ויש לדון לפמש"כ הפו' לענין חו"נ דהמחמיר תע"ב האם הוא גם בעו"ב, ובפרט דשיטת רבים מהראשונים דבעו"ב יש רק חיוב בדיקה ולא חיוב פרישה עיין בגר"ז דס"י קפ"ט בקו"א, ויל"ע.

"during these two 24 hour periods" — כרתי ופלתי סי' קפ"ט ס"ק ט"ו ושו"ע הרב שם ס"ק א'. ועיין ב"ח רס"י קפ"ט דבעו"ב חוששת רק עונה אחת וכ"ה בסד"ט שם ס"ק ל"א, ומ"מ יש להחמיר כדעת הכו"פ. ולענין חו"נ עיין מש"כ לעיל, וביום ל' שלא בעונת ראיתה וכן ביום ל"א [אם אינו וסת החודש], יותר יש לצדד להקל.

"or during the night" — ולכאורה נראה מסתימת הפוסקים דלעונת או"ז לפני יום השלשים אין צריך לחוש, ואף אם ראיתה האחרונה היתה בלילה אינה חוששת לעונת או"ז ביום כ"ט. ועוד, דיסוד עונת או"ז הוא דמלבד חיוב פרישה של שעת וסתה הוסיפו חז"ל פרישה בעונה הסמוכה לוסתה וכמו"ש הש"ך והחת"ס [כל א' כשיטתו], וע"ז קאי מ"ש בגמ' לפרוש מאשתו סמוך לוסתה דהיינו חיוב פרישה קודם שעת הוסת, אבל בדין עונה בינונית אמרו חז"ל את חלק ההיתר וכדתנן במתני' דף י"ד דבא ומצאה תוך ימי עונתה הרי היא בחזקת טהרה, דהיינו עד יום ל', וסתמא כפירושו דתוך ל' ואפילו ביום כ"ט אי"צ לפרוש. והטעם בזה פשוט, דדוקא היכא דחזינן דאשה זו ראתה ביום מסויים החמירו חז"ל להוסיף עונה שמא תקדים משא"כ היכא דכל החשש הוא דשמא תראה כרוב נשים דאינו חשש גמור על יום זה כמו ביום הוסת [ומוכח כן בפו', דברואה מחמת תשמיש מבואר בשו"ע סי' קפ"ז סע' ד' דתולה בוסתה ואילו בעו"ב דעת כמה פוסקים דאינה תולה בעו"ב, עיין בזה בתשו' קנאת סופרים להגר"ש קלוגר בהשמטות לשו"ת טוטו"ד סי' מ"ב ותשו' בית שלמה יו"ב ח"ב סי' י"ט, ובכו"פ סי' קפ"ז נסתפק בזה], ועוד יש לצרף דעת הרבה ראשונים דס"ל דדין עו"ב הוא רק חיוב בדיקה וכמו"ש הגר"ז בקו"א רס"י קפ"ט, וגם כל החשש להלכה להחמיר כאו"ז הוא חומרא. אמנם בספר מלבושי טהרה רס"י קפ"ט כתב להחמיר בזה, וכ"כ בשו"ת שבט הלוי ח"ח סי' קצ"ח אות א', ואפשר דהשבה"ל לשיטתו בזה בהבנת האו"ז דכתב כן לחומרא ולא מדינא ועל כן אין קושיא מהגמ', אבל להש"ך והחת"ס דס"ל דהאו"ז כ"כ מדינא יותר נראה כמו שנתבאר, שיעורי הגרמ"ש קליין שליט"א.

3. "she must check herself" — שו"ע סי' קפ"ד סע' ט'. ובעונת או"ז דחיוב

הפרישה הוא מחשש דשמא תקדים לראות ואינו חשש עצמי שמא תראה כמו בעונת הוסת, אין צריך לבדוק וכהא דכתב החוו"ד סי' קפ"ד ס"ק ט' דביש לה שעה קבועה אינה צריכה בדיקה כי אם בשעת וסתה. ומש"כ בשיעורי שבה"ל להצריך בדיקה בעונת או"ז הוא על דרך חומרא, שיעורי הגרמ"ש קליין שליט"א.

"from sleeping in the same bed" — ואף שכיבה בלבד אסור, דהחשש הוא שמא ע"י הקירוב יבואו לידי תשמיש.

3. "close to sunrise" — שו"ע סי' קפ"ד סע' ד' ושם בש"ך.

"The same rule applies if she forgot etc." — שיעורי הגרמ"ש קליין שליט"א.

"If she arose etc." — דיש לה חזקת טהרה, ועי' ספר האשכול סי' ל"ב. ולא דמי ללעיל בראתה עם הנה"ח או עם השקיעה ולא שמה על לבה לידע אם היה לפני הנה"ח או השקיעה או אח"כ דחוששת לחומרא גם לעונה הקודמת, דהתם יודעת אימתי התחילה ראיתה אלא שאינה יודעת אם היה זה יום או לילה, והוי ספק, ולכן לחומרא יש לחוש לעונה הקודמת, משא"כ הכא שיודעת שראתה עתה, אלא שאנו דנין אם לחוש שהתחילה ראיתה קודם, בזה אמרינן דכיון שיש לה חזקת טהרה לא חיישינן לזה, שיעורי הגרמ"ש קליין שליט"א.

"If she forgot entirely etc." — חוו"ד סי' קפ"ד סוס"ק ד'.

"If she knows when her last period occurred etc." — עיין חוו"ד הנ"ל, ופשוט.

4. "she checks once after getting up ... and once before sunset" — עיין חזו"א סי' פ' ס"ק כ' דלכתחילה יש לדמות בדיקת יום הוסת לז"נ דצריך בדיקה בתחילת העונה ובסופה, ועי' להלן.

"It is commendable ... also after getting up etc." — דכיון שישינה ואינה בודקת בסוף העונה תועיל בבדיקה שלאחר העונה לברר את הזמן של סוף הלילה שלא ראתה.

"In the case of the *onah beinonis* the following etc." — הטעם לכל זה, דכשראיתה האחרונה היתה בלילה, מדינא בודקת בלילה שאז הוא עונת הוסת שלה, ומ"מ תבדוק גם ביום פעם אחת קרוב לסוף העונה כיון דגם בעלמא בעונת הוסת ראוי לבדוק בסוף העונה כדי לברר על זמן זה של סוף העונה, ולכן גם בעו"ב להכו"פ דחוששת כל מעל"ע, אף שכבר בדקה בלילה מ"מ ראוי שתבדוק שוב בסוף עונה בינונית דהיינו בסוף עונת היום. וכשראיתה האחרונה היתה ביום, מדינא עליה לבדוק עצמה רק ביום שהוא עונת וסתה, ואף להכו"פ דחוששת לעו"ב כל המעל"ע מ"מ מדינא סגי במה שבודקת בעונת היום ואפילו בדיקה אחת בלבד בעונת הוסת סגי, וא"כ מן הדין אי"צ בדיקה בלילה [וכבר נתבאר לעיל דבעונת או"ז אי"צ בדיקה], ומ"מ טוב להדר לבדוק גם בתחילת הלילה דסו"ס גם בעונת הוסת לכתחילה ראוי לבדוק גם בתחילת העונה.

4. "the couple may be together etc." — שו"ע שם.

5. "If she did not check herself" — שו"ע שם.

"relations are still prohibited" — אולם חיבוק ונישוק מותר, דהא גם בעונת הוסת מותר מן הדין אלא דהמחמיר תע"ב, והרי לדעת הרי"ף והרמב"ם בעבר הוסת מותרת אף בתשמיש בלא בדיקה, ואף להחולקים דבעבר הוסת צריכה בדיקה מ"מ י"ל דאינו אלא חובת בירור ואין כאן חשש גמור שמא ראתה, דאילו היה חשש גמור שמא ראתה הרי היה אסור בכל הדברים והיה צריך לנהוג גם שאר הרחקות כבנדה וזה הרי מבואר בסד"ט סי' קפ"ד ס"ק י"ג דבעבר הוסת אינו אסור אלא כעונת הוסת ולא יותר, ולפ"ז א"כ גם בחו"נ יש להתיר. ותו, דהא דהמחמיר בחו"נ בעונת הוסת תע"ב הוא מחשש שמא יבוא עליה וכדכתב הט"ז וכ"מ בב"ח, ואילו בעבר הוסת דעל ידי בדיקה מותרת גם בתשמיש לא שייך לאסור מחשש שמא יבוא עליה, דאכן מותר לבוא עליה ע"י בדיקה, שיעורי הגרמ"ש קליין שליט"א.

"It is commendable ... the start of the night etc." — עיין לעיל בסמוך משנ"ת, ואף דכאשר ראיתה האחרונה היתה בלילה נכתב דראוי שתבדוק גם בסוף עונת היום ולא רק בגדר של הידור, היינו משום דאיחור הבדיקה בסוף עונת הוסת יש לו יותר מקום מן הדין דמברר את כל סוף העונה, משא"כ הקדמת הבדיקה בתחילת העונה הוא ענין של הידור בלבד, ודו"ק.

"If she finds it difficult etc." — עיין חזו"א סי' פ' ס"ק כ"ב דבעונת הוסת סגי בבדיקה פעם אחת, ואפילו למ"ד וסתות דאורייתא. [וצ"ל דמש"כ בס"ק כ' דבודקת ב"פ היינו לכתחילה וכמו בז"נ דהבדיקה ב"פ הוא ג"כ לכתחילה, אבל מדינא גם אי וסתות דאורייתא סגי בבדיקה אחת].

"In the case of the *onah beinonis* she etc." — דכשראיתה האחרונה ביום לכו"ע עדיף שתבדוק בסוף עונת היום, דיוצאת בזה הן שיטת הפליתי דעו"ב הוא מעל"ע והן שיטת הב"ח והסד"ט דעו"ב הוא ביום הל' בעונת ראיתה האחרונה. ואף גם בראתה בלילה, דלכאורה היה מקום לדון להכו"פ דעו"ב הוא מעל"ע למה לא תבדוק בסוף עונת היום ותברר את עונת היום וכלול בזה גם עונת הלילה, ובפרט דהרי מהני בדיקה גם אחר עו"ב וכמבואר בשו"ע סע' ט', מ"מ כיון דלהב"ח והסד"ט חששא דעו"ב הוא רק בלילה וסו"ס גם להפליתי יוצאת יד"ח בדיקה כשבודקת בליל השלושים כמו כשבודקת בתוך העונה, לכן עדיף שתבדוק בליל השלושים, וכמ"כ לענין יום ל"א, דכשראיתה האחרונה היתה בלילה, תבדוק בליל ל"א מהטעם הנ"ל.

6. "she should not wash etc." — ע"פ פרישה שם ס"ק י"ח.

"*Bedi'eved*, the check is valid" — עיין ב"ח בקו"א וחזו"א סי' פ' ס"ק כ"ב, וכ"פ בשו"ת שבט הלוי ח"ב סי' ע"א אות א'.

"Some authorities contend" — קצשו"ע סי' קנ"ה סע' ט'.

"even if she did wash the area" — דגם הפרישה לא החמיר אלא כשבודקת אחר שעבר הוסת דס"ל דהבדיקה מבררת על למפרע שלא ראתה ביום הוסת, אבל כאן שבודקת בעונת הוסת עצמה, דהיינו בזמן שמועילה הבדיקה לברר על ההוה, אפילו כשרחצה מהני הבדיקה אף להפרישה, שיעורי הגרמ"ש קליין שליט"א.

7. "Before embarking on a trip" — במחבר שם סע' י' כתב דיקיים עונתו, ושם ברמ"א כתב שמעיקר הדין מותר אף בתשמיש, והמחמיר שלא לפקדה רק בדברי ריצוי תבוא עליו ברכה. ודעת הש"ך שיפקדנה בחיבוק ונישוק, והט"ז מחמיר. ובגר"ז פירש שדברי ריצוי היינו שיבקש ממנה שתמחל על עונתה. ובשו"ת חת"ס יו"ד סי' ק"ע (הו"ד בפת"ש שם ס"ק כ"ב) כתב שיש להחמיר מדינא שלא לפקדה אלא בדברי ריצוי, דס"ל דחיוב פרישה סמוך לוסת הוא מה"ת. אולם זהו דוקא בוסת קבוע, אבל בושא"ק דחיוב פרישה לכו"ע הוא מדרבנן וכמו"ש החת"ס בתשו' סוס"י קע"ט, א"כ בושא"ק לכו"ע רק משום המחמיר תע"ב יש לימנע מלפקדה בתשמיש.

8. "Colored ... should not be worn" — דחזינן שצריכה לברר טהרתה בעונת הוסת ע"י בדיקה וא"כ בודאי לא תלבש צבעוני להצילה מכתם. וכ"ה בספר פרדס

"It is commendable to perform additional *bedikahs* etc." — משנה י"ג ע"א, ושו"ע שם סוף סע' א' אפילו שלא בשעת וסתה. ובשעת וסתה ודאי דכן הוא, דהא שיטת החוו"ד סוס"ק ט' דכשאין לה שעה קבועה צריכה מוך דחוק כל העונה, והנודע ביהודה מהדו"ק יו"ד סי' מ"ו בד"ה מעתה כתב שתבדוק בבוקר, בערב ובאמצע היום כמה פעמים. ודעת הגר"ש ואזנר שליט"א דטוב שתוסיף עוד בדיקה אחת באמצע העונה. — כל סעיף זה משיעורי הגרמ"ש קליין שליט"א.

7. "due to *veset haguf*" — ט"ז סי' קפ"ט ס"ק ל"ח.

10. "One may be lenient etc." — עיין תשו' חת"ס חיו"ד סי' ק"ע בד"ה יהיה. והנה, לענין עונה בינונית לא נתפרש להדיא בפוסקים אי שרי בתשמיש ביוצא לדרך, ואפשר דיש להקל בזה ולסמוך על שיטת הרבה ראשונים דבעו"ב יש רק חיוב בדיקה ולא חיוב פרישה עיין בגר"ז דס"י קפ"ט בקו"א. וביום ל"א דלדעת רוב הפו' אינו בכלל עו"ב וכן

הגדול לרש״י סי׳ רע״א וז״ל: ״ואותו יום או לילה שקבעה לה וסת וכו׳ בודקת עצמה תדיר ולובשת חלוק לבן ומצעת לבנים פרושים על מיטתה, שאם תראה דם כלום יהא ניכר בהן בטוב״. ועי׳ פ״ת סי׳ ק״צ ס״ק כ״ב שנראה שכיון לדין זה, וספר ויחי יוסף סי׳ ו׳, ואג״מ יו״ד ח״ג סי׳ מ״ח. גם תועיל בזה לחוש לדברי החו״ד סי׳ קפ״ד סעי׳ ט׳ שהצריך מוך דחוק כל עונת הוסת.

"If she started menstruating, stopped, and then started again" .9-13 מדינא דגמ׳ אין אשה קובעת וסת בימי נדה ובימי זיבה. ודעת הראב״ד דדינא הכי גם בזה״ז. אבל דעת הרמב״ן שבזה״ז שבנות ישראל החמירו שאינן מונות ימי זיבה לפי שעלולות לטעות, הן קובעות וסת אף בימי נדה וזיבה, וכן קי״ל לדינא. ובש״ך סי׳ קפ״ט ס״ק ע״א ובנה״כ שם נוקט שהוא דווקא להחמיר אבל לא להקל. ולדבריו צריכות בנות ישראל בזה״ז לחשב ימי נדותן וזיבתן. אבל בתוה״ש ס״ק כ״ז נוקט שאין משגיחין בימי נדה וזיבה בין להחמיר ובין להקל, וכן נקטינן עיקר. (והטעם מבואר באחרונים, שבראיה רצופה אין חוששים שמא התחילה בימי זיבה והמשיכה בימי נדה. ורק בראיה שנפסקה והתחדשה אחר כך יש מקום לחשוש כן. ודעת החו״ד (קפ״ד סק״ז) שאפ׳ הפסקה של שעה מועטת חשובה הפסקה. ודעת שועה״ר (קפ״ד ס״ק ז׳, וקפ״ט ס״ק קי״ב) שרק אם פסקה ביום אחד וחידשה את ראיתה ביום אחר חשוב הפסקה). וחידש בשועה״ר (ס׳ קפ״ט ס״ק קי״ב) שכשהאשה מתחילה לראות דם וסת רגיל כדרך נשים, נקטינן בפשיטות שזהו התחלת ימי נדותה. ולכן אם תראה שוב בתוך ז׳ ימי נדה אינה חוששת בחדא זמנא לושא״ק. ורק אם תראה אחרי ז׳ ימים תחוש לו. וטעמו נראה, שאף שאינה קובעת וסת בימי נדה וזיבה, מ״מ חוששת בימי זיבה לושא״ק כמבואר בנדה ס״ד ע״א וברש״י. (ועי׳ בית שלמה ח״ב סי׳ ז׳ בהג״ה מבן המחבר מש״כ בשם הרמב״ם והראב״ד). משא״כ בימי נדה אינה חוששת לושא״ק. אמנם אם תראה בתוך ימי נדותה ג״פ באופן שיכולה לקבוע וסת, חוששת שמא זהו תחילת נדותה. עכ״ד. ובחו״ד סי׳ קפ״ד סק״ז סתם להקל שלעולם אינה חוששת עד שתראה ג״פ, ובלבד שראיה ראשונה היא ושא״ק. ובפרדס רימונים סי׳ קפ״ד ס״ק ט״ז מתבאר שאם הפסיקה למשך יום שלם חוששת אף בתוך ז׳ ימים, ואף בושא״ק, ויש להחמיר כדבריו אם ראתה כן אחרי משך הימים שרגילה להיות שופעת דם. ומה שכתבנו שאם בפעם הראשונה ראתה דם מועט ובפעם השניה דם מרובה וכו׳, טעמו פשוט, שלא מסתבר שהראיה הראשונה המועטת היא העיקר. והראיה השניה של דם מרובה טפלה לה.

פרק עשירי

1. "During these times etc." — ראה לעיל פרק ט' ובמקורות.

2. "If her previous periods began according to a clear pattern" — ראה במקורות להלן בהמשך הפרק.

"at the following three times" — ואף שישנם כמה סוגי וסתות, וכפי שמנה הב"י סי' קפ"ט [נא.] ה' מיני וסתות יעו"ש, מ"מ לחוש שמא תקבע וסת אינה חוששת אלא לשלשה סוגי הוסתות הללו, מלבד בוסת הגוף שחוששת לו אף בפעם אחת וכמבואר בשו"ע שם סע' כ"א. והטעם שאינה חוששת לוסת הדילוג ולוסת הסירוג עד שתקבענו מבואר בראב"ד בבעה"נ שער תיקון הוסתות [בדפו"ח סי' ג' ה"י] ומובא בגר"ז שם ס"ק ל"ב ובמקור מים חיים בסע' י"א, ועיין לחו"ש ס"ק י"ז מה שביאר בטעמו של הראב"ד. וע"ע בבעה"נ שם [סי' ג' הי"ב] מה שכתב הראב"ד לענין וסת השבוע שאינה חוששת עד שתקבע, וביאר שם הטעם. וע"ע חכמ"א כלל קי"ב ס"ח.

"The *veset haflagah* etc." — שו"ע סי' קפ"ט סע' ב' וברמ"א סע' י"ג.

"The *veset hachodesh*" — שו"ע שם סע' ב' וברמ"א סע' י"ג.

"The *onah beinonis* ... the 30th day" — עיין טור ב"י וב"ח רס"י קפ"ט, שו"ע סע' א', פרישה ולבוש שהובאו בש"ך ס"ק ל', ט"ז ס"ק י"ז.

"This is the accepted ruling" — עיין פתחי תשובה ס"ק י' בשם תשו' חכ"צ סי' קי"ד וכו"פ ס"ק ט"ו שהסכימו לדעת הט"ז. וכ"ה בסדרי טהרה ס"ק י"ב מחה"ש בש"ך ס"ק ל' גר"ז סק"א וחכמ"א כלל קי"ב ס"ה. ודלא כש"ך ס"ק ל' דס"ל שאינה חוששת אלא ליום החודש. וגם החוו"ד דס"ל דהוא יום ל"א, מ"מ כתב דחוששת ג"כ ליום ל' כהט"ז והחכ"צ.

"According to other opinions ... on the 31st day" — חוו"ד שם ביאורים ס"ק י"ב.

ביום ל' שלא בעונת הראיה [אם אינו וסת החודש] ודאי יש לצדד להקל.

פרק עשירי

4. "then she has an established *veset* for the longer interval" — נראה שהקביעות היא רק לענין שבעינן ג' פעמים לעקירתה, אבל אינה מסולקת דמים עד זמן הוסת, דהרי

"Ideally etc." — מדברי החוו״ד, ועיין עוד בלחו״ש ס״ק א׳ וכ״ג, תשו׳ חת״ס חיו״ד סי׳ קס״ו בד״ה והוא, שכתבו כהחוו״ד.

ולפי״ז כשהחודש האחרון היה מלא, חוששת ליום ל׳ ולל״א מעיקר הדין, דהא יום הל׳ הוא עונה בינונית לדעת רוב הפו׳ וכנ״ל, ויום ל״א מלבד שהוא עונה בינונית להחוו״ד, הרי הוא גם יום וסת החודש.

וכשהחודש האחרון היה חסר, חוששת ליום ל׳ מעיקר הדין, שהוא גם עונה בינונית לדעת רוב הפוסקים וגם יום וסת החודש, ולכתחילה חוששת גם ליום ל״א שהוא עונה בינונית לשי׳ החוו״ד, וכמשנ״ת דלכתחילה חוששים לשיטה זו.

"The *veset haguf* etc." — שו״ע שם סע׳ כ״א.

3. "**The number of interval days is counted etc.**" — עיין סתימת לשון השו״ע סי׳ קפ״ד סע׳ ו׳, רמ״א סי׳ קפ״ט סע׳ י״ג, תשו׳ חת״ס חיו״ד סי׳ קס״ו אות ג׳ תשו׳ בית שלמה יו״ד ח״ב סי׳ ט״ו ותשו׳ שו״מ תנינא ח״א סי׳ ל״ג. [ושיטת הגר״ז בחישוב מנין ימי הפלגה, דקביעות ההפלגה היא ע״פ הזמן שאינה רואה ולא ע״פ הזמן שרואה, וא״כ ההפלגה צריכה להיות מסוף ראיה לתחילת ראיה, דאלו הם הימים שלא ראתה בהם, ועל ידם קובעת וסת להפלגה. ודוקא בעו״ב הוא דמחשבין מתחילת ראיה לתחילת ראיה, ולא גבי וסת ההפלגה, עיין בדבריו סי׳ קפ״ד ס״ק כ״ב ובקו״א שם אות ד׳, אך כאמור דעת רוב הפו׳ דלא כהגר״ז בזה, ועי׳ שבה״ל ח״ד סוס״י צ״ז].

"**an additional rule is etc.**" — עיין שו״ע ונו״כ סי׳ קפ״ט, ומפורש כן גם בב״י שם בד״ה לשון הרמב״ן.

4. "**there is no further need etc.**" — שו״ע סי׳ קפ״ט סע׳ ב׳.

רגילה לראות קודם זמן וסתה, וע״כ אם הפלגתה לשלושים וחמש יום יש לומר שצריכה לחוש לעו״ב לראייתה, דהרמב״ן בחידושיו בדף ט״ו כתב הטעם דבוסת קבוע לל״ה אינה חוששת לעו״ב הוא מטעם דהוי מסולקת דמים עד זמן וסתה, א״כ י״ל דבכה״ג אינה מסולקת דמים, ואפשר דיש לחוש לחומרא גם לוסת החודש מראייתה כיון שדעת הש״ך בסימן קפ״ט ס״ק מ׳ דבכה״ג לא קבעה וסת דוסת קצר עוקר וסת ארוך, ואף דיש להחמיר דלא כוותיה כמ״ש בשו״ע הרב ובשאר האחרונים, מ״מ לקולא י״ל דאין להקל נגד דעת הש״ך.

5. "**she must anticipate ... on the *onah* when those periods originally occurred**" שיעורי הגרמ״ש קליין שליט״א.

5. "the veset is not considered uprooted" — עיין רמ"א שם סע' י"ג וט"ז ס"ק י"ח, ודלא כב"ח וש"ך ס"ק ל"א. וכדעת הרמ"א וט"ז דהפלגה קצרה אינה עוקרת הפלגה ארוכה כתבו בכו"פ ס"ק י"ח, תפארת למשה בש"ך ס"ק מ', סד"ט ס"ק י"ד וי"ט, בית מאיר סע' י"ג וגר"ז ס"ק מ"ג ומ"ד, והוכיחו כן מהל' נדה להרמב"ן פ"ה הט"ז ופ"ו ה"ב דמפורש כן, וכן מוכח מהראב"ד בבעלי הנפש.

"She must now anticipate etc." — לשון הגר"ז שם ס"ק מ"ד "כללו של דבר אשה שראתה בתחלה הפלגה מרובה, וחזרה וראתה בהפלגה מועטת, וחזרה וראתה בהפלגה מועטת מהשניה, וכן כמה פעמים במיעוט אחר מיעוט שלא בסדר השוה בענין שאין כאן וסת הדילוג, צריכה לחוש לכל ימי ההפלגות, כי לא נעקרו במה שהקדימה לראות אלא עד שיבא יומן ולא תראה וכו'".

6. "always counted from the first day of her most recent period" — רמב"ן בהל' נדה ומובא בטור סי' קפ"ט, רמ"א סע' י"ג, ופשוט.

"dates from two different intervals etc." — עיין בנקוה"כ על הט"ז ס"ק י"ח דבהי' לה וסת קבוע לל', וראתה בהפלגת כ', חוששת ל' ימים אחר ראיה זו, שהוא יום הפלגת ל' מראית ל', ומבואר בדבריו דרק מחמת דהפלגת ל' קבוע לכן הוא דאין מונין הפלגה מהראיה האחרונה, דתולין ראית הכ' בתוספת דמים ואינו סותר החשבון של הפלגת ל', אבל באינו קבוע, אף אילו הפלגה קצרה לא היתה עוקרת את הארוכה, היו מונין מהראיה האחרונה.

וכן יש להוכיח מעצם מש"כ הש"ך ס"ק ל"א דהפלגה קצרה עוקרת את הארוכה, ואילו לא היו מונין מהראיה האחרונה, א"כ למה סותרת ההפלגה הקצרה את ההפלגה הארוכה, והלא אם תראה ביום שהי' ראוי להיות ההפלגה הארוכה, הוי חשבינן לההפלגה הקצרה כדמים יתידים והוי חשיב הפלגה ארוכה, ומוכח דבוסת שאינו קבוע לעולם מונים מהראיה האחרונה. וכ"ה דעת הכו"פ ושאר פו' שהובאו לעיל בסע' הקודם, דחוששת לכל ההפלגות שצריכה לחוש, מראיתה האחרונה.

7. "she must anticipate ... after various time intervals" — עיין לשון הגר"ז שהובא לעיל במקורות לסע' ה'. והנה, לדעת הראב"ד בבעה"נ אם היתה לה וסת קבוע קצר לכ' ושינתה לראות לל', ושוב ראתה בכ', לא נעקר חשש הוסת לל', ועדיין חוששת להפלגת ל' משום וסת שאינו קבוע, שאין וסת קבוע קצר עוקר חשש וסת

שאינו קבוע ארוך. אבל הרמב״ן בהל׳ נדה פ״ו ה״ב חולק ע״ז וסובר דמשקבעה וסת לכ׳ אינה חוששת עוד לל׳ דאי אפשר שתראה כל ימיה לכ׳ ותחוש לל׳, ע״ש. ומיהו גם להרמב״ן היינו דוקא כשהוסת הקצר הוא קבוע והארוך אינו קבוע, אבל כשב׳ הוסתות אינן קבועים, עדיין חוששת לארוך, ואין וסת קצר עוקר החשש דוסת הארוך.

8. "On the other hand ... she need not anticipate etc." — כן הוא לכל הדיעות, הואיל ועבר יום וסתה ולא ראתה בו, הוי עקירה לחשש הוסת, עי׳ שו״ע סי׳ קפ״ט סע׳ ב׳.

9. "Accordingly etc." — כנ״ל בסעיפים הקודמים.

10. "It depends on the *onah* of one's last period" — שו״ע סי׳ קפ״ט סע׳ י״ג. ולענין וסת הפלגה עיין תשו׳ נו״ב תנינא סי׳ פ״ג.

"since it serves only as a starting point etc." — עיין תשו׳ נו״ב שם.

11. "must anticipate menstruation on the same date of the month etc." שו״ע סי׳ קפ״ט סע׳ ב׳ רמ״א סע׳ י״ג.

"only during the same *onah*" — עיין שו״ע סי׳ קפ״ד סע׳ ב׳ וסי׳ קפ״ט סע׳ ב׳ וסע׳ י״ג. ועי׳ חכמ״א כלל קי״ב סי׳ ט״ז.

12. "she no longer needs to anticipate ... on the 1st of the month" שו״ע שם סע׳ ב׳.

13. "on two dates" — עיין בכל זה ברמ״א סע׳ י״ג.

14. "is not rescinded" — גר״ז סי׳ קפ״ט ס״ק ל״ח.

15. "she must anticipate ... on *Rosh Chodesh*" — דיעויין בב״ח בסי׳ קפ״ט שכתב דהא דכתב הטור שם דבראתה בא׳ בניסן ובכ׳ בו חוששת לא׳ באייר מפני ראש חודש ניסן, הפירוש בזה דחוששת רק ליום ב׳ דר״ח, שהוא יום א׳ בחודש

---

13. "she is regarded ... an established cycle for the 10th" — עי׳ לעיל הערה 4 ולפי מש״כ שם דאינה מסולקת דמים עד זמן וסת א״כ י״ל דיש לחוש לעו״ב מראייתה, והיינו דאם החודש מלא ויום החודש הוא יום ל״א יש לחוש ג״כ ליום ל׳ משום עו״ב.

14. "However etc." — עיין במקורות ליסוד הטהרה, ובשיעורי הגרמ״ש קליין שליט״א.

שוה לראית א׳ בניסן, אבל אינה חוששת לל׳ בניסן, וביאר הב״ח ״ואע״ג דבסמוך כתבתי דאם ראתה בר״ח ניסן וביום ראשון דר״ח אייר [דהיינו בל׳ בניסן], וביום כ״ט אייר לא ראתה דחוששת לר״ח סיון, התם היינו טעמא דכיון דחזינן דראתה תרי זימני בראש חודש, אע״ג שזה אחד בניסן וזה אינו אחד באייר אלא הוא יום שלשים של חודש העבר, חיישינן שמא יום הנקרא בשם ראש חודש הוא הגורם ראיתה, אבל לחוש ליום ראשון דר״ח אייר [דהיינו לל׳ בניסן] לכתחילה לא חיישינן, אלא ליום ב׳ דר״ח אייר חוששת לפי שהוא אחד באייר שוה לאחד בניסן, ולכן דקדק רבינו [הטור] בלשונו למעלה שלא אמר אלא באחד באייר באחד בתמוז״ עכ״ל. ובפשוטו היה אפשר לבאר בדעת הב״ח, דרק בראתה ב״פ בראש חודש, בזה הוא דחיישינן דשם ראש חודש גורם ראיתה, ולכן חוששת לא׳ בסיון, משא״כ בראתה פעם אחת בא׳ בניסן, אי״צ לחוש דשם ראש חודש גורם ראיתה, אלא חיישינן רק דא׳ בחודש גורם לראיתה, ולכן חוששת לא׳ באייר ולא לל׳ בניסן, [אא״כ לא ראתה עדיין דאז חוששת לל׳ בניסן משום עונה בינונית]. ולפי״ז הא דבראתה בא׳ בניסן אינה חוששת לשם ראש חודש שהוא הגורם לראיתה, הוא מחמת דבראיה אחת אין חוששין לגרמת שם ראש חודש. - ונפק״מ לפי״ז בראתה בל׳ בחודש, דאין אנו חוששים שמא שם ראש חודש הוא הגורם לראיתה, ורק לכשתראה עוד ראיה באחד מימי ראש חודש אז הוא שנחוש דשם ראש חודש גורם לראיתה. - אבל באמת דיותר נראה לפרש בדברי הב״ח באופן אחר, דאין החילוק בין ב׳ המקרים דלעיל, מחמת דחלוק הוא ראיה אחת לר״ח לבין ב׳ ראיות לר״ח, דבראיה אחת לר״ח אין חוששין דגרמת ראיתה הוא שם ר״ח ואילו בב׳ ראיות לימי החודש חוששים לגרמת יום החדש, אלא יותר נראה בדברי הב״ח, דהא דבראתה בא׳ בניסן אינה חוששת לגרמת שם ראש חודש, הוא משום דבסתם ראיה יש לנו חששות דחודש ודהפלגה וכיו״ב, ואילו גרמת שם ראש חודש הוא מהלך מחודש דבסתם אינה חוששת לזה, ולכן כשראתה בא׳ בניסן אינה צריכה לחוש אלא לגרמת יום החודש, דהיינו לא׳ באייר, ואינה חוששת לל׳ בניסן מחמת גרמת שם ר״ח, דמהיכ״ת לחוש לזה, ורק בראתה בא׳ בניסן ובל׳ בניסן, דאין שום דבר שוה לב׳ ראיות אלו, דזה א׳ בחודש וזה ל׳ בחודש, אבל יש דבר שוה לב׳ ראיות אלו דתרוויהו הם ימי ראש חודש, אז הוא דבאנו לחששא דשם ראש חודש, דכיון דלפנינו ב׳ ראיות שיש להם צד שוה של ימי ראש חודש, אז הוא דחוששת לגרמת שם ראש חודש. ומה שכתב הב״ח

דכיון דחזינן דראתה תרי זימני וכו׳ אין כונתו דמחמת דהוי תרי זימני ולא חדא זימנא לכן הוא דחוששת לגרמת שם ר״ח, אלא כונתו דכיון דהם תרי זימני שוים לגרמת שם ר״ח לכן חוששין לראש חודש, משא״כ בראתה בא׳ בניסן דאין סיבה לחוש לגרמת שם ראש חודש. - ונפק״מ דלפי״ז אם ראתה פעם אחת בל׳ בחודש, אע״פ דאין מפורש בב״ח האיך הדין בזה, מ״מ לפמשנ״ת בסברת הב״ח דרק היכא דיש לנו צד לפרש את גרמת הראיה שאינה בגרמת יום החודש אלא בגרמת שם ראש חודש וכהא דראתה בא׳ בניסן ובל׳ בו, דאין צד שוה לב׳ הראיות ביום החודש כי אם דתרווייהו הם ביום ראש חודש, אז הוא דחוששת לגרמת שם ראש חודש, א״כ ה״ה בראתה פעם אחת בל׳ בחודש, כיון דבפשטות צריך שיהא לה יום בחודש שתחוש לחודש הבא, והרי בחודש הבא אין יום ל׳ דחודש חסר הוא, על כן עליה לחוש לגרמת שם ראש חודש, ולא בא הב״ח להוציא מן הכלל רק סתם ראיה של א׳ בחודש, דאינה חוששת לשם ראש חודש כיון דיש לה למה לחוש, לא׳ בחודש, אבל בראתה בל׳ בחודש דאין לה יום בחודש לחוש, יותר מסתבר לן לומר דשם ראש חודש הוא זה שגרם ראיתה. - ועיין עוד בפרי דעה סי׳ קפ״ט בט״ז ס״ק י״ז שכתב דלא זו כונת הב״ח לחלק בין ראתה פ״א ביום ל׳ לראתה ב״פ ביום ל׳, וכנ״ל, אלא דהפרי דעה חידש שם דאחר ראיה אחת ביום ל׳ חוששת לכ״ט בחודש ואם לא תראה בו חוששת גם לגרמת שם ר״ח, וצ״ע מה חשש איכא על יום כ״ט, והיכן מצינו חשש וסת ליום אחרון בחודש, ויותר מחוור לפרש דהחשש הוא על גרמת שם ראש חודש. משיעורי הגרמ״ש קליין שליט״א.

"However, if she had her period on the 1st of the month etc." — כן מבואר מדברי הב״ח שם דרק אם ראתה בא׳ בניסן ובל׳ בו אז הוא שחוששת שמא שם "ראש חודש" הוא הגורם לראיתה, אבל בראתה בא׳ בניסן ובכ׳ בו, אינה חוששת שמא תראה בל׳ בניסן מחמת שם ראש חודש, דבסתם ראיה של א׳ בחודש אינה חוששת אלא לא׳ בחודש ולא לגרמת שם ראש חודש. וכן מבואר מדברי הב״ח לעיל שם שכתב דכשראתה בא׳ בניסן חוששת לב׳ ימי ר״ח משום דל׳ ניסן הוא עונה בינונית וא׳ באייר הוא יום החודש, ומשמע דלל׳ בניסן אינה חוששת אלא משום עו״ב ולא משום וסת דר״ח.

16. **"As stated above in paragraph 2"** — ראה במקורות שם.

17. "the full 24-hrs of that day" — כו"פ סי' קפ"ט ס"ק ט"ו ועיין בגר"ז סי' קפ"ט ס"ק א' שפסק כדברי הכו"פ להלכה דאפילו אם ראתה עכשיו בלילה אסורה ביום ל' בלילה עד למחרת סוף היום, וכתב ע"ז דכ"מ בגמ' ופוסקים.

"Initially one should follow this opinion" — וכדעת הכו"פ והגר"ז. ואף שכמה אחרונים השיגו על מה שכתב הכו"פ דעו"ב לאו מטעם וסת אתינן עלה, ודעתם דשפיר הוי חששא דעו"ב מטעם וסת, מ"מ גם אי נימא דמטעם וסת הוא יש מקום להצריך לחוש לב' העונות, דהא דעת הנו"ב בתנינא יו"ד סי' פ"ג דבוסת ההפלגות דבעינן ד' ראיות, אין חילוק אימתי היתה הראיה הראשונה, דהוא רק היכי תימצי למנות ממנה את ההפלגה הראשונה, [ודלא כסברת השואל בנו"ב הגרד"ט והגר"ז דחישוב וסת הפלגה היא לפי מספר הפלגת עונות, ולשיטתם שפיר איכא נפק"מ באיזה עונה היתה הראיה הראשונה], והרי עו"ב גדרו הפלגת ל' יום, וא"כ כשאנו חוששים שמא תקבע וסת להפלגת ל', אין חשיבות לראיה האחרונה שראתה עתה לידע אם היתה בעונת היום או בעונת הלילה, וכמו בוסת ההפלגה שאם הראיה הראשונה היתה ביום וג' הראיות האחרונות היו בלילה, תקבע וסת ללילה, וכן להיפך, א"כ מה נפק"מ אימתי היתה הראיה האחרונה, הלא אנו חוששין שמא תקבע וסת לל' יום, ויכולה לקבוע הן לעונת הלילה והן לעונת היום, וא"כ לעולם כשחוששת לעו"ב עליה לחוש הן לעונת הלילה והן לעונת היום. וכ"ה בס' סוגה בשושנים סי' ב' ס"ק י"ד וסי' ד' סוס"ק ל"ט. ותו, דאף גם להגרד"ט והגר"ז דמחשבים עונות, נמי יש להבין שיטת הכו"פ דהחשש הוא על כל המעל"ע, כיון דלשיטתם הרי בהפלגות אין כלל קביעות של מספר ימים, ואעפ"כ בעונה בינונית יש חשש קבוע של ל' יום, וא"כ יותר מסתבר דהחשש הוא על כל המעל"ע ולא על עונה מסויימת.

18. "Therefore etc." — כנ"ל במקורות לסע' ב'.

19. "The day ... is counted only from the last period etc." — עיין בסד"ט ס"ק י"ג חוו"ד ס"ק י"ג וחי' רעק"א על הט"ז ס"ק י"ז, וכמש"כ כיו"ב בט"ז ס"ק י"ח בשם הב"ח לענין וסת ההפלגה דכשראתה בינתיים אינה חוששת להפלגה אלא מהראיה האחרונה, וה"ה נמי לענין עונה בינונית. וכ"פ בחכמ"א כלל קי"ב סע' י"ח. ומקו' הט"ז ס"ק י"ז על הב"ח מוכח שהבין דחוששת לעונה בינונית אף אם היתה ראיה נוספת בינתיים, ולשיטתיה אזיל דס"ל הכי בס"ק י"ח לענין וסת ההפלגה דאין

ראיה באמצע מפסקת את ההפלגה. אולם האחרונים הנ״ל השיגו על הט״ז וכתבו דלענין עו״ב כלל אין לחוש לראיה קודמת.

---

16. "In the case of necessity, or when the immersion night falls etc." — עיין סד״ט סי׳ קפ״ט ס״ק ל״א שחולק על הכו״פ וכתב דאינה אסורה אלא ביום ל׳ מראיה הראשונה, אם היתה ביום אסורה ביום ואם היתה בלילה אסורה בלילה. ויעויין עוד בב״ח סי׳ קפ״ט על הטור בשם הרמב״ן [המובא ברמ״א סע׳ י״ג] "נמצאת אומר שהרואה ליום ראש חודש ניסן חוששת לראש חודש אייר", וכתב ע״ז הב״ח "נראה דחוששת לשני הימים דראש חודש, ביום ראשון חוששת לפי שהוא יום שלשים לראייתה שהוא עו״ב דחוששת לו כיון שלא קבעה לה וסת, וביום שני דר״ח חוששת משום ראש חודש וכו׳", והנה, הרי החשש של אחד באייר הוא רק עונה אחת, כעונת ראיתה, וא״כ אילו היה סובר הב״ח דעו״ב הוא מעל״ע היה לו לחלק, דבא׳ דר״ח חוששת מעל״ע, ואילו בב׳ דר״ח חוששת עונה אחת, ומדלא כתב כן משמע דעתו דאף בעו״ב שהוא יום השלשים חוששת לעונה אחת. וכדברי הב״ח כן כתב גם הט״ז בס״ק י״ד, ומשמע דגם דעת הט״ז כן, דאל״כ היה לו לחלק בין ב׳ הימים, וכנ״ל. ובאמת דבדברי הב״ח רס״י קפ״ט הוא ממש מפורש, שכתב "וצריך לפרוש עונה אחת כשיגיע יום שלשים", ומבואר להדיא דלא כהכו״פ. ומאחר דכן הוא דעת הב״ח, וכ״ה משמעות הט״ז, וגם העירו האחרונים דמסתימת הרמב״ן הרשב״א והר״ן שהביאו דין עו״ב ולא כתבו דשונה משאר וסתות דבעו״ב חוששת מעל״ע משמע דאף בעו״ב חוששת רק עונה אחת, וכן הוא גם שיטת הסד״ט, א״כ לענין הלכה, אף דלכתחילה ראוי לחוש לשיטת הכו״פ והגר״ז דעו״ב הוא מעל״ע, מ״מ מעיקר הדין חששא דעו״ב הוא רק עונה אחת. ולכן במקום צורך ושעת הדחק יש צדדים להקל שלא לחוש אלא בעונת ראיתה האחרונה.

17. "Even if her last period was after an interval of 30 days etc." — כיון דמה הוכחה יש מראיה אחת שראתה בלא קביעות, שגם בעתיד תראה בעונה זו, הא גם ראיה זו גופה יש לה גדר של וסת שאינו קבוע שאנו חוששים שמא בעתיד תקבע וסת ליום ל׳ לאחד מב׳ העונות. ואף דבס׳ סוגה בשושנים סי׳ ב׳ ס״ק י״ד וסי׳ ד׳ סוס״ק ל״ט חידש דגם הכו״פ יודה דאם ראתה בהפלגת ל׳ יום, לא תחוש לעו״ב רק בעונת ראיתה האחרונה, כיון דהחשש שתקבע לל׳ יום כבר התחיל בפועל בזה שראתה אכן להפלגת ל׳ יום, וכשאנו באים לחוש שתקבע וסת לל׳ יום אמרינן דמסתמא תקבע באותה עונה שהתחילה דמהיכ״ת שתשנה וסתה ביום ל׳ מעונה לעונה אחרת, וכל דברי הכו״פ הם באשה שעדיין לא ראתה ביום ל׳, אלא רואה בימים אחרים דחוששת לעו״ב כל המעל״ע אבל לא כשכבר התחילה ראיתה לל׳ יום, ע״ש, מ״מ צל״ע בזה וכנ״ל, ובפרט מש״כ שם דגם הכו״פ יודה דחוששת

20. "she need not anticipate ... on the fifty-ninth day etc." — עיין פרי דעה סי׳ קפ״ט ש״ל ס״ק ל׳ ופרדס רמונים שם ש״ח ס״ק ל׳ שפירשו דלזה נתכוין הש״ך במה שהשיג על הלבוש [ובחוו״ד סוס״ק י״ב פירש בענין אחר], ובפרד״ר שם כתב דלזה גם נתכוין התורת השלמים ס״ק ד׳ בביאור דברי הש״ך. ובפרד״ר שם תלה פלוגתת הלבוש והש״ך לשיטתם שנחלקו כן גם לגבי וסת הפלגה, דלהלבוש חוששת לום הראוי ולהש״ך אינה חוששת ליום הראוי, אולם בפר״ד שם כתב דאף להסוברים כה״ג בוסת הפלגה דחוששת ליום הראוי, עי׳ ט״ז ס״ק ל״א, מ״מ מודו דבעו״ב אינה חוששת ליום הראוי, עיי״ש.

21. "Even if the interval ... is always greater than thirty days, etc." — כו״פ סי׳ קפ״ד ס״ק א׳, חוו״ד סי׳ קפ״ו ס״ק ג׳ וכן מסיק הסדרי טהרה סי׳ קפ״ט סוס״ק כ׳ דוסת תרוה״ד הוא רק להקל בבדיקה ולא להשוותו תוך זמן זה כאשה שיש לה וסת קבוע, וכדברי החוו״ד כתבו בפרי דעה סי׳ קפ״ט ש״ל ס״ק ל׳ וישועות יעקב סוס״י קפ״ד, ועוד רבים מהאחרונים. וכן מפורש בב״י סוס״י קפ״ד. ויש להוכיח כן גם מדברי הרשב״א בתוה״ב שהובא בטור סי׳ קפ״ט [אחר דיני וסת הגוף] וז״ל ״כתב הרשב״א חומר בוסת הקפיצות מבשאר הוסתות, שוסת הקפיצות בין שהוא קרוב יותר מעונה בינונית בין שהוא רחוק יותר לעולם היא חוששת לזמן עונה בינונית

רק עונה אחת צ״ע בזה, דודאי דכל ההסבר הנ״ל הוא טעם נכון לחוש לכל המעל״ע, אבל א״א להעמיס כן בכו״פ שכתב מפורש דעו״ב לאו מטעם וסת אתינן עלה.

21. "within a group of more than three days" — שו״ת אבני צדק סי׳ ע״ג שו״ת שבה״ל ח״ד סי׳ צ״ח אות ו׳ וע״ע אגרו״מ יו״ד ח״ב סי׳ ס״ז ענף ג׳.

"Others are meticulous etc." — ע״פ נוב״ק סי׳ מ״ו ולקט יושר לתלמיד התרוה״ד יו״ד עמ׳ י״ח, [וע״ע שו״ת מהרי״ל החדשות סי׳ צ״ג אות ה׳]. ובשלטי הגיבורים בפ״ב דשבועות כתב החשש על ה׳ ימים [ומיהו בפשוטו אין כונת הש״ג לומר בזה דהחשש הוא דוקא על ה׳ ימים ולא יותר]. וע״ע באבני צדק שם דהמחמיר ביותר מג״י יחמיר רק לעצמו.

"but not more than that" — כמפורש בלקט יושר שם, וכ״ה בשם החזו״א זצ״ל, [ובספרו סי׳ פ״ה ס״ק כ״ג כתב דכלל אין להחמיר בדין של ימי המבוכה]. ולדעת החוו״ד סי׳ קפ״ד ס״ק ד׳ אין מקום לחוש אלא כמספר ימי המשך ראיתה וביותר מזה אין מקום לחוש, וזהו לפי שיטתו שם בדין של משנית וסתה.

וכו'", ולכאורה הא כשוסתה מרוחק מעונה בינונית אמאי חוששת לעו"ב, לא יהא אלא כוסת שאינו קבוע, והרי סו"ס יש לה וסת תרוה"ד שלא תראה עד אחר ל', אלא ע"כ דגם אשה שיש לה וסת תרוה"ד עד אחר ל' אעפ"כ חוששת לעונה בינונית.

22. "**A woman who does not have an established cycle etc.**" — עיין בכל זה בתשו' נו"ב קמא יו"ד סי' מ"ו הובא בפת"ש סי' קפ"ד ס"ק ח', וראה להלן בביאורים ומקורות להמשך הסעיף.

"**but usually menstruates etc.**" — ולדעת הש"ג בפ"ב דשבועות הוי גדר של וסת על כל יום ולפי"ז מסתבר דחשש של ימים שנבוכה הוא רק לאחר שהוחזקה לראות [לסירוגין] ג"פ בכל יום מאלו הימים, וכ"ה דעת השבט הלוי למעשה. אולם לדעת הנו"ב שם יסוד החשש הוא מחמת דרגילה שלא יעברו קבוצת ימים אלו בלא ראיה, והחשש הוא על הימים בכללותם ולא על כל עונה ועונה בפנ"ע, ולפי"ז כל שניכר מתוך סדר ראיותיה שתראה בימים אלו חוששת להם, ואף שלא קבעה לראות לסירוגין ג"פ בכל יום מאלו הימים, וכ"ה לביאור הפליתי סי' קפ"ד סק"ה דבימים אלו מודה רחב"א לר"מ דאסורה מחמת שאין לה וסת ע"ש, דלפירושו אין זה קביעות על כל יום אלא דימים אלו בכללותם מוגדרים כימים שרגילה לראות בהם ודינה כאשה שאין לה וסת שאסורה. והנה, אף דמעיקר הדין אפשר לסמוך על דעת הש"ג דהוי גדר של וסת על כל יום דלפי"ז כאמור מסתבר שצריך להתחזק בג"פ על כל יום, מאחר דבלא"ה איכא מרבוואתא דלא סבירא להו הך דינא דמשנית וסתה, מ"מ יש לחוש לכתחילה לדברי הנו"ב והפליתי דכל שניכר מסדר ראיותיה שרגילה לראות בימים אלו חוששת להם ואף שלא קבעה לראות בג"פ בכל יום מאלו הימים, שיעורי הגרמ"ש קליין שליט"א.

"**within a group of three days**" — כתבו החכמת אדם בכלל ק"ח סי' ו' ובשו"ת

---

22. "**she has to do a *bedikah* daily**" — נו"ב שם.

"**whereas others contend etc.**" — כן הוא לדעת הכו"פ סי' קפ"ד סק"ה דמפרש בדין משנית וסתה דדינה בימים אלו כאשה שאין לה וסת ובזה מודה רחב"א לר"מ דאסורה, דלדבריו הוי רק דין פרישה כאשה שאין לה וסת ואין חיוב בדיקה.

"**According to all opinions etc.**" — וכדין וסת שאינו קבוע דבעבר הוסת ולא בדקה מותרת בלא בדיקה, והרי גם להנו"ב אינו אלא כוסת תרוה"ד, דהתרוה"ד עצמו כתב שאין דינו כקבוע ממש, שיעורי הגרמ"ש קליין שליט"א.

לבושי מרדכי חיו"ד סי' ק"ג דאם רגילה תמיד לראות רק בימים ולא בלילות אינה חוששת ללילות, וכן להיפך ברגילה לראות רק בלילות אינה חוששת לימים. והנה, דברי החכמ"א ולבו"מ בזה מסתברים רק לפי המהלך של הש"ג דהוא גדר של וסת על כל יום, דלפי"ז אם רגילה לראות רק בימים ולא בלילות אינה חוששת ללילות שהרי לא הוחזקה לראות בלילות, אך לשיטת הנו"ב והכו"פ דהחשש הוא על הימים בכללותם ולא על כל עונה ועונה בפנ"ע, וכנ"ל, צריכה לחוש גם ללילות אף שאינה רגילה לראות בהם כיון דרגילה לראות בקבוצת ימים אלו. וכבר נתבאר לעיל דלכתחילה יש לחוש לשיטת הנו"ב והכו"פ. וה"ה אם בתוך קבוצת ימים אלו יש עונה אחת או יותר שאינה רגילה לראות בהם, וכגון שסדר הפלגותיה הוא לכ"ו ולכ"ח יום, וביום כ"ז אינה רגילה לראות, הדבר תלוי במה שנתבאר לעיל, דלדעת הש"ג דהחשש לימים שנבוכה הוא גדר של וסת על כל יום מסתבר דצריך דוקא שתוחזק לראות ג"פ בכל אחת מעונות אלו, משא"כ לפירוש הנו"ב והכו"פ דיסוד החשש הוא מחמת דרגילה שלא יעברו קבוצת ימים אלו בלא ראיה, והחשש הוא על הימים בכללותם ולא על כל עונה ועונה בפנ"ע, י"ל דאף שביום כ"ז אינה רגילה לראות אעפ"כ הוא ג"כ בכלל החשש. וכבר נתבאר לעיל דלכתחילה יש לחוש לשיטת הנו"ב והכו"פ. כ"ז משיעורי הגרמ"ש קליין שליט"א.

"if the usual interval etc." — חשש של ימים שנבוכה הוא דוקא בהפלגות סמוכות, דעל ידי שרגילה להפליג ראיותיה במספר ימים קרובים זל"ז, יש שייכות לימים אלו זה עם זה, שבכללותם הם ימים שעלולה לראות בהם, אבל לגבי ימי החודש לכאורה אין שייך להגדיר קבוצת ימים שהם ימים שעלולה לראות בהם, דוסת לימי החודש הוא מיוחד לכל יום בפנ"ע דהיום גורם, וגם אם רגילה לראות

---

23. **"Even if the intervals between her periods range etc."** — כיון די"א שאינו וסת כלל, ואף להנו"ב דהוי גדר של וסת מ"מ אינו אלא כוסת של תרוה"ד, דהתרוה"ד עצמו כתב שאין דינו כקבוע ממש ולכן חוששת לעונה בינונית וכמבואר בפו' [ובקבוע, בכה"ג שהוא ארוך ליותר מל' יום אינה חוששת לעו"ב לכו"ע, עי' דס"י קפ"ט]. ואף דלהש"ג אפשר דהוי גדר של וסת על כל יום בפנ"ע מ"מ אין הכרח דלהש"ג הוא גדר של וסת קבוע ואפשר שפיר דגם להש"ג אינו אלא גדר של וסת שאינו קבוע ושפיר תחוש לעונה בינונית. ואף אי נימא דלהש"ג הוי כו"ק מ"מ אין להקל בזה מאחר דרוב הפוסקים לא ס"ל הכי, וצריכה לחוש לעונה בינונית, שיעורי הגרמ"ש קליין שליט"א.

בימים סמוכים זל״ז אין שייכות ליום זה עם היום האחר הסמוך לו. [ונפק״מ להיכא שהוסיפה עוד ראיות באמצע ימי החודש דלגבי וסת הפלגה אין לה קבוצת ימים קבועים, ולגבי וסת החודש יש לה קבוצת ימים קבועים]. איברא דלביאור החוו״ד סי׳ קפ״ד ס״ק ד׳ בדין משנית וסתה דהטעם דהחמירו הוא דשמא קבעה וסת לכל ימים אלו, ואף בלא קבעה חיישינן שמא תקבע לג׳ ימים סמוכין, שפיר איכא דין משנית וסתה גם לימי החודש, ואפשר דכ״ה גם לדעת הש״ג שהובא לעיל, אולם להפליתי ולהנו״ב שייך זה רק בהפלגה ולא בוסת החודש וכמושנ״ת. ולמעשה אפשר להקל מאחר דרבים מקילים לגמרי בדין של משנית וסתה, שיעורי הגרמ״ש קליין שליט״א.

23. "**on the immersion night**" — חכמ״א כלל ק״ח סי׳ ו׳ ושו״ת לבושי מרדכי חיו״ד סי׳ ק״ג.

"**All the more so, if the husband is about to leave on a journey**" — חכמת אדם כלל ק״ח סי׳ ו׳ דהא יש מקילים בלא״ה סמוך לוסתה ממש, ומעיקר הדין קיי״ל כדבריהם וכמוש״כ ברמ״א סי׳ קפ״ד סע׳ י׳, לכן אין להחמיר בימי המבוכה. וכ״כ בשו״ת לבושי מרדכי חיו״ד סי׳ ק״ג.

"**she should do a *bedikah* before they have relations**" — שבט הלוי בכמ״ק, וע״ע בכו״פ סי׳ קפ״ו סק״ג.

24. "**If she changed her menstruation pattern etc.**" — וק״ו מוסת שאינו קבוע דנעקר בג״פ.

"**Even if she subsequently menstruated etc.**" — כיון די״א דאינו וסת כלל, ואף להנו״ב דהוי גדר של וסת מ״מ אינו אלא כוסת של תרוה״ד, דהתרוה״ד עצמו כתב שאין דינו כקבוע ממש, ולא נימא בזה דחזר הוסת למקומו. ואף להש״ג דהוי

---

24. "**This means on days that are not close etc.**" — דמסתבר שאם ראתה סמוך לימים אלו לא הוי עקירה לימי המבוכה שהיה לה בעבר, ולכן נכתב דשינתה ראיותיה בהפסק של ג׳ ימים מימי המבוכה. ואם שינתה בפחות מג׳ ימים, להשלטי הגיבורים דהוי גדר של וסת על כל יום מסתבר דבכל ענין הוי עקירה, משא״כ להנו״ב והכו״פ דהוי קביעות על כללות קבוצת ימים אלו, לא הוי עקירה אא״כ ניכר שאין ג׳ ראיות אלו שייכים לקבוצת ימים שקבעה בעבר. ולמעשה בפחות מג׳ ימים תלוי בראות עיני המורה אי הוי שינוי מהוסת או לא, שיעורי הגרמ״ש קליין שליט״א.

גדר של וסת על כל יום מ"מ אפשר דאינו אלא כוסת שאינו קבוע דלא אמרינן חזר הוסת למקומו. ואף אי נימא דלהש"ג הוי כו"ק מ"מ כיון דנפישי רבוואתא דכלל אין סוברים הדין של משנית וסתה, לכן אין צריך להחמיר בהא לומר דחזר הוסת למקומו.

.25 "A woman after pregnancy or nursing etc." — וכמו שנתבאר לעיל דלכל היותר דינו כוסת שאינו קבוע, וכבר כתב בתשו' נוב"ת יו"ד סי' פ"ו דכיון שנתעברה ופסקו דמיה שוב אינה צריכה לחוש לו כלל אחר הנקה, כמובא בפת"ש סי' קפ"ט ס"ק ל"ב, שיעורי הגרמ"ש קליין שליט"א.

.26 "must anticipate menstruation etc." — ועיין בכל זה בטושו"ע סי' קפ"ט מסע' י"ט-כ"ו.

.27 "If a stain was found etc." — שו"ע סי' ק"צ סע' נ"ד.

.28 "If she had one of the sensations etc." — עי' סי' ק"צ סנ"ד, דכתמי עד הבדוק כראיות לכל דבר. והיינו לפי שהוא חשש הרגשה, וק"ו כאן שהרגישה.

.29 "upon checking with a *bedikah* cloth" — פשטות השו"ע ס"ס ק"צ דחושש אפ' בחד זמנא. וכן הבין החת"ס סי' קכ"ו, וע' באחרונים שהאריכו. ובפרט למ"ש רע"א סי' פ"א שכל שודאי מגופה לא חשוב כתם אפ' אם לא הרגישה ואף לדעת שועה"ר שפליג (ס"ס ק"צ), מ"מ בבדיקה מודה לפי שחזקת דמים בהרגשה. ועי' שעורי שבה"ל ס"ס ק"צ שמצדד להקל בבדיקה עד ג' פעמים.

פרק אחד עשר

.2 (a) "If the day etc." — שו"ע סי' קפ"ט סע' ד', ועי' שו"ע סי' קפ"ד סע' ט'.

.28 "one may be lenient concerning the *Ohr Zorua onah*" — דעיקר הטעם שחוששין לאו"ז הוא על דרך הזהירות, ולכן דווקא בראיה גמורה דרך וסת מסתבר לחוש כן שמא תקדים לראות, אבל בבדיקת עד הוא דבר מקרי שא"צ לחוש.

פרק אחד עשר

.3 "If she forgot to check herself ... she may rely etc." — מתבאר מדברי החו"ד סי' קפ"ד באו' י' שאף שמהני הך בדיקה זו להתירה לבעלה, מ"מ לא מהני לעקירת הוסת.

(b) "Since we do not know etc." — טור בשם הרמב״ן, שו״ע ורמ״א סי׳ קפ״ט סע׳ י״ג. וע״ש סע׳ א׳ וב׳.

(c) "Regarding ... a non-established cycle etc." — שו״ע סי׳ קפ״ט סע׳ ב׳.

(d) "An established cycle is rescinded only etc." — חו״ד סי׳ קפ״ד ס״ק י׳ ופ״ת ס״ק י״ח.

3. "Furthermore etc." — עיין שו״ע סי׳ קפ״ט סע׳ י״ד ט״ו וט״ז.

4. "A woman who menstruated four times etc." — שו״ע סי׳ קפ״ט סע׳ ב׳.

5. "only if the three periods occurred on the same *onah*" — תשו׳ נו״ב תנינא סי׳ פ״ג הובא בפת״ש סי׳ קפ״ט ס״ק ט׳. ועיין מה שביאר בזה בחזו״א סי׳ פ״ה ס״ק ס״ב. והוא דלא כהגרד״ט השואל בנו״ב שם דהקביעות הוא להפלגת עונות דלפי״ז אי״צ שיהיו כל הראיות באותה עונה, וכדברי הגרד״ט פסקו גם הגר״ז שם ס״ק ל״ט ולחו״ש ס״ק כ״א.

6. "serves only as a starting point etc." — עיין שו״ע סי׳ קפ״ט סע׳ ב׳, וכן הוא לדעת הנו״ב שצויין לעיל בסע׳ הקודם, ואולם לדעת הגרד״ט ודעימיה שפיר נפק״מ לן לידע אימתי היתה הראיה הראשונה, כיון דאם תהא בעונת הלילה יש כאן ב׳ עונות של הלילה ושל היום משא״כ אם הראיה היתה ביום יש כאן ביום זה רק עונה אחת של היום ולא של הלילה.

8. "or on the *onah beinonis* ... However etc." — עיין טושו״ע רס״י קפ״ד וסי׳ קפ״ט סע׳ א׳, ראשונים נדה ט״ו, ר״ן פ״ב דשבועות ושם בשם הרמב״ן דכשוסתה ארוך מעונה בינונית מסולקת דמים היא עד הוסת, ודלא כדמשמע מרש״י דאף בכה״ג אסורה. וכ״ה בבית מאיר רס״י קפ״ט.

אבל דעת הדברי חיים יו״ד־ב׳ סי׳ ע״ח שכשם שמהני הך בדיקה להתירה לבעלה, מהני גם לעקור את וסתה.

5. "However, many opinions disagree etc." — עי׳ לחם ושמלה סי׳ קפ״ט סט״ו שהוכיח שכן דעת הרבה ראשונים.

8. "If she had an established cycle for long intervals etc." — עי׳ שועה״ד סי׳ קפ״ט ס״ק נ״ח, ובשעורי הגרמ״ש קליין שליט״א.

לחוש לדעת הבית — "If, … of less than thirty days … onah beinonis" מאיר דס"י קפ"ט והחוו"ד ס"ק ב' וס"ק כ' דכשוסתה מובלע בתוך עונה בינונית חוששת לעונה בינונית. וכ"ה בס' האשכול סי' ל"ג.

הטעם בזה, דבאמת — "**only on the same *onah* … of her established cycle**" מעיקר הדין דעת רוב הפוסקים להקל בזה דאי"צ לחוש לעונה בינונית, וכמו שכתב הט"ז סי' קפ"ט ס"ק א', ועיין גם בט"ז ס"ק ל"א שהביא מש"כ המהרש"ל להדיא דאינה חוששת לעו"ב, וגם הב"ח הביא דברי מהרש"ל אלו ולא השיג עליו בזה ומשמע דמודי ליה, וכ"ה להדיא בסדרי טהרה בסי' קפ"ט ס"ק י"ב וס"ק ל"ו דאינה חוששת לעו"ב בכל גווני. ובאמת דמצינו כן גם דעת כמה ראשונים להדיא, דעי' בחי' הרשב"א לדף ט"ו דמבואר בדבריו להדיא דבכל גווני אינה חוששת לעו"ב, וכ"מ מדברי הרשב"א בתוה"ב סוף שער הוסתות והובא בטור סי' קפ"ט בדין וסת הקפיצות שכתב דבזה חמור וסת הקפיצות משאר וסתות דחוששת לעו"ב בין אם הוסת מובלע וכו' ומשמע דבשאר וסתות אינה חוששת לעו"ב כלל. וגם משמעות הטור דס"י קפ"ד ודס"י קפ"ט וכן משמעות המחבר דס"י קפ"ט הוא כדפירש הט"ז שם דביש לה וסת קבוע אינה חוששת לעונה בינונית כלל. ומה שבבית מאיר ובחוו"ד הביאו בשם הר"ן והרמב"ן דחוששת לעו"ב, צ"ע מאין הוציאו כן מדבריהם, דהא הר"ן שם כתב כן בשם הרמב"ן אהא דאמר רבב"ח לגבי הבא מן הדרך דאף אם הגיע שעת וסתה נמי מותרת משום דוסתות דרבנן, ואהא הוא דכתבו הר"ן והרמב"ן דאע"פ דלא אסרינן לה אחר שעבר וסתה, מ"מ שפיר אסרינן לה אחר עונה בינונית משום דוכי לעולם לא תראה, אבל לדידן דקיי"ל בשו"ע סי' קפ"ד סע' ט' וע"ש עוד בסע' י"א דבעבר וסתה אסורה עד שתבדוק, א"כ כבר אסרינן לה בעונת וסתה, ומהיכ"ת להוסיף לה עוד זמן איסור בעו"ב, הא כבר קביע לה זמן ליאסר, ואף דכבר עבר זמן זה ולא ראתה, מ"מ אין אנו אחראין לקבוע לה זמן ליאסר, וכי היכי דבעלמא ביש לה וסת להפלגה [ליותר מל' יום] ועבר וסתה ולא ראתה תו אין לה למה לחוש עד שתראה שוב, ולא קבעינן לה זמן ליאסר אף דוכי לעולם לא תראה, כיון דיש לה זמן קבוע ליאסר ואף שעבר הוסת ולא ראתה, כך גם בוסתה קצר מעו"ב לדידן דעבר הוסת ולא בדקה אסורה, א"כ כבר יש לה זמן ליאסר, ולא אסרינן לה בעו"ב. ובלא"ה צ"ע להעמיס כן בשיטת הרמב"ן, וכפי שכבר העיר בזה הגר"ז בקו"א סי' קפ"ט ס"ק א' דבהל' נדה להרמב"ן משמע להדיא דביש לה וסת קבוע אינה חוששת לעו"ב כלל, ואף כשוסתה קצר מעו"ב, ע"ש.

ולענין הלכה, מאחר דבס' האשכול, בית מאיר, חוו"ד ולחו"ש כתבו דכשוסתה קצר מעו"ב ועבר וסתה ולא ראתה חוששת לעו"ב לכתחילה יש לחוש לדבריהם, מ"מ מאידך מאחר דכאמור יסוד דברי האחרונים הוא ע"פ הרמב"ן ובפשוטו אין ראיה מדברי הרמב"ן, ואדרבה חזינן להרמב"ן, הרשב"א והטור דס"ל דבכל גווני אינה חוששת לעו"ב, וכ"ה דעת המהרש"ל, הב"ח והט"ז, וכ"ה דעת הסדרי טהרה, לכן עכ"פ אי"צ להחמיר בזה אלא ליום השלשים ודוקא בעונת ראיתה, ולא לחוש מעל"ע [ובפרט לפמשנ"ת לעיל בפרק הקודם סע' י"ז דמוכח מרוה"פ דס"ל כהסד"ט דחוששת בעו"ב רק לעונת ראיתה ולא מעל"ע], וכן לא לחוש ליום ל"א. וכן פסק בסוגה בשושנים סי' ה' ס"ק כ"ד.

"In case of necessity" — וכמו שנתבאר לעיל דמעיקר הדין נקטינן כדעת רוב הפו' דאינה חוששת לעונה בינונית בכל גווני ואף כשוסתה קצר מעו"ב.

9. "On the day of her regular interval" — עיין שו"ע סי' קפ"ט סע' י"ד ועי' ש"ך ס"ק ל"ט.

10. "A woman can establish etc." — עד סוף הסעיף. עיין שו"ע סע' ה' ושם בט"ז ס"ק ו' וש"ך ס"ק ח'.

11. "The same rule applies ... a day earlier" — עיין ש"ך סי' קפ"ט ס"ק ט' והוא מדברי הראב"ד בבעה"נ ועי' ב"י, וכן פסק הגר"ז. ואולם בכו"פ הובא בפת"ש ס"ק ג' כתב דוסת זה מנגד להטבע ולכן אינה חוששת לו, ועיין בפרי דעה ש"ל ס"ק כ"ג דכשיש לתלותו בוסת אחר יש לסמוך אדברי הפליתי דיותר מסתבר שהוא וסת אחר מאשר לתלותו בוסת הדילוג למפרע, ע"ש.

12. "A *veset haflagah* of incremental intervals is established etc." — ש"ך

---

9. "of twenty-eight days" — חוו"ד סי' קפ"ד ס"ק ד', הו"ד בפתחי תשובה שם ס"ק ח'.

"Nevertheless, since this matter is disputed etc" — סי' קפ"ט מקור חיים סע' י"ג בשם הב"ח.

"If a woman menstruated etc." — חוו"ד סי' קפ"ט ס"ק י"ד הו"ד בפתחי תשובה שם ס"ק י"א, וע"ש במקור מים חיים סע' י"ג בהג"ה בשם הב"ח והפרישה.

12. "She does not need to anticipate etc." — וכמבואר לעיל בסע' הקודם דכשוסתה הקבוע ארוך מעונה בינונית, אינה חוששת לעונה בינונית.

סי' קפ"ט ס"ק י"ב, ומפשטות דברי הש"ך והפוסקים שהביאו דבריו נראה דאף אם קבעה כגון שראתה פ"א בדילוג יום א', ושוב ראתה בדילוג ב' ימים, ושוב ראתה בדילוג ג' ימים, לא קבעה וסת לדילוג כיון שאינו דילוג שווה, ועיין תוספת טהרה מ"ש בשם הפר"ד.

13. "If, however etc." — דבזה לא דמי לוסת החודש דמבואר בשו"ע סע' ח' דקובעת וסת, ובפרט לביאור הראב"ד שהובא בש"ך ס"ק כ"א דהטעם דקובעת כן גבי וסת החודש משום דקובעת וסת בתוך וסת, ולא שייך זה גבי וסת ההפלגה. וכ"כ בהפלאה.

14. "She does not need ... after an interval of thirty-four days" — דחשבינן כאילו ראתה ביום שהיתה ראויה לראות בו, שהוא בהפלגת שלושים וארבעה, ולכן חוששת להבא שתראה בהפלגת עשרים וחמשה, ואף דלא מצינו כן להדיא כי אם גבי וסת החודש בדילוג וכמו"ש בחוו"ד ס"ק ה', ואילו בהפלגה היה מקום לדון דכיון דאין כאן גורם של יום מסויים שנקבע שזהו יום וסתה, אי אפשר להחשיב כאילו ראתה, מ"מ לדינא יש לומר כן גם גבי וסת ההפלגה בכה"ג שאיחרה ראיתה וכנידון סעיף זה, דהא סו"ס הגיע יום חשש הוסת אלא שעקרתו. וראה להלן בסעיף הבא.

15. "only applies ... after a longer interval. If, however etc." — דכיון דהפלגה קצרה אינה עוקרת את הארוכה, א"כ הרי יום חשש וסתה כלל לא בא עדיין, וא"כ אין שייך להחשיב כאילו ראתה בהפלגת שלשים וארבעה, ולכן חוששת בפעם הבא שתראה בהפלגת שלשים וארבעה, וחלוק וסת ההפלגה מוסת החודש לענין זה, דרק בוסת החודש שיש יום מסויים שחוששים לו, שייך להחשיב כאילו ראתה ביום שהיתה ראויה לחוש לו בין אם הקדימה ובין אם איחרה אותו, משא"כ בוסת ההפלגה דאם הקדימה להפלגה קצרה, אין כאן יום שצריכה לחוש לו, שהרי היתה ראיה בינתיים, ורק שייך לחוש להפלגה מראיתה האחרונה.

---

14. "As explained in paragraph 8 etc." — דהיינו דכשוסתה הקבוע קצר מעונה בינונית, ועבר וסתה הקבוע ולא ראתה, הרי נתבאר במקורות לעיל בסע' הקודם דדעת רוב הפוסקים דאינה חוששת לעונה בינונית וכן הוא משמעות הטושו"ע, ואעפ"כ נתבאר שם דלכתחילה חוששת לעונה בינונית לחוש לשיטת החוו"ד ובית מאיר. משא"כ חששא דוסת החודש הוא מעיקר הדין וכבכל אשה שיש לה וסת קבוע ושינתה ראיתה דחוששת לראית השינוי, וכן חוששת מדינא לוסת ההפלגה.

20. "increased each time by an additional day etc." — פרדס רמונים סי' קפ"ט

16. "on the same day" — טושו״ע סי׳ קפ״ט סע׳ ו׳.

17. "in the same *onah*" — טושו״ע סי׳ קפ״ט סע׳ י״ג.

18. "even when there are other periods in between" — עיין רמ״א סע׳ י״ג פרישה סכ״ח וב״ח שם וש״ך ס״ק ל״א, ומוסכם בפוסקים, ולא נחלקו בזה אלא לגבי וסת הפלגה אי ראיה שבינתיים מפסקת את ההפלגה, אבל בוסת חודש כו״ע מודו דאינה מפסקת את ההפלגה.

"A monthly cycle ... on the 1st of each month etc." — עי׳ גר״ז סי׳ קפ״ט ס״ק ל״ח, וקו״א ס״ק ד׳. וע״ע שיעורי הגרמ״ש קליין שליט״א. ונתבאר לעיל בפרק הקודם.

20. "and the flow ... continued ... until the 1st of *Sivan*" — נקודות הכסף סי׳ קפ״ט בהגה שאחר הט״ז ס״ק ל״ב וכן מפורש בהל׳ נדה להרמב״ן פ״ה הט״ו שרגלים לדבר שבפעם השלישית דמים יתירים אתוספו ביה ולכן הקדימה.

21. "she has established a fixed cycle for *Rosh Chodesh*" — ב״ח סי׳ קפ״ט, שו״ת שבה״ל ח״ג סי׳ קכ״ד לט״ז ס״ק י״ז.

22. "a cycle of menstruating ... has been established etc." — שו״ע סי׳ קפ״ט סע׳ ז׳.

"only regarding stringencies etc." — שו״ע ונו״כ שם בסוף הסעיף.

25. "If she menstruated at other times in between these periods etc." ואע״פ שוסת הסירוג גדרו כוסת החודש וא״כ לכאורה אין ראיות שבאמצע

ש״ח ס״ק י״ב. ויל״ע לדבריו אי אף קובעת וסת להפלגה בדילוג החוזר חלילה, וראה להלן. (ומ״מ נראה דאינו אלא ספק קביעות כיון דפשטות דברי הש״ך לא משמע כן, וע״כ אין להקל בזה שלא לחוש לוסת שאינו קבוע).

22. "and her flow continued to the thirty-fourth day etc." — דכיון שנמשך גם ביום שהיתה ראויה לחוש לו, שייך לומר דנחשיב היום השלשים וארבעה שהיתה ראויה לחוש לו דכאילו ראתה בו, שהרי סו״ס ראתה בו ממעין פתוח, וכיון שכבר קבעה וסת לדילוג תלינן שעיקר הראיה היא ביום שאנו חוששין לו, ומה שהקדימה לראות הוא משום תוספת דמים.

31. "and then again another three times etc." — שו״ע סי׳ קפ״ט סע׳ ח׳.

מעכבות מלקבוע וסת, מ"מ מהא דחזינן בשו"ע סע' ט' דנקט הציור רק בכה"ג שראתה ג' ראיות, וגם בסע' י"ב דנקט חשש הוסת קודם שתקבע לא הזכיר כלל דקובעת גם אם הוסיפה ראיה באמצע, ואדרבה מדכתב דמשלא ראתה בא' בתמוז אינה חוששת עוד, משמע דהוא דוקא כשלא היו ראיות באמצע, ואע"פ דהא דרך רוב נשים לראות לל' יום והו"ל לפרושי סדר ראיותיה עד שתקבע באופן שהוסיפה ראיות בין הראיות הקובעות את הוסת, אלא מוכח מפשטות דברי המחבר דהוא דוקא כשלא הוסיפה ראיות באמצע. והסברא בזה, דמאחר שהוסיפה ראיות באמצע אין אנו רואים את ג' הראיות של א' בחודש כשייכים זה לזה, כיון דבלא"ה ראתה באמצע ראיות אחרות שאינם לפי סדר מסויים.

ומשמע כן גם מדברי החוו"ד ס"ק י"א, מדכתב שם נפק"מ בין סירוג להפלגה עד שתקבע בכה"ג שהחדשים אינם שוים כגון בחשוון כסליו דחוששת להפלגה קודם שתקבע לסירוג, ובהא דכתב המחבר דמשלא ראתה בא' בתמוז אינה חוששת עוד ביאר החוו"ד דהיינו דוקא בציור דהמחבר דאיירי בחדשי חמה שוים ע"ש, ולא כתב החוו"ד חילוק פשוט דבכה"ג דהוסיפה ראיות באמצע חוששת להפלגה עד שתראה שוב בא' באב ותקבע את הוסת לסירוג, ומאידך אין ראיות אלו מעכבות מלקבוע וסת לסירוג, משמע דאכן אם תוסיף ראיות בין ראיות הסירוג לא תקבע וסת לסירוג.

וכן משמע בחוו"ד ס"ק ד' לגבי וסת השבוע מדכתב שם החילוק שבין וסת השבוע להפלגה בכה"ג שראתה באמצע הפלגה "שלישית" ע"ש, ולא כתב בפשיטות דבוסת השבוע אין ראיות שבאמצע מעכבות מלקבוע וסת משא"כ בוסת הפלגה, משמע דרק לאחר שכבר קבעה וסת לימי השבוע הוא דראיות שבאמצע אינן מפסיקות ובזה שאני מהפלגה דראיות שבאמצע מפסיקות, אבל קודם שקבעה וסת, שפיר אמרינן דראיות שבאמצע מפסיקות ומעכבות מלקבוע וסת. וכן הדין בוסת הסירוג, דחד דינא לוסת השבוע ולוסת הסירוג וכמבואר בכו"פ ובסד"ט ובחוו"ד סוס"ק י'.

איברא, דבתפארת למשה ובהפלאה לסע' י"ב חזינן דראיות שבאמצע הסירוג אינן מעכבות מלקבוע וסת, מדביארו בדברי המחבר שם דרק כשסירגה מא' בסיון עד א' באב הוא דאינה חוששת עוד משום וסת עד א' באב, אבל אם תוסיף ראיה באמצע שפיר תחוש לראיה זו, משמע דסברי התפאל"מ וההפלאה דראיות שבאמצע הסירוג אינן מעכבות מלקבוע את הסירוג, ואפשר דטעמם דדמי לוסת החודש וכהא דראתה ר"ח ר"ח כ"ה ור"ח, דאמרינן בגמ' דף ל"ט ע"ב דקובעת וסת

לר"ח, וראית כ"ה בחודש תוספת דמים הוא, וא"כ הוא דוקא אם הוסיפה ראיה בין ראית א' בסיון לראית א' באב, דהיינו בין ראיה שניה לשלישית של הסירוג, דבזה הוא דאינו מעכב כיון דתלינן לראיה זו בתוספת דמים, משא"כ אם הוסיפה ראיה בין ראיה ראשונה לשניה של הסירוג, י"ל דגם אינהו מודו דלא תקבע וסת לסירוג. ומ"מ לדעת החוו"ד ופשטות המחבר דמשמע דלא תקבע וסת כשתוסיף ראיות באמצע, לדידהו משמע דאף אם תוסיף לראות בין ראיה שניה לשלישית נמי מעכב מלקבוע לסירוג, דעד כאן לא אמרינן דראיה שבאמצע תוספת דמים הוא, אלא בכה"ג דיכולים לתלות שיש סדר רגיל לראיותיה, וכהך דאמרי' בגמ' דל"ט ע"ב וכנ"ל, דתלינן סדר ראיותיה בר"ח, אבל לגבי קביעת וסת לסירוג דאינו סדר רגיל, י"ל דלא אמרינן דראיה שבאמצע תוספת דמים היא כדי שתקבע וסת לסירוג.

"Some authorities contend etc." — כנ"ל מדברי התפאל"מ וההפלאה, וכמשנ"ת לעיל דגם לדידהו היינו דוקא בהוסיפה לראות בין ראיה שניה לשלישית ולא כשהוסיפה לראות בין ראיה ראשונה לשניה.

26. "three times on the same day of the week" — שו"ע סי' קפ"ט סע' ו' ושם בש"ך ס"ק י"ד.

27. "on the same *onah*" — פשוט, וכמו בוסת החודש.

28. "If three periods occurred etc." — כו"פ סי' קפ"ט ס"ק ח', חוו"ד שם ס"ק ד' וסד"ט ס"ק ד' וע"ע ס"ק ל"א. וכ"ה בפת"ש שם ס"ק ד'.

"four weeks (less one day)" — עיין כו"פ חוו"ד וסד"ט דמוכח כן והשווהו לוסת הסירוג, ודו"ק. וכיו"ב יעויין בחכמ"א כלל קי"ב סי' ט"ו דמוכח כן.

29. "came a day earlier" — שם בכו"פ, חוו"ד וסד"ט וכ"ה בפת"ש שם.

30. "occurs three times etc." — חוו"ד שם וסד"ט ס"ק ד', ועיין בסד"ט ס"ק ל"א שנסתפק בזה וסיים דיש לחוש לחומרא לב' הוסתות וכן העתיק בחכמ"א כלל קי"ב סי' ט"ו. ומ"מ למעשה נראה להקל כיון שדעת כמה ראשונים דאין לחוש כלל לוסת השבוע, עי' במקורות וביאורים להערה 36.

---

34. "Even if she did not menstruate on the 19th of *Av* etc." — חוו"ד סי' קפ"ט ס"ק ה'. וכ"ה בב"ח.

31. "Therefore if menstruation began on Sunday etc." — כו"פ סי' קפ"ט ס"ק א' וגר"ז שם בקו"א סוס"ק ב' וכ"ה בלחו"ש ס"ק י"א. אולם בחוו"ד ס"ק ד' משמע דכה"ג תקבע וסת.

32. "Out-of-the ordinary physical effort etc." — עיין שו"ע סי' ק"צ סע' נ"ד. "*veset hakefizot*" — ולדעת הטור הוי ככל וסת קבוע שצריך עקירה ג' פעמים והוא כדעת רש"י הרמב"ן והרז"ה דקובעת וסת לקפיצות לחודיה אף בלא יום קבוע, וכמובא בב"י. אולם דעת התוספות הרשב"א והרמב"ם דאינה קובעת וסת לקפיצות לחודיה בלא יום קבוע, וכן פסק המחבר בסי' קפ"ט סע' י"ז. אלא שהרמ"א כתב בשם הגה' מיי' דמ"מ לאחר שקפצה וראתה ג"פ חוששת לו כמו לוסת שאינו קבוע. "after jumping or after receiving a blow etc." — עיין תוספתא נדה פ"א ה"ב דקפצה וראתה הכה אותה בעלה וראתה נשאה משא כבד וראתה הוי ראיה שעל ידי אונס. "She must also anticipate the *onah beinonis* etc." — עיין שו"ע סי' קפ"ד סע' י"ב.

"even if she does not then jump" — דהחשש הוא משום וכי לעולם לא תראה, א"כ אף בלא קפיצה חוששת לעונה בינונית. חוו"ד ס"ק כ"ב וכ"ה פשטות השו"ע סי' קפ"ט סע' י"ב.

33. "is rescinded even after just one time" — רמ"א סי' קפ"ט סע' י"ז וככל וסת שאינו קבוע שנעקר בפ"א בלבד.

34. "when she jumps a fourth time etc." — חוו"ד סי' קפ"ט ס"ק כ"ג. "Similarly, etc." — פתחי תשובה סי' קפ"ז ס"ק מ"ט בשם תשו' חת"ס סי' קע"ד. ומש"כ החוו"ד סי' קפ"ז ס"ק ט"ו דבראתה ליל ג' או ד' אחר טבילה לא חיישא, היינו בלא ראתה כן בג"פ, אבל בראתה כן ג"פ י"ל דיסבור כהחת"ס דחוששת אף בליל ד' שאחר הקפיצה. אמנם בסוג"ב סי' ו' סע' ה' נקט דבכה"ג אינה חוששת לקפיצות.

35. "and menstruated two hours later" — חוו"ד ס"ק כ"ב וכמו בוסת השעות, דהשעה קבועה והיום אינו קבוע, ואתי קביעותא דשעה ועקרה לוסת שאינו קבוע.

---

35. "she must anticipate menstruation on the 16th of *Tammuz* etc." — עש"ך שם ס"ק י"ט, ושם בפרי דעה וחי' רעק"א בשו"ע.

"From the time she jumped until two hours afterwards" — עיין ט"ז סי' קפ"ט ס"ק ד' ושו"ע הרב שם ס"ק י' וי"א. וע"ע להלן בסמוך משנ"ת.

"and after the hour etc." — חוו"ד הנ"ל. ועיין ש"ך ס"ק נ' ובתוה"ש ס"ק מ"ד שמדוייק דדק בוסת הקפיצות המורכב לימים הוא דאסורה כל העונה, אבל באינו מורכב י"ל דאינה אסורה אלא בשעת הוסת. וכן הוא בהל' נדה להרמב"ן פ"ו הי"ג. אך דברי החוו"ד צ"ב, דלמד דינו מוסת השעות, דאתי קביעותא דשעה ועקר לאינו קבוע דיום, ולכאורה צ"ע מאי שייטיה דוסת השעות לוסת הקפיצות, דשאני וסת השעות דאיכא חשש וסת על כל העונה, והתם הוא דאמרינן דאתי קביעותא דשעה ועקר חשש העונה, אבל הכא בוסת הקפיצות מאי עדיפא שעת ראיתה מהקפיצה עצמה, והלא אין כאן חשש לגרמת היום כלל, וא"כ במאי עדיפא שעת וסתה מחשש דקפיצה עצמה.

אך י"ל בטעמו של החוו"ד דסברא הוא, דכיון דלא ראתה בג"פ אלא כעבור שעתים מהקפיצה, אין לה לחוש ליותר ממה שראתה, ובפרט שכל עיקר חששא דקפיצות לאו חשש גמור הוא, דהא נקטינן דאין זה קביעות כלל וא"כ גם לא היתה צריכה לחוש כושא"ק כלל אף אחר ג"פ וכדעת רוב הראשונים, ולכן אף דחיישינן להגה' מיי' שהובא ברמ"א דחוששת לזה כושא"ק, מ"מ אינה חוששת טפי ממה שראתה כן בג"פ כשעתיים אחר הקפיצה ולא יותר.

ותו, דבאמת מסברא צל"ע מה שייך חשש של עונה בוסת הקפיצות, וכי מה ענין לקפיצה עם העונה, תינח בושא"ק דחיישינן שתקבע וסת המורכב, ניחא דחיישינן נמי לגרמת היום, אבל בראתה ג"פ אחר קפיצה, מה ענין חשש עונה לחשש דקפיצה, ולכן מסברא פשוט דבראתה ג"פ בשעה קבועה אחר הקפיצה, אינה חוששת אלא בשעה זו בלבד.

אמנם יעויין בשו"ע הרב ס"ק ע"ב שכתב דאסורה כל העונה, וצ"ע טעמו וכנ"ל, ותו צ"ע דבהל' נדה להרמב"ן הא מבואר ההיפך. ובפשוטו י"ל דהשו"ע הרב איירי באין לה שעה קבועה, ואה"נ ביש לה שעה קבועה חוששת רק לאותה שעה בלבד. אך קצת יל"ע דהא בש"ך ותוה"ש הנ"ל משמע דדק בוסת המורכב הוא דחוששת כל העונה משא"כ באינו מורכב חוששת לשעת ראיתה בלבד, וא"כ למה סתם הגר"ז הדין בזה ולא כתב האיך דינה באם יש לה שעה קבועה.

ואפשר דמהש"ך והתוה"ש אין ראיה, דכונתם רק לאפוקי דבאינו מורכב אינה חוששת מהקפיצה ועד שעת ראיתה, וכיו"ב מצינו גבי וסת השעות בט"ז רס"י קפ"ט

ובשו"ע הרב שם, דברגילה לראות זמן מה אחר טבילתה אינה חוששת מהטבילה ועד שעת ראיתה, אבל אחר שעת ראיתה שפיר חוששת עד סוף העונה, ואף דכאמור הא אין מקום לחשש "עונה" בוסת הקפיצות, דלאו משום גרמת העונה חיישינן שתראה אלא משום גרמת הקפיצה ולמה תחוש עד סוף העונה, מ"מ אפשר לומר, דמאחר דהראיה אינה מובלעת בתוך הקפיצה, א"כ דמיא לוסת הפיהוק דבכה"ג הא נפסק בשו"ע סע' כ"ד דבאין הראיה מובלעת בתוך הוסת חוששת עד סוף העונה, וכדעת הראב"ד דחוששת לשעת הוסת, ודלא כהרז"ה, וכהכרעת הב"י שם על פי הרשב"א וכדביאר הב"י דאע"פ דבעלמא גבי וסתות לא חיישינן לשעת הוסת וכהראב"ד, אלא חיישינן לתחילת ראיתה בלבד וכהרז"ה, מ"מ החשש על תחילת ראיתה הוא תמיד עונה אחת ולכן גם גבי פיהוק חוששת עד סוף אותה עונה, ע"ש. וה"נ גבי קפיצות דכיון דאין הראיה מובלעת בתוך הוסת, חוששת עד סוף העונה. והרמב"ן דס"ל דחוששת רק לשעה הקבוע לה בלבד, י"ל דס"ל כהרז"ה וכדקיי"ל בעלמא לחוש רק לתחילת ראיתה, ואף דהרמב"ן ס"ל דבכל חשש וסת חיישינן כמה ימים בימי המשך ראיתה, היינו רק מחששא דטועות דשמא תחילת ראיתה היא בימי זיבה והמשך ראיתה בימי נדה, אבל לעולם ס"ל להרמב"ן דחיישינן רק לתחילת ראיתה, ועל כן גם גבי קפיצות ופיהוק חוששת רק לשעה הקבועה לה ולא עד סוף העונה, ודו"ק.

"but not after any fixed time interval" — עיין לעיל בסמוך.

36. **"for both of these causes etc."** — שו"ע סי' קפ"ד סע' י"ח.

---

36. **"menstruated an additional time between these three times etc."** — וכמו שנתבאר לעיל סע' כ"ה בדין וסת הסירוג, שאינה קובעת וסת באם הוסיפה ראיות באמצע, ואף דבוסת הסירוג יש אומרים שבין ראיה שניה לשלישית אין ראיה באמצע מפסקת את הוסת לסירוג, מ"מ בוסת השבוע דלדעת כמ"פ אינה קובעת כלל וסת לימי השבוע, אי"צ לחוש לקביעות וסת אא"כ ראתה בג"פ לימי השבוע בלא ראיות נוספות באמצע.

"If two of her periods began on Sundays … she does not establish a cycle for days of the week etc." — דאע"פ שהוא ב"פ לימי השבוע שוה ובשלישית ממעין פתוח, דכה"ג בוסת החודש קובעת וסת עכ"פ מספק, ובזה"ז מדין ודאי, מ"מ בוסת השבוע לא תקבע וסת בכך, חדא דגם בדין הגמ' בדל"ט ע"ב בראתה ב"פ בראש חודש ושלישית בכ"ה ובר"ח דקובעת וסת לר"ח, בפשוטו היינו דוקא כשהפסיקה ראיתה בין ראית כ"ה לראית ר"ח, ולא כשראתה בהמשך אחד. ואף אי נימא דה"ה אם ראתה מכ"ה ועד ר"ח בהמשך אחד קובעת

"must also anticipate the *onah beinonis*" — עיין שו"ע סי' קפ"ד סע' י"ב.

37. "This cycle is rescinded etc." — עיין שו"ע סע' י"ח וש"ך ס"ק מ"ט.

38. "has not rescinded etc." — דעת הרמ"א כפי שנתבאר בפת"ש ס"ק כ' בשם חוו"ד ס"ק כ"ג. ועיי"ש שלדעת המחבר הוברר שקביעות דידה הוא לראש חודש לבדו בלי גרמת הקפיצה. [ויל"ע דלכאורה ה"ה באם ברביעית כלל לא קפצה, אלא ראתה בר"ח בלא קפיצה, דג"כ נימא הוברר הדבר, אבל בחוו"ד משמע לא כן].

39. "for that day of the month etc." — חוו"ד ס"ק כ"ג ומובא בפת"ש ס"ק כ'. דמאחר דהיום קבוע, לא אמרינן קפיצה דאתמול גרם.

40. "she has established a cycle for *Rosh Chodesh* only etc." — עיין שו"ע סי' קפ"ט סע' י"ז, וכל שכן בזה. וע"ע בסע' כ' לגבי וסת הפיהוק.

וסת לר"ח, מ"מ י"ל דבוסת השבוע לא תקבע, משום דהא דקיי"ל דקובעת וסת ממע"פ היינו דיותר מסתבר לן למיתלי עיקר ראיתה בר"ח שהוא לפי סדר קבוע מאשר לומר דעיקר ראיתה הוא בכ"ה בחודש שאינו לפי סדר קבוע, משא"כ בוסתות דלא שכיחי כוסת הסירוג וכן וסת השבוע דכי היכי דאינה חוששת להם משום וסת שאינו קבוע, ה"נ דלא נימא דקובעת ממעין פתוח, דמהיכי תיתי לומר דהראיה העיקרית היא יום הכ"ט. וביותר, דכל עיקר דין וסת השבוע לאו מילתא דפסיקא היא כלל, והרמב"ן בהל' נדה לא הביאו כלל, וכמ"כ הראב"ד בבעה"נ לא הזכיר דקובעת וסת לימי השבוע, ואף דבמהדו"ב הוסיף דין וסת השבוע מ"מ בסוף שער הוסתות [בדפו"ח סי' ד'] סידר בקצרה כל סוגי קביעות הוסתות, ולא הזכיר קביעות וסת לימי השבוע, וכן כתב הרמב"ן בחי' לנדה דף ס"ד ע"א בשם הראב"ד דאינה קובעת וסת לימי השבוע. והמקור לוסת השבוע הוא מדברי הרשב"א וכ"ה בטור, ועיין גם ברשב"א בתוה"ב שלא כתב דין וסת השבוע כקביעות וסת מוחלט כמו שהביא שאר סוגי הוסתות, אלא דמדייק כן מהא דאי' בגמ' בדי"א ע"א דקפיץ בחד בשבא וחזאי וכו', וכתב ב' ביאורים, או דחד בשבא לאו דוקא או דקובעת וסת לימי השבוע, בהפרש של כמה שבועות, ולפי הביאור השני אכן איכא קביעות וסת לימי השבוע. ואף דהרשב"א מדייק כן גם מהא דאמרינן בב"ק נגח שבת שבת ושבת נעשה מועד לשבתות, וחזינן דאיכא קביעות לימי השבוע, מ"מ לפירוש התוס' בב"ק שם היינו דוקא בנגיחות דמחמת שינוי הבגדים של שבת נגח ולא מחמת גרמת היום בשבוע, וכנאה דזהו טעמם של הראשונים דלא ס"ל ההוכחה מהתם, ומכל הנ"ל מבואר דאף דלמעשה חיישינן דקובעת וסת לימי השבוע, מ"מ לאו מילתא דפסיקא היא כלל, ואינו מוחלט כ"כ כשאר וסתות. ולכן כל היכי דחזינן קביעות גמורה של ג' ראיות לימי השבוע שפיר קובעת וסת, אבל בכה"ג דלא ראתה תחילת ראיה ג"פ ליום שוה בשבוע, אינה קובעת וסת ממעין פתוח, ודו"ק.

41. "she has established a cycle for jumping only" — פשוט, דהא לא קבעה ליום מסויים, כי אם ע"י ג' קפיצות, וא"כ היינו הך דסעיף א'.

"She does not have to ... on *Rosh Chodesh* alone" — דהא ראית יום ראש חודש האחרון היתה ע"י קפיצה, ואינה חוששת ליום זה כלל משום גרמת היום,

---

40. "her established cycle for Sunday has not been rescinded" — דזה ודאי אי אפשר לומר שראיה שראתה ממעין פתוח תבטל את וסת השבוע, דלא שבקינן וסת ברור של ימי השבוע ולבטלו ע"י ראיה להפלגה ממעין פתוח. וגם עיקר הדין דבראיה רביעית לימי השבוע בטל וסת השבוע וקובעת להפלגה אינו דין מוחלט, ועיין בכו"פ וסד"ט ס"ק ל"א שנסתפקו בזה וכן העתיק החכמ"א, ולכן הבו דלא לוסיף עלה, דאף דלמעשה נקטינן דבקבעה לראות ד' פעמים לימי השבוע בטל וסת השבוע וקבעה וסת להפלגה, מ"מ הוא דוקא כשכל הראיות היו ממעין סתום ולא כשראיה אחרונה היתה ממעין פתוח. ותו, דיש לדון דאינה קובעת וסת ממעין פתוח אלא בוסת לימי החודש ולא בוסת להפלגת ימים, ועיין בזה לעיל. ותו, דגם בדין הגמ' דקובעת וסת ממעין פתוח וכגון שראתה ב"פ בראש חודש ושלישית בכ"ה ובר"ח, אפשר דאינה קובעת וסת אלא כשהפסיקה ראיתה בין ראית כ"ה לראית ר"ח, משא"כ כשנמשך ראיתה מכ"ה ועד ר"ח דאף לדין הגמ' אפשר דלא תקבע וסת לר"ח, וכל שכן בהפלגה.

43. "However ... ordinary jumping or a minor blow etc." — עיין כיו"ב גבי וסת הפיהוק בסי' קפ"ט סע' י"ט דבפיהוק ועיטוש של פעם אחת אין הוסת נקבע אלא כשעושה כן הרבה פעמים זה אחר זה, ועיין בש"ך ס"ק נ"ד שביאר דכשלא עשתה כן הרבה פעמים הוי דרך כל העולם ואין הוסת נקבע בכך, וה"נ י"ל כן גבי קפיצות, דבקפיצה מועטת וחבטה קטנה אי"צ לחוש שתראה, ורק בקפיצה וחבטה שאינה רגילה. ועיין פרדס רמונים בפתיחה לסי' קפ"ט הוסת הי' אות ב' שביאר הטעם דלא קבעה וסת לקפיצות משום דכיון שראיתה אינה מחמת טבעה רק האונס הכריחה להוציא הדם טרם זמנו, המקרה לא יתמיד לעולם באופן אחד, וביאר דלפעמים באה בכח גדול וכגון שקפצה קפיצה יתירה ביותר ולפעמים אינו כל כך בכח, או לפעמים חלושה בטבעה ויזיק לה האונס להוציא דמה ולפעמים טבעה חזק ולא יזיק לה האונס, ולכן כל שבאה הראיה ע"י מעשה מבחוץ אין כאן קביעות וסת, ע"ש, וכיון שכן ודאי שגם החשש לושא"ק היינו דוקא כאשר עכ"פ היתה קפיצה שאינה רגילה ונעשתה בכח וכיו"ב, ולא בסתם קפיצה מועטת.

"exerted herself with three different activities" — דומיא דוסת לאכילת דברים חמים וכמבואר ברמ"א סע' כ"ג וע"ש בחי' רעק"א, וכן נקט בסוגה בשושנים סי' ו' ס"ק ז'.

"following any other unusual physical effort of any kind" — כמו שקובעת לכל דברים חמים. ומ"מ לענין עקירה מבואר בחוו"ד ס"ק כ"ט גבי וסת לאכילת דברים חמים, שאם קבעה

דהא ראתה ע"י קפיצה. ולכשתקפוץ בר"ח בלא"ה חוששת, שהרי גם בשאר ימים שתקפוץ חוששת, ועכ"פ אין כאן חשש מיוחד על יום ראש חודש.

42. **"she has established a cycle for *Rosh Chodesh* alone without jumping"** שו"ע סע' י"ז, דגבי וסת הקפיצות לא אמרינן קפיצה דאתמול גרמה לה, משא"כ גבי פיהוק דאמרינן הכי, ועיין ט"ז ס"ק ל"ב וש"ך ס"ק נ"ט.

43. **"does not need to anticipate its re - occurrence etc."** — שכן אף בראתה ע"י קפיצה ג"פ לא קבעה וסת, אלא דדעת הרמ"א דחוששת לו משום ושא"ק, וא"כ פשיטא דאינה חוששת משום ושא"ק, ופשוט.

44. **"must anticipate menstruation ... on the same day etc."** —ש"ך ס"ק מ"ח וכ"ה בראב"ד בבעה"נ.

"until the end of that *onah*" — שו"ע הרב סי' קפ"ט ס"ק ע"ב, וכן הוא פשטות דברי הש"ך בס"ק מ"ח מדחוששת לוסת המורכב, והרי במורכב חוששת לכל העונה וכמבואר בש"ך ס"ק נ' ותוה"ש ס"ק מ"ד וכנ"ל במקורות לסע' ד', ופשוט. ומש"כ הרמב"ן בהל' נדה דחוששת רק לשעה ושתים שאחר הקפיצה, היינו דוקא בקבעה ג"פ לראות לקפיצות לחודיה, ובכל אלו הג"פ ראתה רק כשעה או שתים אחר הקפיצה, ולכן כתב דאינה חוששת אלא לשעה זו, וכמו כן מש"כ החוו"ד ס"ק כ"ב דביש לה שעה קבועה חוששת רק לאותה שעה, היינו נמי רק בראתה כן ג"פ.

על ידי ג' דברים חריפים שונים, אינה עוקרת וסת זו אלא כאשר תאכל אחד מהדברים החריפים האלו ג' פעמים ולא תראה דם, אבל אם אכלה דבר חריף אחר ולא ראתה דם, אין זה עקירה, וה"ה הכא, דאם קפצה פעם אחת וראתה, ונשאה משא כבד וראתה, ונחבטה וראתה, קבעה וסת לפעולות מאמץ, ואעפ"כ אין הוסת נעקר אלא כאשר תעשה ג"פ אחת מפעולות אלו שעל ידם נקבע הוסת ולא תראה דם, ולא כאשר תעשה פעולת מאמץ אחרת ולא תראה דם, וכן נקט בסוגה בשושנים סי' ו' ס"ק ח'. [ואולם עיין להלן בסמוך מה שיש לדון ולחלק דשפיר תעקור וסתה].
"there is a doubt as to whether etc." — דאע"פ דכה"ג לגבי וסת השום באכלה שום ג"פ וראתה, קבעה וסת לאכילת שום בלבד, ולא לאכילת שאר דברים חריפים, עיין בזה בחי' רעק"א לסע' כ"ג ובחוו"ד ס"ק כ"ט, מ"מ יש לדון דנידו"ד לא דמי להתם, דשאני אכילת שום בצל ופלפלין שהם דברים שונים, ושמא זה גורם ומשפיע שתראה וזה לא, משא"כ פעולות מאמץ, אפשר דכולהו כחדא נינהו, דחוששת לראיה שלאחר מאמץ, ויל"ע. ולצד זה דפעולות מאמץ כולהו כחדא נינהו, וקובעת ע"י ג"פ קפיצה לכל פעולות מאמץ, א"כ הוא הדין במשנ"ת

"because of the *onah beinonis*" — ואפילו בוסת הקפיצות המורכב לימים דקיי"ל דקבעה וסת וכמבואר בשו"ע סע' י"ח אפ"ה חוששת לעונה בינונית וכמבואר בשו"ע סי' קפ"ד סע' י"ב, וכל שכן בוסת שאינו קבוע.

"However, if she menstruated again in the middle of the month etc." עיין פת"ש סי' קפ"ט ס"ק י' ודלא כט"ז שם ס"ק י"ז, וכ"ה בחי' רעק"א על הט"ז שם, ועיין חוו"ד ס"ק כ"ב מה שביאר בזה דעת הש"ך.

.45 "she does not have to anticipate menstruation on the 21st of *Nissan* ... However" — עיין ש"ך סי' קפ"ט ס"ק מ"ח במש"כ "כגון שקפצה וראתה ואחר כ' יום חזרה וקפצה וראתה וכו'". וע"ע שו"ע סי' קפ"ז סע' י"א.

.46 "She establishes ... indicated by physical sensations" — מכאן עד סוף הפרק ראה טושו"ע ונו"כ סי' קפ"ט סע' י"ט עד סע' כ"ו.

.52 "and the menstruation continues also after these sensations pass... until the end of the *onah*" — טושו"ע סי' קפ"ט סע' כ"ד.

"When menstruation occurs etc." — עי' ש"ך שם ס"ק ס"א וחוו"ד ס"ק ל"ב ועש"ך סוס"י קפ"ד.

לעיל לענין עקירה, שאם קבעה לראות על ידי ג' פעולות מאמץ שונים, שפיר תעקור וסתה על ידי שתעשה איזה פעולת מאמץ ולא תראה דם, ואין חילוק בין פעולה זו או אחרת, ודו"ק.

.45 "If she menstruated ... then she rescinds this cycle etc." — עיין לעיל משנ"ת מדברי החוו"ד גבי וסת לאכילת דברים חריפים דכשקבעה לראות ע"י אכילת ג' דברים שונים, עוקרת וסת זה אף ע"י אכילת ג"פ מין אחד מאלו, וכל שכן בוסת הקפיצות דגם אחר ג"פ אינו קביעות וסת גמורה, וחוששת רק כושא"ק, וכיון שעקרה אחת מהפעולות נעקרו כולן.

.47 "since her cycle is also composed of days" — עיין ש"ך ס"ק נ' ותוה"ש ס"ק מ"ד. ולא דמי למשנ"ת לעיל בשם החוו"ד דביש לה שעה קבועה לקפיצה אינה חוששת אלא לשעה הקבוע לה, דהתם איירי בוסת לקפיצות לחודיה ואינו מורכב לימים, משא"כ בנידו"ד בוסת המורכב לקפיצות ולימים, כיון דאיכא גם גרמת היום, חוששת מרגע הקפיצה עד סוף העונה.

.49 "she returns to her previously established cycle" — פת"ש ס"ק כ"ב בשם חוו"ד.

.50 "A bloodstain etc." — עיין שו"ע סי' ק"צ סע' נ"ב.

.51 "a minor jump or blow etc." — עיין במקורות וביאורים להערה 43.

53. "**until the end of the *onah***" — שו"ע סי' קפ"ט סע' כ"ד.
"**Some authorities contend etc.**" — לחוש להחוות דעת שכונת השו"ע שאסורה מיד עם תחילת המיחושים. ועי' פרד"ר שחולק והקיל בזה. וכ"מ בשעה"ר ס' קפ"ט ס"ק צ"ז.
"**In this case etc.**" — שו"ע הרב סוס"י קפ"ד.

54. "**It is proper for her to anticipate etc.**" — כנ"ל בסע' הקודם.
"**If she established ... She does not anticipate menstruation immediately etc.**" ואפילו להחוו"ד שהובא לעיל בסעיפים הקודמים ג"כ אי"צ לחוש רק משעת קביעותה, כיון שאינו באותה עונה. עי' תו"ט סעיף נ"ג ד"ה ויש אומרים.
"**If a woman usually experiences etc.**" — כן מתבאר מתשובת חת"ס הביאו פ"ת סי' קפ"ז ס"ק מ"ט.

55. "**three times on the same day of the month etc.**" — טושו"ע סי' קפ"ט סע' י"ט.

56. "**then she must anticipate ... from the beginning of the *onah* etc.**"

---

54. "**If the 1ST of *Iyar* passed etc.**" — עי' שו"ע הרב, וע"ש טעמו. ולכאורה הוא תרתי דסתרי, דמתחילה אין חוששים לגרמת היום אלא ע"י פיהוק, ואילו משעבר היום ולא פיהקה ולא ראתה תלינן להקל דראתה תחילה בגרמת היום ועקרתו.
"**Some authorities contend etc.**" — שמאחר ולא קפצה בא' באייר הרי לא עקרה וסתה, ושמא אם היתה קופצת בא' באייר היתה רואה דם. עי' חוו"ד.
"**then a difference of opinion exists etc.**" — להשו"ע הרב דלעיל דאפי' בדאיכא תרתי דסתרי אפ"ה ס"ל דתלינן להקל בגרמת היום, כ"ש בזה, שמאחר וראתה בא' באייר בלא קפיצה הוברר שראית א' בניסן היתה ראיה בגרמת היום ולא מחמת הקפיצה. ולהחוו"ד יל"ע, דבפשוטו כיון דעקירה היינו כעין שקבעה, אין כאן עקירה. אלא שהי' מקום לדון להחוו"ד דיודה דתלינן בגרמת היום כי היכי דחזינן בראתה ב"פ בר"ח ע"י קפיצה ובשלישית ראתה בר"ח שלא ע"י קפיצה דנתברר דראתה בגרמת היום, וא"כ ה"נ נימא הכי דנתברר דראתה בגרמת היום, אך יש לדחות דלא מצינו כן אלא בוסת קבוע ולא בושא"ק.
"**according to all opinions etc.**" — שמאחר וראתה בא' באייר בהמשך ראיה, לכל הדיעות אין כאן עקירה לראית א' בניסן, וחוששת לא' בסיון על ידי קפיצה, כפי שבעבר היתה צריכה לחשוש לא' באייר ע"י קפיצה.

60. "**Also any previous dates etc.**" — אך בפרד"ר ש"ח ס"ק נ"ז כתב דעדיין חוששת לושא"ק.

טושו"ע שם סע' י"ט וסע' כ"ה.

57. "The same applies to an equal intervals cycle" — שם סע' י"ט כ"ב וכ"ה.

58. "composed of both a specific date ... and physical sensations etc."
שם ועי' טושו"ע סוס"י קפ"ד ובש"ך שם.

"However etc." — כ"ה לדעת החוו"ד.

61. "Nonetheless...and she again menstruated etc." — עי' סי' קפ"ט סע' י"ד.

62-63. "eating a pungent food etc." — שו"ע ורמ"א סע' כ"ג, וחוו"ד שם ס"ק כ"ט.

---

62. "only if the sensations etc. ... However etc." — כן מתבאר בשיטת החו"ד באורים ל"א, שכשמתחילה לפהק חזינן שזו העונה שמפהקת בה, ופורשת בעונה זו. ולכן אם אינה רואה בעונה שמפהקת בה אלא בעונה שאחריה, חוששת בעונה שאחריה.

63. "Some opinions rule etc." — דעת היש אומרים היא החו"ד חי' סי' קפ"ט סק"ב. ופליג בזה על השועה"ר ס"ס קפ"ד. וכנראה אזלו לשיטתייהו, שהשועה"ר שמקל בהופיעו מיחושי הגוף עד עבור השעתיים, מקל גם בעו"ב. והחו"ד שמחמיר בהגיע וסת הגוף מחמיר גם בעו"ב. ונראה שבעו"ב אפשר להקל טפי מאשר הגיע וסת הגוף גרידא, לפי שבעו"ב ליכא ריעותא קמן כיון שעדיין לא הגיע וסת הגוף, משא"כ בהגיע וסת הגוף. גם בלש' השו"ע סעיף כ"ד גבי וסת הגוף משמע כהחו"ד, אבל בעו"ב ליכא ראיה. ובפרט שאף בקבעה וסת הגוף המורכב עם יום קבוע, ורגילה שוסת הגוף מופיע בסוף העונה, מקל הט"ז ס"ק ל"ט כהראב"ד שכל זמן שלא הגיע וסת הגוף אין צריכה לחשוש. ואף שמחמירין בזה כשאר פוסקים שפליגו עליה וחוששת מתחילת העונה, מ"מ בעו"ב א"צ לחשוש שעדיין לא התברר שהיום גורם.

65. "more than two days ... and this occurred on three occasions etc." — איתא בחת"ס (הביאו פ"ת סי' קפ"ז ס"ק מ"ט) שאשה שרגילה לקפוץ ולראות רק לאחר מספר ימים קבוע, אמרינן שכך טבעה, שהקפיצה פועלת עליה רק לאחר שעוברים מספר ימים, וכ"ש בוסת הגוף. וע"ע בפ"ת שם ס"ק מ"ג בשם הגהות מיימוניות ואמונת שמואל שאם ראתה בליל שני מהטבילה חיישינן שמא הטבילה דאתמול גרמה, וחזינן שאפשר לתלות את ראות הדם בקפיצה במרחק של יותר מעת לעת אף שאינו קבוע. ואף שכתב החו"ד (באו' ט"ו) שאם ראתה בליל שלישי או רביעי מהטבילה אין לתלות הדם בטבילה, הוא מיירי בוסת שאינו קבוע, אבל בוסת קבוע י"ל שמודה לחת"ס.

67. "the first menstruation must also be accompanied etc." — כפשטות לשון השו"ע סע' כ"ב "אם פיהקה היום" וכו'.

פרק שנים עשר

1. "Before marriage, every woman etc." — שו"ע אבהע"ז סי' ס"א סע' ב', לחשוש לשיטת הרמב"ם פ"י ה"ב וה"ו מהל' אישות דחופת נדה אינה קונה.

"Ideally etc." — רמ"א יו"ד סי' קצ"ב סע' ב', והטעם דבנדה ס"ו ע"א קאמר רבא "תבעוה לינשא ונתפייסה צריכה לישב שבעה נקיים", ומפרש הגמ' דחיישינן שמא ראתה דם מחמת חימוד הנישואין, וחיישינן בכל עת לחימוד חדש.

"If that is not possible etc." — רמ"א שם.

"In any event etc." — משמעות לשון הרמ"א "ואם לא תבעל עד מו"ש יש לה לבדוק עצמה בכל יום עד בעילת מצוה" משמע קצת דעד מו"ש אינה צריכה לבדוק א"ע, אבל בב"ח משמע דצריך לבדוק גם עד מו"ש, וכ"נ בסד"ט ס"ק ח'.

2. "If the wedding date was set etc." — רמ"א אבהע"ז שם.

"The groom should be told beforehand etc." — רמ"א שם.

"should make an effort not to touch her etc." — עי' באר היטב אהע"ז שם ס"ק ח'.

3. "they cannot be alone etc." — שו"ע ורמ"א יו"ד סי' קצ"ב סע' ד'.

פרק שנים עשר

1. "This applies even to a woman who has never menstruated" — גמ' נדה ס"ו ע"א ושו"ע יו"ד סי' קצ"ב סע' א', והטעם נתבאר במקו"ב ליסוד הטהרה.

"an elderly woman" — פת"ש שם ס"ק ב'.

"even if the divorcee is remarrying etc." — שו"ע שם סע' ה'.

"then this immersion is valid *bedi'eved* etc." — שו"ע שם סע' א', ועי' ש"ך שם ס"ק א' שהמנהג להחמיר [מש"כ הש"ך אף לבתולה, כונתו לבתולת דמים שלא ראתה מעולם].

2. "A virgin, who cannot check herself deeply" — ב"ח סי' קצ"ב.

3. "If after she began the seven clean days ... the wedding was postponed etc." שו"ע שם סע' ג' וש"ך ס"ק ו' בשם הב"ח.

"Likewise, if both sides resolved not to marry at all etc." — משמעות הט"ז ס"ק ו', שו"ת שבט הלוי ח"ה סי' קי"א ס"ק ג'.

4. "Even if several days pass after the marriage etc." — ועי' סד"ט ס"ק ט' דנראה

4. "If the bride immersed etc." — ש"ך סי' קצ"ב ס"ק י"א.
"they must separate etc." — מסקנת הסוגיא נדה ס"ה ע"ב שו"ע סי' קצ"ג.
"Even if she did not notice any hymenal blood etc." — שו"ע שם.
"If there was some contact etc." — הרמ"א שם כתב שנהגו להקל בהעראה כשלא ראתה דם, אבל בשו"ת בית שלמה ח"ב סי' ע"ו כתב שלמעשה קשה להקל בזה, כיון שקשה להבחין אם היתה רק העראה או יותר מזה, ועיין בשיעורי שבה"ל שם ס"ק ז' שהאריך. ואם לא הוציא זרע, החכמ"א כלל קט"ו ס"ק ט"ו כתב להחמיר, ובשיעורי שבה"ל שם ס"ק ה' כתב שאם לא היתה ביאה גמורה, אפילו אם היה ברוב אבר אפשר להקל, וכיון שיש בזה הרבה פרטים ואופנים, יש לשאול תמיד חכם.

5. "and recite the following *bracha*" — שו"ע אבהע"ז סי' ס"ג סע' ב' ומקורו בטור שם בשם בה"ג. ובב"ח וט"ז שם כתבו לברך בלא שם ומלכות, כיון שאינה ברכה שנזכרת בש"ס.

6. "at the time of anticipated menstruation" — שו"ת נודע ביהודה מהדו"ת יו"ד סי' קי"ז הו"ד בפת"ש סי' קפ"ד ס"ק כ"ב שו"ת שבטל הלוי ח"ג סי' קי"ב.
"*Ohr Zarua onah*" — שיעורי שבה"ל סי' קפ"ד סע' ב' בשיטת האור זרוע.

7. "four days" — שו"ע סי' קצ"ג וט"ז ס"ק ד'.

8. "If, after etc." — שו"ע סי' קפ"ז סע' י"ג.
"In a case where blood was not noticed etc." — עי' שו"ע רמ"א וש"ך שם, וראה בשיעורי שבה"ל שם שיש הרבה פרטים ואופנים ולכן ישאלו חכם.

מפירושו בכונת הרמ"א סי' קצ"ב סע' ב' דאם עברו ז' ימים אחר ז"נ ולא בדקה עצמה אפילו פעם אחת תוך ז"י אלו, אסור אפילו דיעבד, ע"ש. אמנם בט"ז סוס"ק ג' מוכח דאף אם עברו ז"י אחר טבילה מותר דיעבד אפילו לא בדקה כלל דלא כסד"ט.

5. "external contact" — עי' שו"ת שבט הלוי ח"ה סי' ק"כ.

6. "In case of difficulty ... during the day" — דבלבו גס בה יש מחלוקת אי מהני פתח פתוח, וכיון די"א דמהני, וגם יש סוברים דביום אי"צ שמירה כלל וכמו"ש רמ"א סי' קצ"ב סע' ד', ע"כ בשעת הדחק יש להקל בלא שומר ע"י פ"פ לדה"ר. הגרמ"ש קליין שליט"א.

7. "it is permitted to finish the marital act" — גמ' ושו"ע שם, והטעם, שאם נצריכו לפרוש מיד יהא לבו נוקפו מיד ופורש.

9. "on *leil Shabbos*" — שו"ע או"ח סי' ר"פ סע' ב' ומשנ"ב שם.

10. "the next three times" — שו"ע סי' קפ"ו סע' ב' וכשיטת הרי"ף בב"י שם.

"They may not engage in relations etc." — מקור מים חיים שם דלא כחוו"ד.

"If after relations blood was found etc." — עי' שו"ע סי' קפ"ז סע' א'.

11. "as soon as possible" — שו"ע הרב סי' קפ"ו ס"ק ג' בשם הרמב"ן.

12. "After she checked herself etc." — כדעה הראשונה בשו"ע סי' קפ"ו סע' ב', שהביא המחבר בסתמא.

"for a scrupulous woman etc." — לחשוש לשיטת הרא"ש שהובאה בשו"ע שם סע' ב' בשם יש אומרים.

"at a time interval corresponding etc." — אבל לפני שעבר מספר ימים זה דינה לענין הבדיקות בשעת תשמיש כאשה שיש לה וסת, כמ"ש בשו"ע שם סע' ג' ובחוו"ד שם בביאור דברי התרוה"ד שהובא בב"י שם.

13. "Women normally stop menstruating etc." — שו"ת שבט הלוי ח"ג ס"ס קט"ז.

14. "Although according to the letter of the law etc." — שעורי שבט הלוי, סי' קפ"ד סעיף ז' אות ד'.

---

9. "But *yichud* ... is permitted" — והטעם, מאחר שיחוד בעל ואשתו אף כשהיא נדה ועדיין לא בעל, אינו אלא מדרבנן, כמו שכתבו כמה גדולים וכ"כ בחזו"א, וע"כ דעת הראב"ד שביום מותר ביחוד לגמרי, והטעם דכיון שתהיה מותרת לו לאחר זמן לא תקפו יצרו, וא"כ בעונת הוסת יש להקל ביחוד, וכן משמעות הפוסקים, שיעורי הגרמ"ש קליין שליט"א.

11. "surgically removed" — שו"ת שבט הלוי ח"ה סי' קי"ט.

13. "forbidden to check" — שלא יהא לבו נוקפו ופורש, שו"ע ורמ"א שם סע' א' וסי' קפ"ד סע' א'.

"her husband instructs her to check" — כרתי ופלתי סי' קפ"ו ושו"ה הרב סי' קפ"ד.

14. "One should be meticulous etc." — הגהות חת"ס לשו"ע שם, ולדעתו גם אינה צריכה לבדוק קודם הימים שהיא עשויה לראות בהם. ויש להחמיר לבדוק מיד בשלושת הפעמים הראשונות שאחר הנישואין אף שהיא בתוך הימים שאינה עשויה לראות, ומלבד זאת להדר לבדוק גם בזמנים שעשויה לראות בהם. עי' בשיעורי שבה"ל שם סע' ב' אות

פרק שלשה עשר

1. "She should therefore anticipate menstruation etc." — נדה דף ז' ע"ב מעוברת משהוכר עוברה וכו', ושם בגמ' ח' ע"ב מבואר דהכרת העובר הוא בשלשה חדשים. ובשו"ת שבט הלוי ח"ג סי' קי"ד הוכיח מדברי המאירי דאף אם נודע ההריון לפני ג' חדשים איננה מסולקת דמים עד שיעברו ג' חדשים מתחילת ההריון, דרק לאחר ג"ח מהעיבור העובר מכביד עליה וגורם לסילוק הדם, וכמבואר בגמ' שם דע"י הכבדת העובר הוא דמסתלק הדם.

2. "she must separate etc." — עי' שו"ע סי' קפ"ד סע' ז' וסי' קפ"ט סע' ל"ג.

3. "If she has an established cycle for the day of the month etc." — ואולם אם היה לה וסת קבוע להפלגה וכו' עיין בכל זה בט"ז סי' קפ"ט ס"ק כ"ז וש"ך שם ס"ק מ"ה חכמ"א כלל קי"ב סי' כ"ה.

4. "When she begins the fourth month etc." — שו"ע סי' קפ"ד סע' ז' וסי' קפ"ט סע' ל"ד.

5. "and on the day of the *onah beinonis*" — עי' פת"ש סי' קפ"ט ס"ק ל"א בשם סד"ט שמיקל, אבל בהגה' דרישה ובגר"ז שם ס"ק קי"ד וכן בהפלאה בשם תשו' מהר"ם פאדווה מחמירים.

"as is the case with a woman with a non - established cycle" — משמעות השו"ע סי' קפ"ט סע' ל"ג ודלא כהמהרש"ל המובא בש"ך סי' קפ"ד ס"ק י"ט, וכ"ה גם דעת הש"ך לדינא וכמש"כ הסד"ט והחוו"ד סי' קפ"ד שם מובא בפת"ש שם ס"ק י"ד וכ"ה בחי' רעק"א שם.

ד'. ובדיעבד יש להקל, כמש"כ בשיעורי שבה"ל שם סע' ב' אות ד'. וראה מה שהאריך בכל זה הגרמ"ש קליין שליט"א בסו"ס מראה כהן.

פרק שלשה עשר

4. "In this case etc." — פת"ש סי' קפ"ט ס"ק ל"א בשם סד"ט.

9. "This is only etc." — משום שאין ימים שבתוך כ"ד חודש מצטרפים להחשיבם כימי הפלגה עם הימים שאחר כ"ד חודש, הואיל ותוך כ"ד חודש דינה כמסולקת דמים, ודק

"However ... according to the interval etc." — דאי אפשר לצרף את מספר ימי ההפלגה של אחר ג״ח ראשונים ולמספר ימי הפלגה של תוך ג״ח ראשונים, דמה שלא ראתה לאחר גח״ר י״ל דהוא משום דמסולקת דמים היא, ועיין היטב בחוו״ד סי׳ קפ״ט ביאורים ס״ק כ׳ מש״כ אדברי המהרש״ל בדין אשה שלא ראתה ג׳ עונות. ורק כשב׳ הראיות היו בזמן סילוק דמים הוא דחוששת להפלגה שבין ב׳ הראיות.

"whether that menstruation was etc." — פירוש דאין הטעם במה שאינה חוששת להפלגה זו מחמת דהוי הפלגת ג׳ עונות, אלא אף אם אינה הפלגה ארוכה של ג׳ עונות ג״כ אינה חוששת לה.

6. "Even if she menstruates three times etc." — שו״ע שם סע׳ ל״ג.

7. "During the Talmudical era etc." — עיין נדה ט׳ ע״א מחלוקת תנאים בזה, ובשו״ע סי׳ קפ״ד סע׳ ז׳ וסי׳ קפ״ט סע׳ ל״ג ול״ד פסק כדעת ר׳ יהודה ור׳ יוסי ור׳ שמעון דכל כ״ד חודש מסולקת דמים היא דע״י הלידה איבריה מתפרקין ואין נפשה חוזרת אליה עד לאחר שעברו כ״ד חודש. ואף בשנה מעוברת יש לה רק כ״ד חודש וכמו״ש הפת״ש סי׳ קפ״ד ס״ק י״ג בשם הפליתי ודלא כש״ך שם. וע״ש בפרד״ר שפירש כן גם בכונת הש״ך ורק כלפי עקירת הוסת חשש הש״ך שלא יעקר בחודש הכ״ה, ע״ש.

"If she menstruated however once etc." — עיין שו״ע סי׳ קפ״ט סע׳ ל״ג ובמקורות לעיל סע׳ ה׳.

"and the *onah beinonis*" — כנ״ל במקורות לסע׳ ה׳.

8. "*veset kavuah* with respect to stringencies" — שיעורי שבט הלוי סי׳ קפ״ד סע׳ ז׳ אות ד׳ וסי׳ קפ״ט סע׳ ל״ג אות ג׳.

"However, if she had an established cycle before the pregnancy" דקביעות וסת זו היא לחומרא לחוש לשינוי הטבעים, אבל לא לקולא לעקור וסת קבוע שהיה לה לפני העיבור דהיא קביעות וסת מדין הש״ס, עיין שיעורי שבה״ל שם.

9. "as long as she has menstruated at least one time etc." — ש״ך סי׳ קפ״ט ס״ק ע״ה, וכ״ה דעת רוב האחרונים וכמש״כ בחכמ״א כלל קי״ב סי׳ ל״ח.

לגבי חודש חוששת שפיר לוסתה מיד ביום וסתה הראשון שאחר כ״ד חודש.

10. "The husband should not be present etc." — שו״ת מנחת יצחק ח״ח סי׳ ל׳.

10. "If before becoming pregnant she had an established cycle" — עיין שו"ע סי' קפ"ט סע' ל"ד.

11. "If she had a non-established cycle before becoming pregnant" פתחי תשובה סי' קפ"ט ס"ק ל"ב בשם תשו' נודע ביהודה, וכן נהגו ודלא כההפלאה והלחם ושמלה.

12. "If she checked ... she remains clean" — פתחי תשובה סי' ק"צ ס"ק ז' בשם הרבה אחרונים.

13. "Every woman who gives birth etc." — ויקרא פרק י"ב שו"ע סי' קצ"ד סע' א'.

(a) "or experiences copious discharge of placenta fluid" — כיון שיש לחשוש שנתערב דם במים, הוראת הגר"ש ואזנר שליט"א.

(b) "strong and very frequent contractions" — עי' סד"ט שם ס"ק כ"ה ופתחי תשובה ס"ק ח' ושיעורי שבט הלוי שם סע' ב' אות ד'.

(c) "she cannot walk etc." — סדרי טהרה שם ע"פ משנה באהלות פ"ז מ"ד.

15. "may strictly speaking immerse etc." — ויקרא שם, שו"ע סי' קצ"ד סע' א'.
"However, it is worthwhile etc." — שיעורי שבט הלוי שם ס"ק ב'.

16. "A woman who miscarried etc." — מתני' נדה ל' ע"א, שו"ע שם סע' ב' ג'.

17. "As women become older etc." — שו"ע סי' קפ"ט סכ"ח.

19. "If after menopause etc." — רמ"א שם סכ"ח. ומחבר סל"א.

20. "If after ... she menstruates three times etc." — ט"ז שם ס"ק מ"ג שלא כנה"כ.

---

12. "A woman who bleeds during the 'pure days - *yemei tohar*' etc." — אף שמדין תורה דם זה טהור, כמש"כ בתחילת פ' תזריע, מ"מ נהגו מימי הגאונים להחמיר בזה ואין להקל כלל וכמש"כ הרמ"א בסי' קצ"ד סע' א'.
"even the immersion must be performed with a blessing" — פתחי תשובה שם ס"ק ב'.

13. "she cannot automatically assume etc." — עיין פתחי תשובה שם ס"ק ג'.

קול קורא

מכתבים מגדולי תורה שליט"א
בענין חיזוק לימוד ושינון הלכות טהרה

Letters from the Gedolei Yisrael to Strengthen the Importance of Learning and Reviewing the Laws of Family Purity

המכתבים דלהלן ניתנו למכון טהרת ישראל
לצורך חיזוק השיעורים בהלכות טהרה ולעורר לחיזוק ושינון ההלכות

דברים אחדים

בס"ד, כסליו תשנ"ח לפ"ק

נקדים בזה בשורות אחדות לבאר את הכונה ב"קול קורא" הנלהב מאת גדולי תורה שליט"א לחיזוק הידיעה ושינון הלימוד בהלכות נדה, לאברכים בני תורה ולהמון עם בית ישראל.

אין זה סוד, כי הלימוד הראשוני של הלכות אלו לפני החתונה, הוא בזמן שאין באפשרות החתן להשכיל ולהבין את פרטי הדינים המרובים, מהם אשר דורשים שימת לב לפרטים שבשעתו עדיין לא הבין החתן את פירושם ואת משמעותם, שהרי הדברים עדיין אינם מעשיים אז כדי שיתיישבו על הלב, מהם הכרוכים בחישובים שונים של חשבונות הוסתות, ולא הרי חשבון זה כחבירו, מהם דברים שאינם מחיי היום יום אלא כל מקרה כשלעצמו הוא עראי ומקרי, ומהם דברים הקשורים עם סיבות רפואיות בלתי שגרתיות כבדיקת רופאים, ימי עיבור וימי הנקה וכיוצא באלו, ובלא ידיעה ברורה של ההלכות, בנקל עלולים לבוא לידי מכשול ח"ו.

זאת ועוד, לימוד ראשוני זה של תמצית ההלכות הנחוצות, נלמדים בפרק זמן קצר הסמוך לנישואין, בו החתן מוקף בחבילי דטרדי, ואין ישוב הדעת כראוי לסכם לעצמו את הדברים שלמד, עד שלא מעט מהחתנים ניגשים לקראת החתונה עם דברים מעורפלים, שכל שינוי קל עלול להיות שינוי מהמותר לאסור.

יתירה מכך, לפי עדות מהרבנים מורי ההוראה שליט"א, נתקלים לא אחת במקרים בו מתברר שהיתה הבנה מוטעית בהלכה נחוצה שגרמה למכשול ח"ו, מהם שנבעו מחמת אי שימת לב, ומהם שנבעו מחמת חוסר ידיעה של דברים שהיה מן ההכרח לדעת אותם. אפשר גם, שהדברים בשעתו נלמדו, אך מחמת שלא היה נוגע למעשה מיד, נשכחו עם הזמן, ואילו היו שונים את פרקם שוב, או היו משתתפים בשיעורים הנמסרים ע"י הרבנים שליט"א, היו מונעים מעצמם מכשול ועון.

מן הדומה, שהדברים מדברים בעד עצמם וכל לב מבין ידע את חובתו לשוב לחזור ולשנן הלכות אלו, ולהשתתף בשיעורים הנמסרים על ידי הרבנים שליט"א.

ובזה אנו מפרסמים את קריאת הרבנים לחייב כל יחיד ויחיד לידע ההלכות המעשיות על בוריין, ובו מעוררים הם לכל האברכים לקבוע לימודם בהלכות נדה אחר החתונה, ואף מדגישים הם, כי עיקר הלימוד המחוייב הוא דוקא אחר החתונה, ומכאן הקריאה לכל מי שעדיין לא קבע את לימודו אחר החתונה, שיצטרף לשיעורי הלכות נדה הנמסרים על ידי תלמידי חכמים מוסמכים ובקיאים בהלכות אלו.

וזאת לדעת, כי גם אם נמצאים תקופה בזמן שמסולקת מדמים, מעוברת או מניקה, עליו ללמוד דינים אלו, כי לא זו בלבד שגם בתקופה זו ישנם שאלות המתעוררות ומהן השכיחות דוקא בתקופה זו, ובלי לימוד לא יעלה על הדעת מה הן השאלות בכלל, והרבה מכשולים נבעו מכך שהדברים לא היו מעשיים ולכן לא ידעו את המעשה אשר יעשון, זאת ועוד, מיד בסיום תקופה זו הדברים נוגעים הלכה למעשה, ואז יהא מאוחר מדי להקיף את כל הנחוץ לדעת, והחכם עיניו בראשו.

הדברים מוגשים לרבים על ידי מכון "טהרת ישראל" שהוקם לפני מספר שנים בעידודם ובברכתם של גדולי התורה שליט"א, ועומד בראשותו ותחת שרביט הנהגתו של הגאון רבי משה שאול קליין שליט"א דומ"צ בבית דינו של הגר"ש ואזנר שליט"א ורב שכונת אור החיים. המכון שם לו למטרה להפיץ ידיעת הלכות טהרה לחתנים, לאברכים, ולהמון העם. מאז הוקם המכון, נמסרו בערים שונות עשרות סדרות שיעורי הלכה לאברכים ולבעלי בתים, על ידי מגידי שיעורים הבקיאים ביותר בדינים אלו, בהם השתתפו רבים מכל שכבות הציבור. מבוגרים כצעירים, בעלי בתים לצד אברכים בני תורה.

לא נכחד, כי מתוך עבודת הקודש זו, בהרבצת תורה ע"י מסירת השיעורים הללו, ומתוך ההיכרות של מגידי השיעורים עם ציבור גדול של שומעים ומבקשים לדעת דבר ד' זו הלכה, גברה ונתחזקה אצלינו משימה קדושה זו, לעורר ולהעיר עוד ועוד, על הצורך לחזור ולשנן את ההלכות, כי למרבה הצער, הכרנו מקרוב הרבה בורות בשטח זה.

מכון "טהרת ישראל" שהוקם למען מטרה קדושה זו, יעמוד בעז"ה בעתיד כבעבר, לימין כל אלו המבקשים לארגן שיעורי תורה על ידי תלמידי חכמים

הבקיאים בהלכות אלו, הן בערים הגדולות והן בערי השדה, ויעמוד בעז"ה לצד אברכים יראי שמים שלמדו היטב הלכות נדה ומעונינים להבחן ולקבל את ההכשרה המתאימה להפיץ שיעורי טהרה בכל אתר.

הכו"ח למען הרחבת גבולות הקדושה והטהרה בישראל

הלל ורטהיימר

יו"ר מכון "טהרת ישראל"

משה שאול קליין

מו"ץ בבד"ץ דמרן הגר"ש ואזנר שליט"א
ורב שכונת אור-החיים בני-ברק

בס"ד, יום י' באדר ב' תשנ"ז

באתי בדברים אלו לעורר לב האברכים החשובים שזכו לבנות בית בישראל, על דבר החיוב הגדול המוטל עליהם ללמוד טהרה לדעת את הדרך ילכו בה והמעשה אשר יעשון, כי הנה אינו דומה הלכות אלו להלכות אחרות שיש בהם מסורת בית אבא ורגילות איך לנהוג, ואף בזה המכשלה רבה כשאין יודעים פרטי ההלכות, ק"ו בהלכות טהרה שמפני הצניעות אין בזה מסורת ורגילות מאבות לבנים, וכל הנושא הוא תורה חדשה בשביל האברכים החשובים, וע"כ חובה כפולה ומכופלת ללמוד הלכות טהרה הלכה למעשה, ואף אלו שכבר למדו עליהם לחזור על תלמודם כי גדול התלמוד שמביא לידי מעשה.

ומתורתו של רבינו עמוד ההוראה מרן הגר"ש הלוי ואזנר שליט"א למדנו גודל הנחיצות להפיץ תורת הטהרה בישראל, ע"י שהרביץ תורה ברבים בעיון הלכה למעשה בהלכות אלו לאלפי ת"ח מופלגי תורה, ועי"ז רבתה הדעת זה סדר טהרות בישראל, כי הת"ח החלו להעמיק בהלכות אלו הן ביחיד והן בחבורה בכוללי האברכים, ועי"ז רבו גם הספרים שנתחדשו בנושא זה בדורנו.

והנה מן הנסיון שאחר החתונה נכנס האברך לכולל ושם יש סדרי לימוד המחייבים אותו ואינו יכול ללמוד בעיון הלכות נדה החמורות, ואף אלו שכבר למדו קשה עליהם ללמוד שוב בעיון, וגם לאו כל מוחא סביל דא ללמוד הלכות אלו בעיון, ע"כ מוטל על הרבנים ומו"צ ללמד לרבים הלכות נדה בקוצר, ומוטל על האברכים חיוב להשתתף בשיעורים אלו, ומי לנו גדול מגדולי הראשונים הרמב"ן והרא"ש ועוד שכתבו הלכות נדה בקוצר ללמד לבני ובנות ישראל.

עלינו להחזיק טובה ולאמץ ידי הרה"ג ר' הלל ורטהיימר שליט"א שהקים מכון "טהרת ישראל" שנטל על עצמו תפקיד להרבות רוח טהרה בישראל, ומתייעץ איתי על כל צעד ושעל, ואחד מפעולותיו הברוכות הוא שנשלחים על ידו רבנים ומורי צדק חשובים שעשו שימוש חכמים ובקיאים במיוחד בהלכות אלו, ומוסרים שיעורים מתומצתים לרבים, ופסקי ההלכות הם ע"פ פסקי ההלכות שקיבלתי ממורי ורבי גאון ההוראה מרן הגר"ש הלוי ואזנר שליט"א, ועי"ז רבתה הדעת זה סדר טהרות, וכבר נמסרו עשרות שיעורי תורה הן בבני ברק והן בשאר ערי הארץ אפילו במקומות רחוקים.

ובודאי שראוי לכל יראי ה' להשתתף בשיעורי הטהרה ללמוד ע"מ לעשות ועי"ז נזכה בעזר ה' להקים דורות ישרים וכשרים להקים לגיון של מלך מלכי המלכים הקב"ה הראויים לקבל פני משיח צדקינו במהרה בימינו אמן.

ועי"ז באתי עה"ח

משה שאול קליין

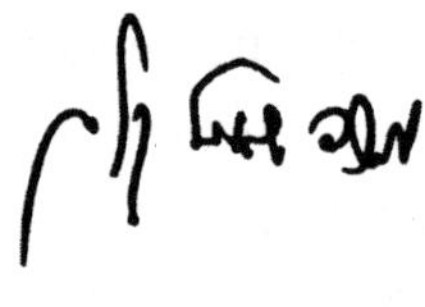

ב"ה

דברים אמתיים הנ"ל א"צ חיזוק כי מדברים בעד עצמן, אבל מצוה לחזק **כי אין לך גורם יסוד לבנין בית ישראל שיהי' ראוי לקיום ולישועת ה' כטהרת הבית שהוא יתד שהכל תלוי בו** ע"כ לבי ונפשי עם העושים ומעשים אלה להרבות כבוד ד' ולהטיב לבנ"י הכשרים.

ע"ז בעה"ח מצפה לרחמי ה'

שמואל הלוי ואזנר

רב אב"ד ור"מ זכרון מאיר - בני ברק

הנני מצטרף וקורא גם אני לאחב"י לחזק את המכון טהרת ישראל כי דבר גדול מאד להרבות שיעורים לאברכים צעירים ללמדם ההלכות הנחוצות ולהצילם שלא יכשלו ח"ו באיסורים ואשרי חלקם וחלק כל המחזיק בהם

ובעה"ח ג' טבת תשנ"ח לפ"ק

הק' יוחנן סופר

בס״ד אור ליום ערש״ק פ׳ כי תשא תשנ״ז

כתוב [דברים ז-ו] כי עם קדוש אתה וגו׳ בך בחר ד׳ להיות לו לעם סגולה מכל העמים וגו׳ חשק ד׳ בכם ויבחר בכם וגו׳ כי מאהבת ד׳ אתכם, מבואר כאן בכתובים גודל מעלת כלל ישראל, שרק בנו בחר ד׳ להיות לעם סגולה דפירושה סגולה אוצר חביב כלי יקר ואבנים טובות שהמלכים גונזים אותם כך אתם תהיו לי סגולה משאר אומות כו׳ כי לי כל הארץ והם בעיני ולפני לכלום [רש״י פ׳ יתרו י״ט־ה].

מה שחשק ד׳ בנו כתב הרמב״ן שם שנקשר עמכם בקשר אמיץ שלא יפרד מכם לעולם כו׳ שתהיו אתם סגולה ונחלה לו כו׳ כי מאהבת ד׳ אתכם בחר בכם, שראה אתכם ראויים להתאהב לפניו ונבחרים לאהבה יותר מכל העמים.

ומה שכתוב בפ׳ יתרו ואתם תהיו לי ממלכת כהנים וגוי קדוש כתב הספורנו כמו שיהיה הענין לעתיד לבא כאמרו והי׳ הנשאר בציון והנותר בירושלים קדוש יאמרו לו ואחז״ל סנהדרין צ״ב ע״א מה קדוש לעולם קיים אף הם לעולם קיימים כי אמנם היתה כונת הבו״ע במתן תורה לתת להם כל הטוב העתיד וכו׳ ע״ש, הרי מפורש יוצא מפרשיות תוה״ק את האושר החיים הנצחי שכל אחד מהכלל ישראל יש לו, ושיכול להשיג במשך שנות חייו, והסיבה היסודית והעקרית היא מה שכתוב כי עם קדוש אתה.

הרבה דרגות יש בקדושה, אך עד כמה שמשתדל עצמו לקיים דברי רבא [יבמות כ׳] קדש עצמך במותר לך הוא הפתח והשער הגדול שיוכל להשיג ולהרבות במעלה זו.

והרי ידוע שבאלו ההלכות העסוקים בהם זוכים שהקב״ה מגין על הלומד שח״ו לא יכשל בהם ומי שעסוק כדוגמא בהל׳ שבת אז קדושת השבת הוא אצלו באיכות יותר גדולה, והעוסק בדי״מ הוא נזהר יותר ונשמר שלא יכשל בהם.

ולכן באנו להעיר הלבבות האברכים גדולי התורה שיח׳ הגם כשהגיעו לפרקם למדו הלכות נדה וכל סימני הלכות הקשורים בזה שלא יכשלו באיסורי נגיעה וכדומה וגם שעי״ז נפרץ הגדר והסייג של הצניעות אשר נסיונות יקיפו אותו ומתרחק מהמעלות העליונות הנתבאר בתחלת דברינו, **לכן חובה על כל א׳ וא׳ שיקבע זמן ללימוד ההלכות אף לאחר הנשואין ובזה יוכל להיות בטוח שישמר מכל מכשול.**

ויש להחזיק טובה למכון טהרת ישראל מיסודו של הרב הג״ר הלל וורטהיימר שליט״א שעושה הרבה במסירת שיעורים לחתנים ומבחנים ע״י רבנים מובהקים, והכל

נעשה ע״י הדרכתו של הגאון ר׳ משה שאול קליין שליט״א שמשמיא זיכו לו להרבות טהרה בישראל.

הכו״ח למען הרבות קדושה בישראל,

מיכל יהודה ליפקוביץ

הכו״ח למען הרבות קדושה בישראל,

מיכל יהודה ליפקוביץ

ג. א. כו״ח למען הסיר מכשול ולחזק קדושה בבית ישראל

א.י.ל. שטינמן

ג״א כו״ח למען הסיר מכשול ולחזק קדושה בבית ישראל

א.י.ל. שטינמן

הרב ש. י. נסים קרליץ

רמת אהרן
רח' ר' מאיר 6, בני-ברק

בס"ד, יום ב' אד"ב תשנ"ז

כאשר דוד המלך אמר שמרתי דרכי ה' ולא רשעתי מה' כי כל משפטיו לנגדי חוקותיו לא אסור ממנה. היינו איך להיות בטוח ששמרתי ולא רשעתי, כשכל משפטיו לנגדי ע"י שחוקותיו לא אסור ממנה, היינו שעוסק בהם תמיד.
והנה ענין הלכות טהרה שפרטיו מרובים, **גם אחרי שלמדו היטב ההלכות צריך להיות קביעות לחזור וללמד הדברים.**

ועלינו להחזיק טובה להרבנים הגאונים שליט"א שעוסקים בחיזוק "טהרת ישראל" ולהשתתף בשיעורים ברב עם, ועי"ז נגרם גם חיזוק לרחוקים להתקרב לתורה ומצוות.

החותם בברכה לכל העוסקים ומשתתפים בדבר

נסים קרליץ

החותם בברכה לכל העוסקים ומשתתפים בדבר
נסים קרליץ

הנני להצטרף לכל הנ"ל כיהודה ועוד לקרא ובאמת שדברי תורה צריכין חזוק וביחוד בהלכות טהרה שעינינו הרואות עד כמה החמירו בזה חכמי הדורות והוסיפו חומר על חומר וכבר האריכו למעניתם בספרי הפוסקים מה ראו להחמיר בזה, ועל הכל מכיון שהלכות אלו מסורות ביד כל אדם להיות כל איש שורר בביתו והשכחה מצוי', ואפי' אברכים יקרים נכשלים בענינים אלה, ע"כ יבורכו המעוררים להתחזק בלמוד ההלכות האלה ועל ידי כך תרבה הטהרה בישראל להיות ראויים להשראת השכינה.

הצב"י שמעון בעדני

הצב"י שמעון בעדני

נתן געשטעטנער

אבד"ק קרית אגודת ישראל

ור"מ מתיבתא "פנים מאירות" בני-ברק

בס"ד, קרית אגו"י בני-ברק ח"י כסליו תשנ"ח לפ"ק

אפריון נמטייה להאי גברא יקירא הרה"ג איש חי רב פעלים לתורה מוה"ר הלל ורטהיימר שליט"א, אשר זה כמה עבר עליו רוח טהרה להרבות טהרה בישראל, על ידי הפצת לימוד הלכות טהרת הבית בשיעורי תורה הנלמדים במקומות קרובים ורחוקים.

והנה אך למותר לבאר את עוצם החובה ללמוד ולדעת הלכות חמורות אלו, אשר שמירתן הוא יסוד קדושת בית ישראל ויחוסו, וכמבואר בשו"ע אהע"ז (סימן ד' סי"ג) שאם אינו שומרם ח"ו הולד פגום ומקולקל ואין משפחתו מיוחסת, עיין בב"ש וח"מ שם. והפגם הוא אף כשנכשל בשוגג, ומכל שכן ששגגת תלמוד עולה זדון (ב"מ לג:). ומי שאינו לומד הלכות אלו בדקדוק כמעט לא ימלט מלהכשל בחמורות, ועל דרך שכתב א"ז הגאון מהר"י אייבשיץ זצ"ל בס' יערות דבש (והובא בהקדמת ס' משנה ברורה על הלכות שבת) כי אי אפשר כלל במציאות שינצל מאיסור שבת אם לא ילמד כל הדינים על בוריים היטב היטב עיי"ש. והלכות אלו הן הן גופי תורה, וכאמרם ז"ל (אבות פ"ג מי"ח) קנין ופתחי נדות הן הן גופי תורה, ופירש"י "כלומר אל יהיו קלות בעיניך אלא שים לבך עליהן כי חמורין הן יותר מדאי ותמצא בהם עומק גדול". ובתוס' יו"ט גם הביא מכסף משנה (סופ"ד מה' יסודי התורה) "ופתחי נדה נושאם דבר מכוער, אעפ"כ אלו הן גופי הלכות, כלומר עיקרי תורה מצד השכר הגדול הצפון להעוסקים בהם". וק"ז רבינו החתם סופר ז"ל למד מסכת נדה עם תלמידיו הקדושים, וכמו שכתב בסיום חידושי מס' נדה וז"ל "סימנו מסכת נדה בעזה"י בישיבה הרמה בק"ק מאטערשדארף, יום ג' פורים קטן בשמחה רבה לפ"ק, עם תלמידים הגונים אלופים ומסובלים, לקבל טהרה וקדושה עלולים".

ולכן בואו ונחזיק טובה להרה"ג היקר הנ"ל המזכה את הרבים בלימוד שיעורים בהלכות גדולות אלו, הנחוצים אף לתלמידי חכמים הזוכים לשבת בחצרות ה', ומכל שכן לעם ה' הטרודים כל היום על המחיה ועל הכלכלה, **ואני קורא לכל החרדים לדבר ה' להתחזק בלימוד ההלכות של טהרת בית ישראל,** יבואו טהורים ויתעסקו בלימוד טהרה ובזכות זה נזכה לראות במהרה ביעוד הנביא, וישב מצרף וגו' וטהר את בני לוי וגו' והיו לה' מגישי מנחה בצדקה.

נתן געשטעטנער

משה שטרנבוך

סגן נשיא העדה החרדית בעיה"ק
מח"ס "מועדים וזמנים", שו"ת "תשובות והנהגות" ועוד
ראב"ד דק"ק חרדים ביוהנסבורג

שמחתי בבשורה טובה, שקבוצת אברכים ת"ח, בחברת "טהרת ישראל" עוסקים במצוה רבה לעורר גם אצל בני תורה, ללמוד ולחזור הלכות נדה, שמצוי שלומדים סמוך לחתונה רק מקופיא ראשי פרקים ונשאר כן, או נשכח אצלם הלכות, ועלולים ח"ו ליכשל בחמורות, ודבר גדול עושים לסדר שיעורים עם בחינות.

והלכות נדה הם יסוד קדושת ישראל, ובו יצירת הנפש, ובעונם היא כרת ר"ל, והילדים הם פגומים, וכמה אזהרות הוסיפו חכמינו ז"ל לא ליכשל באסור נדה, וכבר אמרו חז"ל שאם נכשל משגגת תלמוד זהו זדון.

ובזמן האחרון ב"ה חיברו ספרים הרבה בקיצור הלכות, ומועיל בס"ד ללמוד בקיצור עיקרי הדינים, אבל צריך גם תורה שבע"פ להזהיר לפרש לברר וללבן הדברים, ובשניהם כאחד הברכה מצויה, וכבר נוכחתי כמה וכמה פעמים שאברכים שהצטרפו ללימודים אלו בירכו על התועלת, וצריך שיעורים לנשים גם כן, או הבעל הוא שילמד אשתו.

והאמת בכל פעם שלומדים, נוסף ללומד הלכות אלו חידושים למעשה, ובעצם הלימוד מוסיף קדושה, שאינו אלא כמצות אנשים מלומדה, רק אדרבה מבינים ליזהר יותר, ובזה לבד שכרו רב מאד בס"ד.

וראיתי גאוני ישראל ובעלי הוראה משבחים פעולת "טהרת ישראל" שבראשו עומד ידידי הרב הגאון רבי משה שאול קליין שליט"א, והנני בחפץ לב מצטרף בקריאה לסדר שיעורים כאלו לחזקם ולעודדם בכל ארה"ק בס"ד.

והנני מצפה בכליון לישועת ה' ורחמי שמים מרובים

משה שטרנבוך

משה הלברשטאם

חבר הבד"צ העדה החרדית
ראש ישיבת "דברי חיים" טשאקאווע
מח"ס שו"ת "דברי משה"
פעיה"ק ירושלים תובב"א

בס"ד, יום ד' לסדר הנותן אמרי שפר, ט' טבת תשנ"ח

תורה צוה לנו משה וגו' לכן שמחתי באומרים לי יד שלוחה אלי לבוא בכתובים אודות אחד ממפעלי התורה החשובים אשר מטרתו קודש להפיץ טהרה בקרב ישראל עם קדוש באצה"ק אשר בשם "טהרת ישראל" יכונה אשר יסד וכונן ידידנו וידיד כל בית ישראל איש חי ורב פעלים מקבציאל בתורה ובהוראה הגאון הצ' רבי משה שאול קליין שליט"א רב שכונת אור החיים ומחשובי וגדולי המורים בעיה"ת בני ברק ת"ו, אשר היא מהלכות ודינים החמורות, **שהחובה על כאו"א ללמוד ולשנן להיות שגור בפיו יסודות דינים אלו לידע המעשה אשר יעשון לבלתי הכשל בהם ח"ו.** ומטרת המכון הוא להיות לעזר לאלו שרצונם לדעת את המותר והאסור ע"י מתן שעורים קבועים ע"י מורי הוראה אשר משנתם סדורה בפיהם ללמוד עם האברכים הצעירים אחר נשואיהם הלכתא רבתא הדין, ובפרט אשר זכה לצרופא דרבנן כתב עוז חביון מאת מו"ר הגאון האדיר עמוד ההוראה מרן בעל "שבט הלוי" אשר יצא בשבח רעיון נשגב זה. ופוק חזי לשונו הזהב של כ"ק זקיני הגה"ק בעל ישמח משה זי"ע בספרו שו"ת "השיב משה" וזל"ק: "ונכון להודיע דינים הרבה בדיני נדה וטבילה וחציצה שאינם ידועים כלל", עיי"ש. ותועלת מרובה יש בדבר זה שהוא בכפילא הן לטובת אלו שמפאת קוצר הזמן מעת חתונתם לא היה סיפק בידם לעבור על כל ההלכות ממקודם בשו"ע וגם לאלו אשר למדו שורש הלכה למען דעת ההכרעה בהלכה זו. **ועצם שינון הלכות אלו בתמידות הוא סגולה לינצל מכל מכשול** בבחינת בא ליטהר מסיעין לו, והשי"ת יהיה בעזרם של כל העוסקים בזה להרבות טהרה בארה"ק מדן ועד באר שבע, עדי שיקוים ומלאה הארץ דעה - זו טהרות - את ד',

ובעה"ח למען טהרת ישראל עם קדוש.

משה הלברשטאם

פעיה"ק ירושלים תובב"א

מסעוד בן שמעון

דיין ומו"צ
ורב דקהל הספרדים
רמת אלחנן בני ברק

בס"ד, יום ח"י כסליו תשנ"ח

אמרו חז"ל במדרש, אמר רבי חלפתא, אשריה, ואשרי יולדתה, ואשרי בעלה, ואשרי משפחתה של כל אשה המשמרת דיני הטהרה כראוי, שמשמרת את עצמה ואת בעלה מדינה של גיהנם, ומביאתן לחיי העולם הבא. במדרש זה מבואר כי ענין טהרת הבית הוא היסוד של אושר האדם בעולמו, שלו ושל משפחתו, לנצח נצחים, ולאשר קיום השמירה בפועל הוא באשה, תלוי הדבר באשה. אך פשוט הדבר, כי בראש ובראשונה חייב הבעל ללמוד ההלכות במקורן ובשרשן שידעם על בוריין, שאז יהיי סמוך לבו שאכן ביתו מתנהג עפ"י ההלכה וטהור הוא, ואם לאו עלולים להכשל בחסרון ידיעה בהרבה גופי הלכה, וכמו שהאריך בזה בהקדמת ספר "טהרת ישראל" יעוי"ש, ושם כתב שהצדיק ר' אורי מסטרעלסק **חזר הלכות הטהרה אלף פעמים!**

על כן בואו ונחזיק טובה לשומרי משמרת הטהרה שהקימו מכון בשם "טהרת ישראל" שמטרתו להפיץ לימוד ההלכות של הטהרה ע"י ששולחים ת"ח ומורי צדק ללמד ההלכות למעשה בכללותם ובפרטותם, בכל ישוב להרבות הטהרה בישראל.

ובודאי **חובה קדושה על כל יראי ה', ואף לאברכים שתורתם אומנותם להשתתף בשעורים אלו לדעת את ההלכות למעשה** ואף אם אין בה אלא חזרה בלבד, ומכש"כ שהנסיון הוכיח שהרבה הלכות נעלמות מחסרון ידיעה בהוראה למעשה.

החותם לכבודה של תורה ולחזוק הקדושה והטהרה

מסעוד בן שמעון

החותם לכבודה של תורה ולחזוק הקדושה והטהרה
מסעוד בן שמעון

Glossary of Hebrew – English Terms

alos hashachar – dawn

bedikah – check
bedieved – post factum
bracha – blessing

chasan – groom
chatzitzah – intervening substance
Chol ha'moed – intermediary days of Pesach / Sukkos
chupah – wedding canopy

daven – pray

eid bedikah – examination cloth
eiruv – area enclosed to allow carrying on Shabbos
erev Shabbos – Friday

gezeirah – rabbinical enactment

haflagah – interval
hefsek taharah – a check to see if flow has ceased
hanetz hachamah – sunrise

iyun – inspection of body prior to immersion

kallah – bride
kesem – stain
kesubah – marriage document
leil Shabbos – Friday night

mikveh – ritualarium
mincha ketanah – approximately two and a half hours before end of day
motzei Shabbos / Yom Tov – eve. after the conclusion of Shabbos / Yom Tov

netz hachamah – sunrise

onah – daytime /nighttime when period is to be anticipated
onah beinonis – average cycle

poskim – Halachic authorities

Rosh Chodesh – the beginning of the Jewish month (the 30th / 1st)

sechita – squeezing
shivah – seven days of mourning
shloshim – thirty day mourning period
shul – synagogue

tamei – unclean
tevilah – immersion

veset – menstrual period
veset kavuah – established menstruation cycle
veset hachodesh – menstruation cycle according to same lunar calendar date
veset haflagah – menstruation cycle after a certain interval of days
veset haguf – menstruation cycle due to bodily symptoms /sensations
veset hakefitzot – jump induced cycle
veset she'aina kavuah – non established menstruational cycle

yamim hanevochim – days of confusion (menstruation within a group of specific days)
yichud – man and woman being alone in private quarters

Index

Key:
kesem regarding veset day **10** 27; **11** (50)
= Chap. **10** par. 27; Chap. **11** footnote (50)

A

B

C

D

E

F

G

H

I

J

K

L

M

N

O

P

R

S

U

V

W

במעמד מרנן ורבנן גדולי תורה שליט"א

הוענקו מילגות לע"ב אברכים מצטיינים

מאות אנשים ובראשם גדולי התורה התאספו לכנס מיוחד שנערך בבני ברק מטעם מכון "טהרת ישראל".

הכנס נועד לתת ביטוי והוקרה ל-72 אברכים שעמדו בהצלחה בכור המבחן על ספר "יסוד הטהרה" וכמו"כ להגביר בתודעת רבים אחרים את חשיבות הענין ולזרזם שיצטרפו למעגלי הלומדים.

בין גדולי התורה שכיבדו את המעמד בהופעתם נראו הגאונים: רבי גרשון אדלשטיין שליט"א ראש ישיבת פוניבז', רבי ניסים קרליץ שליט"א ראש כולל חזון איש.

פתח והנחה את הכנס יו"ר המכון הרה"ג ר' הלל ורטהיימר שליט"א, שקידם בברכה את הנאספים וציין את הצלחת המבחן שנערך כמעט ללא פירסומת ולהפתעתנו נרשמו אליו כ-400 אברכים מכל גווני הקשת, מהם עברו את כור המבחן בהצלחה ע"ב אברכים שהם חתני הכנס אשר חוט של חן וטהרה נסוך עליהם.

כמו"כ הזכיר שמלאו 10 שנים ליסוד המכון והפליא את מסירותו של העומד בראשו הגאון רבי משה שאול קליין שליט"א שמקדיש הרבה מזמנו לסייע בהכוונה מלאה של כל פעולות המכון.

במרוצת העשור נאמרו ע"י רבני המכון המכתתים רגליהם במסירות רבה מאות שיעורים בהלכות טהרה ברחבי הארץ ובחו"ל אף לארצות רחוקות, עוד הזכיר את פעולות המכון בשטח ההסברה ובהוצאה לאור של הספרים "יסוד הטהרה" ו"משמרת טהרה" ו"ידיעת הטהרה", שנתקבלו בציבור בהתלהבות רבה, וכבר שוקדים צוות ת"ח על תרגום הספר בשפות נוספות.

רושם מרטיט עשתה הופעתו בכנס של ראש הישיבה מרן הגאון הגדול רבי מיכל יהודה ליפקוביץ שליט"א שדיבר בהתרגשות גדולה על חשיבות המשימה להרבות טהרה בישראל המקשר את ישראל לאבינו שבשמים.

כמו״כ נשא דברים הגה״ח רבי אהרן טויסיג שליט״א משגיח רוחני בישיבת אלכסנדר והגאון רבי שמואל אליעזר שטרן שליט״א רב מערב בני ברק, שהקריא את מכתב הברכה ששיגר לכנס מרן בעל שבט הלוי הגאון הגדול הגר״ש ואזנר שליט״א שבו נאמר:

״הנה כבוד תלמידי וידיד נפשי הגאון הג׳ ר׳ משה שאול קליין שליט״א רב שכונת אור החיים ומובהק ההוראה בביד״צ ובית הוראה זוכה היום לחזק כמאה אברכים מופלגי תורה בענין טהרת בית ישראל - ואשר בידו נסיון רב של עשרות בשנים מעבודת הק׳ של בית הוראה ז״מ ועוד, והכל נעשה ע״י מכון טהרת ישראל ומספר שראוי למחברו הג׳ בעל ס׳ יסוד הטהרה - על דרך המקובל לנו בעזרת חי החיים ויהי ה׳ אלוקיו אתו לבנות עוד חומה בצורה לטהרת בנות ישראל, הכ״ד מצפה להרמת קרן הטהרה בישראל שמואל הלוי ואזנר״.

את המשא המרכזי השמיע ראש המכון הגאון רבי משה שאול קליין שליט״א שתיאר את ההשתלשלות ההיסטורית שבעקבותיה נתחדש בדורינו הלימוד הנפוץ בהל׳ טהרה, לעומת ההווי בדור הקודם שלא נמסר לימוד זה כי אם ביחידות עד שבא מרן הגר״ש ואזנר שליט״א בראותו את העזובה בתחום זה סלל דרך ישרה להפיץ את ידיעת הטהרה בבתי ישראל ע״י שיעוריו ברוב עם וע״י העידוד שנתן לבעלי הוראה שילמדו את העם.

מצבת זכרון

לנשמות הורי היקרים אישי סגולה
ועתירי מעש וטובי הלב
רבי הפעלים ואנשי חסד

אבי מורי ורבי הרה"ח
מוהר"ר **אפרים חיים** ב"ר **אברהם נח הלוי** זצ"ל **קליין**
נלב"ע צום העשירי י' טבת תשמ"ט
עמוס במעש"ט ומוכתר בכתר שם טוב

ואמי מורתי נפש זכה ועדינה
מרת **מרים רחל** ב"ר **חיים הכהן** (דרשן) ע"ה
נלב"ע ט"ז אלול תשמ"ז

ת. נ. צ. ב. ה.

זכרם לא ימוש מאתנו ומזרענו עד עולם

אברהם נח הלוי קליין

הנדיבים הנכבדים אשר נדבה רוחם לפרקים חשובים בספר לתוספת קדושה וטהרה בעמ״י
We thank the generous philanthropists who kindly donated towards large sections in this *sefer*, with the pure intentions of spreading more purity and holiness in *Klal* Yisroel.

לעילוי נשמת

האישה החשובה
אשת חיל עטרת בעלה
שמה נודע בשערים לתהילה
עדינת הנפש ואצילת הרוח
מגזע היחס

מרת **מלכה הגר** ע״ה
אלמנת הרה״ח ר׳ משה הגר זצ״ל - תל אביב
בת הרב מרדכי זיסקינד סג״ל לנדא זצוק״ל - מריישא גליצי׳

נלב״ע ג׳ אייר תשס״ו

ת.נ.צ.ב.ה.

הונצח ע״י בנה ידידנו היקר
הר״ר יוסף דוד הגר וב״ב הי״ו
Rabbi & Mrs. Yosef Dovid Hager
Los Angeles, California

הנדיבים הנכבדים אשר נדבה רוחם לתרום פרקים חשובים בספר לתוספת קדושה וטהרה בעמ״י

We thank the generous philanthropists who kindly donated towards large sections in this *sefer*, with the pure intentions of spreading more purity and holiness in *Klal Yisroel*.

לזכרון עולם ולעילוי נשמת

אבי מורי הרה״ח

הר״ר אברהם משה ב״ר אליעזר יוסף הכהן ז״ל

נלב״ע ח׳ אדר א׳ תשס״ג

ת.נ.צ.ב.ה.

הונצח ע״י בנו ידידנו החשוב רב פעלים לתורה וחסד, הנגיד המפואר

הר״ד יעקב מאיר הכהן הי״ו ומשפ׳

Mr. & Mrs. Yaakov Meir HaKohen, Woodmere, NY

לברכה והצלחה מתוך בריאות הגוה״נ

ולמילוי כל משאלות ליבם לטובה

לזכרון עולם ולעילוי נשמת

אבינו מורנו הרה״ג הנכבד ירא מרבים

מוה״ר **שלום גוטמאן** זצ״ל

בן הר׳ **יעקב ישראל** ז״ל ומרת **רחל** ע״ה

נפטר בשם טוב י״ט תשרי, תש״ן

איש ירא אלוקים, ישר ונאמן, מעוטר במידות טובות ומוזהבות, מוכתר בכתר שם טוב

עסק הרבה במשך ל״ה שנים לטובת ק״ק אנשי מארמאראש בקליוולנד, אהיא.

ואמנו מורתנו הנכבדה, רודפת צדקה וחסד

מרת **פיגא סעריל** ע״ה

ב״ר ר׳ **יוסף מרדכי** ע״ה ומרת **בילא** ע״ה

נלב״ע כ״א אדר א׳ תשס״א

ת.נ.צ.ב.ה.

הונצחו ע״י בניהם הנכבדים והחשובים אנשי חסד נודעים לתהילה

הרה״ח ר׳ יוסף מרדכי גוטמאן שליט״א ורעיתו תחי׳

Mr. and Mrs. Joseph Gutman

ור׳ יעקב ישראל ג-אטמאן שליט״א ורעיתו תחי׳

Mr. and Mrs. Jacob Gutman

הנדיבים הנכבדים אשר נדבה רוחם לתרום פרקים חשובים בספר לתוספת קדושה וטהרה בעמ״י

We thank the generous philanthropists who kindly donated towards large sections in this *sefer*, with the pure intentions of spreading more purity and holiness in *Klal Yisroel*.

לזכרון עולם ולעילוי נשמת

אבי מורי

הר״ר **דוד** ב״ר **אברהם שרעבי** ז״ל

נלב״ע ב׳ תשרי ר״ה תשס״ה

ת.נ.צ.ב.ה.

הונצח ע״י בנו ידידנו היקר

*הר״ר **אליעזר ירמיהו שרעבי** וב״ב הי״ו*

Rabbi & Mrs. Eliezer Sharabi, Baltimore, MD

לזכרון עולם ולעילוי נשמת

הרה״ח ר׳ **מנחם מנדל** בן הרה״ח ר׳ **שמעון שרייבר** ז״ל

עסק בצרכי ציבור באמונה, נלב״ע כ״ו אדר א׳ תשנ״ב

האשה החשובה מרת **חיה רבקה** בת ר׳ **סיני זונדל** ע״ה

אשת חיל נזדככה ביסורים, נלב״ע כ״ד אדר א׳ תשס״ג

ת.נ.צ.ב.ה.

*הונצחו ע״י בנם ידידנו היקר הר״ר **שמעון שרייבר** שליט״א*

Rabbi Shimon Shreiber

Bnei Brak, Israel

לזכרון עולם ולעילוי נשמת

אבי מורי הר״ר **אברהם** ב״ר **נחום טמבור** ז״ל נלב״ע ה׳ חשון תשי״א

ואמי מורתי מרת **נעכא** בת ר׳ **דוד** ע״ה נלב״ע כ״ה אייר תשנ״ו

דודי ר׳ **אברהם** ב״ר **מאיר צבי אסטרייכר** ז״ל נלב״ע כ״א תשרי תשנ״ט

ודודתי מרת **פרידה** ב״ר **נחום אריה** ע״ה נלב״ע א׳ דר״ח אלול תשנ״ז

ת.נ.צ.ב.ה.

*הונצח ע״י משפחתם, הרה״ח ר׳ **משה** ורעייתו **מרים פוגל** הי״ו*

Rabbi & Mrs. Moshe Fogel,

Brooklyn, NY

הנדיבים הנכבדים אשר נדבה רוחם לתרום פרקים חשובים בספר לתוספת קדושה וטהרה בעמ״י
We thank the generous philanthropists who kindly donated towards large sections in this *sefer*, with the pure intentions of spreading more purity and holiness in *Klal Yisroel.*

לזכרון עולם ולעילוי נשמת

הר״ר **אברהם מאיר** ב״ר **מרדכי דויד** ז״ל
נלב״ע כ״ז אדר א׳ תשל״ו

זוג׳ האשה מרת **טובא רבקה** ב״ר **אברהם מאיר דויד** ע״ה
נלב״ע ו׳ כסלו תשס״א

הר״ר **ישראל** ב״ר **מנחם מנדל צביק** ז״ל
נלב״ע עריו״כ תשכ״ו

האשה **שושנה רוזא** ב״ר **ראובן צביק** ע״ה
נלב״ע ר״ח ניסן תשנ״ח

ולע״נ הר״ר **רפאל שלמה** ב״ר **לוי יצחק כהנא** ז״ל
נלב״ע כ״ח ניסן תשס״ד

וזוג׳ **חיה בלומא** ב״ר **אברהם מאיר** ע״ה
נלב״ע י״ד סיון תש״מ

ת. נ. צ. ב. ה.

הונצח ע״י משפחתם ידידינו היקרים
הר״ר מנדי ורעייתו גיטי צביק, Brooklyn, NY
להצלחתם ולמילוי כל משאלות ליבם לטובה ולברכה

יחקו בספר לטובה ולברכה

ידידנו **הרב משה מלכא** ומשפ׳ הי״ו
Rabbi & Mrs. Moshe Malka

להצלחת חינוך ילדיהם
מתוך קדושה וטהרה
וסייעתא דשמיא
בכל העניינים

הנדיבים הנכבדים אשר נדבה רוחם לתרום פרק בספר לתוספת קדושה וטהרה בעם ישראל
We thank the generous philanthropists who kindly donated towards different chapters in this *sefer*, with the pure intentions of spreading more purity and holiness in *Klal Yisroel*.

ידידנו הר"ר מאיר יעקב ווינרוב הי"ו
ורעייתו חנה חיה צביה תחי'

Rabbi Meir Yaakov and
Mrs. Chana Chaya Tzivia Weinrob

Passaic, NJ

לשפע ברכה הצלחה ונחת מכל יוצ"ח
מתוך בריאות ואושר

ידידנו הר"ר יצחק מאיר סטטפלד הי"ו ורעייתו תחי'

Rabbi and Mrs. Yitzchak Meir Statfeld

Brooklyn, NY

לשפע ברכה והצלחה פרנסה ונחת
מכל יוצ"ח מתוך בריאות הגוה"נ

ידידינו היקרים הר"ר חיים ב"ר קלמן הכהן הי"ו
ורעייתו מרת לאה אסתר ב"ר חיים ברוך תחי'

Rabbi Chaim and Mrs. Leah Esther
Brooklyn, NY

לשפע ברכה והצלחה, עושר ואושר, ונחת מכל יוצ"ח אמן.

לרפואת האשה מרת שיינדל בת מיימעל פרומט תחי'
ומרת צביה דבורה מלכה רות בת גולדה פריידה תחי'
לאורך ימים ושנים נעימים

הקהילות והנדיבים הנכבדים אשר נדבה רוחם לתרום להוצאת הספר, לזכות והפצת טהרה בישראל.
הקב"ה ישלח להם ולב"ב שפע ברכה והצלחה מתוך בריאות הגוה"נ וכט"ס.

We thank all the philanthropists who generously donated towards the publishing of this *sefer*, for the zchus of spreading Tahara in Yisroel. May Hakadosh Baruch Hu send them all Bracha and Hatzlacha in everything they do.

The venerable Congregation Moses Montefiore Anshe Emunah, Baltimore, MD
Headed by ***Rabbi Elan Adler***

הקהילה החשובה **"משה מונטיפיורי אנשי אמונה"** הי"ו

ולעומד בראשה הרה"ג רבי **אילן אדלר** שליט"א

The venerable congregation Beth Israel, Norwalk, CT
Headed by ***Rabbi Yehoshua Hecht***

הקהילה החשובה **"בית ישראל"** הי"ו

ולעומד בראשה הרה"ג רבי **יהושע העכט** שליט"א

The venerable congregation Young Israel Ezras Israel of Potomac
Headed by ***Rabbi Yosef Singer***

הקהילה החשובה **"עזרת ישראל יונג ישראל"**

ולעומד בראשה הרה"ג רבי **יוסף סינגער** שליט"א

האשה החשובה רודצו"ח תומכת נלהבת למוסדות תורה וחסד

ה"ה **חנה סטרוטש** הי"ו וכל משפ' הכבודה

A great supporter of any Torah and Chessed cause

Mrs. ***Hannah Storch*** *and family*

תזכה לראות רב נחת מכל יוצא"ח שפע ברכה והצלחה מתוך בריאות הגוה"נ לאורך ימים ושנים טובות

May she see nachas from all her children and have success in all her endeavors, health and wealth for many more years to come

The venerable Congregation of Agudas Yisroel, "Bais Binyomin" Flatbush
Headed by ***Rabbi Pinchas Breuer,*** *Flatbush, NY*

שלמי תודה

לקהילה המפוארת **"אגודת ישראל- בית בנימין"**, פלטבוש, נ.י.

ולמורם ורבם, תלמיד מובהק למרן הגר"ש ואזנר שליט"א בעל "שבט הלוי"

ידיד נאמן למורנו הגרמ"ש קליין שליט"א, ראש מכון "טהרת ישראל"

הגאון רבי **פנחס ברייער** שליט"א

שעומד לימיננו בכל עת

יאריך ה' ימיו ושנותיו מתוך בריאות הגוה"נ

כל אחד בשמו הטוב יבורך בברכה והצלחה, אורך ימים ושנים טובים הם ומשפ' מתוך בריאות הגוה"נ עד עולם

יזכו בספר לטובה ולברכה

הנדיבים הנכבדים אשר נדבה רוחם להוצאת הספר. יבורכו בכל מילי דמיטב,
בברכה, הצלחה וסייעתא דשמיא בכל מעשה ידיהם, אמן.
We thank all the individuals who generously donated towards the publishing of this *sefer*.
May they and their families be blessed.

הר"ר **אלן אנגלנדר** הי"ו
Allan S. Englander

הר"ר **הרשל בוים** הי"ו
Hershel Boehm

הר"ר **שמואל ארי' בנג'מאן** הי"ו
Arie Benjamin

הר"ר **צבי גאטמן** הי"ו
Zvi Guttman

הר"ר **דניאל נח גורדון** הי"ו
Daniel Gordon

הר"ר **אילן גייבער** הי"ו
Allan J. Gibber

הר"ר **רענן י. גלברמן** הי"ו
Ranan J. Gilberman

הר"ר **ריצארד הסקינס** הי"ו
Richard P. Haskins

הר"ר **מנדל וואקס** הי"ו
Mendel Wax

הר"ר **עקיבא ווגשל** הי"ו
Akiva Wagschal

ד"ר **פאול וולסוב** הי"ו
Dr. Paul S. Volosov, M.D.

הר"ר **יעקב וולקטש** הי"ו
Jacob Wealcatch

הר"ר **שמואל א. וולקטש** הי"ו
Samuel A. Wealcatch

הר"ר **יהושע זלצברג** הי"ו
Joshua Salzberg

הר"ר **ברוך לוין** הי"ו
Bruce I. Levine

הרב **צבי לזרוף** הי"ו
Herschel Lazaroff

הר"ר **פלטיאל מאיירס** הי"ו
Paul B. Myers

הר"ר **שמואל מייזלמן** הי"ו
Samuel A. Meiselman

הר"ר **אהרן נודל** הי"ו
Aron Nudell

הר"ר **אנדרו סינגר** הי"ו
Andrew Mark Singer

הר"ר **מתתיהו סלטקין** הי"ו
Mathew Slatkin

הר"ר **שלמה ספטנר** הי"ו
Solomon A. Spetner

הר"ר **שמואל ספרלינג** הי"ו
Samuel Sperling

הר"ר **יוסף פולאק** הי"ו
Joseph E. Pollak

הר"ר **שלום י. פולען** הי"ו
Shalom Y. Pollen

הר"ר **בנימין פריד** הי"ו
Bruce M. Fried

הר"ר **אמיאן פרוסט קלמר** הי"ו
Amian Frost Kelemer

הר"ר **חנניה קרמר** הי"ו
Chananya Kramer

הר"ר **לואיס רומר** הי"ו
.Dr. Lewis H. Romer, M.D

הר"ר **חיים יעקב רינגו** הי"ו
Chaim Yaakov Ringo

הר"ר **ברנרד שטיינהרטר** הי"ו
Bernard Steinharter

הר"ר **משה שרמן** הי"ו
Moshe Sherman

גב' **רחל ניוברגר** תחי'
Mrs. Newberger

גב' **פנינה רוז** תחי'
Mrs. P. Ros

Of Baltimore, MD

הנדיבים הנכבדים אשר נדבה רוחם לתרום להוצאת הספר, לזכות והפצת טהרה בישראל.
הקב"ה ישלח להם ולב"ב שפע ברכה והצלחה מתוך בריאות הגוה"נ וכט"ס.

We thank all the individuals who generously donated towards the publishing of this *sefer*, for the *zchus* of spreading *Tahara* in *Yisroel*. May *Hakadosh Baruch Hu* send them all *Bracha* and *Hatzlacha* in everything they do.

יוחקו בספר לטובה ולברכה

הר"ר זבולון בגלייטר הי"ו
Arnold Begleiter, Baltimore, MD

הר"ר שמואל שפרלינג הי"ו
Shmuel Sperling, Baltimore, MD

הר"ר דן לנדר הי"ו
Dan Lender, Baltimore, MD

הר"ר מאיר דייאמנט הי"ו ומשפ'
Marc W. Diamond, Providence, RI

הר"ר מרדכי ד. הכהן קרמר הי"ו ומשפ'
Dr. Mordechai Kramer, Baltimore

משפחת גודמן
Goodman Family, Pikesville, MD

הר"ר גרשון ל. וואגל הי"ו
Gershon L. Vogel, Pikesville, MA

הר"ר יאיר ורעייתו **אורלי שלם** הי"ו
Ron & Orly Shalem, Baltimore, MD

לרפו"ש ר' משה בן רחל לאה שיחי'
ורבקה בת צפורה תחי'
נתרם ע"י בנם
הר"ר נפתלי צבי בעער הי"ו
Naftali Zvi Bier, Brooklyn, NY

לרפואת האשה מרת כידיה בת חנה תחי'
ורחמים בן לונה הי"ו לרפו"ש בקרוב
נדבת ר' חיים בן ניסים חסון מבוסטון
Chaim Ben Nissim Chason
Jota Inc., Brookline, MA

הר"ר שלמה אריה פוגל הי"ו
Shlomo Arye Fogel, Brooklyn, NY

הר"ר יוסף טבק הי"ו
Josef Tabak, Brooklyn, NY

הר"ר משה צבי פוקס הי"ו
Shmuel Fuchs Foundation, Brooklyn, NY

הר"ר יצחק גולדברנר הי"ו
I. Goldbrenner, Brooklyn, NY

הר"ר ט. רוזנטל הי"ו
Tomas Rosenthal, Brooklyn, NY

הר"ר משה קופמן הי"ו
Moishe Kofman, Brooklyn, NY

הר"ר יעקב פיינסטון הי"ו
Dr. Jacob Finestone, Brooklyn, NY

הר"ר א. הנדלר הי"ו
Isidor Handler, Brooklyn, NY

הר"ר שמאי הרטמן הי"ו
Shamai Hartman, Brooklyn, NY

הר"ר משה צוקער הי"ו
Dr. Martin Cukier

הר"ר יוסף ברכפלד הי"ו
Joseph Brachfeld

הר"ר יעקב פריד הי"ו
Yaakov Fried

כל אחד בשמו הטוב יבורך בברכה והצלחה, אורך ימים ושנים טובים
הם ומשפ' מתוך בריאות הגוה"נ עד עולם

הנדיבים הנכבדים אשר נדבה רוחם לתרום להוצאת הספר. יבורכו בכל מילי דמיטב,
בברכה, הצלחה וסייעתא דשמיא בכל מעשי ידיהם, אמן.

We thank all the individuals who generously donated towards the publishing of this *sefer*. May they and their families be blessed.

יוחקו בספר לטובה ולברכה

הר"ר חיים נפתלי דובק הי"ו
Chaim N. Dovek, Boston, MA

הר"ר משה וואג הי"ו
Moses & Eva Vegh, PA

הר"ר אברהם סדלוף הי"ו
The Pandanarum Company LLC

ישיבת מקדש מלך
Yeshivat Mikdash Melech

הר"ר עמרם סננט הי"ו, **הר"ר עזרא הרני** הי"ו
Amram Sananes, Ezra Erani, Brooklyn, NY

הר"ר שמואל דוד סטיילער הי"ו
Dr. Shmuel Dovid Styler, Brooklyn, NY

הר"ר יונה בלומנפרוכט הי"ו
Jonah Blumenfrucht, Brooklyn, NY

הרבנית **שקאפ** תליט"א
נשי עזרת ישראל
N-shei Ezras Israel, Brooklyn, NY

הר"ר משה שארר הי"ו
ובנו היקר **הר"ר ישראל שארר** הי"ו
Sruli Schorr, Brooklyn, NY

הר"ר ישראל לפקוביץ הי"ו
Yisrael Lefkowitz, Brooklyn, NY

הר"ר אברהם באקנרוט הי"ו
Avraham Backenroth, Brooklyn, NY

הר"ר שלום אוברלנדר הי"ו
Sholem Oberlander, Brooklyn, NY

הר"ר אברהם טרייעביטש הי"ו
Avrahavm Treivitch, Brooklyn, NY

הר"ר יוסף לשקוביץ הי"ו
Joseph Leshkowitz

הר"ר זאב וינברג הי"ו
The Lease Pro, Lakewood, NJ

הר"ר י. קלוגמן הי"ו
Jack Y. Klugmann, Passaic, NJ

הר"ר טוביה ליברמן הי"ו
T.G. Liberman, Monsey, NY

הר"ר דוד באום הי"ו
David Baum, Passaic, NJ

הר"ר וולף כץ הי"ו
Volvi Katz, Monsey, NY

הר"ר בנימין פיליפסון הי"ו
Beni Philipson, Monsey, NY

הר"ר משה ליכטנשטיין הי"ו
Morris Lichtenstein, Monsey, NY

הר"ר ברנט הי"ו
Profeel Marketing, Monsey, NY

הר"ר אברהם רייך הי"ו
Comp-U-Plus Rockland, Monsey

הר"ר חיים ראזמאן הי"ו
Chaim Rausman, Monsey, NY

הגב' פיין רפורטינג הי"ו
Mrs. F. Reporting, Monsey, NY

הר"ר דניס ברמן הי"ו
Dennis Berman, Potomac, VA

הר"ר יהושע וולף הי"ו
Joshua Wolff, Brighton, MA

הר"ר ג'ור הלפארט הי"ו ומשפ'
Juar Elfrat, Brooklyn, NY

הנדיבים הנכבדים אשר נדבה רוחם ותרמו להוצאת הספר, לזכות ולעילוי נשמת יקיריהם
הקב"ה ישלח להם ולב"ב ברכה והצלחה, אורך ימים ושנים נעימים.
We thank all the individuals who generously donated towards the publishing of this *sefer*, for the *zchus* and *leiluy nishmas* deceased family members. May they and their families be blessed.

לזכרון עולם ולעילוי נשמת

האשה החשובה והנודעת במעשיה הטובים
מרת **לאה רוזנברג** בת הר"ר **שמואל אלימלך** ע"ה
נלב"ע י"א מנחם אב תשנ"ו
הונצחה ע"י בנה וכלתה יונתן ואסתר רוזנברג הי"ו
Dedicated by her son and daughter-in-law
Jonathan and Esther Rosenberg, Edison, NJ

האשה החשובה
מרת **אסתר** ב"ר **יצחק** ע"ה
נפטרה ביום הקדוש יום כיפור, תשס"ד
הונצחה ע"י משפחתה, משפחת וגנר, Passaic, NJ

הרה"ח ר' **שלמה** ב"ר **פנחס נתן** ע"ה נלב"ע י"ח טבת, תשס"ה
וזוג' מרת **אלטע אסתר יכט** ב"ר **זאב** ע"ה נלב"ע כ"ג סיון תשס"ב
הונצח ע"י משפחת לויבעד הי"ו, מאנסי, ניו יארק

הר"ר **אברהם יצחק** ב"ר **משה צוקער** ז"ל נלב"ע ז' אדר תשס"ב
הונצח ע"י בנם ר' ד"ר משה צוקער הי"ו
Dr. Martin Cukier, Brooklyn, NY

הר"ר **משה צבי** ב"ר **יודא ליב הלוי** ז"ל נלב"ע י"ב אדר תשכ"ט
מרת **שרה** ב"ר **יצחק אייזיק** ז"ל נלב"ע כ"א שבט תש"ס
מרת **מינדל** ב"ר **אשר** ז"ל נלב"ע ט"ז אב תשנ"ב
הונצח ע"י הרה"ח ר' יהודה לאונגר הי"ו

הרה"ח ר' **יונה צבי** ב"ר **יוחנן** ז"ל וזוג' מרת **שרה** ב"ר **משה יהושע** ז"ל
הרה"ח ר' **אפרים** ב"ר **שמואל חיים** ז"ל וזוג' מרת **רבקה** ב"ר **משה אהרן** ז"ל
הונצח ע"י הרה"ח ר' אהרן הרצוג הי"ו, ברוקלין, נ.י.

ת.נ.צ.ב.ה.

הנדיבים הוררדים אשר נדבה רוחם להוצאת הספר, לזכות ולעילוי נשמת יקיריהם
הקב"ה ישלח להם ולב"ב ברכה והצלחה, אורך ימים ושנים נעימים.

We thank all the individuals who generously donated towards the publishing of this *sefer*, for *the zchus and leiluy nishmas* deceased family members. May they and their families be blessed.

לזכרון עולם ולעילוי נשמת

א"מ ר' צבי אריה ב"ר אתמר אפרים ז"ל נלב"ע כ' טבת תשס"ד
הונצח ע"י בנו הר"ר יעקב מנחם פאללאק הי"

הילד אברהם ישראל ז"ל
בן יבלחט"א ר' דוד יעקב הכהן הי"ו למשפ' סאקס
נלב"ע כ' אדר א' תשס"ה
הונצח ע"י זקנו הרה"ח ר' חיים פאללק הי"ו לברכה ושובע נחת, Baltimore, MD

א"מ ר' זלמן מיכאל ב"ר יהודה לייב ז"ל גודדון נלב"ע י"ז תמוז תשס"ב
הונצח ע"י בנו הר"ר דניאל נח גודדון הי"ו, בולטימור
Daniel Gordon, Baltimore, MD

סבתי האשה מרת **זהרה אסתר ב"ר שאול ע"ה**
נלב"ע ח' סיון תשנ"ו
הונצח ע"י נכדה הר"ר שמואל ווילקאטש הי"ו, Baltimore, MD

אבי וחמי הר"ר יואל ב"ר יוסף ז"ל התלמן
נלב"ע כ"ג אלול תשס"ד
הונצח ע"י משפ' סילברברג, Baltimore, MD

נר תמיד ומצבת זכרון לעילוי נשמת איש היקר באדם, צנוע ומעלי ולא מחזיק טיבותא לנפשיה
שקבע עיתותיו לתורה וחסד, נשא ונתן באמונה, הקפיד על דקדוק המצוות והמנהגים בכל המצבים והתקופות
מוה"ר יהודה בהר"ר יוסף הערצאג זצ"ל מבודפסט - וינה יצ"ו
תלמיד הגה"צ ר' יוסף אלימלך כהנא מצעהלים ומהרש"נ מסעמיהאלי ובעל הויגד יעקב מפאפא זצללה"ה
נלב"ע י"ג אייר תשס"א
ולע"נ זוגתו מרת ריזל לאה בת מוה"ר שמואל בנימין ע"ה
שהיתה ידועה באצילות נפשה, בטוב ליבה ובצניעתה המופלגת והצטיינה בחכמתה וביראתה
נלב"ע כ"ח שבט תשס"ה

הונצח ע"י בנם ידידנו הרה"ח ר' שמואל בנימין הערצאג שליט"א

ת.נ.צ.ב.ה.